Sentence Skills

A Workbook for Writers

Seventh Edition

Form B

Annotated Instructor's Edition

Sentence Skills

A Workbook for Writers

Seventh Edition

Form B

Annotated Instructor's Edition

John Langan

Atlantic Cape Community College

Boston   Burr Ridge, IL   Dubuque, IA   Madison, WI   New York
San Francisco   St. Louis   Bangkok   Bogotá   Caracas   Kuala Lumpur
Lisbon   London   Madrid   Mexico City   Milan   Montreal   New Delhi
Santiago   Seoul   Singapore   Sydney   Taipei   Toronto

The **McGraw·Hill** Companies

 **Higher Education**

SENTENCE SKILLS, FORM B
Published by McGraw-Hill, a business unit of The McGraw-Hill Companies, Inc., 1221 Avenue of
the Americas, New York, NY, 10020. Copyright © 2004, 1994, 1990, 1987, 1983, and 1979
by the McGraw-Hill Companies, Inc. All rights reserved. No part of this publication may be reproduced or
distributed in any form or by any means, or stored in a database or retrieval system, without the prior
written consent of The McGraw-Hill Companies, Inc., including, but not limited to, in any network
or other electronic storage or transmission, or broadcast for distance learning.
Some ancillaries, including electronic and print components, may not be available to customers outside
the United States.

This book is printed on acid-free paper.

1 2 3 4 5 6 7 8 9 0 DOC/DOC 0 9 8 7 6 5 4 3

ISBN 0-07-282087-X (student edition)
ISBN 0-07-282088-8 (annotated instructor's edition)

President of McGraw-Hill Humanities/Social Sciences: Steve Debow
Sponsoring editor: Alexis Walker
Development editor: Carla Samodulski
Senior marketing manager: David S. Patterson
Media producer: Todd Vaccaro
Project manager: Jean R. Starr
Production supervisor: Carol A. Bielski
Coordinator of freelance design: Jean Mailander
Supplement associate: Kathleen Boylan
Cover illustration: Paul D. Turnbaugh
Interior design: Rick Soldin
Typeface: 11/13 Times Roman
Compositor: Electronic Publishing Services, Inc., TN
Printer: R. R. Donnelley

www.mhhe.com

Praise for *Sentence Skills*

"John Langan's Sentence Skills . . . is the one book that has it all: a text easy for students to read and understand; a thorough covering of all the major and minor errors; a plethora of exercises and tests with answer key; a host of both CD-ROM and Web-based supplements; availability in multiple forms for alternation between semesters."

Sherry Lusk, *Northwest Mississippi Community College*

"An excellent text for remedial grammar and writing courses."

Michele A. Adams, *Wentworth Institute of Technology*

"You absolutely must have a copy of this book. It has some of the best proofreading drills I have ever found."

Jeannine Edwards, *The University of Memphis*

"Probably the most thorough approach to sentence and paragraph level development and structure I have ever seen."

Kathryn Mincey, *Morehead State University*

"I am so impressed with this text that I would not only suggest but fight for its adoption."

Dorothea D. Burkhart, *Davidson County Community College*

"It is thorough, well organized, well developed, and easy to use for both students and instructors."

Theresa Zeleznik, *Cuyahoga Community College, Western Campus*

"There is enough in here to keep students interested, busy—and learning!"

Sara Jane Richter, *Oklahoma Panhandle State University*

"The appendices, the section on how to use a computer to compose, the walkthrough of a student's drafts in "Brief Guide," and the section on reading really pump this book up. The checklists are very good while the reflective activities add a deeper dimension to the composing process."

Michele Mohr, *Morton College*

"The greatest strength of the text remains its easy-to-use style."

William Muller, *Moraine Valley Community College*

About the Author

John Langan has taught reading and writing at Atlantic Cape Community College near Atlantic City, New Jersey, for over twenty-five years. The author of a popular series of college textbooks on both subjects, he enjoys the challenge of developing materials that teach skills in an especially clear and lively way. Before teaching, he earned advanced degrees in writing at Rutgers University and in reading at Glassboro State College. He also spent a year writing fiction that, he says, "is now at the back of a drawer waiting to be discovered and acclaimed posthumously." While in school, he supported himself by working as a truck driver, a machinist, a battery assembler, a hospital attendant, and an apple packer. He now lives with his wife, Judith Nadell, near Philadelphia. Among his everyday pleasures are running, working on his Apple computer, and watching Philadelphia sports teams on TV. He also loves to read: newspapers at breakfast, magazines at lunch, and a chapter or two of a recent book ("preferably an autobiography") at night.

The Langan Series

Essay-Level

College Writing Skills, Media Edition
ISBN: 0-07-281892-1 (Copyright © 2003)

College Writing Skills with Readings, Fifth Edition
ISBN: 0-07-238121-3 (Copyright © 2001)

Paragraph-Level

English Skills, Seventh Edition
ISBN: 0-07-238127-2 (Copyright © 2001)

English Skills with Readings, Fifth Edition
ISBN: 0-07-248003-3 (Copyright © 2002)

Sentence-Level

Sentence Skills: A Workbook for Writers, Form A, Seventh Edition
ISBN: 0-07-238132-9 (Copyright © 2003)

Sentence Skills: A Workbook for Writers, Form B, Seventh Edition
ISBN: 0-07-282087-X (Copyright © 2004)

Sentence Skills with Readings, Second Edition
ISBN: 0-07-238132-9 (Copyright © 2001)

Grammar Review

English Brushup, Third Edition
ISBN: 0-07-281890-5 (Copyright © 2003)

Reading

Reading and Study Skills, Seventh Edition
ISBN: 0-07-244519-8 (Copyright © 2002)

Contents

Contents

Part Three: Reinforcement of the Skills 383

To the Instructor

Note: The Annotated Instructor's Edition you are holding is identical to the student version except for the answers, which are included for all the activities and tests.

Key Features of the Book

Sentence Skills will help students learn to write effectively. It is an all-in-one text that includes basic rhetoric and gives full attention to grammar, punctuation, mechanics, and usage.

The book contains eight distinctive features to aid instructors and their students:

1   **Coverage of basic writing skills is exceptionally thorough.** The book pays special attention to fragments, run-ons, verbs, and other areas where students have serious problems. At the same time, a glance at the table of contents shows that the book also treats skills (such as dictionary use and spelling improvement) not found in other texts. In addition, parts of the book are devoted to the basics of effective writing, to practice in editing and proofreading, and to achieving variety in sentences.

2   **The book has a clear and flexible format.** It is organized in three easy-to-use parts. Part One is a guide to the goals of effective writing followed by a series of activities to help students practice and master those goals. Part Two is a comprehensive treatment of the rules of grammar, mechanics, punctuation, and usage needed for clear writing. Part Three provides a series of mastery, editing, and proofreading tests to reinforce the sentence skills presented in Part Two.

   Since parts, sections, and chapters are self-contained, instructors can move easily from, for instance, a rhetorical principle in Part One to a grammar rule in Part Two to a mastery test in Part Three.

3   **Opening chapters deal with the writer's attitude, writing as a process, and the importance of specific details in writing.** In its opening pages, the book helps students recognize and deal with their attitude toward writing—an important part of learning to write well. In the pages that follow, students are encouraged to see writing as a multistage process that moves from prewriting to proofreading. Later, a series of activities helps students understand the nature of specific details and how to generate and use those details. As writing teachers well know, learning to write concretely is a key step for students to master in becoming effective writers.

4   **Practice activities are numerous.** Most skills are reinforced by activities, review tests, and mastery tests, as well as tests in the *Instructor's Manual.* For many of the skills in the book, there are more than one hundred practice sentences.

5   **Practice materials are varied and lively.** In many basic writing texts, exercises are monotonous and dry, causing students to lose interest in the skills presented. In *Sentence Skills,* many exercises involve students in various ways. An inductive opening project allows students to see what they already know about a given skill. Within chapters, students may be asked to underline answers, add words, generate their own sentences, or edit passages. And the lively and engaging practice materials in the book both maintain interest and help students appreciate the value of vigorous details in writing.

6   **Terminology is kept to a minimum.** In general, rules are explained using words students already know. A clause is a *word group;* a coordinating conjunction is a *joining word;* a nonrestrictive element is an *interrupter.* At the same time, traditional grammatical terms are mentioned briefly for students who learned them somewhere in the past and are comfortable seeing them again.

7   **Self-teaching is encouraged.** Students may check their answers to the introductory activities and the practice activities in Part One by referring to the answers in Appendix E. In this way, they are given the responsibility for teaching themselves. At the same time, to ensure that the answer key is used as a learning tool only, answers are *not* given for the review tests in Part One or for any of the reinforcement tests in Part Two. These answers appear in the *Annotated Instructor's Edition* and the *Instructor's Manual;* they can be copied and handed out to students at the discretion of the instructor.

8   **Diagnostic and achievement tests are provided.** These tests appear in Appendixes C and D of the book. Each test may be given in two parts, the second of which provides instructors with a particularly detailed picture of a student's skill level.

Changes in the Seventh Edition

Here are the major changes in this new edition of *Sentence Skills:*

- Collaborative and reflective activities have been added to key chapters of the book. The *collaborative activities* build on the idea that students' interaction can increase learning. Group discussion, team writing, and student-generated examples are all used to lend energy to the classroom and strengthen students' mastery of essential writing skills.

The *reflective activities* build on the idea that getting students to think about what they are learning can increase mastery. These activities engage students' higher-order thinking skills and encourage them to be active participants in their own learning.

- Many of the sentence skills in the book are in a simpler, more intuitive sequence. This framework, which places related topics in the same section, seems better suited to the way students learn. For example, the first grammar section, "Sentences," begins with the simple sentence and subjects and verbs; the second chapter in this section treats fragments; the third chapter examines run-ons; and the final chapter presents the four basic kinds of sentences and the main techniques for joining sentences (subordination and coordination).

  The second grammar section groups together verbs, pronouns, and matters of agreement, and the third section presents modifiers and parallelism. The final two sections are more traditional: punctuation and mechanics, followed by chapters relating to word use.

- Another addition to the book is an appendix titled "ESL Pointers," complete with practice activities which address common trouble spots faced by nonnative speakers of English.

- Here are some of the other changes in this revision. There is now a section on the use of computers in the writing process. An appendix on the parts of speech has been added to the end of the book. In certain paragraph and essay assignments, a greater emphasis is placed on the importance of prewriting and revising. Practice sentences and passages have been freshened and updated throughout the text. Finally, visual interest has been added to the book in the form of a more student-friendly design.

Helpful Learning Aids Accompany the Book

Supplements for Instructors

- Access to a toll-free support line dedicated to users and potential users of the Langan Series: 800-MCGRAWH (800-624-7294). E-mail inquiries may be sent to **langan@mcgraw-hill.com**.

- An *Annotated Instructor's Edition* (ISBN 0-07-282088-8) consists of the student text complete with answers to all activities and tests.

- The comprehensive *Instructor's Manual and Test Bank,* available on line at **www.mhhe.com/langan** and on the *Instructor's Resource CD-ROM,* includes (1) a model syllabus along with suggestions for teaching the course, (2) an answer key, and (3) a complete set of additional mastery tests. The pages of the manual are 8½ × 11 inches, so that both the answer pages and the added mastery tests can be conveniently printed and reproduced on copying machines.

- An *Online Learning Center* (**www.mhhe.com/langan**) offers a host of instructional aids and additional resources for instructors, including a comprehensive computerized test bank, the Instructor's Manual and Test Bank, online resources for writing instructors, and more.

- An *Instructor's Resource CD-ROM* (0-07-282091-8) offers all the above supplements and M.O.R.E. (McGraw-Hill Online Resources for English, also available online at **www.mhhe.com/english**) in a convenient offline format.

- *PageOut!* helps instructors create graphically pleasing and professional web pages for their courses, in addition to providing classroom management, collaborative learning, and content management tools. PageOut! is **FREE** to adopters of McGraw-Hill textbooks and learning materials. Learn more at **www.mhhe.com/pageout**.

Supplements for Students

- An *Online Learning Center* (**www.mhhe.com/langan**) offers a host of instructional aids and additional resources for students, including self-correcting exercises, writing activities for additional practice, a PowerPoint grammar tutorial, guides to doing research on the Internet and avoiding plagiarism, useful web links, and more.

AllWrite! 2.1 is an interactive, browser-based tutorial program that provides an online handbook, comprehensive diagnostic pretests and posttests, plus extensive practice exercises in every area. Throughout the text, marginal icons, or TextLinks, alert students to additional help in *AllWrite!*

You can contact your local McGraw-Hill representative or consult McGraw-Hill's web site at **www.mhhe.com/langan** for more information on the supplements that accompany *Sentence Skills,* Seventh Edition. You may also send an e-mail to **langan@mcgraw-hill.com**.

Acknowledgments

Reviewers who have contributed to this edition through their helpful comments on *Sentence Skills,* Forms A and B, include

Kris Acquistapace, Crafton Hills College

Michelle A. Adams, Wentworth Institute of Technology

Beth Ashburn, Piedmont Baptist College

Gary Bennett, Santa Ana College

Amelia Billingsley, Floyd College

Dorothea D. Burkhart, Davidson County Community College

Judy D. Covington, Trident Technical College

LaNelle Daniel, Floyd College

Jane Dominik, San Joaquin Delta College

Jeannine Edwards, University of Memphis

Jeanne Gilligan, Delaware Technical Community College

Vera Holder, University of Maryland

Adam Kempler, College of the Canyons

Sherry Lusk, Northwest Mississippi Community College

Judy I. Marks, Rio Hondo College

H. Brown Miller, City College of San Francisco

Kathryn Mincey, Morehead State University

Michele Mohr, Morton College

Stephanie Mood, Grossmont College

William Muller, Moraine Valley Community College

Kathleen Perryman, Joliet Junior College

Tracy Peyton, Pensacola Junior College

Charles Pierce, Tidewater Community College

Sara Jane Richter, Oklahoma Panhandle State University

Drema Stringer, Marshall Community/Technical College

Ellen Taylor, Davenport University

Glenda Whalon, Cochise College

Theresa Zeleznick, Cuyahoga Community College, Western Campus

I owe thanks as well for help provided by Eliza Comodromos, Susan Gamer, and Jean Starr as well as for the support of my McGraw-Hill editors: Carla Samodulski and Alexis Walker.

John Langan

Part One

Effective Writing

Introduction

Part One is a guide to the goals of effective writing followed by a series of activities to help you practice and master these goals. Begin with the introductory chapter, which makes clear the reasons for learning sentence skills. Then read the second chapter carefully; it presents all the essentials you need to know to become an effective writer. Finally, work through the series of activities in the third chapter. Your instructor may direct you to certain exercises, depending on your needs. After completing the activities, you'll be ready to take on the paragraph and essay writing assignments at the end of the chapter.

At the same time that you are writing papers, start working through the sentence skills in Parts Two and Three of the book. Practicing the sentence skills in the context of actual writing assignments is the surest way to master the rules of grammar, mechanics, punctuation, and usage.

Note: A writing progress chart on pages 585–591 (in Appendix F) will help you track your performance.

1 Learning Sentence Skills

Why Learn Sentence Skills?

Why should someone planning a career as a nurse have to learn sentence skills? Why should an accounting major have to pass a competency test in grammar as part of a college education? Why should a potential physical therapist or graphic artist or computer programmer have to spend hours on the rules of English? Perhaps you are asking questions like these after finding yourself in a class with this book. On the other hand, perhaps you *know* you need to strengthen basic writing skills, even though you may be unclear about the specific ways the skills will be of use to you. Whatever your views, you should understand why sentence skills—all the rules that make up standard English—are so important.

Clear Communication

Standard English, or "language by the book," is needed to communicate your thoughts to others with a minimal amount of distortion and misinterpretation. Knowing the traditional rules of grammar, punctuation, and usage will help you write clear sentences when communicating with others. You may have heard of the party game in which one person whispers a message to the next person; the message is passed, in turn, along a line of several other people. By the time the last person in line is asked to give the message aloud, it is usually so garbled and inaccurate that it barely resembles the original. Written communication in some form of English other than standard English carries the same potential for disaster.

To see how important standard English is to written communication, examine the pairs of sentences on the following pages and answer the questions in each case.

3

1. Which sentence indicates that there might be a plot against Ted?

   a. We should leave Ted. These fumes might be poisonous.

   b. We should leave, Ted. These fumes might be poisonous.

2. Which sentence encourages self-mutilation?

   a. Leave your paper and hand in the dissecting kit.

   b. Leave your paper, and hand in the dissecting kit.

3. Which sentence indicates that the writer has a weak grasp of geography?

   a. As a child, I lived in Lake Worth, which is close to Palm Beach and Alaska.

   b. As a child, I lived in Lake Worth, which is close to Palm Beach, and Alaska.

4. In which sentence does the dog warden seem dangerous?

   a. Foaming at the mouth, the dog warden picked up the stray.

   b. Foaming at the mouth, the stray was picked up by the dog warden.

5. Which announcer was probably fired from the job?

   a. Outside the Academy Awards theater, the announcer called the guests names as they arrived.

   b. Outside the Academy Awards theater, the announcer called the guests' names as they arrived.

6. Below are the opening lines of two students' exam essays. Which student seems likely to earn a higher grade?

   a. Defense mechanisms is the way people hides their inner feelings and deals with stress. There is several types that we use to be protecting our true feelings.

   b. Defense mechanisms are the methods people use to cope with stress. Using a defense mechanism allows a person to hide his or her real desires and goals.

7. The following lines are taken from two English papers. Which student seems likely to earn a higher grade?

   a. A big problem on this campus is apathy, students don't participate in college activities. Such as clubs, student government, and plays.

   b. The most pressing problem on campus is the disgraceful state of the student lounge area. The floor is dirty, the chairs are torn, and the ceiling leaks.

Continued

8. The following sentences are taken from reports by two employees. Which worker is more likely to be promoted?

   a. The spring line failed by 20 percent in the meeting of projected profit expectations. Which were issued in January of this year.

   b. Profits from our spring line were disappointing. They fell 20 percent short of January's predictions.

9. The following paragraphs are taken from two job application letters. Which applicant would you favor?

   a. Let me say in closing that their are an array of personal qualities I have presented in this letter, together, these make me hopeful of being interviewed for this attraktive position.

   sincerely yours'

   Brian Davis

   b. I feel I have the qualifications needed to do an excellent job as assistant manager of the jewelry department at Horton's. I look forward to discussing the position further at a personal interview.

   Sincerely yours,

   Richard O'Keeney

In each case, the first choice (*a*) contains sentence-skills mistakes. These mistakes include missing or misplaced commas, misspellings, and wordy or pretentious language. As a result of such mistakes, clear communication cannot occur—and misunderstandings, lower grades, and missed job opportunities are probable results. The point, then, is that all the rules that make up standard written English should be a priority if you want your writing to be clear and effective.

Success in College

Standard English is essential if you want to succeed in college. Any report, paper, review, essay exam, or assignment you are responsible for should be written in the best standard English you can produce. If you don't do this, it won't matter how fine your ideas are or how hard you worked—most likely, you will receive a lower grade than you would otherwise deserve. In addition, because standard English requires you to express your thoughts in precise, clear sentences, training yourself to follow the rules can help you think more logically. The basic logic you learn to practice at the sentence level will help as you work to produce well-reasoned papers in all your subjects.

Success at Work

Knowing standard English will also help you achieve success on the job. Studies have found repeatedly that skillful communication, more than any other factor, is the key to job satisfaction and steady progress in a career. A solid understanding of standard English is a basic part of this vital ability to communicate. Moreover, most experts agree that we are now living in an "age of information"—a time when people who use language skillfully have a great advantage over those who do not. Fewer of us will be working in factories or at other types of manual labor. Many more of us will be working with information in various forms—accumulating it, processing it, analyzing it. No matter what kind of job you are preparing yourself for, technical or not, you will need to know standard English to keep pace with this new age. Otherwise, you are likely to be left behind, limited to low-paying jobs that offer few challenges or financial rewards.

Success in Everyday Life

Standard English will help you succeed not just at school and work but in everyday life as well. It will help you feel more comfortable, for example, in writing letters to friends and relatives. It will enable you to write effective notes to your children's schools. It will help you get action when you write a letter of complaint to a company about a product. It will allow you to write letters inquiring about bills—hospital, medical, utility, or legal—or about any kind of service. To put it simply, in our daily lives, those who can use and write standard English have more power than those who cannot.

How This Book Is Organized

- A good way to get a quick sense of any book is to turn to the table of contents. By referring to pages ix–xii, you will see that the book is organized into three basic parts. What are they?

  Part One: Effective Writing

  Part Two: Sentence Skills

  Part Three: Reinforcement of the Skills

- In Part One, the final section of Chapter 2 describes how a __computer__ can help in the writing process.

- Part Two deals with sentence skills. The first section is "Sentences." How many sections (skills areas) are covered in all? Count them. __five__

- Part Three reinforces the skills presented in Part Two. What are the four kinds of reinforcement activities in Part Three?

  Mastery Tests

  Combined Mastery Tests

  Editing and Proofreading Tests

  Combined Editing Tests

- Helpful charts in the book include (*fill in the missing words*) the __spelling__ __list__ on the inside front cover, the __progress__ charts in Appendix F, and the __checklist__ of sentence skills on the inside back cover.

- Finally, the six appendixes at the end of the book are:

  (A) Parts of Speech, (B) ESL Pointers, (C) Diagnostic Test,

  (D) Achievement Test, (E) Answers to Introductory Activities and

  Practice Exercises, (F) Progress Charts

How to Use This Book

Here is a way to use *Sentence Skills*. First, read and work through Part One, Effective Writing—a guide to the goals of effective writing followed by a series of activities to help you practice and master these goals. Your instructor may direct you to certain activities, depending on your needs.

Second, take the diagnostic test on pages 554–559. By analyzing which sections of the test give you trouble, you will discover which skills you need to concentrate on. When you turn to an individual skill in Part Two, begin by reading and thinking about the introductory activity. Often, you will be pleasantly surprised to find that you know more about this area of English than you thought you did. After all, you have probably been speaking English with fluency and ease for many years; you have an instinctive knowledge of how the language works. This knowledge gives you a solid base for refining your skills.

Your third step is to work on the skills in Part Two by reading the explanations and completing the practices. You can check your answers to each practice activity in this part by turning to the answer key at the back of the book (Appendix E). Try to figure out *why* you got some answers wrong—you want to uncover any weak spots in your understanding.

Your next step is to use the review tests at the ends of chapters in Part Two to evaluate your understanding of a skill in its entirety. Your instructor may also ask you to take the mastery tests or other reinforcement tests in Part Three of the book. To help ensure that you take the time needed to learn each skill thoroughly, the answers to these tests are *not* in the answer key.

The emphasis in this book is on writing clear, error-free sentences. And the heart of the book is the practice material that helps reinforce the sentence skills you learn. A great deal of effort has been taken to make the practices lively and engaging and to avoid the dull, repetitive skills work that has given grammar books such a bad reputation. This text will help you stay interested as you work on the rules of English that you need to learn. The rest is a matter of your personal determination and hard work. If you decide—and only you can decide—that effective writing is important to your school and career goals and that you want to learn the basic skills needed to write clearly and effectively, this book will help you reach those goals.

2 A Brief Guide to Effective Writing

This chapter and Chapter 3 will show you how to write effective paragraphs and essays. The following questions will be answered in turn:

1   Why does your attitude toward writing matter?
2   What is a paragraph?
3   What are the goals of effective writing?
4   How do you reach the goals of effective writing?
5   What is an essay?
6   What are the parts of an essay?
7   How can a computer help?

Why Does Your Attitude toward Writing Matter?

Your attitude toward writing is an important part of learning to write well. To get a sense of just how you feel about writing, read the following statements. Put a check beside those statements with which you agree. (This activity is not a test, so try to be as honest as possible.)

_____   1.   A good writer should be able to sit down and write a paper straight through without stopping.

_____   2.   Writing is a skill that anyone can learn with practice.

_____   3.   I'll never be good at writing because I make too many mistakes in spelling, grammar, and punctuation.

_____   4.   Because I dislike writing, I always start a paper at the last possible minute.

_____   5.   I've always done poorly in English, and I don't expect that to change.

Now read the following comments about these five statements. The comments will help you see if your attitude is hurting or helping your efforts to become a better writer.

1   *A good writer should be able to sit down and write a paper straight through without stopping.*

The statement is *false*. Writing is, in fact, a process. It is done not in one easy step but in a series of steps, and seldom at one sitting. If you cannot do a paper all at once, that simply means you are like most of the other people on the planet. It is harmful to carry around the false idea that writing should be an easy matter.

2   *Writing is a skill that anyone can learn with practice.*

This statement is *absolutely true*. Writing is a skill, like driving or word processing, that you can master with hard work. If you want to learn to write, you can. It is as simple as that. If you believe this, you are ready to learn how to become a competent writer.

Some people hold the false belief that writing is a natural gift which some have and others do not. Because of this belief, they never make a truly honest effort to learn to write—and so they never learn.

3   *I'll never be good at writing, because I make too many mistakes in spelling, grammar, and punctuation.*

The first concern in good writing should be *content*—what you have to say. Your ideas and feelings are what matter most. You should not worry about spelling, grammar, and punctuation while working on content.

Unfortunately, some people are so self-conscious about making mistakes that they do not focus on what they want to say. They need to realize that a paper is best done in stages and that the rules can and should wait until a later stage in the writing process. Through review and practice, you will eventually learn how to follow the rules with confidence.

4   *Because I dislike writing, I always start a paper at the last possible minute.*

This is all too common. You feel you are *going to* do poorly, and then your behavior ensures that you *will* do poorly! Your attitude is so negative that you defeat yourself—not even allowing enough time to really try.

Again, what you need to realize is that writing is a process. Because it is done in steps, you don't have to get it right all at once. Just get started well in advance. If you allow yourself enough time, you'll find a way to make a paper come together.

5 *I've done poorly in English in the past, and I don't expect that to change now.*

How you may have performed in the *past* does not control how you can perform in the *present*. Even if you did poorly in English in high school, it is in your power to make this one of your best subjects in college. If you believe writing can be learned, and if you work hard at it, you *will* become a better writer.

In brief, your attitude is crucial. If you believe you are a poor writer and always will be, chances are you will not improve. If you realize you can become a better writer, chances are you will improve. Depending on how you allow yourself to think, you can be your own best friend or your own worst enemy.

What Is a Paragraph?

A *paragraph* is a series of sentences about one main idea, or *point*. A paragraph typically starts with a point, and the rest of the paragraph provides specific details to support and develop that point.

Consider the following paragraph, written by a student named Gary Callahan.

Returning to School

Starting college at age twenty-nine was difficult. For one thing, I did not have much support from my parents and friends. My father asked, "Didn't you get dumped on enough in high school? Why go back for more?" My mother worried about where the money would come from. My friends seemed threatened. "Hey, there's the college man," they would say when they saw me. Another reason that starting college was hard was that I had bad memories of school. I had spent years of my life sitting in classrooms completely bored, watching clocks tick ever so slowly toward the final bell. When I was not bored, I was afraid of being embarrassed. Once a teacher called on me and then said, "Ah, forget it, Callahan," when he realized I did not know the answer. Finally, I soon learned that college would give me little time with my family. After work every day, I have just an hour and ten minutes to eat and spend time with my wife and daughter before going off to class. When I get back, my daughter is in bed, and my wife and I have only a little time together. Then the weekends go by quickly, with all the homework I have to do. But I am going to persist because I believe a better life awaits me with a college degree.

The preceding paragraph, like many effective paragraphs, starts by stating a main idea, or point. A *point* is a general idea that contains an opinion. In this case, the point is that starting college at age twenty-nine was not easy.

In our everyday lives, we constantly make points about all kinds of matters. We express all kinds of opinions: "That was a terrible movie." "My psychology instructor is the best teacher I have ever had." "My sister is a generous person." "Eating at that restaurant was a mistake." "That team should win the playoff game." "Waitressing is the worst job I ever had." "Our state should allow the death penalty." "Cigarette smoking should be banned everywhere." In *talking* to people, we don't always give the reasons for our opinions. But in *writing,* we *must* provide reasons to support our ideas. Only by supplying solid evidence for any point that we make can we communicate effectively with readers.

An effective paragraph, then, must not only make a point but support it with *specific evidence*—reasons, examples, and other details. Such specifics help prove to readers that the point is reasonable. Even if readers do not agree with the writer, at least they have in front of them the evidence on which the writer has based his or her opinion. Readers are like juries; they want to see the evidence so that they can make their own judgments.

Take a moment now to examine the evidence that Gary has provided to back up his point about starting college at twenty-nine. Complete the following outline of Gary's paragraph by summarizing in a few words his reasons and the details that develop them. The first reason and its supporting details are summarized for you as an example.

Point: Starting college at age twenty-nine was difficult.

Reason 1: Little support from parents and friends

Details that develop reason 1: Father asked why I wanted to be dumped on again, mother worried about tuition money, friends seemed threatened

Reason 2: Bad memories of school

Details that develop reason 2: Boredom; fear of being embarrassed

Reason 3: Little time with family

Details that develop reason 3: About an hour to spend with them between work and school; only a little time before bed; homework on weekends

As the outline makes clear, Gary provides three reasons to support his point about starting college at twenty-nine: (1) he had little support from his friends or parents, (2) he had bad memories of school, and (3) college left him little time with his family. Gary also provides vivid details to back up each of his three reasons.

His reasons and descriptive details enable readers to see why he feels that starting college at twenty-nine was difficult.

To write an effective paragraph, then, aim to do what Gary has done: begin by making a point, and then go on to support that point with specific evidence. Finally, like Gary, end your paper with a sentence that rounds off the paragraph and provides a sense of completion.

What Are the Goals of Effective Writing?

Now that you have considered an effective student paragraph, it is time to look at four goals of effective writing:

Goal 1: Make a Point

It is often best to state your point in the first sentence of your paper, just as Gary does in his paragraph about returning to school. The sentence that expresses the main idea, or point, of a paragraph is called the *topic sentence.* Your paper will be unified if you make sure that all the details support the point in your topic sentence. Activities on pages 44–48 in Chapter 3 will help you learn how to write a topic sentence.

Goal 2: Support the Point

To support your point, you need to provide specific reasons, examples, and other details that explain and develop it. The more precise and particular your supporting details are, the better your readers can "see," "hear," and "feel" them. Activities on pages 39–44 and 48–61 in Chapter 3 will help you learn how to be specific in your writing.

Goal 3: Organize the Support

6.1

You will find it helpful to learn two common ways of organizing support in a paragraph—*listing order* and *time order.* You should also learn the signal words, known as *transitions,* that increase the effectiveness of each method.

Listing Order   The writer can organize supporting evidence in a paper by providing a list of two or more reasons, examples, or details. Often the most important or interesting item is saved for last because the reader is most likely to remember the last thing read.

Transition words that indicate listing order include the following:

one	second	also	next	last of all
for one thing	third	another	moreover	finally
first of all	next	in addition	furthermore	

The paragraph about starting college uses a listing order: it lists three reasons why starting college at twenty-nine is not easy, and each of those three reasons is introduced by one of the transitions above. In the spaces below, write in the three transitions:

<u>   For one thing   </u>   <u>   Another   </u>   <u>   Finally   </u>

The first reason in the paragraph about starting college is introduced with *for one thing,* the second reason by *another,* and the third reason by *finally.*

Time Order   When a writer uses time order, supporting details are presented in the order in which they occurred. *First* this happened; *next* this; *after* that, this; and so on. Many paragraphs, especially paragraphs that tell a story or give a series of directions, are organized in time order.

Transition words that show time relationships include the following:

first	before	after	when	then
next	during	now	while	until
as	soon	later	often	finally

Read the paragraph below, which is organized in time order. See if you can underline the six transition words that show the time relationships.

Della had a sad experience <u>while</u> driving home last night. She traveled along the dark, winding road that led toward her home. She was only two miles from her house <u>when</u> she noticed a glimmer of light in the road. The <u>next</u> thing she knew, she heard a sickening thud and realized she had struck an animal. The light, she realized, had been its eyes reflected in her car's headlights. Della stopped the car and ran back to see what she had hit. It was a handsome cocker spaniel, with blond fur and long ears. <u>As</u> she bent over the still form, she realized there was nothing to be done. The dog was dead. Della searched the dog for a collar and tags. There was nothing. <u>Before</u> leaving, she walked to several nearby houses, asking if anyone knew who owned the dog. No one did. <u>Finally</u> Della gave up and drove on. She was sad to leave someone's pet lying there alone.

The main point of the paragraph is stated in its first sentence: "Della had a sad experience while driving home last night." The support for this point is all the details of Della's experience. Those details are presented in the order in which they occurred. The time relationships are highlighted by these transitions: *while, when, next, as, before,* and *finally.*

More about Transitions   Transitions are words and phrases that indicate relationships between ideas. They are like signposts that guide travelers, showing them how to move smoothly from one spot to the next. Be sure to take advantage of transitions. They will help organize and connect your ideas, and they will help your readers follow the direction of your thoughts.

To see how transitions help, write a check beside the item in each pair that is easier to read and understand.

Pair A

_____   One way to stay in shape is to eat low-calorie, low-fat foods. A good strategy is to walk or jog at least twenty minutes four times a week.

__✓__   One way to stay in shape is to eat low-calorie, low-fat foods. Another good strategy is to walk or jog at least twenty minutes four times a week.

Pair B

_____   I begin each study session by going to a quiet place and setting out my textbook, pen, and notebook. I check my assignment book to see what I have to read.

__✓__   I begin each study session by going to a quiet place and setting out my textbook, pen, and notebook. Then I check my assignment book to see what I have to read.

In each pair, the second item is easier to read and understand. In pair A, the listing word *another* makes it clear that the writer is going on to a second way to stay in shape. In pair B, the time word *then* makes the relationship between the sentences clear. The writer first sets out the textbook and a pen and notebook and *then* checks an assignment book to see what to do.

Activities on pages 62–66 will give you practice in the use of listing order and time order, as well as transitions, to organize the supporting details of a paragraph.

Goal 4: Write Error-Free Sentences

If you use correct spelling and follow the rules of grammar, punctuation, and usage, your sentences will be clear and well written. But by no means must you have all that information in your head. Even the best of writers need to use reference materials to be sure their writing is correct. So when you write your papers, keep a good dictionary and grammar handbook nearby.

In general, however, save them for after you've gotten your ideas firmly down in writing. You'll see in the next part of this guide that Gary made a number of sentence errors as he worked on his paragraph. But he simply ignored them until he got to a later draft of his paper, when there would be time enough to make the needed corrections.

How Do You Reach the Goals of Effective Writing?

Even professional writers do not sit down and write a paper automatically, in one draft. Instead, they have to work on it a step at a time. Writing a paper is a process that can be divided into the following steps:

- *Step 1:* Getting Started through Prewriting
- *Step 2:* Preparing a Scratch Outline
- *Step 3:* Writing the First Draft
- *Step 4:* Revising
- *Step 5:* Editing and Proofreading

These steps are described on the following pages.

Step 1: Getting Started through Prewriting

What you need to learn first are strategies for working on a paper. These strategies will help you do the thinking needed to figure out both the point you want to make and the support you have for that point.

There are several *prewriting strategies*—strategies you use before writing the first draft of your paper:

- Freewriting
- Questioning
- Clustering
- Making a list

Freewriting   *Freewriting* is just sitting down and writing whatever comes into your mind about a topic. Do this for ten minutes or so. Write without stopping and without worrying at all about spelling, grammar, or the like. Simply get down on paper all the information about the topic that occurs to you.

Here is the freewriting Gary did on his problems with returning to school. Gary had been given the assignment "Write about a problem you are facing at the present time." Gary felt right away that he could write about his college situation. He began prewriting as a way to explore and generate details on his topic.

Example of Freewriting

One thing I want to write about is going back to school. At age twenty-nine. A lot to deal with. I sometimes wonder if Im nuts to try to do this or just stupid. I had to deal with my folks when I decided. My dad hated school. He knew when to quit, I'll say that for him. But he doesn't understand Im different. I have a right to my own life. And I want to better myself. He teases me alot. Says things like didnt you get dumped on enough in high school, why go back for more. My mom doesnt understand either. Just keeps worring about where the money was coming from. Then my friends. They make fun of me. Also my wife has to do more of the heavy house stuff because I'm out so much. Getting back to my friends, they say dumb things to get my goat. Like calling me the college man or saying ooh, we'd better watch our grammer. Sometimes I think my dads right, school was no fun for me. Spent years just sitting in class waiting for final bell so I could escape. Teachers didnt help me or take an intrest, some of them made me feel like a real loser. Now things are different and I like most of my teachers. I can talk to the teacher after class or to ask questions if I'm confused. But I really need more time to spend with family, I hardly see them any more. What I am doing is hard all round for them and me.

Notice that there are problems with spelling, grammar, and punctuation in Gary's freewriting. Gary is not worried about such matters, nor should he be. He is just concentrating on getting ideas and details down on paper. He knows that it is best to focus on one thing at a time. At this stage, he just wants to write out thoughts as they come to him, to do some thinking on paper.

You should take the same approach when freewriting: explore your topic without worrying at all about being "correct." Figuring out what you want to say should be your focus at this early stage of the writing process.

Questioning   *Questioning* means that you think about your topic by writing down a series of questions and answers about it. Your questions can start with words like *what, when, where, why,* and *how.*

Here are some questions that Gary might have asked while developing his paper, as well as some answers to those questions.

Example of Questioning

Why do I have a problem with returning to school? My parents and friends don't support me.

How do they not support me? Dad asks why I want to be dumped on more. Mom is upset because college costs lots of money. Friends tease me about being a college man.

When do they not support me? When I go to my parents' home for Friday night visits, when my friends see me walking toward them.

Where do I have this problem? At home, where I barely see my wife and daughter before having to go to class, and where I have to let my wife do house things on weekends while I'm studying.

Why else do I have this problem? High school was bad experience.

What details back up the idea that high school was bad experience? Sat in class bored, couldn't wait to get out, teachers didn't help me. One embarrassed me when I didn't know the answer.

Clustering   Clustering is another prewriting strategy that can be used to generate material for a paper. It is helpful for people who like to do their thinking in a visual way.

In *clustering,* you begin by stating your subject in a few words in the center of a blank sheet of paper. Then as ideas come to you, put them in ovals, boxes, or circles around the subject, and draw lines to connect them to the subject. Put minor ideas or details in smaller boxes or circles, and also use connecting lines to show how they relate.

Keep in mind that there is no right or wrong way of clustering. It is a way to think on paper about how various ideas and details relate to one another. Below is an example of clustering that Gary might have done to develop his idea.

Example of Clustering

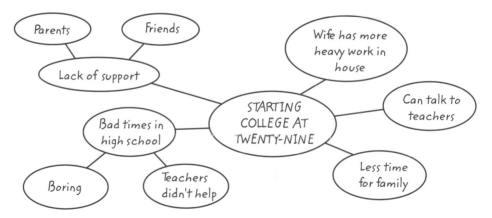

Making a List   In *making a list*—a prewriting strategy also known as *listing, list making,* and *brainstorming*—you make a list of ideas and details that could go into your paper. Simply pile these items up, one after another, without worrying about putting them in any special order. Try to accumulate as many details as you can think of.

After Gary did his freewriting about returning to school, he made up the list of details shown below.

Example of Listing

parents give me hard time when they see me

Dad hated school

Dad quit school after eighth grade

Dad says I was dumped on enough in high school

Dad asks why I want to go back for more

Mom also doesnt understand

keeps asking how Ill pay for it

friends give me a hard time too

friends call me college man

say they have to watch their grammar

my wife has more heavy work around the house

also high school had been no fun for me

just sat in class after class

couldnt wait for final bell to ring

wanted to escape

teachers didnt help me

teachers didnt take an interest in me

one called on me, then told me to forget it

I felt like a real loser

I didnt want to go back to his class

now I'm more sure of myself

OK not to know an answer

talk to teachers after class

job plus schoolwork take all my time

get home late, then rush through dinner

then spend evening studying

even have to do homework on weekends

One detail led to another as Gary expanded his list. Slowly but surely, more supporting material emerged that he could use in developing his paper. By the time he had finished his list, he was ready to plan an outline of his paragraph and to write his first draft.

Notice that in making a list, as in freewriting, details are included that will not actually end up in the final paragraph. Gary decided later not to develop the idea that his wife now has more heavy work to do in the house. And he realized that several of his details were about why school is easier in college ("now I'm more sure of myself," "OK not to know an answer," and "talk to instructors after class"); such details were not relevant to his point.

It is natural for a number of such extra or unrelated details to appear as part of the prewriting process. The goal of prewriting is to get a lot of information down on paper. You can then add to, shape, and subtract from your raw material as you take your paper through the series of writing drafts.

Important Points about Prewriting Strategies   Some writers may use only one of the prewriting strategies described here. Others may use bits and pieces of all four strategies. Any one strategy can lead to another. Freewriting may lead to questioning or clustering, which may then lead to a list. Or a writer may start with a list and then use freewriting or questioning to develop items on the list. During this early stage of the writing process, as you do your thinking on paper, anything goes. You should not expect a straight-line progression from the beginning to the end of your paper. Instead, there probably will be a constant moving back and forth as you work to discover your point and decide just how you will develop it.

Keep in mind that prewriting can also help you choose from among several topics. Gary might not have been so sure about which problem to write about. Then he could have made a list of possible topics—areas in his life in which he has had problems. After selecting two or three topics from the list, he could have done some prewriting on each to see which seemed most promising. After finding a likely topic, Gary would have continued with his prewriting activities until he had a solid main point and plenty of support.

Finally, remember that you are not ready to begin writing a paper until you know your main point and many of the details that can be used to support it. Don't rush through prewriting. It's better to spend more time on this stage than to waste time writing a paragraph for which you have no solid point and not enough interesting support.

Step 2: Preparing a Scratch Outline

A *scratch outline* is a brief plan for a paragraph. It shows at a glance the point of the paragraph and the main support for that point. It is the logical backbone on which the paper is built.

4.1

This rough outline often follows freewriting, questioning, clustering, or listing—or all four. Or it may gradually emerge in the midst of these strategies. In fact, trying to outline is a good way to see if you need to do more prewriting. If a solid outline does not emerge, then you know you need to do more prewriting to clarify your main point or its support. Once you have a workable outline, you may realize, for instance, that you want to do more listing to develop one of the supporting details in the outline.

In Gary's case, as he was working on his list of details, he suddenly discovered what the plan of his paragraph could be. He went back to the list, crossed out items that he now realized did not fit, and added the following comments.

Example of List with Comments

Starting college at twenty-nine isn't easy—three reasons

parents give me hard time when they see me
Dad hated school
Dad quit school after eighth grade
Dad says I was dumped on enough in high school
Dad asks why I want to go back for more
Mom also doesnt understand
keeps asking how Ill pay for it
friends give me a hard time too
friends call me college man
say they have to watch their grammar
~~my wife has more heavy work around the house~~

Parents and friends don't support me

also high school had been no fun for me
just sat in class after class
couldnt wait for final bell to ring
wanted to escape
teachers didnt help me
teachers didnt take an interest in me
one called on me, then told me to forget it
I felt like a real loser
I didnt want to go back to his class
~~now I'm more sure of myself~~
~~OK not to know an answer~~
~~talk to teachers after class~~

Bad memories of school

job and schoolwork take all my time
get home late, then rush through dinner
then spend evening studying
even have to do homework on weekends

Not enough time with family

Under the list, Gary was now able to prepare his scratch outline:

Example of Scratch Outline

Starting college at age twenty-nine isn't easy.
1. Little support from parents or friends
2. Bad memories of school
3. Not enough time to spend with family

After all his preliminary writing, Gary sat back, pleased. He knew he had a promising paper—one with a clear point and solid support. Gary was now ready to write the first draft of his paper, using his outline as a guide.

Step 3: Writing the First Draft

4.2

When you write your first draft, be prepared to put in additional thoughts and details that didn't emerge in your prewriting. And don't worry if you hit a snag. Just leave a blank space or add a comment such as "Do later" and press on to finish the paper. Also, don't worry yet about grammar, punctuation, or spelling. You don't want to take time correcting words or sentences that you may decide to remove later. Instead, make it your goal to develop the content of your paper with plenty of specific details.

Here is Gary's first draft:

First Draft

Last fall, I finaly realized that I was stuck in a dead-end job. I wasnt making enough money and I was bored to tears. I figured I had to get some new skills which meant going back to school. Beginning college at age twenty-nine turned out to be much tougher than I thought it would be. My father didnt understand, he hated school. That's why he quit after eighth grade. He would ask, Didnt you get dumped on enough in high school? Then wondered why I wanted to go back for more of the same thing. My mother was worried about where the money were coming from and said so. When my friends saw me coming down the st. They would make fun of me with remarks like Hey theres the college man. They may have a point. School never was much fun for me. I spent years just siting in class waiting for the bell to ring. So I could escape. The teachers werent much help to me. One time, a teacher called on me then told me to forget it. I felt like a real loser and didnt want to go back to his class. College takes time away from my family. ADD MORE DETAILS LATER. All this makes it very hard for me.

After Gary finished the draft, he was able to put it aside until the next day. You will benefit as well if you can allow some time between finishing a draft and starting to revise.

Step 4: Revising

4.3

Revising is as much a stage in the writing process as prewriting, outlining, and writing a first draft. *Revising* means rewriting a paper, building on what has been done, to make it stronger. One writer has said about revision, "It's like cleaning house—getting rid of all the junk and putting things in the right order." It is not just "straightening up"; instead, you must be ready to roll up your sleeves and do whatever is needed to create an effective paper. Too many students think that the first draft *is* the paper. They start to become writers when they realize that revising a rough draft three or four times is often at the heart of the writing process.

Here are some quick hints that can help make revision easier:

- Ideally, set your first draft aside for a while. A few hours are fine, but a day or two is best. You can then come back with a fresh, more objective point of view.

- Work from typed or printed text. You'll be able to see the paper more impartially in this way than if you were just looking at your own familiar handwriting.

- Read your draft aloud. Hearing how your writing sounds will help you pick up problems with meaning as well as style.

- As you do all these things, add your thoughts and changes above the lines or in the margins of your paper. Your written comments can serve as a guide when you work on the next draft.

Here is Gary's second draft.

Second Draft

Starting college at age twenty-nine turned out to be really tough. I did not have much support from my parents and friends. My father hated school, so he asked, Didnt you get dumped on enough in high school? Why go back for more? My mother asking about where the money were coming from. Friends would be making fun of me. Hey theres the college man they would say as soon as they saw me. Another factor was what happened to me in high school. I spent years just sitting in class waiting for the bell to ring. I was really bored. Also the teachers liked to embaras me. One teacher called on me and then said forget it. He must of relized I didnt know the answer. I felt like a real loser and didnt want to go back in his class for weeks. Finally

I've learned that college takes time away from my family. I have to go to work every day. I have a little over one hour to eat dinner and spend time with my wife and daughter. Then I have to go off to class and when I get back my daughter is in bed asleep. My wife and I have only a little time together. On weekends I have lots of homework to do, so the time goes by like a shot. College is hard for me, but I am going to stay there so I can have a better life.

Notice the improvements made in the second draft:

- Gary started by clearly stating the point of his paragraph. He remembered the first goal in effective writing: *Make a point.*

- To keep the focus on his own difficulties, he omitted the detail about his father quitting school. He remembered that the first goal in effective writing is also to *stick to one point,* so the paper will have unity.

- He added more details so that he would have enough support for his reasons why college was hard. He remembered the second goal in effective writing: *Support the point.*

- He inserted transitions to set off the second reason ("Another factor") and the third reason ("Finally") why starting college at twenty-nine was difficult for him. He remembered the third goal in effective writing: *Organize the support.*

Gary then went on to revise the second draft. Since he was doing the paper on a computer, he was able to print it out quickly. He double-spaced the lines, allowing room for revisions, which he added in longhand during his third draft. (Note that if you are not using a computer, you may want to do each draft on one side of a page, so that you see your entire paper at one time.) Shown below are some of the changes that Gary made in longhand as he worked on his third draft.

Part of Third Draft

Starting college at age twenty-nine ~~turned out to be really tough~~ was difficult. For one thing I did

not have much support from my parents and friends. My father ~~hated school,~~

~~so he~~ asked, Didnt you get dumped on enough in high school? Why go back

for more? My mother ~~asking~~ woried about where the money were coming from.

Friends would ~~be making~~ make fun of me. Hey theres the college man they would

reason that starting college was hard

say as soon as they saw me. Another ~~factor~~ was what happened to me in

final

high school. I spent years just siting in class waiting for the bell to ring. I was

really bored. Also the teachers liked to embaras me. . . .

After writing these and other changes, Gary typed them into his computer file and printed out the almost-final draft of his paper. He knew he had come to the fourth goal in effective writing: *aim for error-free sentences.*

Step 5: Editing and Proofreading

ALLWRITE!

4.4

The next-to-last major stage in the writing process is *editing*—checking a paper for mistakes in grammar, punctuation, usage, and spelling. Students often find it hard to edit a paper carefully. They have put so much work into their writing, or so little, that it's almost painful for them to look at the paper one more time. You may simply have to *will* yourself to carry out this important closing step in the writing process. Remember that eliminating sentence-skills mistakes will improve an average paper and help ensure a strong grade on a good paper. Further, as you get into the habit of checking your papers, you will also get into the habit of using sentence skills consistently. They are an integral part of clear, effective writing.

The checklist of sentence skills on the inside back cover of the book will serve as a guide while you are editing your paper.

Here are hints that can help you edit the next-to-final draft of a paper for sentence-skills mistakes:

Editing Hints

1. Have at hand two essential tools: a good dictionary (see page 336) and a grammar handbook (you can use Part Two of this book).

2. Use a sheet of paper to cover your essay so that you can expose only one sentence at a time. Look for errors in grammar, spelling, and typing. It may help to read each sentence out loud. If the sentence does not read clearly and smoothly, chances are something is wrong.

3. Pay special attention to the kinds of errors you tend to make. For example, if you tend to write run-ons or fragments, be especially on the lookout for these errors.

4. Try to work on a typewritten or word-processed draft, where you'll be able to see your writing more objectively than you can on a handwritten page; use a pen with colored ink so that your corrections will stand out.

Shown below are some of the corrections in spelling, grammar, and punctuation that Gary made when editing his paper.

Part of Gary's Edited Draft

Starting college at age twenty-nine was difficult. For one thing, I did not

have much support from my parents and friends. My father asked, "Didn't

you get dumped on enough in high school? Why go back for more?" My

mother ~~woried~~ *worried* about where the money ~~were~~ *was* coming from. Friends would

make fun of me. "Hey, there's the college man," they would say as soon as they

saw me. . . .

All that remained for Gary to do was to enter in his corrections, print out the final draft of the paper, and proofread it (see below for hints on proofreading) for any typos or other careless errors. He was then ready to hand the paper in to his instructor.

Proofreading, the final stage in the writing process, means checking a paper carefully for errors in spelling, grammar, punctuation, and so on. You are ready for this stage when you are satisfied with your choice of supporting details, the order in which they are presented, and the way they and your topic sentence are worded.

At this point in his work, Gary used his dictionary to do final checks on his spelling. He used a grammar handbook (such as the one in Part Two of this text) to be sure about grammar, punctuation, and usage. Gary also read through his paper carefully, looking for typing errors, omitted words, and any other errors he may have missed before. Proofreading is often hard to do—again, students have spent so much time with their work, or so little, that they want to avoid it. But if it is done carefully, this important final step will ensure that your paper looks as good as possible.

Proofreading Hints

1   One helpful trick at this stage is to read your paper out loud. You will probably hear awkward wordings and become aware of spots where the punctuation needs to be improved. Make the changes needed for your sentences to read smoothly and clearly.

2   Another helpful technique is to take a sheet of paper and cover your paragraph so that you can expose just one line at a time and check it carefully.

3   A third strategy is to read your paper backward, from the last sentence to the first. This helps keep you from getting caught up in the flow of the paper and missing small mistakes—which is easy to do, since you're so familiar with what you mean to say.

What Is an Essay?

An essay does the same thing a paragraph does: it starts with a point, and the rest of it provides specific details to support and develop that point. However, a paragraph is a series of *sentences* about one main idea or point, while an *essay* is a series of *paragraphs* about one main idea or point—called the *central idea.* Since an essay is much longer than one paragraph, it allows a writer to develop a topic in more detail. Despite the greater length of an essay, the process of writing it is the same as that for writing a paragraph: prewriting, preparing a scratch outline, writing and revising drafts, editing, and proofreading.

Here are the major differences between a paragraph and an essay:

Paragraph	*Essay*
Made up of sentences.	Made up of paragraphs.
Starts with a sentence containing the main point (topic sentence).	Starts with an introductory paragraph containing the central idea, expressed in a sentence called the *thesis statement* (or *thesis sentence*).
Body of paragraph contains specific details that support and develop the topic sentence.	Body of essay contains paragraphs that support and develop the central idea. Each of these paragraphs has its own main supporting point, stated in a topic sentence.
Paragraph often ends with a closing sentence that rounds it off.	Essay ends with a concluding paragraph that rounds it off.

Later in his writing course, Gary was asked to expand his paragraph into an essay. Here is the essay that resulted:

> For a typical college freshman, entering college is fun, and an exciting time of life. It is a time not just to explore new ideas in classes but to lounge on the grass chatting with new friends, to sit having soda and pizza in the cafeteria, or to listen to music and play cards in the student lounge. I see the crowds of eighteen-year-olds enjoying all that college has to offer, and

I sometimes envy them their freedom. Instead of being a typical freshman, I am twenty-nine years old, and beginning college has been a difficult experience for me. I have had to deal with lack of support, bad memories of past school experiences, and too little time for my family.

Few people in my life support my decision to enter college. My father is especially bewildered by the choice I have made. He himself quit school after finishing eighth grade, and he assumes that I should hate school as much as he did. "Didn't you get dumped on enough in high school?" he asks me. "Why go back for more?" My mother is a little more understanding of my desire for an education, but the cost of college terrifies her. She has always believed that college was a privilege only the rich could afford. "Where in the world will all that money come from?" she says. And my friends seem threatened by my decision. They make fun of me, suggesting that I'm going to think I'm too good to hang around with the likes of them. "Ooooh, here comes the college man," they say when they see me approach. "We'd better watch our grammar."

I have had to deal not only with family and friends but with unhappy memories of my earlier school career. I attended an enormous high school where I was just one more faceless kid in the crowd. My classes seemed meaningless to me. I can remember almost none of them in any detail. What I do remember about high school was just sitting, bored, until I felt nearly brain-dead, watching the clock hands move ever so slowly toward dismissal time. Such periods of boredom were occasionally interrupted by moments of acute embarrassment. Once an algebra teacher called on me and then said, "Oh, forget it, Callahan," in disgusted tones when he realized I didn't know the answer. My response, of course, was to shrink down in my chair and try to become invisible for the rest of the semester.

Furthermore, my decision to enter college has meant I have much less time to spend with my family. I work eight hours a day. Then I rush home and have all of an hour and ten minutes to eat dinner and spend time with my wife and daughter before I rush off again, this time to class. When I return from class, I am dead tired. My little girl is already asleep. My wife and I have only a little time to talk together before I collapse into bed. Weekends are a little better, but not much. That's when I try to get my papers written and catch up on a few chores around the house. My wife tries to be understanding, but it's hard on her to have so little support from me these days. And I'm missing out on a lot of special times in my daughter's life. For instance, I didn't realize she had begun to walk until three days after it happened.

So why do I put myself and my family through all these difficulties? Sometimes I'm not sure myself. But then I look at my little girl sleeping, and I think about the kind of life I am going to be able to give her. My college degree may make it possible for me to get a job that is more rewarding, both financially and emotionally. I believe I will be a better provider for my family, as well as a more well-rounded human being. I hope that the rewards of a college degree will eventually outweigh the problems I am experiencing now.

What Are the Parts of an Essay?

When Gary decided to expand his paragraph into an essay, he knew he would need to write an introductory paragraph, several supporting paragraphs, and a concluding paragraph.

Each of these parts of the essay is explained below.

Introductory Paragraph

A well-written introductory paragraph will often do the following.

8.1

1   **Gain the reader's interest.** On pages 30–32 are several time-tested methods used to draw the reader into an essay.

2   **Present the thesis statement.** The thesis statement expresses the central idea of an essay, just as a topic sentence states the main idea of a paragraph. Here's an example of a thesis statement.

> A vacation at home can be wonderful.

An essay with this thesis statement would go on to explain some positive things about vacationing at home

What is the thesis statement in Gary's essay? Find that statement on page 28 and write it here:

. . . beginning college has been a difficult experience for me.

You should have written down the next-to-the-last sentence in the introductory paragraph of Gary's essay.

3   **Lay out a plan of development.** A *plan of development* is a brief statement of the main supporting details for the central idea. These supporting details should be presented in the order in which they will be discussed in the essay. The plan of development can be blended into the thesis statement or presented separately.

Blended into a thesis statement: A vacation at home can be wonderful because you can avoid the hassles of travel, make use of your knowledge of the area, and indulge in special activities.

Presented separately: A vacation at home can be wonderful. At home you can avoid the hassles of travel, make use of your knowledge of the area, and indulge in special activities.

Note that some essays lend themselves better to a plan of development than others do. At the least, your introductory paragraph should gain the reader's interest and present the thesis statement.

What is the plan of development in Gary's essay? Find the sentence on page 28 that states Gary's plan of development and write it here:

I have had to deal with lack of support, bad memories . . . and too little

time for my family.

You should have written down the last sentence in the introductory paragraph of Gary's essay.

Four Common Methods of Introduction

1   **Begin with a broad statement and narrow it down to your thesis statement.** A broad statement can capture your reader's interest while introducing your general topic. It may provide useful background material as well. The writer of the introductory paragraph below begins with a broad statement about her possessions. She then narrows the focus down to the three possessions that are the specific topic of the paper.

I have many possessions that I would be sad to lose. Because I love to cook, I would miss several kitchen appliances that provide me with so many happy cooking adventures. I would also miss the wonderful electronic equipment that entertains me every day, including my large-screen television set and my VCR. I would miss the two telephones on which I have spent many interesting hours chatting in every part of my apartment, including the bathtub. But if my apartment were burning down, I would most want to rescue three things that are irreplaceable and hold great meaning for me—the silverware set that belonged to my grandmother, my mother's wedding gown, and my giant photo album.

2   **Present an idea or situation that is the opposite of what you will be writing about.** One way to gain the reader's interest is to show the difference between your opening idea or situation and the one to be discussed in the essay.

> The role of computers in schools is constantly growing. Such growth is based on a widespread faith that computers can answer many of the learning needs of our students. Many people believe that it is just a matter of time before computers do all but take the place of human teachers. However, educators should be cautious about introducing computers into the curriculum. Computers may interfere with the learning of critical language skills, they may move too fast for students to digest new concepts, and they are poor substitutes for certain real-world experiences.

3   **Tell a brief story.** An interesting incident or anecdote is hard for a reader to resist. In an introduction, a story should be no more than a few sentences, and it should relate meaningfully to—and so lead the reader toward—your central idea. The story you tell can be an experience of your own, of someone you know, or of someone you have read about. For instance, in the following introduction, the author tells a simple personal story that serves as background for his central idea.

> I remember the September morning that I first laid eyes on Jasmin. I'd been calling clients at my desk at work when I heard a warm, musical laugh. There was something so attractive about the sound that I got up to get a cup of coffee and to find the source of that laugh. I discovered the voice to be that of a young, auburn-haired woman we had just hired from a temporary agency. Soon after that, Jasmin and I began going out, and we spent the next two years together. Only recently have we decided to break up because of disagreements about finances, about children, and about our relationship with her family.

4   **Ask one or more questions.** The questions may be those you intend to answer in your essay, or they may show that your topic relates directly to readers. In the following example, the questions are designed to gain readers' interest and convince them that the essay applies to them.

> Does your will to study collapse when someone suggests getting a pizza? Does your social life compete with your class attendance? Is there a huge gap between your intentions and your actions? If the answers to these questions are yes, yes, and yes, read on. You can benefit from some powerful ways to motivate yourself: setting goals and consciously working to reach them, using rational thinking, and developing a positive personality.

Which of these four methods of introduction does Gary use in his essay?

method 2

Gary begins with an idea that is the opposite of what he is writing about. His essay is about his difficulties with college life, but he begins with the idea that college "is fun, and an exciting time" for some students.

Supporting Paragraphs

The traditional college essay has three supporting paragraphs. But some essays will have two supporting paragraphs, and others will have four or more. Each supporting paragraph should have its own topic sentence, stating the point to be developed in that paragraph.

Notice that each of the supporting paragraphs in Gary's essay has its own topic sentence. For example, the topic sentence of his first supporting paragraph is "Few people in my life support my decision to enter college."

What is the topic sentence of Gary's second supporting paragraph?

I have had to deal . . . with unhappy memories of my earlier school career.

What is the topic sentence of Gary's third supporting paragraph?

Furthermore, . . . I have much less time to spend with my family.

In each case, Gary's topic sentence is the first sentence of the paragraph.

Concluding Paragraph

8.2

An essay that ended with its final supporting paragraph would probably leave the reader wondering if the author was really done. A concluding paragraph is needed for a sense of completion. Here are two common methods of conclusion.

Two Common Methods of Conclusion

1   **Provide a summary and a final thought.** Using wording different from your introduction, restate your thesis and main supporting points. This review gives readers an overview of your essay and helps them remember what they've read. A final thought signals the end of the paper, as in the following concluding paragraph from an essay about personal possessions.

> If my home ever really did burn down, I would hope to be able to rescue some of the physical things that so meaningfully represent my past. My grandmother's silver set is a reminder of the grandparents who enriched my childhood, my mother's wedding gown is a glamorous souvenir of two

important weddings, and my photo album is a rich storage bin of family and personal history. I would hate to lose them. However, if I did, I would take comfort in the fact that the most important storage place for family and personal memories is my own mind.

2   **Focus on the future.** Focusing on the future often involves making a prediction or a recommendation. This method of conclusion may refer in a general way to the central idea, or it may include a summary. The following conclusion from an essay about self-motivation combines a summary with a prediction. The prediction adds further support for the central idea.

> So get your willpower in gear, and use the three keys to self-motivation—set goals and work to reach them, think rationally, and develop a positive personality. You will find that a firm commitment to this approach becomes easier and easier. Progress will come more often and more readily, strengthening your resolve even further.

What kind of conclusion does Gary use in his essay?

method 2
_____

In his conclusion, Gary refers to his central idea in the context of the future. He makes hopeful points about what his and his family's life will be like after he gets a college degree.

How Can a Computer Help?

If you don't yet write on a computer, it's time to start. In today's world, word processing is an essential mechanical skill, just as effective writing is a vital communication skill.

The computer can be a real aid in the writing process. You can quickly add or delete anything, from a word to an entire section. You can "cut" material and "paste" it elsewhere in seconds. A word-processing program makes it easy to set margins, space lines, and number pages. It can also help you check your spelling, your grammar, and to some extent your style. And at any point during your work, you can print out one or more copies of your text.

Word processing is not hard to learn. Just as you don't need to know how a car works to drive one, you don't need to understand how a computer functions to use it. Once you have learned a few simple keystrokes, you can begin. You do not even need to own your own computer. Nearly every college has at least one computer center, complete with rows of computers and staff members to provide assistance. Free classes in word processing may be available as well.

Tips on Using a Computer

- If you are using your school's computer center, allow enough time. You may have to wait for a computer or printer to be free. In addition, you may need several sessions at the computer and printer to complete your paper.

- Every word-processing program allows you to "save" your writing by hitting one or more keys. Save your work frequently as you work on a draft. Work that is saved is preserved by the computer. Work that is not saved is lost when the file you are working on is closed or when the computer is turned off—or if there's a power or system failure.

- Keep your work in two places—the hard drive or disk you are working on and a backup disk. At the end of each session with the computer, copy your work onto the backup disk. Then if the hard drive or working disk becomes damaged, you'll have the backup copy.

- Print out your work at least at the end of every session. Then not only will you have your most recent draft to work on away from the computer; you'll also have a copy in case something should happen to your disks.

- Work in single spacing so that you can see as much of your writing on the screen at one time as possible. Just before you print out your work, change to double spacing.

- Before making major changes in a paper, create a copy of your file. For example, if your file is titled "Worst Job," create a file called "Worst Job 2." Then make all your changes in that new file. If the changes don't work out, you can always go back to the original file.

Using a Computer at Each Stage of the Writing Process

Following are some ways to make word processing a part of your writing.

Prewriting

If you're a fast typist, many kinds of prewriting will go well on the computer. With freewriting in particular, you can get ideas onto the screen almost as quickly as they occur to you. A passing thought that could be productive is not likely to get lost. You may even find it helpful, when freewriting, to dim the screen of your monitor so that you can't see what you're typing. If you temporarily can't see the screen, you won't have to worry about grammar or spelling or typing errors (all of which do not matter in prewriting); instead, you can concentrate on getting down as many ideas and details as possible about your subject.

After any initial freewriting, questioning, and list-making on a computer, it's often very helpful to print out a hard copy of what you've done. With a clean print-out in front of you, you'll be able to see everything at once and revise and expand your work with handwritten comments in the margins of the paper.

Word processing also makes it easy for you to experiment with the wording of the point of your paper. You can try a number of versions in a short time. After you have decided on the version that works best, you can easily delete the other versions—or simply move them to a temporary "leftover" section at the end of the paper.

Preparing a Scratch Outline

If you have prepared a list of items during prewriting, you may be able to turn that list into an outline right on the screen. Delete the ideas you feel should not be in your paper (saving them at the end of the file in case you change your mind), and add any new ideas that occur to you. Then use the cut and paste functions to shuffle the supporting ideas around until you find the best order for your paper.

Writing Your First Draft

Like many writers, you may want to write out your first draft by hand and then type it into the computer for revision. Even as you type your handwritten draft, you may find yourself making some changes and improvements. And once you have a draft on the screen, or printed out, you will find it much easier to revise than a handwritten one.

If you feel comfortable composing directly on the screen, you can benefit from the computer's special features. For example, if you have written an anecdote in your freewriting that you plan to use in your paper, simply copy the story from your freewriting file and insert it where it fits in your paper. You can refine it then or later. Or if you discover while typing that a sentence is out of place, cut it out from where it is, and paste it wherever you wish. And if while writing you realize that an earlier sentence can be expanded, just move your cursor back to that point and type in the added material.

Revising

It is during revision that the virtues of word processing really shine. All substituting, adding, deleting, and rearranging can be done easily within an existing file. All changes instantly take their proper places within the paper, not scribbled above the line or squeezed into the margin. You can concentrate on each change you want to make, because you never have to type from scratch or work on a messy draft. You can carefully go through your paper to check that all your supporting evidence is relevant and to add new support as needed here and there. Anything you decide to eliminate can be deleted in a keystroke. Anything you add can be inserted precisely where you choose. If you change your mind, all you have to do is delete or cut and paste. Then you can sweep through the paper, focusing on other changes, such as improving word choice, increasing sentence variety, eliminating wordiness, and so on.

If you are like many students, you will find it convenient to print out a hard copy of your file at various points throughout the revision. You can then revise in longhand—adding, crossing out, and indicating changes—and later quickly make these changes in the document.

Editing and Proofreading

Editing and proofreading also benefit richly from word processing. Instead of crossing or whiting out mistakes, or rewriting an entire paper to correct numerous errors, you can make all necessary changes within the most recent draft. If you find editing or proofreading on the screen hard on your eyes, print out a copy. Mark any corrections on that copy, and then transfer them to the final draft.

If the word-processing package you're using includes spelling and grammar checks, by all means use them. The spell-check function tells you when a word is not in the computer's dictionary. Keep in mind, however, that the spell-check cannot tell you how to spell a name correctly or when you have mistakenly used, for example, *their* instead of *there.* To a spell-check, *Thank ewe four the complement* is as correct as *Thank you for the compliment.* Also, use the grammar check with caution. Any errors it doesn't uncover are still your responsibility.

A word-processed paper, with its clean appearance and handsome formatting, looks so good that you may feel it is in better shape than it really is. Do not be fooled by your paper's appearance. Take sufficient time to review your grammar, punctuation, and spelling carefully.

Even after you hand in your paper, save the computer file. Your instructor may ask you to do some revising, and then the file will save you from having to type the paper from scratch.

Chapter Review

Answer each of the following questions by filling in the blank or circling the answer you think is correct.

1. *True or false?* ___T___ Writing is a skill that anyone can learn with practice.

2. An effective paragraph or essay is one that
   a. makes a point.
   b. provides specific support.
   c. makes a point and provides specific support.
   d. does none of the above.

3. The sentence that states the main idea of a paragraph is known as the ___topic___ sentence; the sentence that states the central idea of an essay is known as the ___thesis___ statement.

4. Prewriting can help a writer find
   a. a good topic to write about.
   b. a good main point to make about the topic.
   c. enough details to support the main point.
   d. all of the above.

5. One step that everyone should use at some stage of the writing process is to prepare a plan for the paragraph or essay known as a(n) ___scratch___ ___outline___.

6. When you start writing, your first concern should be
   a. spelling.
   b. content.
   c. grammar.
   d. punctuation.

7. Two common ways of organizing a paragraph are ___listing___ order and ___time___ order.

8. A thesis statement
   a.   is generally part of an essay's introduction.
   b.   states the central idea of the essay.
   c.   can be followed by the essay's plan of development.
   (d) all of the above.

9. The words *first, next, then, also, another,* and *finally* are examples of signal words, commonly known as ___transitions___.

10. A computer can help a writer
    a.   turn a list into an outline.
    b.   find just the right words to express a point.
    c.   add and delete supporting evidence.
    (d) all of the above.

Preview: A Look Ahead

Chapter 3 provides a series of activities to help you master three of the four goals of effective writing: (1) making a point, (2) supporting the point with specific details, and (3) organizing the support. Part Two of this book and a dictionary will help you with the fourth goal—writing error-free sentences. Part Three provides various tests to reinforce the sentence skills studied in Part Two.

3 Practice in Effective Writing

The following series of activities will strengthen your understanding of the writing guidelines presented in Chapter 2. Through practice, you will gain a better sense of the goals of effective writing and how to reach those goals. You will also help prepare yourself for the writing assignments that follow the activities.

Your instructor may ask you to do the entire series of activities or may select the activities that are most suited to your particular needs.

1 Understanding General versus Specific Ideas

A paragraph is made up of a main idea, which is general, and the specific ideas that support it. So to write well, you must understand the difference between general and specific ideas.

It is helpful to realize that you use general and specific ideas all the time in your everyday life. For example, in choosing a video to rent, you may think, "Which should I rent, an action movie, a comedy, or a romance?" In such a case, *video* is the general idea, and *action movie, comedy,* and *romance* are the specific ideas.

Or you may decide to begin an exercise program. In that case, you might consider walking, jumping rope, or lifting weights. In this case, *exercise* is the general idea, and *walking, jumping rope,* and *lifting weights* are the specific ideas.

Or if you are talking to a friend about a date that didn't work out well, you may say, "The dinner was terrible, the car broke down, and we had little to say to each other." In this case, the general idea is *the date didn't work out well,* and the specific ideas are the three reasons you named.

The four activities here will give you experience in recognizing the relationship between general and specific. They will also provide a helpful background for all the information and activities that follow.

Activity 1

Each group of words consists of one general idea and four specific ideas. The general idea includes all the specific ideas. Underline the general idea in each group.

Example   cooking   dusting   vacuuming   <u>chore</u>   washing dishes

1. hammer	drill	saw	screwdriver	<u>tool</u>
2. sprain	fracture	<u>injury</u>	scrape	cut
3. gold	<u>metal</u>	silver	aluminum	brass
4. gas	food	rent	taxes	<u>expense</u>
5. come here	stop	go	<u>command</u>	hurry
6. sneakers	boots	<u>footwear</u>	sandals	high heels
7. <u>entertainment</u>	television	concerts	movies	sporting events
8. long lines	stuck doors	junk mail	slow waiters	<u>annoyances</u>
9. factory	<u>business</u>	hardware store	supermarket	restaurant
10. nail biting	tardiness	smoking	<u>bad habits</u>	interrupting

Activity 2

In each item below, one idea is general and the others are specific. The general idea includes the specific ones. In the spaces provided, write in two more specific ideas that are covered by the general idea.

Example   *General:* exercises
            Specific: chin-ups, jumping jacks, ____*sit-ups*____ , ____*push-ups*____

Answers will vary. Some possibilities are shown.

1. *General:* college subjects
    Specific: American history, psychology, ____English____ , ____sociology____

2. *General:* cookies
    Specific: gingersnap, chocolate chip, ____oatmeal____ , ____Fig Newton____

3. *General:* dogs
    Specific: beagle, collie, ____poodle____ , ____German shepherd____

4. *General:* jobs
    Specific: waitress, judge, ____cook____ , ____editor____

5. *General:* sports
    Specific: tennis, baseball, ____basketball____ , ____hockey____

6. *General:* cooking methods
   Specific: boil, steam, _____bake_____ , _____roast_____

7. *General:* seafood
   Specific: clams, lobster, _____shrimp_____ , _____flounder_____

8. *General:* emotions
   Specific: anger, embarrassment, _____fear_____ , _____love_____

9. *General:* disasters
   Specific: plane crash, tornado, _____fire_____ , _____flood_____

10. *General:* circus performers
    Specific: lion tamer, human cannonball, _____clown_____ , _____trapeze artist_____

Activity 3

Read each group of specific ideas below. Then circle the letter of the general idea that tells what the specific ideas have in common. Note that the general idea should not be too broad or too narrow. Begin by trying the example item, and then read the explanation that follows.

Example   *Specific ideas:* peeling potatoes, washing dishes, cracking eggs, cleaning out refrigerator

The general idea is

a.   household jobs.

(b)   kitchen tasks.

c.   steps in making dinner.

Explanation   It is true that the specific ideas are all household jobs, but they have in common something even more specific—they are all tasks done in the kitchen. Therefore answer *a* is too broad, and the correct answer is *b*. Answer *c* is too narrow because it doesn't cover all the specific ideas. While two of them could be steps in making a dinner ("peeling potatoes" and "cracking eggs"), two have nothing to do with making dinner.

1. *Specific ideas:* "She's picking on me." "He teased me." "He started it." "Why does she get to stay up later than I do?"

   The general idea is:

   a.   complaints.

   (b.)   kids' complaints.

   c.   kids' complaints about bedtime.

2. *Specific ideas:* fleece-lined boots, wool scarf, mittens, ski jacket
   The general idea is:
   a. clothing.
   (b.) winter clothing.
   c. winter footwear.

3. *Specific ideas:* horse, cow, tiger, elephant
   The general idea is:
   a. living things.
   b. animals.
   (c.) four-legged animals.

4. *Specific ideas:* rain, hurricane, snow, wind
   The general idea is:
   (a.) weather conditions.
   b. wet weather conditions.
   c. unusual weather conditions.

5. *Specific ideas:* dictionary, atlas, encyclopedia, almanac
   The general idea is:
   a. books.
   b. nonfiction books.
   (c.) reference books.

6. *Specific ideas:* no smoking, speed limit 40 miles per hour, exit, gentlemen
   The general idea is:
   (a.) signs.
   b. warning signs.
   c. road signs.

7. *Specific ideas:* "I didn't see the speed limit sign," "My car's speedometer was broken," "I was late for a wedding," "I didn't realize how fast I was going"
   The general idea is:
   a. statements.
   b. excuses.
   (c.) excuses for driving too fast.

8. *Specific ideas:* go on a camping trip, take a trip to the seashore, visit a national park, go on a cruise

   The general idea is:

   a.   things to do.

   (b.)   things to do on a vacation.

   c.   things to do on a rainy Sunday afternoon.

9. *Specific ideas:* pretzels, cookies, tortilla chips, popcorn

   The general idea is:

   a.   foods.

   (b.)   snack foods.

   c.   health foods.

10. *Specific ideas:* bike, car, wheelbarrow, vacuum cleaner

    The general idea is:

    a.   common items.

    b.   things for riding.

    (c.)   things with wheels.

Activity 4

In the following items, the specific ideas are given but the general ideas are unstated. Fill in the blanks with the unstated general ideas.

Example   *General idea:*   car problems _____

               Specific ideas: flat tire   dented bumper

                              cracked windshield   dirty oil filter

Wording of answers may vary.

1. *General idea:*   toys _____

   Specific ideas: teddy bear   dollhouse

                        rocking horse   building blocks

2. *General idea:*   performers _____

   Specific ideas: violinist   actor

                        ballerina   singer

3. *General idea:*   things that fly _____

   Specific ideas: airplane   kite

                        bird   bee

4. *General idea:* _____ *beverages* _____
   Specific ideas: milk   tea
                       coffee   lemonade

5. *General idea:* _____ *tests* _____
   Specific ideas: SAT   midterm
                       final   surprise quiz

6. *General idea:* _____ *things for passing from one level to another* _____
   Specific ideas: elevator   escalator
                       stairs   ladder

7. *General idea:* _____ *foods made from corn* _____
   Specific ideas: popcorn   caramel corn
                       cream of corn soup   corn muffins

8. *General idea:* _____ *containers (or carriers)* _____
   Specific ideas: suitcase   briefcase
                       shopping bag   backpack

9. *General idea:* _____ *annoyances* _____
   Specific ideas: mosquitoes   telephone salespeople
                       nosy neighbors   loud engines

10. *General idea:* _____ *free items (or lucky finds)* _____
    Specific ideas: Food samples at the supermarket
                        A good chair on someone's curb on garbage pickup day
                        A five-dollar bill on a street corner
                        A car wash you get for filling your tank with gas

2 Understanding the Paragraph

A *paragraph* is made up of a main idea and a group of related sentences developing the main idea. The main idea often appears in a sentence known as the *topic sentence.*

It is helpful to remember that a topic sentence is a *general* statement. The other sentences provide specific support for the general statement.

Activity

Each group of sentences below could be written as a short paragraph. Circle the letter of the topic sentence in each case. To find the topic sentence, ask yourself, "Which is a general statement supported by the specific details in the other three statements?"

Begin by trying the example item below. First circle the letter of the sentence you think expresses the main idea. Then read the explanation.

Example   a.   Newspapers are a good source of local, national, and world news.

           b.   The cartoons and crossword puzzles in newspapers are entertaining.

           (c.) Newspapers have a lot to offer.

           d.   Newspapers often include coupons worth far more than the cost of the paper.

Explanation   Sentence *a* explains one important benefit of newspapers. Sentences *b* and *d* provide other specific advantages of newspapers. In sentence *c*, however, no one specific benefit is explained. Instead, the words "a lot to offer" refer only generally to such benefits. Therefore sentence *c* is the topic sentence; it expresses the main idea. The other sentences support that idea by providing examples.

1. a.   We tend to drive everywhere, instead of walking.

    (b.) Many Americans don't get enough exercise.

    c.   Automatic machines do much of our work for us, so we don't need to use our own muscles.

    d.   Many of us have little leisure time for regular exercise.

2. a.   The songs have catchy tunes and clever lyrics.

    b.   The dancing is great—lively and athletic.

    (c.) The new musical movie is bound to be a hit.

    d.   The plot is funny and fast-paced.

3. a.   The knife—at first just a sharp edge on a piece of stone—may have been humanity's first invention.

    b.   Language, spoken and then written, is fundamental to human society.

    (c.) Some of the greatest inventions were very early developments in human history.

    d.   Another early invention that made a great deal of other technology possible was a very simple one: the wheel.

4. (a.) Americans send greeting cards for a wide variety of occasions.

    b.   Cards are sent for almost every holiday: Valentine's Day, Mother's Day, and so on.

    c.   Personal occasions calling for greeting cards include birthdays, a new baby, and moving to a new home.

    d.   In addition to the traditional sympathy card when a person dies, today there are sympathy cards for a divorce, losing a job, and the death of a pet.

5. a. Television broadcasts of the World Cup draw more than a billion viewers.

   b. Soccer is a sport anyone can play because it requires no expensive equipment and no special physical traits.

   c. Worldwide, more than 200 million people play soccer, on 4 million teams.

   (d.) Soccer is the world's most popular sport, for both participants and spectators.

3 Understanding the Topic Sentence

ALLWRITE!

3.2

As already explained, most paragraphs center on a main idea, which is often expressed in a topic sentence. An effective topic sentence does two things. First, it presents the topic of the paragraph. Second, it expresses the writer's attitude or opinion or idea about the topic. For example, look at the following topic sentence:

Professional athletes are overpaid.

In the topic sentence, the topic is *professional athletes;* the writer's idea about the topic is that professional athletes *are overpaid.*

Activity

For each topic sentence below, underline the topic and double-underline the point of view that the writer takes toward the topic.

Examples   Living in a small town has many advantages.

         Car phones should be banned.

1. College textbooks are very expensive.
2. Cat owners and dog owners are two different types of people.
3. Public speaking is terrifying to many people.
4. The best things in life are free.
5. Disasters often bring out the best in people.
6. Serving on a jury can be an educational experience.
7. Our landlord is a strange man.
8. Loud car stereos should be made illegal.
9. The food in the cafeteria is unfit for humans to eat.
10. Divorce is not always the right answer to marriage problems.

4 Identifying Topics, Topic Sentences, and Support

The following activity will sharpen your sense of the differences between topics, topic sentences, and supporting sentences.

Activity

Each group of items below includes one topic, one main idea (expressed in a topic sentence), and two supporting details for that idea. In the space provided, label each item with one of the following:

> *T* — Topic
> *MI* — main idea
> *SD* — supporting details

1. __T__ a. Supermarkets.

   __MI__ b. Supermarkets make food shopping very convenient.

   __SD__ c. It saves time to buy most or all of your food in one store.

   __SD__ d. Most supermarkets provide plenty of parking.

2. __SD__ a. Children whose mothers smoke are more likely to have behavioral disorders.

   __MI__ b. Children of smoking mothers suffer harmful effects.

   __SD__ c. Research shows that secondhand smoke increases children's chances of getting lung diseases.

   __T__ d. Mothers who smoke cigarettes.

3. __MI__ a. Beethoven's deafness did not prevent him from composing magnificent music.

   __SD__ b. His Ninth Symphony, with its powerful chorus, was written when he was totally deaf.

   __T__ c. Beethoven's deafness.

   __SD__ d. He wrote the famous Third Symphony, one of his most popular works, after his hearing had begun to fail.

4. _SD_ a. Many refuges and parks have walkways where people in wheelchairs can pass through various bird environments.

_MI_ b. Bird watching can be enjoyed even by people with physical handicaps.

_SD_ c. Many birding hotspots feature an auto-tour, allowing birds to be viewed from a vehicle.

_T_ d. Bird watching.

5. _SD_ a. Vocational school graduates often become some of the best-paid professionals in the United States.

_MI_ b. Vocational training can have significant benefits in life.

_T_ c. Vocational education.

_SD_ d. Many vocational school graduates eventually start their own successful businesses.

5 Recognizing Specific Details I

Specific details are examples, reasons, particulars, and facts. Such details are needed to support and explain a topic sentence effectively. They provide the evidence needed for us to understand, as well as to feel and experience, a writer's point.

Below is a topic sentence followed by two sets of supporting sentences. Write a check mark next to the set that provides sharp, specific details.

Topic sentence: Ticket sales for a recent U2 concert proved that the rock band is still very popular.

_____ a. Fans came from everywhere to buy tickets to the concert. People wanted good seats and were willing to endure a great deal of various kinds of discomfort as they waited in line for many hours. Some people actually waited for days, sleeping at night in uncomfortable circumstances. Good tickets were sold out extremely quickly.

_✓_ b. The first person in the long ticket line spent three days standing in the hot sun and three nights sleeping on the concrete without even a pillow. The man behind her waited equally long in his wheelchair. The ticket window opened at 10:00 A.M., and the tickets for the good seats—those in front of the stage—were sold out an hour later.

Explanation The second set (*b*) provides specific details. Instead of a vague statement about fans who were "willing to endure a great deal of various kinds of discomforts," we get vivid details we can see and picture clearly: "three days standing in the hot sun," "three nights sleeping on the concrete without even a pillow," "The man behind her waited equally long in his wheelchair."

Instead of a vague statement that tickets were "sold out extremely quickly," we get exact and vivid details: "The ticket window opened at 10:00 A.M., and the tickets for the good seats—those in front of the stage—were sold out an hour later."

Specific details are often like a movie script. They provide us with such clear pictures that we could make a film of them if we wanted to. You would know just how to film the information given in the second set of sentences. You would show the fans in line under a hot sun and, later, sleeping on the concrete. The first person in line would be shown sleeping without a pillow under her head. You would show tickets finally going on sale, and after an hour you could show the ticket seller explaining that all the seats in front of the stage were sold out.

In contrast, the writer of the first set of sentences (*a*) fails to provide the specific information needed. If you were asked to make a film based on set *a,* you would have to figure out on your own just what particulars to show.

When you are working to provide specific supporting information in a paper, it might help to ask yourself, "Could someone easily film this information?" If the answer is yes, your supporting details are specific enough for your readers to visualize.

Activity

Each topic sentence below is followed by two sets of supporting details. Write *S* (for *specific*) in the space next to the set that provides specific support for the point. Write *G* (for *general*) next to the set that offers only vague, general support.

1. *Topic sentence:* Watching a rented movie at home is cheaper and more convenient than going to a movie theater.

   _G_ a. Going to a first-run movie with the whole family costs us much more than it would to enjoy some pretty good movies at home. Also, food of all kinds at the theater is certainly more expensive than food we can easily make at home or even have delivered. It's not crowded at home, either. And if we have to leave our seats at the theater for some reason or other, we end up missing several minutes of the movie. But at home, we don't have that problem at all.

   _S_ b. For the $24 it cost to take the family to a movie last night, we could have rented five recent movies. Instead of waiting in line for ten minutes to spend $2 per soda and $2.50 per box of popcorn, we could have had pizza delivered. And at the theater, when we left to take a kid to the restroom, it took us five minutes to figure out what was happening on the screen when we got back. At home, we could have paused the movie for a few minutes.

   Hint: Which set of supporting details could you more readily use in a film?

2. *Topic sentence:* Young children can be difficult travel partners.

_S_ a. First, they constantly ask, "Are we there yet?" even minutes after you have left your driveway. Then, they always forget things—such as going to the bathroom or bringing their favorite toy—so that you have to stop or go back home. Worst of all is their constant arguing over such things as who is "making noises" or "looking me in a funny way" and their pestering an adult to make the other child stop.

_G_ b. First, just a short time after you roll out of your driveway, they begin to ask about the trip. Then, they always want to stop for something little that they need or something they have forgotten to do. Finally, the most annoying thing they do is get mad at each other for unimportant things. When this happens they often drag whichever adult is present into their arguments, pestering him or her over and over.

3. *Topic sentence:* I find life much easier in summer than in winter.

_S_ a. In the summer, I don't have to spend half an hour putting on sweaters, heavy socks, boots, coat, hat, and gloves. When I'm driving, I don't have to crawl at a snail's pace to avoid slipping off icy roads. And when I'm walking outside, I don't have to climb over snowbanks or wade through slush.

_G_ b. For one thing, I save a great deal of time in the summer every day because I don't have to put on heavy clothing to keep from freezing to death. The summer weather is very comfortable. In summer, also, it is much easier to get from place to place, whether I'm driving my car or going somewhere on foot.

4. *Topic sentence:* Contrary to popular opinion, eating chocolate is not as unhealthy as most people think.

_G_ a. As chocolate lovers know, eating chocolate in any form can make you feel better at certain times. It is a wonderful treat. Of course, snacking on too much of any food, especially sweets, can be bad for you. We all know that. But eating chocolate doesn't seem to have any lasting effect on your health. And that's definitely good news.

_S_ b. Chocolate can raise your spirits because it contains small amounts of a natural substance that doctors prescribe as an antidepressant. Eating too much chocolate candy can make you gain weight, of course, just like any other fattening food. However, because of its unique chemical makeup, the fat in the chocolate won't raise your cholesterol no matter how much you eat.

5. *Topic sentence:* Television sportscasters have some annoying habits.

_G_ a. They pile up overly dramatic words, acting like everything they say is the most important thing in the world. They make statements that are too obvious to need saying, but they announce each one as if it were an original or very deep thought everyone will be glad to hear. To top it all off, they keep making annoyingly off-the-wall comments about the players, especially at crucial moments in a game.

_S_ b. They never let a word stand on its own. A team isn't just in trouble; it's in *deep* trouble or *serious* trouble or *the worst kind* of trouble. And they'll say something that everyone knows, such as "He'd sure like to score now," as if it were amazing. And at two strikes with the bases loaded, they'll add a totally unrelated comment like, "Johnny was born in Flint, Michigan, and collects butterflies."

6 Recognizing Specific Details II

Activity

At several points in each of the following paragraphs, you are given a choice of two sets of supporting details. Write *S* (for *specific*) in the space next to the set that provides specific support for the point. Write *G* (for *general*) next to the set that offers only vague, general support.

Paragraph 1

When my friends and I heard that a restaurant was opening up in town, we were excited that there would be a new place to go for dinner. But, now that I have had my first meal there, I do not think I will be visiting that restaurant ever again. From the moment my friends and I walked in the door, our time at the restaurant was disappointing.

_G_ a. Reservations are not honored anywhere near on time; the wait for our table was uncomfortably long. We saw many customers who had come before we did waiting very impatiently, just like we were.

_S_ b. Even with a reservation, we had to wait in the lounge for forty-five minutes before getting our table. Others there said they had been waiting nearly an hour, and we saw two couples give up and leave in disgust.

The service was also a problem.

_S_ c. Just to get a menu, we had to wait half an hour. After the soup, we had to wait another half hour for the main course—or, rather, for some of it, since the clam spaghetti ordered by one of my friends never arrived until the rest of us were nearly finished with our steaks. Dessert came faster, the only problem being that the waiter brought apple pie rather than the lemon sherbet we had ordered.

_G_ d. We had to wait much too long even to get a menu; and after we had eaten our soup we had another lengthy wait for the main course. And unfortunately, the main dish ordered by one of my guests didn't arrive until long after the rest of us had been served and were almost done. We didn't have to wait nearly as long to get our dessert, but it was the wrong dessert—we had ordered something else.

The food was equally disappointing.

_G_ e. The soup was not very tasty, to say the least. The clam spaghetti seemed rather skimpy; there were not enough clams in it. The steaks were done properly, but the meat did not seem to be of the highest quality, to say the least. The dessert did not taste really fresh; in fact, it was quite stale.

_S_ f. The soup was so bland that we couldn't be sure what was in it other than water and a few limp vegetables. The person who had the clam spaghetti counted precisely two clams in it. The steaks were rare, as requested, but so tough that we could hardly cut them. The pie was soggy and seemed to be at least a week old.

Paragraph 2

Today's job market is more competitive than ever. To get a job these days, a person must have more than strong work skills; he or she must also possess strong interview skills. Here are a few steps you can take to strengthen the impression you make at a job interview. First, arrive early.

_G_ a. By arriving a few minutes early for the job interview, you make your interviewer think some positive things about you. This can certainly affect what hiring decisions your potential employer makes. Also, if you are early, you will have the chance to do a few things to get ready, such as calm down, check your appearance, and prepare yourself to say the things you want to say to your interviewer.

_S_ b. Arrive at least ten minutes early to show that you are serious about getting the job. Being early also shows that you will be a punctual and reliable employee. In addition, with the extra time, you can fix your shirt, comb your hair, and wipe any sweat from your palms or forehead. A few extra minutes can also help you review the things that you want to say to your interviewer—where you worked before, what skills you have, and why you think you can do the job.

Have a professional appearance when you go to an interview.

__G__ c. Remember, you are up against strong competition, and you have only a short time to make an impression, so clothes are important. Don't wear clothes that seem to say you don't care what you look like. Make sure you have groomed yourself properly so that you send the right message to your potential boss.

__S__ d. Remember, your interviewer may be speaking to thirty other job candidates. With so much competition and such little time to make an impression, twenty minutes on average, show that you pay attention to detail. Wear clothing similar to what is worn at that job. Put on clean, wrinkle-free clothes; shine your shoes; and have your hair neat and clean.

Be sure to behave in a professional manner.

__S__ e. When you talk to an interviewer, speak clearly. Do not mumble, whisper, or rush through your response. Also, as you talk, look directly at your interviewer. Keeping eye contact—not looking at the floor or the pictures on the wall—will show you are a confident speaker. In addition, sit with your back straight and your feet flat on the floor. Do not slouch forward or sit back in the chair. A relaxed posture suggests that you are not serious about the interview or your work.

__G__ f. When you talk to an interviewer, be sure to speak in a manner that suggests you are a confident professional. Keep your eyes in the right place throughout the entire interview, and be conscious of your body language. All these factors will show the type of speaker and person you are. Also pay attention to your posture throughout the interview. You should make an effort to sit on your chair in a serious position. Appearing to be relaxed will weaken your effect on the interviewer.

7 Providing Specific Details

Activity

Each of the following sentences contains a general word or words, set off in *italic* type. Substitute sharp, specific words in each case.

Example   After the parade, the city street was littered with *garbage.*
             After the parade, the city street was littered with multicolored
             confetti, dirty popcorn, and lifeless balloons.

Answers will vary.

1. It took me *a long time* to complete my chores.

_____

_____

2. When the relationship broke up, I felt *various emotions.*

_____

_____

3. In the accident, the car was *damaged.*

_____

_____

4. When the party started, there were *a lot of snacks* on the table.

_____

_____

5. *Different kinds of insects* invaded our home this summer.

_____

_____

6. Ray *has some unpleasant eating habits.*

_____

_____

7. Our new teacher *did some surprising things.*

_____

_____

8. *The weather has been dreadful* all weekend.

_____

_____

9. My dog can *do a wonderful trick.*

_____

_____

10. The children *acted up* when ordered to come in the house.

_____

_____

8 Selecting Details That Fit

5

The details in your paper must all clearly relate to and support your opening point. If a detail does not support your point, leave it out. Otherwise, your paper will lack unity. For example, see if you can circle the letter of the two sentences that do *not* support the topic sentence below.

> *Topic sentence:* Mario is a very talented person.
>
> (a.) Mario is always courteous to his professors.
> b.   He has created beautiful paintings in his art course.
> c.   Mario is the lead singer in a local band.
> d.   He won an award in a photography contest.
> (e.) He is hoping to become a professional photographer.

Explanation   Being courteous may be a virtue, but it is not a talent, so sentence *a* does not support the topic sentence. Also, Mario's desire to become a professional photographer tells us nothing about his talent; thus sentence *e* does not support the topic sentence either. The other three statements all clearly back up the topic sentence. Each in some way supports the idea that Mario is talented—in art, as a singer, or as a photographer.

Activity

In each group below, circle the two items that do *not* support the topic sentence.

1. *Topic sentence:* Leaving car windows open during a rainstorm can damage a car.
    (a.) Any books or newspapers sitting on the car seats can be ruined.
    b.   Wet carpets have a tendency to get moldy and eventually rot.
    (c.) Sitting on a wet seat can soak a passenger's clothing.
    d.   Getting an instrument panel wet can cause short circuits.
    e.   Water can permanently stain leather seats and dashboards.

2. *Topic sentence:* Rosa is a perfect employee.

    a.   She always arrives at work on time.

    (b.) She saves most of her paycheck for bills.

    c.   Rosa never misses a day of work.

    d.   She is very polite to coworkers.

    (e.) She often tries to persuade her friends to get a job.

3. *Topic sentence:* Popcorn popped and served without fat is a healthy choice for a snack.

    a.   Popcorn itself is very low in fat and in calories.

    b.   It's high in the complex carbohydrates that are better for many people than the simple carbohydrates in sugary snacks.

    (c.) Many people love popcorn as much as other snacks that aren't as good for them.

    d.   Unlike many snacks, popcorn helps digestion because it is a good source of fiber.

    (e.) Popcorn tastes best freshly made.

4. *Topic sentence:* It's hard being the little brother of an award-winning student and athlete.

    (a.) When you were both in grade school, your brother always managed to protect you from the school bullies.

    b.   At the start of each school year, teachers and coaches exclaim, "We expect you to live up to your brother's standards!"

    c.   When you get less than perfect grades, all you hear is, "It's a shame you can't be more like your brother."

    (d.) Your brother leaves for college next year, but promises to help you with your homework over the phone whenever you want.

    e.   At family reunions, everyone crowds around your big brother to hear all the details of his latest accomplishments.

5. *Topic sentence:* In recent years, several factors have caused people to move out of large cities and into nearby suburbs.

    a.   A loss of jobs within cities has forced people to seek work outside of the city.

    b.   High city taxes have driven people out of the cities in search of cheaper living.

ⓒ Improved pollution-control methods have lowered air pollution in many cities.

ⓓ Big cities have more cultural and artistic resources than smaller cities and suburbs.

e. The wish for open space and less crowded neighborhoods has drawn many people to the suburbs.

9 Providing Details That Fit

Activity 1

Each topic sentence below is followed by one supporting detail. See if you can add a second detail in each case. Make sure your detail supports the topic sentence.
Answers will vary.

1. *Topic sentence:* There are good reasons why the movie rental store is losing so many customers.

    a. The store stocks only one copy of every movie, even the most popular titles.

    b. _____

2. *Topic sentence:* The little boy did some dangerous stunts on his bicycle.

    a. He rode down a flight of steps at top speed.

    b. _____

3. *Topic sentence:* Craig has awful table manners.

    a. He stuffs his mouth with food and then begins a conversation.

    b. _____

4. *Topic sentence:* There are many advantages to living in the city.

    a. One can meet many new people with interesting backgrounds.

    b. _____

5. *Topic sentence:* All high school students should have summer jobs.

    a. Summer jobs help teens learn to handle a budget.

    b. _____

Activity 2

See if you can add *two* supporting details for each of the topic sentences below.
Answers will vary.

1. *Topic sentence:* The managers of this apartment building don't care about their tenants.

   a.   Mrs. Harris has been asking them to fix her leaky faucet for two months.

   b.   _____

   c.   _____

2. *Topic sentence:* None of the shirts for sale were satisfactory.

   a.   Some were attractive but too expensive.

   b.   _____

   c.   _____

3. *Topic sentence:* After being married for forty years, Mr. and Mrs. Lambert have grown similar in odd ways.

   a.   They both love to have a cup of warm apple juice just before bed.

   b.   _____

   c.   _____

4. *Topic sentence:* It is a special time for me when my brother is in town.

   a.   We always go bowling together and then stop for pizza.

   b.   _____

   c.   _____

5. *Topic sentence:* Our neighbor's daughter is very spoiled.

   a.   When anyone else in the family has a birthday, she gets several presents too.

   b.   _____

   c.   _____

10 Providing Details in a Paragraph

Activity

The following paragraph needs specific details to back up its three supporting points. In the spaces provided, write two or three sentences of convincing details for each supporting point.

Answers will vary.   **A Disappointing Concert**

   Although I had looked forward to seeing my favorite musical group in concert, the experience was disappointing. For one thing, our seats were terrible, in two ways. _____

_____

_____

_____

_____

In addition, the crowd made it hard to enjoy the music. _____

_____

_____

_____

_____

And finally, the band members acted as if they didn't want to be there. _____

_____

_____

_____

_____

_____

11 Omitting and Grouping Details in Planning a Paper

One common way to develop material for a paper involves three steps: (1) First, make up a list of details about your point. (2) Then omit details that don't truly support your point. (3) Finally, group the remaining details together in logical ways. Omitting details that don't fit and grouping related details together are part of learning how to write effectively.

See if you can figure out a way to put the following details into three groups. Write *A* in front of the details that go with one group, *B* in front of the details that go with a second group, and *C* in front of the details that make up a third group. Cross out the four details that do not relate to the topic sentence.

Topic sentence: My brother Shawn caused our parents lots of headaches when he was a teenager.

__A__ In constant trouble at school

__A__ While playing a joke on his lab partner, nearly blew up the chemistry lab

__B__ Girlfriend was eight years older than he and had been married twice

____ ~~Girlfriend had a very sweet four-year-old son~~

__B__ Parents worried about people Shawn spent his time with

__C__ Several signs that he was using drugs

__A__ Failed so many courses that he had to go to summer school in order to graduate

__A__ Was suspended twice for getting into fights between classes

____ ~~Our father taught math at the high school we attended~~

__C__ His money just disappeared, and he never had anything to show for it

__B__ His best pal had been arrested for armed robbery

__C__ Often looked glassy-eyed

__B__ Hung around with older kids who had dropped out of school

____ ~~Until he was in eighth grade, he had always been on the honor roll~~

__C__ No one was allowed in his room, which he kept locked whenever he was away from home

____ ~~Has managed to turn his life around now that he's in college~~

Explanation   After thinking about the list for a while, you probably realized that the details about Shawn's trouble at school form one group. He got in trouble at school for nearly blowing up the chemistry lab, failing courses, and fighting between classes. Another group of details has to do with his parents' worrying about the people he spent time with. His parents were worried because he had an older girlfriend, a best friend who was arrested for armed robbery, and older friends who were school dropouts. Finally, there are the details about signs that he was using drugs: his money disappearing, his glassy-eyed appearance, and not allowing others in his room.

The main idea—that as a teenager, the writer's brother caused their parents lots of headaches—can be supported with three kinds of evidence: the trouble he got into at school, his friends, and the signs indicating that he was on drugs. The other four items in the list do not logically go with any of these three types of evidence and so should be omitted.

Activity

This activity will give you practice in omitting and grouping details. See if you can figure out a way to put the following details into three groups. Write *A* in front of the details that go with one group, *B* in front of the details that go with a second group, and *C* in front of the details that make up a third group. Cross out the four details that do not relate to the topic sentence.

Topic sentence: There are interesting and enjoyable ways for children to keep their classroom skills strong over summer vacation.

__C__ Kids can help figure out how big a tip to leave in a restaurant.

__A__ They can keep their reading skills sharp in various ways.

____ ~~Summer is a good time for learning to swim.~~

__A__ Reading the newspaper with Mom or Dad will keep kids in touch with challenging reading.

__C__ Adults can ask a child to do such tasks as count their change.

__B__ Kids can have fun improving their writing skills.

__B__ A child might enjoy writing a diary of his or her summer activities.

__A__ Weekly visits to the library will keep them in touch with good books.

____ ~~After returning to school, children can write about their summer vacation.~~

____ ~~Kids should also have plenty of physical exercise over the summer.~~

__C__ Arithmetic skills can be polished over the summer.

__B__ Parents can encourage kids to write letters to relatives.

____ ~~Parents should take children to the library during the school year too.~~

__C__ In the grocery store, a child can compare prices and choose the best bargains.

__A__ Even the comic strips provide reading practice for a young child.

__B__ Getting a pen-pal in another state can give a child an enjoyable reason to write over the summer.

12 Using Transitions

6.1

As already stated, transitions are signal words that help readers follow the direction of the writer's thought. To see the value of transitions, look at the two versions of the short paragraph below. Check the version that is easier to read and understand.

_____ a. Where will you get the material for your writing assignments? There are several good sources. Your own experience is a major resource. For an assignment about childhood, for instance, you can draw on your own numerous memories of childhood. Other people's experience is extremely useful. You may have heard people you know or even people on TV or radio talking about their childhood. Or you can interview people with a specific writing assignment in mind. Books and magazines are a good source of material for assignments. Many experts, for example, have written about various aspects of childhood.

✓ b. Where will you get the material for your writing assignments? There are several good sources. First of all, your own experience is a major resource. For an assignment about childhood, for instance, you can draw on your own numerous memories of childhood. In addition, other people's experiences are extremely useful. You may have heard people you know or even people on TV or radio talking about their childhood. Or you can interview people with a specific writing assignment in mind. Finally, books and magazines are a good source of material for assignments. Many experts, for example, have written about various aspects of childhood.

Explanation   You no doubt chose the second version, _b_. The listing transitions—_first of all, in addition,_ and _finally_—make it clear when the author is introducing a new supporting point. The reader of paragraph _b_ is better able to follow the author's line of thinking and to note that three main sources of material for assignments are being listed: your own experience, other people's experience, and books and magazines.

Activity

The following paragraphs use listing order or time order. In each case, fill in the blanks with appropriate transitions from the box that comes before the paragraph. Use each transition once.

1.

after	before	later	then	when

On those miserable days when everything goes wrong, I like to fantasize about a day when everything would go right. On my fantasy day, I'd wake up early, a few minutes _____before_____ the alarm would have gone off, and outside my window I'd see sparkling sunshine and blue sky. _____After_____ dressing unhurriedly, I'd stroll to the bus stop, arriving just as the bus pulled up. I'd get a nice window seat, and _____then_____ the bus would roll into town with no traffic tie-ups. When I arrived at work, my boss would greet me with a big smile and tell me he was giving me a raise. _____Later_____, at lunch time, he'd take me to a plush restaurant to celebrate. And _____when_____ I got home that evening, my neighbor would be waiting for me—with tickets to the ball game.

2.

third	finally	for one thing	second	in addition

Though not all migraine headaches are alike, they tend to have typical features. _____For one thing_____, migraines may come every few days or weeks, or months may go by without an attack. A _____second_____ feature is that while a migraine can be set off by stress, it usually doesn't develop until after the stressful event is over. _____Third_____, a migraine is one-sided: the pain is on the left or right side of the face or head, and for any individual it's usually on the same side. _____In addition_____, the pain is throbbing and may be accompanied by nausea. _____Finally_____, a coming attack is often signaled by an "aura": a period during which the individual may feel tired or depressed or may have difficulties with vision, such as seeing flashes of light or being unable to read.

3.

when	later	during

_____During_____ the winter of 1928, a terrible flu epidemic raged across the United States. Many employees of Miles Laboratories, a pharmaceutical company in Elkhart, Indiana, were home sick. But _____when_____ the president of Miles Labs visited the office of the Elkhart newspaper, he found every employee healthy and at work. The paper's editor explained that at the first hint of a cold symptom, he dosed staff members with a combination of aspirin and baking soda. The president was impressed with the idea. He _____later_____ asked his company chemists to come up with a tablet that combined the two ingredients. In 1931 the resulting product, Alka-Seltzer, was put on the market.

4.

another	last	first of all	also

Date rape has become a serious issue for high-school and college students. There are some basic strategies for protecting yourself from date rape and its consequences. _____First of all_____, double-date or group-date, especially if you are going out with someone you don't know very well. _____Another_____ thing to remember is not to drink alcoholic beverages. Alcohol can cloud your judgment and harm your memory. _____Also_____, avoid parties that are not chaperoned. At a party, stay with the crowd. Never allow anyone to lure you or force you into an empty room or hidden area. _____Last_____, if all of the precautions fail and you fall victim to date rape, go immediately to a hospital or rape-crisis center and seek medical help and counseling.

13 Organizing Details in a Paragraph

The supporting details in a paragraph must be organized in a meaningful way. The two most common methods of organizing details are listing order and time order. The activities that follow will give you practice in both methods of organization.

Activity 1

Use *listing order* to arrange the scrambled list of sentences below. Number each supporting sentence 1, 2, 3, . . . so that you go from the least important item to what is presented as the most important item.

Note that transitions will help by making clear the relationships between some of the sentences.

Topic sentence: You can protect yourself and your valuables while traveling by keeping a few guidelines in mind.

___7___ Keep an immediate store of cash in your purse or wallet, but hide the rest of your money and your credit cards in a money belt.

___3___ Second, be aware of your surroundings and of the people around you.

___1___ The first rule is plain common sense: Pack light.

___2___ The less you have to carry, the less you'll have to lose, and the less vulnerable you'll look to a would-be thief.

___6___ But the biggest favor you can do yourself is not to keep all your valuables in one place.

___4___ Don't discuss where you are staying, where you are going, or other personal details so that strangers can overhear you.

___8___ That way, if your purse or wallet is stolen, you won't lose everything.

___5___ In addition, make photocopies of your driver's license, credit cards, and other important documents, so you have all that information on hand in case the originals are stolen.

Activity 2

Use *time order* to arrange the scrambled sentences below. Number the supporting sentences in the order in which they occur in time (1, 2, 3, . . .).

Note that transitions will help by making clear the relationships between sentences.

Topic sentence: If you're interviewing for a job, following these steps will help you make a good impression.

___5___ One way to make sure you're on time is to do a "practice run" to figure out exactly how long it takes you to get to the office and find a parking spot, or walk from the bus or subway stop.

___8___ After the interview, be sure to send a thank-you note that says again how much you are interested in the job.

___3___ You can find out the company "look" by going by the office at quitting time and seeing what employees are wearing.

___1___ As soon as you've scheduled the interview, decide what outfit you will wear.

___4___ On the big day, do whatever is necessary to arrive for the appointment on time—even a few minutes early.

___7___ For example, if you are interviewing for a sales job, say, "As a psychology major, I've learned a lot about what makes people want to buy."

___2___ Choose an outfit that makes you look as though you already work for the company.

___6___ During the interview itself, make it clear how your abilities make you a good choice for the position.

14 Understanding the Plan of Development in an Essay

Activity

Complete each thesis statement below by adding a third supporting idea. Use wording that is parallel to the two supporting ideas already provided.
Answers will vary.

1. Among the smartest things I've ever done in my life were giving up smoking, learning to use a computer, and _____.

2. Three ingredients for a perfect vacation are a good traveling companion, good weather, and _____.

3. If I could take only three courses at college, they would be in literature, psychology, and _____.

4. The three modern inventions I'd find it hardest to do without are the automobile, the telephone, and _____.

5. Not coming to work on time, taking long lunch breaks, and _____ _____ are certain ways to annoy your boss and lose your job.

6. To reduce stress, it is helpful to take a brisk walk, talk things over with a friend, and _____.

7. Having a sense of humor, being a good listener, and _____ _____ are qualities I enjoy in my friends.

8. The reasons I like gardening so much are that I enjoy being outside, getting exercise, and _____.

9. Crowded aisles, rude fellow shoppers, and _____

_____ make going to the supermarket an unpleasant
experience.

10. Three good ways to prepare for a test are reviewing your notes, studying with

classmates, and _____.

15 Recognizing Specific Details in an Essay

Activity

For each supporting paragraph in the essay below, there are two sets of supporting details. Write *S* (for *specific*) in the blank next to the set that provides specific
support for the topic sentence. Write *G* (for *general*) in the blank next to the set
with only vague, general support.

Introduction

What do you do if you're a college student who could use some extra
money? You may already have a part-time job and still need some extra cash.
A full-time job is out of the question—what's the point of being in school if
you don't have time to study? Well, there are ways to make some extra bucks
by using free time here and there plus your special skills and experience and
some old-fashioned get-up-and-go. You can give your finances a boost by cre-
ating your own business in a field such as arts and crafts, house and yard
work, and animal care.

Supporting Paragraph 1

"Arts and crafts" may sound like a summer camp activity, but it is actually a good way to pick up some extra money.

_G_ a. Even if you think you have no artistic talent, you can probably make
something lovely that someone else would like to buy. There are many
types of arts and crafts, and most do not require drawing or painting.
By making use of those spare moments everyone has—during the
day, in the evenings, and on weekends—you can accomplish a lot
more than you think. You can even make money on something that
you up till now have thought of only as a hobby. By now you may
be very good at that hobby, and people will be happy to pay you for
your high-quality work.

_S_ b. For example, Rashid, a freshman, makes great wire-wrap and beaded jewelry. He works on the jewelry during odd hours—for a half hour or so in the morning before leaving for his first class, when he wants a break from studying, and even while "watching" TV. He gets inexpensive supplies from various sources. For instance, he gets some of his beads from cheap old jewelry he picks up at yard sales. At a recent one-day craft show, Rashid made $150. He sells his work at many such shows during the year.

Supporting Paragraph 2

Perhaps you don't have the interest or patience needed for arts-and-crafts work. Well, you can still make considerable cash doing work almost anybody can do—housework and yard work.

_S_ a. Maybe, like Olga, an accounting major, you have been helping with the cleaning of your family's home. Then, like her, you might not mind spending several hours once a week to clean someone else's home. For your efforts, you can take home from $30 to as much as the $60 per week that Olga makes. Or you can make an average of about $20 for each lawn you mow. Like Tim, you could pass out flyers advertising your skills and end up earning over $3,000 during the mowing months.

_G_ b. Like many people, you may have already spent a good deal of time on such work. You may be one of those "volunteered" at your house to help every week in keeping things tidy throughout the house. Or your contribution may be to do something or other outdoors, in the yard or garden. While you may have been doing some form of upkeep over the years for your family without earning a cent, believe it or not, there are a lot of families who will pay you to do those same activities.

Supporting Paragraph 3

If you have any experience caring for animals, you can profit from that experience in several ways.

_G_ a. Working people will sometimes pay a responsible person to spend time with their dog during the day. People who go on vacation will often choose to use a pet-sitter rather than board their pets at a commercial kennel, where the pet is locked up in a caged area. Restaurants and other businesses, such as dental offices, that display fish tanks will often pay someone to take care of the tanks regularly, rather than tie up their own employees with the task.

_S_ b. For example, Cesar, a business major, has a couple of hours each morning before classes begin. So he charges $3 a day to walk dogs for people in his center-city apartment complex. Walking eight dogs at a time, he makes about $500 a month—in addition to his week-end job. Patricia, a freshman, charges businesses $10 a week to clean fish tanks. She has ten regular clients and can arrange the work to fit her class schedule.

Conclusion

So if you feel that life would be so much easier if you only had a few more bucks in your pocket, don't just moan about it. There are ways to fatten your wallet by making good use of the time you may now be spending sleeping late, watching TV, or talking on the phone. You will find that it pays to be willing to find the right place to sell your services and do the necessary promotion. As a bonus, you will get some great experience in dealing with people and in running your own business.

16 Providing Details in an Essay

Activity

The supporting paragraphs of the following essay need more specific details. In the spaces provided, add a sentence or two of convincing details for each idea. Answers will vary.

Introduction

Living at home with my family had many advantages. Since my mother didn't charge me anything to live at home, it was definitely cheaper—I had no rent or food bills. There was always someone at home to take my phone messages, to provide encouragement when I was feeling low, and to worry about me when I was sick. But living at home was not perfect. In fact, I recently decided to move out and rent an apartment with a friend. My main reasons for moving out were to give me a better environment for my college work, to have more freedom and privacy, and to build a better relationship with my mother.

Supporting Paragraph 1

First of all, a place of my own will provide a better place to study. It will undoubtedly be more quiet than it was at home. _____

_____

_____

_____

_____

Also, I will have fewer interruptions in my own place than I had at home.

_____

_____

_____

_____

And if I need to study with a friend, I will feel freer to invite someone over to my own apartment. _____

_____

_____

_____

_____

Supporting Paragraph 2

In addition, having my own apartment will give me more freedom and privacy. At home, there were all kinds of demands on my time. _____

_____

_____

_____

Second, at home it was difficult to make phone calls in private. _____

_____

_____

_____

_____

Furthermore, it was almost impossible to spend some private time when my friends came over. _____

_____

_____

_____

_____

Supporting Paragraph 3

Finally, by moving into my own place, I am establishing a better relationship with my mother. My bad habits no longer annoy her and cause her to constantly yell at me. _____

_____

_____

_____

_____

Also, since she now doesn't expect me to take much responsibility around the house, I don't resent her as much. _____

_____

_____

_____

_____

Simply being apart for much of the time has helped our relationship. _____

_____

_____

_____

_____

Conclusion

I love my mother and my sisters and little brother, but I am much happier living in my own place. Now that the problems I had with studying, gaining control over my own life, and arguing with my mother have improved, I am happier, and my family is happier too. In fact, I've noticed that when I go back to my family's house to visit and help out, everyone is happy to see me, and I have a better time.

17 Providing Transitions in an Essay

Activity 1

6.1

The following essay uses time order. Fill in the blanks with appropriate transitions from the box. Use every transition once. You will probably find it helpful to check off (✔) each transition as you use it.

as	during	while	after
when	later	until	then
immediately	before	finally	

Volunteering at a wildlife rehabilitation center can be very rewarding. Watching sick and injured animals mend and orphans grow strong and independent is very satisfying. It is especially thrilling to see an animal being returned to the wild soon _____after_____ you have helped nurse it back to health. But there can be a downside. As my sons and I found out, when you volunteer at the center, your time is never your own. Recently, my family's plans for a day of fishing on my day off from work were upset by some very active babies, a large bird who liked fast food, and a fishhook.

It all began when my phone rang just _____as_____ the boys and I were stepping out the door to leave for the lake. The supervisor at the rehabilitation center wanted to know if I could pick up a few orphaned chipmunks someone had found and bring them to the center. Since the chipmunks and the center were on our way, I agreed. _____When_____ we arrived at the address, however, we found that the chipmunks had escaped and were running loose in the house. It took almost two hours to urge them out of hiding and recapture them. But then we delivered the babies to the center.

The task accomplished, the boys and I decided that we should eat lunch _____before_____ continuing. _____During_____ lunch at a fast-food restaurant, my sons looked out the window and saw a laughing gull sitting on a nearby trash can. The bird's feathers were dripping with grease. Often these birds become coated with discarded cooking oil while rummaging through trash cans looking for a meal. _____Immediately_____, the boys and I left our lunch and went to the rescue. Forty minutes _____later_____, the bird was being washed at the center, and the boys and I were on the road again.

Following a long drive, we ___finally___ arrived at the lake. Soon we were unpacking our fishing gear, but ___then___ fate struck again. A great black-backed gull had snagged a fisherman's bait and got a fishhook caught in its throat. Fishing was put on hold ___until___ we could capture the big bird and make our third trip of the day to the rehabilitation center.

Later, ___while___ fishing, the boys and I discussed our adventures. We all agreed that we were glad we had been able to help the unfortunate animals. However, we hope that animal emergencies won't intrude on our next fishing trip.

Activity 2

The following essay uses listing order. Fill in the blanks with appropriate transitions from the box. Use every transition once. You will probably find it helpful to check off (✓) each transition as you use it.

one	for one thing	moreover	first	in addition
another	second	furthermore	finally	third

Parents come in all sorts, shapes, and sizes, and we might suppose that no two are alike. One researcher, however, has examined parents' methods of child rearing and has suggested that their styles fall into three general types: (1) permissive, (2) authoritarian, or (3) authoritative. These terms may sound highly technical, but the three styles they identify seem to be in line with everyday observations; in other words, they describe familiar types of parents. Each type has distinct characteristics.

In the ___first___ category is the permissive parent. Permissive parents are every child's dream. ___One___ characteristic of permissive parents is that they give a child as much freedom as possible. "Anything goes" is their motto. ___Another___ characteristic is that they don't make demands on their children. Permissive parents seldom set rules for their kids, and when they do, they are sure to explain why. ___Moreover___, these parents rarely punish their children. Instead of imposing rules and punishment, they encourage their kids to take part in family decisions. Emotionally, permissive parents are warm toward their children.

In the _____second_____ category are authoritarian parents—who might be called a kid's nightmare. _____For one thing_____, these parents exert enormous control over their children. They want and expect instant obedience to their orders; and they are likely to give orders constantly and to set very high, rigid standards. Their motto is, "I'm the boss." _____In addition_____, they are quick to punish a child (sometimes harshly) for not living up to their standards, or for any other kind of disobedience. Authoritarian parents are typically less warm toward their kids than parents in the other two categories.

_____Finally_____, in the _____third_____ category are authoritative parents. Scientific researchers do not often make value judgments, but in this case they do: authoritative parents are the researchers' dream. These parents love and respect their kids, and they value independence for children. But they do make rules and they do set standards. _____Furthermore_____, they will impose discipline when necessary. They are warm and encouraging, and they reason with their kids, but they are firm about the things they consider important. And, according to the researchers, it is the children of authoritative parents, on the whole, who turn out best.

What about your parents—which category would you place them in? And what about you yourself? If you are already a parent, which style is yours? If parenthood is still in your future, which style would you like to make yours?

Note: "Furthermore," "in addition," and "moreover" could be interchanged.

18 Introductory and Concluding Paragraphs

ALLWRITE!
8.1

Activity 1

Four common methods of introducing an essay are as follows:

a Begin with a broad statement and narrow it down to your thesis statement.
b Present an idea or situation that is the opposite of the one you will develop.
c Tell a brief story.
d Ask one or more questions.

Following are four introductions. In the space provided, write the letter of the method of introduction used in each case.

_____d_____ 1. Does it seem like every time you try to get ahead, something unexpected comes along to set you back again? Do you sometimes feel overwhelmed by your financial commitments? Have you postponed important milestones in your life, such as buying a house or having a child, because you are afraid you won't be able to afford them? By following a few simple guidelines, you can begin to gain control of your financial future, build confidence in your ability to manage your resources, and start making your dreams come true.

_____ c _____

2. A couple awake one morning to find that their elderly cat has died during the night. So as not to distress their children with the sight of the corpse, the husband wraps it up, puts it in a shopping bag, and takes it with him when he leaves for work. He commutes on a ferry, and his plan is to dispose of the body by tossing it overboard. The shopping bag happens to be from a very classy store. On the ferry, the man leaves the bag unattended while he is getting coffee; when he returns, it has been stolen. The Dead Cat in the Shopping Bag is an "urban legend," one of many such stories that have always fascinated ordinary people and are now also beginning to draw the attention of sociologists. Urban legends have three notable features: they spread rapidly, they are always described as factual, and they keep reappearing in new versions.

_____ b _____

3. When you can't sleep, it may seem logical to take a sleeping pill. After all, insomnia—sleeplessness—not only gives you a miserable night but also lowers your productivity the next day by making you weary, irritable, and fuzzy-minded. So it's tempting to reach for a pill that promises to spare you all this—but you should resist the temptation. Here's why that pill can actually make things worse, and why you should try some safer remedies.

_____ a _____

4. I've shared my life and home with many marvelous pets over the years. I've had dogs that have helped with the farm chores, herding the sheep and cattle. I've had parrots that have called me by name and warned me, "Don't be late for dinner," each time I've left the house. But without a doubt, the most special animal in my life was a huge, three-legged, cross-eyed, bob-tailed cat that enriched my life for almost ten years. She was an efficient exterminator, a loving foster mother, and the best conversation piece I've ever known.

Activity 2

Two common methods of concluding an essay are as follows:

a   Provide a summary and a final thought.
b   Focus on the future.

Following are two conclusions. In the space provided, write the letter of the method of conclusion used in each case.

_____b_____   1. You may be glad to know that the oven was finally fixed, and we had our real Thanksgiving dinner the next day. Since then, I have already started thinking about Thanksgiving next year. My frustrating experience has made me wonder if my sister has the right idea. Maybe I should start doing what she has done the last few years—accept our aunt's invitation to come and have Thanksgiving dinner with her in Florida.

_____a_____   2. When I first joined Mr. Yo's class, studying karate seemed to be a constructive way for me to spend my free time. After three years, I've had no cause to change that opinion. I've learned self-discipline, trained myself to be physically fit, and gained a core of inner peace. Every minute of my time spent studying karate has been worth it.

19 Prewriting

2.3

These activities will give you practice in some of the prewriting strategies you can use to generate material for a paper. While the focus here is on writing a paragraph, the strategies apply to writing an essay as well. See if you can do two or more of these prewriting activities.

Note: Responses to these activities will vary.

Activity 1: Freewriting

On a sheet of paper, freewrite for several minutes about the best or most disappointing friend you ever had. Don't worry about grammar, punctuation, or spelling. Try to write, without stopping, about whatever comes into your head concerning your best or most disappointing friend.

Activity 2: Questioning

On another sheet of paper, answer the following questions about the friend you've started to write about.

1. When did this friendship take place?

2. Where did it take place?

3. What is one reason you liked or were disappointed in this friend? Give one quality, action, comment, etc. Also, give some details to illustrate this quality.

4. What is another reason that you liked or were disappointed in your friend? What are some details that support the second reason?

5. Can you think of a third thing about your friend that you liked or were disappointed in? What are some details that support the third reason?

Activity 3: Clustering

In the center of a blank sheet of paper, write and circle the words *best friend* or *most disappointing friend*. Then, around the circle, add reasons and details about the friend. Use a series of boxes, circles, or other shapes, along with connecting lines, to set off the reasons and details. In other words, try to think about and explore your topic in a very visual way.

Activity 4: Making a List

On separate paper, make a list of details about the friend. Don't worry about putting them in a certain order. Just get down as many details about the friend as occur to you. The list can include specific reasons you liked or were disappointed in the person and specific details supporting those reasons.

20 Outlining, Drafting, and Revising

Here you will get practice in the writing steps that follow prewriting: outlining, drafting, revising, editing, and proofreading.

Note: Responses to these activities will vary.

Activity 1: Scratch Outline

On the basis of your prewriting, see if you can prepare a scratch outline made up of your main idea and the three main reasons you liked or were disappointed in your friend. Use the form below:

_____ was my best *or* most disappointing friend.

Reason 1: _____

Reason 2: _____

Reason 3: _____

Activity 2: First Draft

Now write a first draft of your paper. Begin with your topic sentence, stating that a certain friend was the best or most disappointing one you ever had. Then state the first reason to support your main idea, followed by specific details supporting that reason. Next, state the second reason, followed by specific details supporting that reason. Finally, state the third reason, followed by support.

Don't worry about grammar, punctuation, or spelling. Just concentrate on getting down on paper the details about your friend.

Activity 3: Revising the Draft

Ideally, you will have a chance to put your paper aside for a while before writing the second draft. In your second draft, try to do all of the following:

1. Add transition words such as *first of all, another,* and *finally* to introduce each of the three reasons you liked or were disappointed in the friend you're writing about.

2. Omit any details that do not truly support your topic sentence.

3. Add more details as needed, making sure you have plenty of support for each of your three reasons.

4. Check to see that your details are vivid and specific. Can you make a supporting detail more concrete? Are there any persuasive, colorful specifics you can add?

5. Try to eliminate wordiness (see page 378) and clichés (see page 374).

6. In general, improve the flow of your writing.

7. Be sure to include a final sentence that rounds off the paper, bringing it to a close.

Activity 4: Editing and Proofreading

When you have your almost-final draft of the paper, proofread it as follows:

1. Using your dictionary, check any words that you think might be misspelled. Or use a spell-check program on your computer.

2. Using Part Two of this book, check your paper for mistakes in grammar, punctuation, and usage.

3. Read the paper aloud, listening for awkward or unclear spots. Make the changes needed for the paragraph to read smoothly and clearly. Even better, see if you can get another person to read the draft aloud to you. The spots that this person has trouble reading are spots where you may have to do some rewriting.

4. Take a sheet of paper and cover your writing so that you can expose and carefully check one line at a time. Or read your writing backward, from the end of the paragraph to the beginning. Look for typing errors, omitted words, and other remaining errors.

Don't fail to edit and proofread carefully. You may be tired of working on your paper at this point, but you want to give the extra effort needed to make it as good as possible. A final push can mean the difference between a higher and a lower grade.

21 Paragraph and Essay Writing Assignments

Your instructor may ask you to do some of the following paragraph and essay writing assignments. Be sure to refer to the activities on pages 39–78 as you write. Also, check the rules for paper format on page 260.

Note: Responses to these activities will vary.

Five Paragraph Assignments

■ Paragraph Assignment 1: Providing Examples

Listed below are three topic sentences, followed by specific examples, the supporting details. On a piece of paper, invent two additional examples to support each point. Try to make your examples as specific and as realistic as the ones shown.

Point: My friend Mac has several dangerous driving habits.

1. For one thing, he never signals when he's going to make a left-hand turn. The only warning a car behind Mac has is when he slows down suddenly.

2. …

3. …

Point: My apartment is in need of repairs.

1. When it rains, water runs down through the ceiling light fixture in the bedroom. The ceiling is always damp and soggy, and there is a musty odor that grows stronger every day.

2. …

3. …

Point: There are three kinds of everyday happenings that really annoy me.

1. First of all, I hate waiting in long lines at a store, especially when several employees are standing around nearby when they could be opening up another register.

2. …

3. …

■ Paragraph Assignment 2: A Great Snack

Everyone has a favorite snack. What is yours? Maybe it is a huge plate of tortilla chips coated with cheese, a bowl of vanilla ice cream sprinkled with semisweet chocolate chips, or a stack of chocolate graham crackers to dip in hot cocoa with marshmallows floating on top. Write a paragraph about preparing and eating your perfect snack, including any special way, place, or time you prefer to eat the snack.

Begin your paragraph with a statement that summarizes the details you plan to write about, such as this: "One of my favorite snacks is a ham and cheese sandwich with pickle chips, which must be made and eaten in just the right ways." Then go on to explain in detail just how you prepare your snack. For the example above, you would include what kind of bread you use, how many slices of ham and cheese you put on, and where exactly you position the pickle chips. You would then go on to write about how you like to eat your creation. For instance, perhaps the best way to eat your favorite snack is late at night while sitting on your living-room couch with a good book in your hand and the TV turned on with the sound turned down.

Your paragraph will be organized in time order, describing the different steps that are involved in your enjoyment of the snack. Help your reader follow your supporting details by using time transition words, such as *first, next, then,* and *finally.*

■ Paragraph Assignment 3: A Special Photograph

Pictures have a magical power. They freeze moments in time forever, allowing us to look back to places and events that happened long ago. Find a photograph that has special meaning for you. Perhaps it is a photo of a family member who has passed away or a childhood picture of you and a close friend. Write a paragraph describing the picture and explaining its significance. Begin with your topic sentence, perhaps similar to one of the following:

> A photo I have of me with my first girlfriend, Dana, is very special for two reasons.

> A photograph of a funny scene during my tenth birthday party reminds me of the most fun—and the funniest—birthday party I ever had.

Since your readers will not actually see the picture, it is up to you to provide descriptive details so that they will know just what the picture looks like. You might use that description as a starting point for the specific details needed to support your topic sentence.

After describing the photo referred to in the first topic sentence above, for example, you would go on to explain the two reasons mentioned. One reason might be that the photo was taken on a particularly wonderful date. A colorful description of that date will help readers see just how terrific it was. Your second reason might be that Dana is the person you ended up marrying, and that photo is the earliest one of you two together. A few more details about the photo—how you two posed, the expressions on your faces—may tell how the photo shows you suspected even then you would end up together. (You may wish to attach a copy of the photo to the draft of the paper that you hand in.)

■ Paragraph Assignment 4: Your Position in the Family

Psychologists have concluded that there are significant differences in being an only, oldest, middle, or youngest child. Which of these are you, and how did it influence the way you were brought up? Did you have more responsibilities than your brothers and sisters? If you were an only child, did you spend a lot of time with adults? Were you a spoiled youngest child? Jot down the advantages and disadvantages that come to mind.

Use the most important ideas on your list to develop a paragraph on how you think your position in your family affected you. Begin with your topic sentence, a statement such as this: "As the second of three children, I received less attention, was given more independence, and was pushed less to achieve than my brother and sister." Use specific examples to illustrate each part of your topic sentence. Try to make your examples interesting and colorful by including very specific relevant details, such as how things looked and what was said.

■ Paragraph Assignment 5: An Embarrassing Moment

Each of us has been embarrassed at some time or other. Thankfully, we often look back at our embarrassing moments years later and smile. Write a paragraph about an embarrassing incident that happened to you which you can smile about today. The paragraph should provide lots of specific detail so that readers can feel and understand your embarrassment.

Begin your paragraph with a topic sentence that tells readers the general situation in which you were embarrassed, such as any of these:

> My first day on the job as a waiter ended with an embarrassing accident that still makes me cringe a little today.

> When I met my girlfriend's parents, something happened that was so embarrassing it took me many months to be able to smile about it.

> One of the most embarrassing moments in my life happened in high school when I was walking in the cafeteria with a platter of meat loaf on my tray.

You might find freewriting to be a useful way of quickly getting down on paper the story you want to tell. Then you can use that freewriting as a starting point by adding, subtracting, and refining. As you tell events in the order in which they happened, help your readers follow your narrative by using time transitions like *first, next, then,* and *finally.*

Five Essay Assignments

■ Essay Assignment 1: Leaving Home

Sooner or later most young people leave the home they have grown up in to begin life on their own. While the feeling of independence may be thrilling, flying the coop also involves numerous problems. Write about three problems that many people are likely to meet when they live away from home for the first time. Your thesis statement should be similar to either of these:

When young adults move out on their own for the first time, they are likely to experience problems with _____, _____, and _____.

When I moved out of my parents' home to live on my own for the first time, I experienced problems with _____, _____, and _____.

Note that each of these thesis statements incorporates a plan of development.

Before beginning this essay, you may want to make a list of problems that young people on their own for the first time are likely to experience, or problems that you experienced when you were first on your own. Select three of those problems to write about—each one will be the subject of its own topic sentence. To avoid going from a strong beginning to a weaker ending, save the problem you feel is most important for last.

The first paragraph of your essay, of course, will be your introduction. Use one of the four common methods of introducing an essay listed and explained on pages 30–31. The last sentence of this introduction will probably be your thesis statement, such as this one:

When I finally moved out of my parents' home to live on my own for the first time, I experienced problems with using my time well, doing household chores, and facing loneliness.

The three supporting paragraphs will develop the areas of problems listed in your thesis statement. Develop each of those paragraphs with plenty of specific details. For instance, here's a sample outline for the first supporting detail of an essay with the above thesis statement:

Topic sentence for supporting paragraph 1: For one thing, I felt such freedom living alone that I at first did a poor job of managing my time.

1. I started going to bed entirely too late.

2. I skipped classes without thinking of the consequences.

3. I began coming in to work late.

Here are sample second and third topic sentences for this essay:

Topic sentence for supporting paragraph 2: Unused to running a household (and my life) all on my own, I have taken many months to figure out how to handle a few simple household chores well.

Topic sentence for supporting paragraph 3: Probably the worst problem I have faced since moving out on my own is one that I never expected: loneliness.

Before starting to write your final paragraph, check the suggestions for conclusions on pages 32–33.

■ Essay Assignment 2: Life on the Job

At some point or other, each of us has had a job that we have strong feelings about. Write an essay about the best or worst job you have ever had. In your introduction, you might begin with a general description of your job, explaining what it was and what you were supposed to do. Then end the paragraph with your thesis statement and plan of development.

Here are some thesis statements that may help you think about your own paper.

Thesis statement with plan of development: I hated my government office job because the building was in bad condition, the rules were ridiculous, and many of the workers were unhappy.

(A supporting paragraph on the condition of the government office building, for example, might focus on the fact that the building had a leaky roof; worn, dirty carpets; and several bathrooms that did not work.)

Thesis statement: I love my job as a waiter because my boss is friendly, the schedule is flexible, and the pay is good.

(A supporting paragraph about the boss could begin with this topic sentence: "One thing that makes my job at the restaurant so great is that my boss is a pleasant person who really likes and appreciates her employees." Such a sentence might then be followed by some very carefully worded, concrete specifics and perhaps a revealing anecdote.)

■ Essay Assignment 3: A Letter of Praise or Criticism

Most of us watch some television, listen to the radio, or read the newspaper. We have each seen, heard, or read things that we have found enjoyable or offensive. Write a letter to a television network, radio station, or newspaper in which you compliment or criticize something that you saw, listened to, or read. Don't just say you liked or disliked your topic. Instead give two or three detailed reasons that support your feelings either way.

Your letter should use the essay form already discussed—it should have an introduction, a paragraph for each supporting reason, and a conclusion. Also, it should use a standard address format and begin "Dear Sir or Madam:" (a common opening for a business letter to an unknown person).

After your letter has been revised, you might even mail it. The media are sensitive to the views of members of their audience. If your letter is carefully constructed and neatly written, you are likely to get a reply.

■ Essay Assignment 4: The Most Important Qualities in a Person

TV ads, music videos, and many popular TV shows suggest to us that our culture values physical beauty, strength, and wealth. But are these the most important qualities a person can have? Can you think of others that are more important? For example, which is better: for a teenager to learn how to be cool or how to be kind? Think about the most important qualities a person can have and choose the three that you think are most important. Write a five-paragraph essay in which you show why the three traits you chose are so crucial.

A good prewriting strategy is to write a list of personal qualities that are important to you. Then choose the three that you feel most strongly about. You can freewrite on some of these potential topics to see if they make strong subjects for this essay. In this way, you'll be able to determine whether a particular quality will work for this assignment. Each characteristic will be the topic of a supporting paragraph in your essay. For each of those paragraphs, focus on why you feel the quality you selected is so important. Make your support as specific as possible, perhaps using examples or anecdotes that show how important the quality that you selected is.

In planning your introduction, consider beginning with a situation that contrasts with your thesis statement. Here, for example, is one such introduction for this essay.

> As a child, I spent many years hoping that I would have the qualities of the heroes I saw on TV. The TV stars I wanted to be like seemed to have everything I wanted. They were attractive, rebellious, and confident. These prime-time muscle-bound TV heroes were also tough, intense, and cool— qualities which, as a twelve-year-old kid, I thought were the most important things anyone could have. But today, my feelings have changed. Now when

I think of the top three qualities a person could have, cool is not even on the list. Today, in our hectic, stress-filled world, I think the qualities that are most important for people to have are kindness, humor, and perseverance.

Alternatively, write instead an essay titled "The Three Most Unpleasant Qualities in People."

■ Essay Assignment 5: An Analysis of Spending Habits

Like many people, you probably would be happy if you could put more of your money aside for future needs, perhaps next year's tuition, another car, or even a new home. But—also like many people—you may find that by the end of each month, there is nothing much left of your paycheck. Often, a careful analysis of spending habits turns up several ways a person can find some cash to squirrel away. To prepare for this assignment, do a careful analysis of your own spending and shopping patterns. Then write an essay about three ways you feel that you can change your spending habits in order to feed more to your bank account.

Here's a sample scratch outline for this assignment:

Thesis statement: An analysis of my spending habits has shown me that I can do a better job of saving money by spending less at the supermarket, on eating out, and on clothing.

Topic sentence for supporting paragraph 1: I now see that I can spend much less at the supermarket by being more disciplined.

Topic sentence for supporting paragraph 2: In addition, I also realize now that I have been spending much more than is reasonable on restaurant food.

Topic sentence for supporting paragraph 3: Finally, I believe I can have a satisfying wardrobe without spending as much money as I have been on clothes.

And here's a sample scratch outline for the paragraph with the first topic sentence above:

Topic sentence: I now see that I can spend much less at the supermarket by being more disciplined.

(1) I can be more careful about using coupons.

(2) I can take better advantage of sales.

(3) I can buy less junk food.

To help you think about your essay, here are some areas in which people often find that it would be worthwhile to cut back on spending:

Rent	Jewelry	Exercise classes
Eating out	Cosmetics	First-run movies
Clothing	Haircuts	Sporting events

If after analyzing your spending habits you feel that you have been doing a good job of making the most of your paycheck, write an essay instead about your success. A thesis statement for that essay might go like this: "An analysis of my spending habits shows that I have been doing a pretty good job of keeping down my food, clothing, and recreation expenses."

Part Two

Sentence Skills

Introduction

Part Two explains the basic skills needed to write clear, error-free sentences. While the skills are presented within five traditional categories (sentences; verbs, pronouns, and agreement; modifiers and parallelism; punctuation and mechanics; word use), each section is self-contained so that you can go directly to the skills you need to work on. Note, however, that you may find it helpful to cover "Subjects and Verbs" before turning to other skills. Typically, the main features of a skill are presented on the first pages of a section; secondary points are developed later. Numerous activities are provided so that you can practice skills enough to make them habits. The activities are varied and range from underlining answers to writing complete sentences involving the skill in question. One or more review tests at the end of each section offer additional practice activities.

4 Subjects and Verbs

Introductory Activity

Understanding subjects and verbs is a big step toward mastering many sentence skills. As a speaker of English, you already have an instinctive feel for these basic building blocks of English sentences. See if you can insert an appropriate word in each space below. The answer will be a subject. *Answers will vary.*

1. The _____ will soon be over.

2. _____ cannot be trusted.

3. A strange _____ appeared in my backyard.

4. _____ is one of my favorite activities.

Now insert an appropriate word in the following spaces. Each answer will be a verb.

5. The prisoner _____ at the judge.

6. My sister _____ much harder than I do.

7. The players _____ in the locker room.

8. Rob and Marilyn _____ with the teacher.

Finally, insert appropriate words in the following spaces. Each answer will be a subject in the first space and a verb in the second.

9. The _____ almost _____ out of the tree.

10. Many _____ today _____ sex and violence.

11. The _____ carefully _____ the patient.

12. A _____ quickly _____ the ball.

Answers are on page 566.

The basic building blocks of English sentences are subjects and verbs. Understanding them is an important first step toward mastering a number of sentence skills.

Every sentence has a subject and a verb. Who or what the sentence speaks about is called the *subject;* what the sentence says about the subject is called the *verb.* In the following sentences, the subject is underlined once and the verb twice:

People gossip.

The truck belched fumes.

He waved at me.

Alaska contains the largest wilderness area in the United States.

That woman is a millionaire.

The pants feel itchy.

A Simple Way to Find a Subject

To find a subject, ask *who* or *what* the sentence is about. As shown below, your answer is the subject.

Who is the first sentence about? People

What is the second sentence about? The truck

Who is the third sentence about? He

What is the fourth sentence about? Alaska

Who is the fifth sentence about? That woman

What is the sixth sentence about? The pants

It helps to remember that the subject of a sentence is always a *noun* (any person, place, or thing) or a pronoun. A *pronoun* is simply a word like *he, she, it, you,* or *they* used in place of a noun. In the preceding sentences, the subjects are persons (*People, He, woman*), a place (*Alaska*), and things (*truck, pants*). And note that one pronoun (*He*) is used as a subject.

A Simple Way to Find a Verb

14.1c

To find a verb, ask what the sentence *says about* the subject. As shown below, your answer is the verb.

What does the first sentence *say about* people? They gossip.

What does the second sentence *say about* the truck? It belched (fumes).

What does the third sentence *say about* him? He waved (at me).

What does the fourth sentence *say about* Alaska? It contains (the largest wilderness area in the United States).

What does the fifth sentence *say about* that woman? She is (a millionaire).

What does the sixth sentence *say about* the pants? They feel (itchy).

A second way to find the verb is to put *I, you, he, she, it,* or *they* in front of the word you think is a verb. If the result makes sense, you have a verb. For example, you could put *they* in front of *gossip* in the first sentence above, with the result, *they gossip,* making sense. Therefore, you know that *gossip* is a verb. You could use the same test with the other verbs as well.

Finally, it helps to remember that most verbs show action. In "People gossip," the action is gossiping. In "The truck belched fumes," the action is belching. In "He waved at me," the action is waving. In "Alaska contains the largest wilderness area in the United States," the action is containing.

Certain other verbs, known as *linking verbs,* do not show action. They do, however, give information about the subject of the sentence. In "That woman is a millionaire," the linking verb *is* tells us that the woman is a millionaire. In "The pants feel itchy," the linking verb *feel* gives us the information that the pants are itchy.

Practice 1

In each of the following sentences, draw one line under the subject and two lines under the verb.

To find the subject, ask *who* or *what* the sentence is about. Then, to find the verb, ask what the sentence *says about* the subject.

1. Fran froze six pounds of hamburger patties.

2. The company offered a ten-dollar rebate on every toaster oven.

3. The sports announcer talked nonstop during the game.

4. Brenda peeled the bandage off her cut finger.

5. The warm sunshine felt good on my bare legs.

6. Our backyard is knee-deep in weeds.

7. Alicia snagged her stocking with her broken fingernail.

8. The steel comb scratched my scalp.

9. The pen leaked all over my finger.

10. That outlet store carries only damaged or outdated goods.

Practice 2

Follow the directions given for Practice 1. Note that all of the verbs here are linking verbs.

1. The best shows on television this week were the ads.

2. In some countries, an after-dinner burp is a compliment to the cook.

3. Mirror sunglasses always look eerie, like a robot's eyes.

4. My voice sounds terrible in the morning.

5. Tamika became engaged to Hassan after just three dates.

6. Harold's new after-shave lotion smells like cleaning fluid.

7. Visitors often appear fearful at my German shepherd's bark of greeting.

8. To a female fly, a male's wing vibrations are a love song.

9. My head cold feels like a combination of fatal headache and torture by sneezing.

10. In some ways, the change from tadpole to frog seems as much of a miracle as the change from frog to prince.

Practice 3

Follow the directions given for Practice 1.

1. One lonely neon light glowed in the distance.

2. The kite soared into the sky at the end of a taut, vibrating string.

3. Manuel caught a foul ball at the game.

4. The skaters shadowed each other's movements perfectly.

5. Fluorescent lights emphasized the tired lines in the man's face.

6. Tracy <u>reads</u> to her bedridden grandmother every night.

7. Marsha's oversized <u>glasses</u> <u>slipped</u> down her nose twenty times a day.

8. Carelessly, <u>Jane</u> <u>allowed</u> the children to light the kerosene heater.

9. The <u>squirrel</u> <u>jumped</u> from one tree branch to another.

10. <u>Carpenters</u> <u>constructed</u> a wooden wheelchair ramp next to the stone steps of the church.

More about Subjects and Verbs

Distinguishing Subjects from Prepositional Phrases

The subject of a sentence never appears within a prepositional phrase. A *prepositional phrase* is simply a group of words beginning with a preposition and ending with the answer to the question *what, when,* or *where.* Here is a list of common prepositions.

Common Prepositions				
about	before	by	inside	over
above	behind	during	into	through
across	below	except	of	to
among	beneath	for	off	toward
around	beside	from	on	under
at	between	in	onto	with

When you are looking for the subject of a sentence, it is helpful to cross out prepositional phrases.

~~In the middle of the night,~~ we heard footsteps ~~on the roof.~~
The magazines ~~on the table~~ belong ~~in the garage.~~
~~Before the opening kickoff,~~ a brass band marched ~~onto the field.~~
The hardware store ~~across the street~~ went ~~out of business.~~
~~In spite of our advice,~~ Sally quit her job ~~at Burger King.~~

Practice

Cross out prepositional phrases. Then draw a single line under subjects and a double line under verbs.

1. Stripes ~~of sunlight~~ glowed ~~on the kitchen floor~~.
2. The black panther draped its powerful body ~~along the thick tree branch~~.
3. A line ~~of impatient people~~ snaked ~~from the box office to the street~~.
4. ~~At noon~~, every siren ~~in town~~ wails ~~for fifteen minutes~~.
5. The tops ~~of my Bic pens~~ always disappear ~~after a day or two~~.
6. Joanne removed the lint ~~from her black socks with Scotch tape~~.
7. The mirrored walls ~~of the skyscraper~~ reflected the passing clouds.
8. Debris ~~from the accident~~ littered the intersection.
9. ~~Above the heads of the crowd~~, a woman swayed ~~on a narrow ledge~~.
10. The squashed grapes ~~in the bottom of the vegetable bin~~ oozed sticky purple juice.

Verbs of More Than One Word

Many verbs consist of more than one word. Here, for example, are some of the many forms of the verb *help:*

Some Forms of the Verb Help

helps	should have been helping	will have helped
helping	can help	would have been helped
is helping	would have been helping	has been helped
was helping	will be helping	had been helped
may help	had been helping	must have helped
should help	helped	having helped
will help	have helped	should have been helped
does help	has helped	had helped

Below are sentences that contain verbs of more than one word:

Yolanda is working overtime this week.

Another book has been written about the Kennedy family.

We should have stopped for gas at the last station.

The game has just been canceled.

Notes

1   Words like *not, just, never, only,* and *always* are not part of the verb, although they may appear within the verb.

Yolanda is not working overtime next week.

The boys should just not have stayed out so late.

The game has always been played regardless of the weather.

2   No verb preceded by *to* is ever the verb of a sentence.

Sue wants to go with us.

The newly married couple decided to rent a house for a year.

The store needs extra people to help out at Christmas.

3   No *-ing* word by itself is ever the verb of a sentence. (It may be part of the verb, but it must have a helping verb in front of it.)

We planning the trip for months. (This is not a sentence, because the verb is not complete.)

We were planning the trip for months. (This is a complete sentence.)

Practice

Draw a single line under subjects and a double line under verbs. Be sure to include all parts of the verb.

1. Only Einstein could have passed that math test.

2. She could have been killed by that falling rock.

3. The children did not recognize their father in his Halloween costume.

4. The hunger strikers have been fasting for four days.

5. I could not see the tiny letters on the last row of the eye doctor's chart.

6. People may be wearing paper clothing by the year 2050.

7. He should have studied longer for the final.

8. Rosa has been soaking in the bathtub for an hour.

9. Long lines of southbound geese were flying overhead.

10. My little brother can ask the same stupid question five times in a row.

Compound Subjects and Verbs

A sentence may have more than one verb:

> The dancer stumbled and fell.
> Lola washed her hair, blew it dry, and parted it in the middle.

A sentence may have more than one subject:

> Cats and dogs are sometimes the best of friends.
> The striking workers and their bosses could not come to an agreement.

A sentence may have several subjects and several verbs:

> Holly and I read the book and reported on it to the class.
> Pete, Nick, and Eric caught the fish in the morning, cleaned them in the after-
> noon, and ate them that night.

Practice

Draw a single line under subjects and a double line under verbs. Be sure to mark *all* the subjects and verbs.

1. The trees creaked and shuddered in the powerful wind.

2. The little girl fell off the jungle gym and landed in the dirt.

3. On Sunday, I will vacuum the upstairs rooms and change the linens.

4. The late afternoon sun shone on the leaves and turned them to gold.

5. Sam and Billy greased their chapped lips with Vaseline.

6. The tall, masked man and his Native American friend rode off into the sunset.

7. My sister and I always race each other to the bathroom in the morning.

8. Nia breathed deeply and then began her karate exercises.

9. At the party, Phil draped a tablecloth around his shoulders and pretended to be Dracula.

10. The professional wrestler and his opponent strutted around the ring and pounded on their chests.

■ Review Test 1

Draw one line under the subjects and two lines under the verbs. As necessary, cross out prepositional phrases to help find subjects. Underline all the parts of a verb. And remember that you may find more than one subject and more than one verb in a sentence.

1. The endings of most movies are happy.

2. I should have filled the car with gas before work.

3. The female of many animals is larger than the male.

4. Three buildings on our block are for sale.

5. Dozens of ants gathered around a scoop of pink ice cream on the sidewalk.

6. Many shoppers saw the pennies on the floor but would not pick them up.

7. Squirrels can collect thousands of nuts in one season.

8. Fruits and vegetables with dangerous sprays should be banned from this country.

9. An extra key was placed under the big empty planter by the front door.

10. Ved dieted for a year, lost a hundred pounds, and cured his high blood pressure.

■ Review Test 2

Follow the directions given for Review Test 1.

1. A collection of watercolor paintings was damaged in the flood.

2. Everything in that linen store is on sale at 40 percent off.

3. My son is looking for dinosaur bones in the backyard.

4. According ~~to surveys~~, most people talk ~~to their dogs~~.

5. Jay and Elise were married two years ago and are divorced already.

6. ~~At dinnertime~~, my cat meows and rubs ~~against my leg~~.

7. The huge tree ~~outside our kitchen window~~ throws lovely shadows ~~on the kitchen wall in the afternoon~~.

8. My parents and the Greens played bridge ~~for hours~~ and argued constantly.

9. Deanna took a chocolate ~~from the box~~, took one bite, and put the piece back.

10. Mona removed Ed's arm ~~from her shoulders~~ and ran ~~from the theater with tears in her eyes~~.

5 Fragments

Introductory Activity

Every sentence must have a subject and a verb and must express a complete thought. A word group that lacks a subject or a verb and that does not express a complete thought is a fragment.

Listed below are a number of fragments and sentences. See if you can complete the statement that explains each fragment.

1. Children.   *Fragment*

   Children cry.   *Sentence*

"Children" is a fragment because, while it has a subject *(Children)*, it lacks a ___verb___ *(cry)* and so does not express a complete thought.

2. Dances.   *Fragment*

   Lola dances.   *Sentence*

"Dances" is a fragment because, while it has a verb *(Dances)*, it lacks a ___subject___ *(Lola)* and so does not express a complete thought.

3. Staring through the window.   *Fragment*

   Bigfoot was staring through the window.   *Sentence*

"Staring through the window" is a fragment because it lacks a ___subject___ *(Bigfoot)* and also part of the ___verb___ *(was)* and because it does not express a complete thought.

4. When the dentist began drilling.   *Fragment*

   When the dentist began drilling, I closed my eyes.   *Sentence*

"When the dentist began drilling" is a fragment because we want to know what happened when the dentist began drilling. The word group does not follow through and ___express a complete thought___.

Answers are on page 567.

What Fragments Are

ALLWRITE!
15.2

Every sentence must have a subject and a verb and must express a complete thought. A word group that lacks a subject or a verb and does not express a complete thought is a *fragment*. Following are the most common types of fragments that people write:

1 Dependent-word fragments

2 *-ing* and *to* fragments

3 Added-detail fragments

4 Missing-subject fragments

Once you understand the specific kind or kinds of fragments that you might write, you should be able to eliminate them from your writing. The following pages explain all four types of fragments.

1 Dependent-Word Fragments

Some word groups that begin with a dependent word are fragments. Here is a list of common dependent words:

Common Dependent Words	
after	unless
although, though	until
as	what, whatever
because	when, whenever
before	where, wherever
even though	whether
how	which, whichever
if, even if	while
in order that	who
since	whose
that, so that	

Whenever you start a sentence with one of these dependent words, you must be careful that a dependent-word fragment does not result. The word group beginning with the dependent word *After* in the selection below is a fragment.

After I stopped drinking coffee. I began sleeping better at night.

A *dependent statement*—one starting with a dependent word like *After*—cannot stand alone. It depends on another statement to complete the thought. "After I stopped drinking coffee" is a dependent statement. It leaves us hanging. We expect in the same sentence to find out *what happened after* the writer stopped drinking coffee. When a writer does not follow through and complete a thought, a fragment results.

To correct the fragment, simply follow through and complete the thought:

After I stopped drinking coffee, I began sleeping better at night.

Remember, then, that *dependent statements by themselves* are fragments. They must be attached to a statement that makes sense standing alone.*

Here are two other examples of dependent-word fragments.

Brian sat nervously in the dental clinic. While waiting to have his wisdom tooth pulled.

Maria decided to throw away the boxes. That had accumulated for years in the basement.

"While waiting to have his wisdom tooth pulled" is a fragment; it does not make sense standing by itself. We want to know in the same statement *what Brian did* while waiting to have his tooth pulled. The writer must complete the thought. Likewise, "That had accumulated for years in the basement" is not in itself a complete thought. We want to know in the same statement what *that* refers to.

How to Correct Dependent-Word Fragments

In most cases, you can correct a dependent-word fragment by attaching it to the sentence that comes after it or to the sentence that comes before it:

After I stopped drinking coffee, I began sleeping better at night.

(The fragment has been attached to the sentence that comes after it.)

---

*Some instructors refer to a dependent-word fragment as a *dependent clause*. A *clause* is simply a group of words having a subject and a verb. A clause may be *independent* (expressing a complete thought and able to stand alone) or *dependent* (not expressing a complete thought and not able to stand alone). A dependent clause by itself is a fragment. It can be corrected simply by adding an independent clause.

Brian sat nervously in the dental clinic while waiting to have his wisdom tooth pulled.

(The fragment has been attached to the sentence that comes before it.)

Maria decided to throw away the boxes that had accumulated for years in the basement.

(The fragment has been attached to the sentence that comes before it.)

Another way of correcting a dependent-word fragment is to eliminate the dependent word and make a new sentence:

I stopped drinking coffee.

He was waiting to have his wisdom tooth pulled.

They had accumulated for years in the basement.

Do not use this second method of correction too frequently, however, for it may cut down on interest and variety in your writing style.

Notes

1 Use a comma if a dependent-word group comes at the *beginning* of a sentence (see also page 311):

After I stopped drinking coffee, I began sleeping better at night.

2 However, do not generally use a comma if the dependent-word group comes at the end of a sentence:

Brian sat nervously in the dental clinic while waiting to have his wisdom tooth pulled.

Maria decided to throw away the boxes that had accumulated for years in the basement.

3 Sometimes the dependent words *who, that, which,* or *where* appear not at the very start but *near* the start of a word group. A fragment often results.

Today I visited Faye Cooper. <u>A friend who is in the hospital.</u>

"A friend who is in the hospital" is not in itself a complete thought. We want to know in the same statement *who* the friend is. The fragment can be corrected by attaching it to the sentence that comes before it:

Today I visited Faye Cooper, a friend who is in the hospital.

(Here a comma is used to set off "a friend who is in the hospital," which is extra material placed at the end of the sentence.)

Practice 1

Turn each of the dependent-word groups into a sentence by adding a complete thought. Put a comma after the dependent-word group if a dependent word starts the sentence.

Examples   After I got out of high school

After I got out of high school, I spent a year traveling.

The watch that I got fixed

The watch that I got fixed has just stopped working again.

Answers will vary.

1. After I got home from the party

   _____

   _____

2. Because I finished all my assignments

   _____

   _____

3. When my grandfather died

   _____

   _____

4. The discount store that just opened

   _____

   _____

5. Although my daughter is only five years old

   _____

   _____

Practice 2

Underline the dependent-word fragment (or fragments) in each item. Then correct each fragment by attaching it to the sentence that comes before or the sentence that comes after—whichever sounds more natural. Put a comma after the dependent-word group if it starts the sentence.

1. <u>Since she was afraid of muggers.</u> Barbara carried a small can of Mace on her key ring. A hat pin was hidden under her coat lapel.

   Since she was afraid of muggers, Barbara carried a small can of Mace on her key ring.

2. <u>When I began watching the TV mystery movie.</u> I remembered that I had seen it before. I already knew who had murdered the millionaire.

   When I began watching the TV mystery movie, I remembered that I had seen it before.

3. Tulips had begun to bloom. <u>Until a freakish spring snowstorm blanketed the garden.</u> The flowers perished in the unseasonable cold.

   Tulips had begun to bloom until a freakish spring snowstorm blanketed the garden.

4. <u>Whenever I'm in the basement and the phone rings.</u> I don't run up to answer it. <u>If the message is important.</u> The person will call back.

   Whenever I'm in the basement and the phone rings, I don't run up to answer it. If the message is important, the person will call back.

5. <u>Since she is a new student.</u> Carla feels shy and insecure. She thinks she is the only person. <u>Who doesn't know anyone else.</u>

   Since she is a new student, Carla feels shy and insecure. She thinks she is the only person who doesn't know anyone else.

2 *-ing* and *to* Fragments

When a word ending in *-ing* or the word *to* appears at or near the start of a word group, a fragment may result. Such fragments often lack a subject and part of the verb.

Underline the word groups in the examples below that contain *-ing* words. Each is an *-ing* fragment.

Example 1

I spent all day in the employment office. <u>Trying to find a job that suited me.</u> The prospects looked bleak.

Example 2

Lola surprised Tony on the nature hike. <u>Picking blobs of resin off pine trees.</u> Then she chewed them like bubble gum.

Example 3

Mel took an aisle seat on the bus. <u>His reason being that he had more legroom.</u>

People sometimes write *-ing* fragments because they think the subject in one sentence will work for the next word group as well. In the first example above, they might think the subject *I* in the opening sentence will also serve as the subject for "Trying to find a job that suited me." But the subject must actually be *in* the sentence.

How to Correct *-ing* Fragments

1   Attach the fragment to the sentence that comes before it or the sentence that comes after it, whichever makes sense. Example 1 above could read, "I spent all day in the employment office, trying to find a job that suited me." (Note that here a comma is used to set off "trying to find a job that suited me," which is extra material placed at the end of the sentence.)

2   Add a subject and change the *-ing* verb part to the correct form of the verb. Example 2 could read, "She picked blobs of resin off pine trees."

3   Change *being* to the correct form of the verb *be (am, are, is, was, were).* Example 3 could read, "His reason was that he had more legroom."

How to Correct *to* Fragments

As noted above, when *to* appears at or near the start of a word group, a fragment sometimes results.

> To remind people of their selfishness. Otis leaves handwritten notes on cars that take up two parking spaces.

The first word group in the example above is a *to* fragment. It can be corrected by adding it to the sentence that comes after it.

> To remind people of their selfishness, Otis leaves handwritten notes on cars that take up two parking spaces.

(Note that here a comma is used to set off "To remind people of their selfishness," which is introductory material in the sentence.)

Practice 1

Underline the *-ing* fragment in each of the following selections. Then make the fragment a sentence by rewriting it, using the method described in parentheses.

Example   The dog eyed me with suspicion. Not knowing whether its master was at home. I hesitated to open the gate.
(Add the fragment to the sentence that comes after it.)

Not knowing whether its master was at home, I hesitated to open

the gate.

1. Julie spent an hour at her desk. Staring at a blank piece of paper. She didn't know how to start her report.
(Add the fragment to the preceding sentence.)

Julie spent an hour at her desk, staring at a blank piece of paper.

_____

2. Rummaging around in the kitchen drawer. Tyrone found the key he had misplaced a year ago.
(Add the fragment to the sentence that comes after it.)

Rummaging around in the kitchen drawer, Tyrone found the key he had

misplaced a year ago.

3. I went back to get a carton of Tropicana. <u>As a result, losing my place in the checkout line.</u>
(Add the subject *I* and change *losing* to the correct form of the verb, *lost.*)

As a result, I lost my place in the checkout line.

Practice 2

Underline the *-ing* or *to* fragment in each item. Then rewrite the item correctly, using one of the methods of correction described on pages 105–106.

1. Last night, my bedroom was so hot I couldn't sleep. <u>Tossing and turning for hours.</u> I felt like a blanket being tumbled dry.

   Tossing and turning for hours, I felt like a blanket being tumbled dry.

   Or: I tossed and turned for hours.

2. A sparrow landed on the icy windowsill. <u>Fluffing its feathers to keep itself warm.</u>

   A sparrow landed on the icy windowsill, fluffing its feathers to keep itself warm. Or: It fluffed its feathers to keep itself warm.

3. Alma left the party early. <u>The reason being that she had to work the next day.</u>

   Alma left the party early, the reason being that she had to work the next day. Or: The reason was that she had to work the next day.

4. <u>Grasping the balance beam with her powdered hands.</u> The gymnast executed a handstand. Then she dismounted.

   Grasping the balance beam with her powdered hands, the gymnast executed a handstand.

5. <u>To cover his bald spot.</u> Walt combed long strands of hair over the top of his head. Unfortunately, no one was fooled by this technique.

   To cover his bald spot, Walt combed long strands of hair over the top of his head.

3 Added-Detail Fragments

Added-detail fragments lack a subject and a verb. They often begin with one of the following words or phrases.

also	except	including
especially	for example	such as

See if you can underline the one added-detail fragment in each of these examples:

Example 1

Tony has trouble accepting criticism. <u>Except from Lola.</u> She has a knack for tact.

Example 2

My apartment has its drawbacks. <u>For example, no hot water in the morning.</u>

Example 3

I had many jobs while in school. <u>Among them, busboy, painter, and security guard.</u>

People often write added-detail fragments for much the same reason they write *-ing* fragments. They think the subject and verb in one sentence will serve for the next word group as well. But the subject and verb must be in *each* word group.

How to Correct Added-Detail Fragments

1   Attach the fragment to the complete thought that precedes it. Example 1 could read: "Tony has trouble accepting criticism, except from Lola." (Note that here a comma is used to set off "except from Lola," which is extra material placed at the end of the sentence.)

2   Add a subject and a verb to the fragment to make it a complete sentence. Example 2 could read: "My apartment has its drawbacks. For example, there is no hot water in the morning."

3   Change words as necessary to make the fragment part of the preceding sentence. Example 3 could read: "Among the many jobs I had while in school have been busboy, painter, and security guard."

Practice 1

Underline the fragment in each selection below. Then make it a sentence by rewriting it, using the method described in parentheses.

Example   My husband and I share the household chores. <u>Including meals.</u> I do the cooking and he does the eating.
(Add the fragment to the preceding sentence.)
My husband and I share the household chores, including meals.

1. My father has some nervous habits. <u>For instance, folding a strip of paper into the shape of an accordion.</u>
(Correct the fragment by adding the subject *he* and changing *folding* to the proper form of the verb, *folds.*)
For instance, he folds a strip of paper into the shape of an accordion.

2. Marco stuffed the large green peppers. <u>With hamburger meat, cooked rice, and chopped parsley.</u> Next, using toothpicks, he reattached the stemmed pepper tops.
(Add the fragment to the preceding sentence.)
Marco stuffed the large green peppers with hamburger meat, cooked rice, and chopped parsley.

3. My little brother is addicted to junk foods. <u>For example, Bugles and Doritos.</u> If something is good for him, he won't eat it.
(Correct the fragment by adding the subject and verb *he craves.*)
For example, he craves Bugles and Doritos.

Practice 2

Underline the added-detail fragment in each selection. Then rewrite that part of the selection needed to correct the fragment. Use one of the three methods of correction described on page 108.
Answers may vary.

1. My husband keeps all his old clothes. <u>For instance, his faded sweatshirt from high school.</u> He says it's the most comfortable thing he owns.
For instance, he has his faded sweatshirt from high school.

2. My sister has some very bad habits. <u>For example, borrowing my sweaters.</u> She also returns them without washing them.

   For example, she borrows my sweaters.

3. To improve her singing, Amber practiced some odd exercises. <u>Such as flapping her tongue and fluttering her lips.</u>

   To improve her singing, Amber practiced some odd exercises, such as flapping her tongue and fluttering her lips.

4. When she spotted her ex-husband, Leona left the party. She did not want him to see how much she had changed. <u>For example, put on forty pounds.</u>

   For example, she had put on forty pounds.

5. Stanley wanted a big birthday cake. <u>With candles spelling out STAN.</u> He wanted to see his name in lights.

   Stanley wanted a big birthday cake with candles spelling out STAN.

4 Missing-Subject Fragments

In each example below, underline the word group in which the subject is missing.

Example 1

One example of my father's generosity is that he visits sick friends in the hospital. <u>And takes along get-well cards with a few dollars folded in them.</u>

Example 2

The weight lifter grunted as he heaved the barbells into the air. <u>Then, with a loud groan, dropped them.</u>

People write missing-subject fragments because they think the subject in one sentence will apply to the next word group as well. But the subject, as well as the verb, must be in *each* word group to make it a sentence.

How to Correct Missing-Subject Fragments

1   Attach the fragment to the preceding sentence. Example 1 could read: "One illustration of my father's generosity is that he visits sick friends in the hospital and takes along get-well cards with a few dollars folded in them."

2   Add a subject (which can often be a pronoun standing for the subject in the preceding sentence). Example 2 could read: "Then, with a loud groan, he dropped them."

Practice

Underline the missing-subject fragment in each selection. Then rewrite that part of the selection to correct the fragment. Use one of the two methods of correction described above.

Rewritten versions may vary.

1. Embarrassed, Sandra looked around the laundromat. <u>Then quickly folded her raggedy towels and faded sheets.</u>

    Then she quickly folded her raggedy towels and faded sheets.

    _____

2. Wally took his wool sweaters out of storage. <u>And found them full of moth holes.</u>

    Wally took his wool sweaters out of storage and found them full of moth

    holes.

3. My sister is taking a word processing course. <u>Also, is learning two computer languages.</u> Machines don't frighten her.

    Also, she is learning two computer languages.

    _____

4. When someone comes to the door, my dog races upstairs. <u>Then hides under the bed.</u> Strangers really terrify him.

    Then he hides under the bed.

    _____

5. A tiny bug crawled across my paper. <u>And sat down in the middle of a sentence.</u> There was suddenly one comma too many.

    A tiny bug crawled across my paper and sat down in the middle of a

    sentence.

A Review: How to Check for Fragments

1   Read your paper aloud from the *last* sentence to the *first*. You will be better able to see and hear whether each word group you read is a complete thought.

2   If you think any word group is a fragment, ask yourself: Does this contain a subject and a verb and express a complete thought?

3   More specifically, be on the lookout for the most common fragments.

- Dependent-word fragments (starting with words like *after, because, since, when,* and *before*)

- *-ing* and *to* fragments (*-ing* or *to* at or near the start of a word group)

- Added-detail fragments (starting with words like *for example, such as, also,* and *especially*)

- Missing-subject fragments (a verb is present but not the subject)

Collaborative Activity

Part A: Editing and Rewriting

Working with a partner, read carefully the short paragraph below and underline the five fragments. Then use the space provided to correct the fragments. Feel free to discuss the rewrite quietly with your partner and refer back to the chapter when necessary.

¹Did you ever wonder how trainers get porpoises to do all those tricks, like leaping over a high bar or jumping through a hoop? ²Wild porpoises are first taught to eat fish from their trainer's hand. ³The trainer blows a ~~whistle.~~ *whistle when* ⁴~~When~~ the animal accepts a fish. ⁵The porpoise associates the whistle with "correct" behavior. ⁶Once the porpoise

Continued

touches a human hand to get a fish, it will touch other ~~things.~~ *things, like* ~~⁷Like~~ a

red target ball. ⁸For example, the trainer will hold the ball high above

the water while leaning over a kind of pulpit. ⁹Seeing the ~~ball.~~ *ball, the* ~~¹⁰The~~

porpoise leaps out of the ~~water.~~ *water because* ~~¹¹Because~~ it knows it will be rewarded

with a fish. ¹²A hoop can then be substituted for a ball, and the

porpoise's behavior can be "shaped" so it will jump through the

hoop. ¹³If the porpoise misses the hoop by jumping too ~~low.~~ *low, the* ~~¹⁴The~~

fish reward is withheld. ¹⁵The intelligent mammal will associate "no

fish" with "wrong" behavior. ¹⁶Very quickly, the porpoise will be

leaping gracefully through the center of the hoop.

_____

_____

_____

_____

_____

_____

_____

_____

_____

_____

_____

_____

Continued

Part B: Creating Sentences

Working with a partner, make up your own short fragments test as directed.

Answers will vary.

1. Write a dependent-word fragment in the space below. Then correct the fragment by making it into a complete sentence. You may want to begin your fragment with the word *before*, *after*, *when*, *because*, or *if*.

   Fragment _____

   Sentence _____

   _____

2. Write an *-ing* fragment in the space below. Then correct the fragment by making it into a complete sentence. You may want to begin your fragment with the word *laughing*, *walking*, *shopping*, or *talking*.

   Fragment _____

   Sentence _____

   _____

3. Write an added-detail fragment in the space below. Then correct the fragment by making it into a complete sentence. You may want to begin your fragment with the word *also*, *especially*, *except*, or *including*.

   Fragment _____

   Sentence _____

   _____

Reflective Activity

Answers will vary.

1. Look at the paragraph that you revised above. How has removing fragments affected the reading of the paragraph? Explain.

2. Explain what it is about fragments that you find most difficult to remember and apply. Use an example to make your point clear. Feel free to refer to anything in this chapter.

■ **Review Test 1**

Turn each of the following word groups into a complete sentence. Use the space provided.

Examples   Feeling very confident

Feeling very confident, I began my speech.

Until the rain started

We played softball until the rain started.

Answers will vary.

1. Before you leave work today

_____

2. When the game show came on

_____

3. Since I have to gain some weight

_____

4. While I was looking in the store window

_____

5. Will be in town next week

_____

6. Stanley, who has a terrible temper

_____

7. Down in the basement

_____

8. Flopping down on the couch

_____

9. Who fixed my car

_____

10. To wake up early

_____

■ **Review Test 2**

Underline the fragment in each selection. Then correct the fragment in the space provided.

Example   Sam received all kinds of junk mail. <u>Then complained to the post office.</u> Eventually, some of the mail stopped coming.

Then he complained to the post office.

1. <u>Since she was afraid of mussing her hair.</u> Terry refused to go swimming.

   Since she was afraid of mussing her hair, Terry refused to go swimming.

2. The first time I took a college course, I was afraid to say anything in class. I didn't open my mouth. <u>Not even to yawn.</u>

   I didn't open my mouth, not even to yawn.

3. <u>Looking like a large dish of vanilla fudge ice cream.</u> Our brown-and-white cat went to sleep on the table.

   Looking like a large dish of vanilla fudge ice cream, our brown-and-white

   cat went to sleep on the table.

4. Fran read that a sure sign of age is forgetting things. She wanted to show the article to her doctor. <u>But couldn't remember where it was.</u>

   She wanted to show the article to her doctor but couldn't remember

   where it was.

5. Dave insisted on wearing a silly hat. <u>Which his girlfriend hated.</u> It had two horns like a Viking helmet.

   Dave insisted on wearing a silly hat which his girlfriend hated.

6. A box of frozen vegetables slipped out of Mark's grocery bag. <u>And split open on the sidewalk.</u> Little green peas rolled in every direction, while hard white onions bounced down the street.

   A box of frozen vegetables slipped out of Mark's grocery bag and split

   open on the sidewalk.

7. Even though Laurie isn't disabled. She used to park in "handicapped only" parking spaces. After receiving several tickets, however, she gave up this selfish habit.

Even though Laurie isn't disabled, she used to park in "handicapped only"

parking spaces.

8. Thinking that the Halloween get-together was a costume party. Vince came dressed as a boxer. Unfortunately, the other guests were dressed normally.

Thinking that the Halloween get-together was a costume party, Vince

came dressed as a boxer.

9. My doctor is using disposable equipment. Such as paper examining gowns and plastic thermometers. He says these are more hygienic.

My doctor is using disposable equipment, such as paper examining gowns

and plastic thermometers.

10. Stanley painted his house lemon-yellow. With orange shutters and a lime-green roof. People say his house looks like a fruit salad.

Stanley painted his house lemon-yellow, with orange shutters and a

lime-green roof.

■ **Review Test 3**

In the space provided, write *C* in front of the five word groups that are complete sentences; write *frag* in front of the five fragments. The first two items are done for you.

frag	1. As I was driving my car to work last Monday morning.
_C_	2. I saw an animal die.
_C_	3. It was a beautiful, breezy fall day.
frag	4. With colorful leaves swirling across the road.
_C_	5. Suddenly, a squirrel darted out from the bushes.
frag	6. And began zigzagging in the path of approaching cars.
_C_	7. Soundlessly, the car in front of me hit the animal.
frag	8. Sending its tiny gray-brown body flying off the road in a flurry of leaves.
_C_	9. After the incident, I thought about how fragile life is.
frag	10. And how easily and quickly it can be taken away.

Now correct the fragments you have found. Attach each fragment to the sentence that comes before or after it, or make whatever other change is needed to turn the fragment into a sentence. Use the space provided. The first one is corrected for you.
Wording of answers may vary.

1. _As I was driving my car to work last Monday morning, I saw an animal die._

2. It was a beautiful, breezy fall day, with colorful leaves swirling across the road.

3. Suddenly, a squirrel darted out from the bushes and began zigzagging in the path of approaching cars.

4. Soundlessly, the car in front of me hit the animal, sending its tiny gray-brown body flying off the road in a flurry of leaves.

5. After the incident, I thought about how fragile life is and how easily and quickly it can be taken away.

■ Review Test 4

Answers will vary.

Write quickly for five minutes about the high school you attended. Don't worry about spelling, punctuation, finding exact words, or organizing your thoughts. Just focus on writing as many words as you can without stopping.

After you have finished, go back and make whatever changes are needed to correct any fragments in your writing.

6 Run-Ons

Introductory Activity

A run-on occurs when two sentences are run together with no adequate sign given to mark the break between them. Shown below are four run-on sentences and four correctly marked sentences. See if you can complete the statement that explains how each run-on is corrected.

1. A man coughed in the movie theater the result was a chain reaction of copycat coughing.   *Run-on*

    A man coughed in the movie theater. The result was a chain reaction of copycat coughing.   *Correct*

The run-on has been corrected by using a ____period____ and a capital letter to separate the two complete thoughts.

2. I heard laughter inside the house, no one answered the bell.   *Run-on*

    I heard laughter inside the house, but no one answered the bell.
    Correct

The run-on has been corrected by using a joining word, ____but____, to connect the two complete thoughts.

3. A car sped around the corner, it sprayed slush all over the pedestrians.
    Run-on

    A car sped around the corner; it sprayed slush all over the pedestrians.
    Correct

The run-on has been corrected by using a ____semicolon____ to connect the two closely related thoughts.

4. I had a campus map, I still could not find my classroom building.
    Run-on

    Although I had a campus map, I still could not find my classroom building.   *Correct*

The run-on has been corrected by using the subordinating word ____Although____ to connect the two closely related thoughts.

Answers are on page 568.

What Are Run-Ons?

A *run-on* is two complete thoughts that are run together with no adequate sign given to mark the break between them. As a result of the run-on, the reader is confused, unsure of where one thought ends and the next one begins. Two types of run-ons are fused sentences and comma splices.

Some run-ons have no punctuation at all to mark the break between the thoughts. Such run-ons are known as *fused sentences:* they are fused or joined together as if they were only one thought.

Fused Sentence

Rochelle decided to stop smoking she didn't want to die of lung cancer.

Fused Sentence

The exam was postponed the class was canceled as well.

In other run-ons, known as *comma splices*, a comma is used to connect or "splice" together the two complete thoughts.* However, a comma alone is *not enough* to connect two complete thoughts. Some connection stronger than a comma alone is needed.

Comma Splice

Rochelle decided to stop smoking, she didn't want to die of lung cancer.

Comma Splice

The exam was postponed, the class was canceled as well.

Comma splices are the most common kind of run-on. Students sense that some kind of connection is needed between thoughts, and so they put a comma at the dividing point. But the comma alone is *not sufficient*. A stronger, clearer mark is needed between the two thoughts.

---

*Notes:
1. Some instructors feel that the term *run-ons* should be applied only to fused sentences, not to comma splices. But for many other instructors, and for our purposes in this book, the term *run-on* applies equally to fused sentences and comma splices. The bottom line is that you do not want either fused sentences or comma splices in your writing.
2. Some instructors refer to each complete thought in a run-on as an *independent clause.* A *clause* is simply a group of words having a subject and a verb. A clause may be *independent* (expressing a complete thought and able to stand alone) or *dependent* (not expressing a complete thought and not able to stand alone). A run-on is two independent clauses that are run together with no adequate sign given to mark the break between them.

A Warning: Words That Can Lead to Run-Ons

People often write run-ons when the second complete thought begins with one of the following words:

I	we	there	now
you	they	this	then
he, she, it		that	next

Remember to be on the alert for run-ons whenever you use these words in your writing.

Correcting Run-Ons

Here are four common methods of correcting a run-on:

1   Use a period and a capital letter to separate the two complete thoughts. (In other words, make two separate sentences of the two complete thoughts.)

Rochelle decided to stop smoking. She didn't want to die of lung cancer.
The exam was postponed. The class was canceled as well.

2   Use a comma plus a joining word (*and, but, for, or, nor, so, yet*) to connect the two complete thoughts.

Rochelle decided to stop smoking, for she didn't want to die of lung cancer.
The exam was postponed, and the class was canceled as well.

3   Use a semicolon to connect the two complete thoughts.

Rochelle decided to stop smoking; she didn't want to die of lung cancer.
The exam was postponed; the class was canceled as well.

4   Use subordination.

Because Rochelle didn't want to die of lung cancer, she decided to stop smoking.
When the exam was postponed, the class was canceled as well.

The following pages will give you practice in all four methods of correcting run-ons. The use of subordination will be explained further on page 145, in a chapter that deals with sentence variety.

Method 1: Period and a Capital Letter

One way of correcting a run-on is to use a period and a capital letter at the break between the two complete thoughts. Use this method especially if the thoughts are not closely related or if another method would make the sentence too long.

Practice 1

Locate the split in each of the following run-ons. Each is a *fused sentence*—that is, each consists of two sentences fused or joined together with no punctuation at all between them. Reading each sentence aloud will help you "hear" where a major break or split in the thought occurs. At such a point, your voice will probably drop and pause.

Correct the run-on by putting a period at the end of the first thought and a capital letter at the start of the second thought.

Example   Craig was not a success at his job. His mouth moved faster than his hands.

1. Michael gulped two cups of strong coffee. His heart then started to flutter.

2. Elena defrosted the freezer in her usual impatient way. She hacked at the thick ice with a screwdriver.

3. The engine was sputtering and coughing. A strong smell of gas came from under the hood.

4. A bright yellow Volkswagen "bug" pulled up beside me. It looked like a deviled egg on wheels.

5. The phone in the next apartment rings all the time. The new tenants keep complaining about the sound.

6. Numbered Ping-Pong balls bounced in the machine. We clutched our raffle tickets tightly.

7. The store clerk watched the girls closely. They must have looked like shoplifters to her.

8. It's hard to discuss things with Lauren. She interprets almost everything as criticism.

9. Kate's books look like accident victims. They have cracked spines and torn covers.

10. I got to the sale too late. The last ceiling fan had been sold just five minutes before.

Practice 2

Locate the split in each of the following run-ons. Some of the run-ons are fused sentences, and some of them are *comma splices*—run-ons spliced or joined together only with a comma. Correct each run-on by putting a period at the end of the first thought and a capital letter at the start of the next thought.

1. Human teenagers must be descended from cockroaches, Both like to stay out late and eat junk food.

2. Only the female mosquito drinks blood. The male lives on plant juices.

3. Sonja has the experience to be an excellent marriage counselor. She's already been married four times.

4. My uncle's final words probably express everyone's feeling about death. He said, "Wait a minute."

5. I remember every rainbow I've ever seen. One actually circled the sun.

6. The beach was once beautiful. Now it is covered with soda cans, plastic six-pack rings, and cigarette butts.

7. In eighteenth-century Russia, smoking carried a death penalty. The same is true of chain-smoking today.

8. The business school near our home just closed down. It ran out of money.

9. The frankfurter or hot dog did not begin in Germany, In fact, it first appeared in China.

10. The man about to be shot by a firing squad had a last request. He wanted to be given a bulletproof vest.

Practice 3

Write a second sentence to go with each sentence below. Start the second sentence with the word given in the margin.

Example   *He*   My dog's ears snapped up. *He had heard a wolf howling on*
                                                 television.

They

Answers will vary.

1. The M&Ms spilled all over the floor. _____

_____

Then

2. I closed every window in the house. _____

_____

She

3. Talia saves everything. _____

_____

It

4. The car needed to be vacuumed. _____

_____

There

5. The street was flooded. _____

_____

Method 2: Comma and a Joining Word

Another way of correcting a run-on is to use a comma plus a joining word to connect the two complete thoughts. Joining words (also called *coordinating conjunctions*) include *and, but, for, or, nor, so,* and *yet.* Here is what the four most common joining words mean:

and   in addition, along with

Lola was watching Monday night football, and she was doing her homework as well.

(*And* means *in addition:* Lola was watching Monday night football; *in addition,* she was doing her homework.)

but   however, except, on the other hand, just the opposite

I voted for the president two years ago, but I would not vote for him today.

(*But* means *however:* I voted for the president two years ago; *however,* I would not vote for him today.)

for   because, the reason why, the cause for something

Saturday is the worst day to shop, for people jam the stores.

(*For* means *because:* Saturday is the worst day to shop *because* people jam the stores.) If you are not comfortable using *for*, you may want to use *because* instead of *for* in the activities that follow. If you do use *because*, omit the comma before it.

so   as a result, therefore

Our son misbehaved again, so he was sent upstairs without dessert.

(*So* means *as a result:* Our son misbehaved again; *as a result,* he was sent upstairs without dessert.)

Practice 1

Insert the comma and the joining word (*and, but, for, so*) that logically connects the two thoughts in each sentence.

Example   I hate to see animals in cages, *so* a trip to the zoo always depresses me.

1. We knew the old desk had a secret drawer, *but* no one could find it.
2. I had to retype my term paper, *for* my little boy had scrawled on it with a purple crayon.
3. Last year my nephew needed physical therapy, *so* the whole family pitched in to work with him.
4. My new car is a pleasure to drive, *for* there isn't the slightest squeak or rattle.
5. A cat food commercial came on, *and* Marie started to sing along with the jingle.
6. It rained a lot this summer, *so* we have not had to water our lawn.
7. I heard the grinding of the garbage truck, *so* I ran downstairs and grabbed the trash bags.
8. Ella wanted to take a break, *but* the boss wanted the inventory list right away.
9. I couldn't read the map, *for* an ink stain had blotted out an entire country.
10. The two little boys had a giggling fit, *so* their father hustled them out of the church.

Practice 2

Add a complete, closely related thought to each of the following statements. When you write the second thought, use a comma plus the joining word shown at the left.

Example   *but*   I was sick with the flu, _but I still had to study for the test._

Answers will vary.

so   1. I couldn't resist the banana cream pie _____

_____

but   2. We tried to follow the directions _____

_____

and   3. Jamal took three coffee breaks before lunch _____

_____

for   4. The car seat was drenched _____

_____

but   5. I don't usually pick up hitchhikers _____

_____

Method 3: Semicolon

A third method of correcting a run-on is to use a semicolon to mark the break between two thoughts. A *semicolon* (;) is made up of a period above a comma and is sometimes called a *strong comma*. The semicolon signals more of a pause than a comma alone but not quite the full pause of a period.

Occasional use of semicolons can add variety to sentences. For some people, however, the semicolon is a confusing mark of punctuation. Keep in mind that if you are not comfortable using it, you can and should use one of the first two methods of correcting a run-on sentence.

Semicolon Alone

Here are some earlier sentences that were connected with a comma plus a joining word. Now they are connected with a semicolon. Notice that a semicolon, unlike a comma, can be used alone to connect the two complete thoughts in each sentence.

Lola was watching Monday night football; she was doing her homework as well.

I voted for the president two years ago; I would not vote for him today.

Saturday is the worst day to shop; people jam the stores.

Practice

Insert a semicolon where the break occurs between the two complete thoughts in each of the following sentences.

Example   She had a wig on; it looked more like a hat than a wig.

1. Alan had to go up the ramp backward; his wheelchair's strongest gear is reverse.
2. A cockroach is almost indestructible; it can live for weeks with its head cut off.
3. Pat read the funny birthday cards; she laughed aloud in the quiet store.
4. My brother captured the fluttering moth; it bumped around inside his hands.
5. Alex couldn't finish the book; it was giving him nightmares.

Semicolon with a Transition

A semicolon is sometimes used with a transitional word and a comma to join two complete thoughts:

I figured that the ball game would cost me about ten dollars; however, I didn't consider the high price of food and drinks.

Fred and Martha have a low-interest mortgage on their house; otherwise, they would move to another neighborhood.

Sharon didn't understand the instructor's point; therefore, she asked him to repeat it.

Note   Sometimes transitional words do not join complete thoughts but are merely interrupters in a sentence (see pages 312–314):

My parents, moreover, plan to go on the trip.

I believe, however, that they'll change their minds.

Transitional Words

Here is a list of common transitional words (also known as *adverbial conjunctions*).

Common Transitional Words

however	moreover	therefore
on the other hand	in addition	as a result
nevertheless	also	consequently
instead	furthermore	otherwise

Practice 1

For each item, choose a logical transitional word from the box above and write it in the space provided. In addition, put a semicolon *before* the transition and a comma *after* it.

Example   It was raining harder than ever __; however,__ Bobby was determined to go to the amusement park.

Answers may vary.

1. Most people can do without food for a month __; on the other hand,__ they need two quarts of water a day to survive.

2. Jean's son was sick __; therefore,__ she delivered his newspapers for him.

3. Linda felt safe living near a fire hydrant __; however,__ she wished that the neighborhood dogs didn't like it so much.

4. The bride's father apologized to the waiting guests __; furthermore,__ he promised to return all the wedding gifts.

5. Andrea thinks gift-wrapping paper is a waste of money __; consequently,__ she wraps presents in newspaper.

Practice 2

Punctuate each sentence by using a semicolon and a comma.

Example   A band rehearses in the garage next door;as a result,I'm thinking of moving.

1. The hostess told us there would be a twenty-minute wait; however, she then seated the couple who came in after us.

2. Ricki knows nothing about computers; as a result, she decided to sign up for a word-processing course.

3. All too many children are emotionally abused; moreover, many are physically abused as well.

4. I insisted that my wife stop smoking; otherwise, I would have suffered the effects of the secondhand smoke from her cigarettes.

5. We packed the groceries carefully; nevertheless, the bread was squashed and two eggs were broken.

Method 4: Subordination

A fourth method of joining related thoughts is to use subordination. *Subordination* is a way of showing that one thought in a sentence is not as important as another thought. Here are three sentences in which one idea is subordinated to (made less emphatic than) the other idea:

> Because Rochelle didn't want to die of lung cancer, she decided to stop smoking.
>
> The wedding reception began to get out of hand when the guests started to throw food at each other.
>
> Although my brothers wanted to watch a *Star Trek* rerun, the rest of the family insisted on turning to the network news.

Dependent Words

Notice that when we subordinate, we use dependent words like *because, when,* and *although.* Following is a brief list of common dependent words (see also the list on page 100). Subordination is explained in full on page 145.

Common Dependent Words		
after	before	unless
although	even though	until
as	if	when
because	since	while

Practice 1

Choose a logical dependent word from the box on the previous page and write it in the space provided.

Example   _____Although_____ going up a ladder is easy, looking down can be
          difficult.

Answers may vary.

1.   _____After_____ an emotional reunion between a mother and son, the
     talk-show host paused for a commercial about chewing gum.

2.   You should have looked at the label _____before_____ you washed that wool
     sweater.

3.   _____When_____ the instructor announced that there were only ten minutes
     left in the test, students began writing even more quickly to finish their essay
     answers.

4.   _____If_____ you open the windows, the paint fumes will disappear
     more quickly.

5.   The directions say to continue on the main highway _____until_____ a
     large red barn and a small road appear on the right.

Practice 2

Rewrite the five sentences below so that one idea is subordinate to the other. Use
one of the dependent words in the box on the previous page. As in the example
below, use a comma if a dependent statement starts a sentence. (All the sentences
are taken from this chapter.)

Example   I hate to see animals in cages; a trip to the zoo always depresses me.
          Because I hate to see animals in cages, a trip to the zoo always

          depresses me.

Answers may vary.

1.   I had a campus map; I still could not find my classroom building.
     Even though I had a campus map, I still could not find my classroom building.

2.   A cat food commercial came on; Marie started to sing along with the jingle.
     When a cat food commercial came on, Marie started to sing along with

     the jingle.

3. The phone in the next apartment rings constantly; I'm beginning to get used to the sound.

Since the phone In the next apartment rings constantly, I'm beginning to
get used to the sound.

4. Michael gulped two cups of strong coffee; his heart began to flutter.

After Michael gulped two cups of strong coffee, his heart began to flutter.

5. A car sped around the corner; it sprayed slush all over the pedestrians.

As a car sped around the corner, it sprayed slush all over the pedestrians.

Collaborative Activity

Part A: Editing and Rewriting

Working with a partner, read carefully the short paragraph below and underline the five run-on sentences. Then use the space provided to correct the five run-ons. Feel free to discuss the rewrite quietly with your partner and refer back to the chapter when necessary.

Wording of rewritten answers may vary.

[1]People do funny things when they get on an elevator. [2]They try to move into a corner or against a wall. [3]They all face forward _forward, and their_ their hands are kept in front or at their sides. [4]Most of all, they avoid eye contact with the other passengers, preferring to stare at the floor numbers. [5]Nobody teaches these people how to behave on an elevator _elevator; however,_ however, everyone seems to obey the same rules. [6]Psychologists have a theory about elevator behavior that they feel explains these actions. [7]Elevators are small, enclosed spaces _spaces. They_ they force people into contact with one

Continued

another. [8]The contact is a violation of a person's "personal space" this is

space." This

the invisible shield we all carry with us. [9]We get nervous when a

us. We

stranger stands too close to us we want to put that invisible shield back.

[10]Therefore, an elevator isn't the place to try to get to know someone.

_____

_____

_____

_____

_____

_____

_____

_____

_____

_____

_____

_____

Part B: Creating Sentences

Working with a partner, make up your own short run-ons test as directed.
Answers will vary.

1. Write a run-on sentence. Then rewrite it, using a period and capital
letter to separate the thoughts into two sentences.

   Run-on _____

   _____

   Rewrite _____

   _____

Continued

2. Write a sentence that has two complete thoughts. Then rewrite it, using a comma and a joining word to correctly join the complete thoughts.

Two complete thoughts _____

_____

Rewrite _____

_____

3. Write a sentence that has two complete thoughts. Then rewrite it, using a semicolon to correctly join the complete thoughts.

Two complete thoughts _____

_____

Rewrite _____

_____

Reflective Activity
Answers will vary.

1. Look at the paragraph that you revised above. Explain how run-ons interfered with your reading of the paragraph.

2. In your own written work, which type of run-on are you more likely to write: comma splices or fused sentences? Why?

3. Which method of correcting run-ons are you most likely to use in your own writing? Which are you least likely to use? Why?

■ Review Test 1

Some of the run-ons that follow are *fused sentences,* having no punctuation between the two complete thoughts; others are *comma splices,* having only a comma between the two complete thoughts.

Correct the run-ons by using one of the following three methods:

- Period and a capital letter
- Comma and a joining word (*and, but, for,* or *so*)
- Semicolon

Use whichever method seems most appropriate in each case.

Example   Fred pulled the cellophane off the cake ~and~ the icing came along with it.

Answers will vary.

1. The runner was called safe, ~but~ even he couldn't believe it.

2. I looked all over for my new shirt. ~A~ all I could find was the empty bag.

3. Lia tried to fold the road map neatly, ~but~ she gave up and stuffed it into the glove compartment.

4. First we can't wait to go on vacation, ~;~ then we can't wait to come home again.

5. One step was sagging ~so~ Martina hired a carpenter to fix the porch.

6. I ran toward the supermarket, ~.T~ the manager had just locked the doors.

7. Ted tried to assemble the barbecue, ~but~ the instructions were impossible to understand.

8. I reached into the pretzel bag; all that was left was salt.

9. Tina was starving, ~so~ she bought a limp sandwich from the vending machine.

10. Bev was bored. ~S~ she drew rocket ships in the margins of her notebook.

■ **Review Test 2**

Correct the run-on in each sentence by using subordination. Choose from among the following dependent words.

after	because	if	until
although	before	since	when
as	even though	unless	while

Example   Tony hated going to a new barber, he was afraid of butchered hair.

Because Tony was afraid of butchered hair, he hated going to a

new barber.

Answers will vary.

1. The fan started throwing beer cans onto the field security guards hustled him away.

    Because the fan started throwing beer cans onto the field, security

    guards hustled him away.

2. I had three cups of coffee, my eyes looked like huge globes.

    After I had three cups of coffee, my eyes looked like huge globes.

3. The boy didn't want to talk to his mother, he pretended to be asleep.

    Because the boy didn't want to talk to his mother, he pretended to be

    asleep.

4. The check arrived in the mail we didn't really believe that we had won the contest.

    Until the check arrived in the mail, we didn't really believe that we had won

    the contest.

5. We forgot to put film in the camera, the only pictures we have of our vacation are the ones in our memory.

    Since we forgot to put film in the camera, the only pictures we have of our

    vacation are the ones in our memory.

6. I left school this afternoon hailstones as big as marbles were falling from the sky.

    When I left school this afternoon, hailstones as big as marbles were falling

    from the sky.

7. The plumber comes quickly our kitchen will look like a swamp.

    Unless the plumber comes quickly, our kitchen will look like a swamp.

8. The man circled the crowded parking lot in their car, his wife ran into the store to return a sweater.

   While the man circled the crowded parking lot in their car, his wife ran into the store to return a sweater.

9. The boy was wearing headphones nearly everyone on the bus could hear the beat of the song on his radio.

   Even though the boy was wearing headphones, nearly everyone on the bus could hear the beat of the song on his radio.

10. The computer went dead a message appeared on the screen saying, "System error."

    Before the computer went dead, a message appeared on the screen saying, "System error."

■ **Review Test 3**
Answers will vary.
On separate paper, write six sentences, each of which has two complete thoughts. In two of the sentences, use a period and a capital letter between the thoughts. In another two sentences, use a comma and a joining word (*and, but, or, nor, for, so, yet*) to join the thoughts. In the final two sentences, use a semicolon to join the thoughts.

■ **Review Test 4**
Answers will vary.
Write quickly for five minutes about something that makes you angry. Don't worry about spelling, punctuation, finding exact words, or organizing your thoughts. Just focus on writing as many words as you can without stopping.

   After you have finished, go back and make whatever changes are needed to correct any run-on sentences in your writing.

7 Sentence Variety I

This chapter will show you how to write effective and varied sentences. You'll learn more about two techniques—subordination and coordination—that you can use to expand simple sentences, making them more interesting and expressive. You'll also reinforce what you have learned in Chapters 5 and 6 about how subordination and coordination can help you correct fragments and run-ons in your writing.

Four Traditional Sentence Patterns

Sentences in English are traditionally described as *simple, compound, complex,* or *compound-complex.* Each is explained below.

The Simple Sentence

A simple sentence has a single subject-verb combination.

> Children play.
> The game ended early.
> My car stalled three times last week.
> The lake has been polluted by several neighboring streams.

A simple sentence may have more than one subject:

> Lola and Tony drove home.
> The wind and sun dried my hair.

or more than one verb:

> The children smiled and waved at us.
> The lawn mower smoked and sputtered.

or several subjects and verbs:

> <u>Manny</u>, <u>Moe</u>, and <u>Jack</u> <u><u>lubricated</u></u> my car, <u><u>replaced</u></u> the oil filter, and <u><u>cleaned</u></u> the spark plugs.

Practice

On separate paper, write:

Answers may vary.

> Three sentences, each with a single subject and verb
>
> Three sentences, each with a single subject and a double verb
>
> Three sentences, each with a double subject and a single verb

In each case, underline the subject once and the verb twice. (See pages 90–91 if necessary for more information on subjects and verbs.)

The Compound Sentence

A compound, or "double," sentence is made up of two (or more) simple sentences. The two complete statements in a compound sentence are usually connected by a comma plus a joining word (*and, but, for, or, nor, so, yet*).

A compound sentence is used when you want to give equal weight to two closely related ideas. The technique of showing that ideas have equal importance is called *coordination.*

Following are some compound sentences. Each sentence contains two ideas that the writer considers equal in importance.

> The rain increased, so the officials canceled the game.
>
> Martha wanted to go shopping, but Fred refused to drive her.
>
> Hollis was watching television in the family room, and April was upstairs on the phone.
>
> I had to give up wood carving, for my arthritis had become very painful.

Practice 1

Combine the following pairs of simple sentences into compound sentences. Use a comma and a logical joining word (*and, but, for, so*) to connect each pair.

Note   If you are not sure what *and, but, for,* and *so* mean, review pages 124–125.

Example   •   We hung up the print.

           •   The wall still looked bare.

We hung up the print, but the wall still looked bare.

Answers may vary; possible answers are given.

1. • I am studying computer science.

    • My sister is majoring in communications.

I am studying computer science, and my sister is majoring in

communications.

2. • The children started hitting each other.

    • I made them turn off the TV.

The children started hitting each other, so I made them turn off the TV.

3. • Betsy put masking tape on her forehead at night.

    • She wanted to stop wrinkles from forming.

Betsy put masking tape on her forehead at night, for she wanted to

stop wrinkles from forming.

4. • The pizza was covered with salty anchovies and pepperoni.

    • He picked up the salt shaker as usual.

The pizza was covered with salty anchovies and pepperoni, but he

picked up the salt shaker as usual.

5. • She felt faint.

    • She grabbed the metal lamppost.

She felt faint, so she grabbed the metal lamppost.

Practice 2

Answers may vary.

On separate paper, write five compound sentences of your own. Use a different joining word (*and, but, for, or, nor, so, yet*) to connect the two complete ideas in each sentence.

The Complex Sentence

A complex sentence is made up of a simple sentence (a complete statement) and a statement that begins with a dependent word.* Here is a list of common dependent words:

Dependent Words

after	if, even if	when, whenever
although, though	in order that	where, wherever
as	since	whether
because	that, so that	which, whichever
before	unless	while
even though	until	who
how	what, whatever	whose

A complex sentence is used when you want to emphasize one idea over another in a sentence. Look at the following complex sentence:

Because I forgot the time, I missed the final exam.

The idea that the writer wants to emphasize here—*I missed the final exam*—is expressed as a complete thought. The less important idea—*Because I forgot the time*—is subordinated to the complete thought. The technique of giving one idea less emphasis than another is called *subordination*.

Following are other examples of complex sentences. In each case, the part starting with the dependent word is the less emphasized part of the sentence.

While Aisha was eating breakfast, she began to feel sick.
I checked my money *before* I invited Pedro for lunch.
When Jerry lost his temper, he also lost his job.
Although I practiced for three months, I failed my driving test.

---

*The two parts of a complex sentence are sometimes called an independent clause and a dependent clause. A *clause* is simply a word group that contains a subject and a verb. An *independent clause* expresses a complete thought and can stand alone. A *dependent clause* does not express a complete thought in itself and "depends on" the independent clause to complete its meaning. Dependent clauses always begin with a dependent or subordinating word.

Practice 1

Use logical dependent words to combine the following pairs of simple sentences into complex sentences. Place a comma after a dependent statement when it starts the sentence.

Examples • I obtained a credit card.
          • I began spending money recklessly.
            When I obtained a credit card, I began spending money recklessly.

          • Alan dressed the turkey.
          • His brother greased the roasting pan.
            Alan dressed the turkey while his brother greased the roasting pan.

Answers may vary; possible answers are given.

1. • The movie disgusted Dena.
   • She walked out after twenty minutes.
     Because the movie disgusted Dena, she walked out after twenty

     minutes.

2. • The house had been burglarized.
   • Dave couldn't sleep soundly for several months.
     After the house had been burglarized, Dave couldn't sleep soundly for

     several months.

3. • My vision begins to fade.
   • I know I'd better get some sleep.
     When my vision begins to fade, I know I'd better get some sleep.

     _____

4. • The family would need a place to sleep.
   • Fred told the movers to unload the mattresses first.
     Since the family would need a place to sleep, Fred told the movers to

     unload the mattresses first.

5. • The hurricane hit the coast.
   • We crisscrossed our windows with strong tape.
     When the hurricane hit the coast, we crisscrossed our windows with

     strong tape.

Practice 2

Rewrite the following sentences, using subordination rather than coordination. Include a comma when a dependent statement starts a sentence.

Example   The hair dryer was not working right, so I returned it to the store.

Because the hair dryer was not working right, I returned it

to the store.

Answers may vary; possible answers are given.

1. The muffler shop advertised same-day service, but my car wasn't ready for three days.

    Although the muffler shop advertised same-day service, my car wasn't

    ready for three days.

2. The high-blood-pressure pills produced dangerous side effects, so the government banned them.

    Because the high-blood-pressure pills produced dangerous side effects,

    the government banned them.

3. Phil lopped dead branches off the tree, and Michelle stacked them into piles on the ground below.

    While Phil lopped dead branches off the tree, Michelle stacked them into

    piles on the ground below.

4. Anne wedged her handbag tightly under her arm, for she was afraid of muggers.

    Anne wedged her handbag tightly under her arm because she was afraid

    of muggers.

5. Ellen counted the cash three times, but the total still didn't tally with the amount on the register tape.

    Although Ellen counted the cash three times, the total still didn't tally

    with the amount on the register tape.

Practice 3

Combine the following simple sentences into complex sentences. Omit repeated words. Use the dependent words _who, which,_ or _that._

Notes

a   The word _who_ refers to persons.

b   The word *which* refers to things.

c   The word *that* refers to persons or things.

Use commas around the dependent statement only if it seems to interrupt the flow of thought in the sentence. (See pages 312–314.)

Examples   • Clyde picked up a hitchhiker.

•   The hitchhiker was traveling around the world.

Clyde picked up a hitchhiker who was traveling around the world.

•   Larry is a sleepwalker.

•   Larry is my brother.

Larry, who is my brother, is a sleepwalker.

Answers may vary; possible answers are given.

1. •   The boy was in a motorcycle accident.

•   The boy limps.

The boy who limps was in a motorcycle accident.

2. •   Raquel is a champion weight lifter.

•   Raquel is my neighbor.

Raquel, who is my neighbor, is a champion weight lifter.

3. •   The two screws were missing from the assembly kit.

•   The two screws held the bicycle frame together.

The two screws that held the bicycle frame together were missing

from the assembly kit.

4. •   The letter is from my ex-wife.

•   The letter arrived today.

The letter that arrived today is from my ex-wife.

5. •   The tall hedge muffled the highway noise.

•   The hedge surrounded the house.

The tall hedge which surrounded the house muffled the highway noise.

Practice 4

Answers will vary.

On separate paper, write eight complex sentences, using, in turn, the dependent words *unless, if, after, because, when, who, which,* and *that.*

The Compound-Complex Sentence

A compound-complex sentence is made up of two (or more) simple sentences and one (or more) dependent statements. In the following examples, a solid line is under the simple sentences and a dotted line is under the dependent statements.

When the power line snapped, Jack was listening to the stereo, and Linda was reading in bed.

After I returned to school following a long illness, the math teacher gave me makeup work, but the history instructor made me drop her course.

Practice 1

Read through each sentence to get a sense of its overall meaning. Then insert a logical joining word (*and, or, but, for,* or *so*) and a logical dependent word (*because, since, when,* or *although*).

Answers will vary.

1. _____Since_____ he had worked at the construction site all day, Tom decided not to meet his friends at the diner, _____for_____ he was too tired to think.

2. _____When_____ the projector broke for a second time, some people in the audience hissed, _____and_____ others shouted for a refund.

3. Nothing could be done _____until_____ the river's floodwaters receded, _____so_____ the townspeople waited helplessly in the emergency shelter.

4. _____When_____ you are sent damaged goods, the store must replace the items, _____or_____ it must issue a full refund.

5. Sears had the outdoor grill I wanted, _____but_____ the clerk wouldn't sell it to me _____because_____ it was the floor sample.

Practice 2

Answers will vary.

On separate paper, write five compound-complex sentences.

Review of Subordination and Coordination

15.5

Subordination and coordination are ways of showing the exact relationship of ideas within a sentence. Through **subordination** we show that one idea is less important than another. When we subordinate, we use dependent words like *when, although, while, because,* and *after.* (A list of common dependent words has been given on page 140.) Through **coordination** we show that ideas are of equal importance. When we coordinate, we use the words *and, but, for, or, nor, so, yet.*

Practice

Use subordination or coordination to combine the following groups of simple sentences into one or more longer sentences. Be sure to omit repeated words. Since various combinations are possible, you might want to jot down several combinations on separate paper. Then read them aloud to find the combination that sounds best.

Keep in mind that, very often, the relationship among ideas in a sentence will be clearer when subordination rather than coordination is used.

Example
- My car does not start on cold mornings.
- I think the battery needs to be replaced.
- I already had it recharged once.
- I don't think charging it again would help.

Because my car does not start on cold mornings, I think the battery needs to be replaced. I already had it recharged once, so I don't think charging it again would help.

Comma Hints

a   Use a comma at the end of a word group that starts with a dependent word (as in "Because my car does not start on cold mornings, . . .").

b   Use a comma between independent word groups connected by *and, but, for, or, nor, so, yet* (as in "I already had it recharged once, so . . .").

Answers will vary.

1. • I needed butter to make the cookie batter.
    • I couldn't find any.
    • I used vegetable oil instead.

    I needed butter to make the cookie batter, but I couldn't find any,

    so I used vegetable oil instead.

    _____

2. • Tess had worn glasses for fifteen years.
    • She decided to get contact lenses.
    • She would be able to see better.
    • She would look more glamorous.

    Although Tess had worn glasses for fifteen years, she decided to get

    contact lenses. She would be able to see better, and she would look

    more glamorous.

    _____

3. • The children at the day-care center took their naps.
    • They unrolled their sleeping mats.
    • They piled their shoes and sneakers in a corner.

    When the children at the day-care center took their naps, they

    unrolled their sleeping mats, and they piled their shoes and sneakers

    in a corner.

4. • Jerry dialed the police emergency number.
    • He received a busy signal.
    • He dropped the phone and ran.
    • He didn't have time to call back.

    When Jerry dialed the police emergency number, he received a busy

    signal. He dropped the phone and ran, for he didn't have time to

    call back.

5. • Louise disliked walking home from the bus stop.
    • The street had no overhead lights.
    • It was lined with abandoned buildings.

    Louise disliked walking home from the bus stop, for the street had no

    overhead lights, and it was lined with abandoned buildings.

    _____

6. • The rain hit the hot pavement.
   • Plumes of steam rose from the blacktop.
   • Cars slowed to a crawl.
   • The fog obscured the drivers' vision.

   When the rain hit the hot pavement, plumes of steam rose from the blacktop. Cars slowed to a crawl, for the fog obscured the drivers' vision.

   _____

7. • His car went through the automated car wash.
   • Harry watched from the sidelines.
   • Floppy brushes slapped the car's doors.
   • Sprays of water squirted onto the roof.

   While his car went through the automated car wash, Harry watched from the sidelines. Floppy brushes slapped the car's doors, and sprays of water squirted onto the roof.

   _____

8. • The pipes had frozen.
   • The heat had gone off.
   • We phoned the plumber.
   • He couldn't come for two days.
   • He had been swamped with emergency calls.

   Since the pipes had frozen and the heat had gone off, we phoned the plumber. He couldn't come for two days because he had been swamped with emergency calls.

   _____

9. • My car developed an annoying rattle.
   • I took it to the service station.
   • The mechanic looked under the hood.
   • He couldn't find what was wrong.

   When my car developed an annoying rattle, I took it to the service station. The mechanic looked under the hood, but he couldn't find what was wrong.

   _____

10. • The childproof cap on the aspirin bottle would not budge.
   • The arrows on the bottleneck and cap were lined up.
   • I pried the cap with my fingernails.
   • One nail snapped off.
   • The cap still adhered tightly to the bottle.

   The childproof cap on the aspirin bottle would not budge even though the arrows on the bottleneck and cap were lined up. When I pried the cap with my fingernails, one nail snapped off, and the cap still adhered tightly to the bottle.

Note: Many other combinations are possible.

■ Review Test 1

Combine each group of short sentences into one sentence. Various combinations are possible. Choose the combination that reads most smoothly and clearly and that sounds most appropriate in the context of the surrounding sentences.

Here is an example of a group of sentences and some possible combinations:

Example • Martha moved in the desk chair.
   • Her moving was uneasy.
   • The chair was hard.
   • She worked at the assignment.
   • The assignment was for her English class.

   Martha moved uneasily in the hard desk chair, working at the assignment for her English class.

   Moving uneasily in the hard desk chair, Martha worked at the assignment for her English class.

   Martha moved uneasily in the hard desk chair as she worked at the assignment for her English class.

   While she worked at the assignment for her English class, Martha moved uneasily in the hard desk chair.

Note In combining short sentences into one sentence, omit repeated words where necessary. Use separate paper.

Our First Camping Trip

- My husband and I went camping for the first time.
- It was an experience.
- The experience is one we will never forget.

Possible answers:

My husband and I went camping for the first time, <u>and</u> it was an experience <u>that</u> we will never forget.

- We borrowed a tent.
- We borrowed a propane stove.
- We borrowed them from my brother-in-law.

We borrowed a tent <u>and</u> a propane stove from my brother-in-law.

- We arrived at the campground.
- We chose a spot.
- The spot was where we could pitch our tents.

<u>When</u> we arrived at the campground, we chose a spot <u>where</u> we could pitch our tents.

- We had forgotten to bring the directions for setting up the tent.
- We had to put up the tent using a trial-and-error process.
- The process took us four hours.

<u>Because</u> we had forgotten to bring the directions for setting up the tent, we had to put up the tent using a trial-and-error process, <u>which</u> took us four hours.

- The tent suddenly collapsed.
- It was nearly dark.
- We had to put it up again.

<u>When</u> it was nearly dark, the tent suddenly collapsed, <u>so</u> we had to put it up again.

- Later, we had difficulty making dinner.
- The stove at first refused to light.
- The food refused to cook.

Later, we had difficulty making dinner <u>because</u> the stove at first refused to light, <u>and</u> the food refused to cook.

- We finished cleaning up.
- We were exhausted.
- We crawled into our sleeping bags.

<u>After</u> we finished cleaning up, we were exhausted, <u>so</u> we crawled into our sleeping bags.

- A brief rain awoke us that night.
- We were so tired.
- We soon fell asleep again.

A brief rain awoke us that night, <u>but</u> we were so tired <u>that</u> we soon fell asleep again.

- Morning came.
- We were damp and miserable.

When morning came, we were
damp and miserable.

- We had learned the important lesson.
- It was that "roughing it" was too rough for us.

We had learned the important
lesson that "roughing it" was
too rough for us.

■ Review Test 2

Combine each group of short sentences into one sentence. Various combinations are possible. Choose the combination that reads most smoothly and clearly and that sounds most appropriate in the context of surrounding sentences.

Notes   In combining short sentences into one sentence, omit repeated words where necessary. Use separate paper.

My Dishwashing Job

Possible answers:

- I had one of the worst experiences of my life.
- This happened when I showed up for my first night of work.
- It was work as a restaurant dishwasher.

I had one of the worst
experiences of my life when I
showed up for my first night of
work as a restaurant
dishwasher.

- I was to load the dirty dishes and silverware into the dishwashing machine.
- The dishes were cleaned and dried.

I was to load the dirty dishes
and silverware into the
dishwashing machine, where the
dishes were cleaned and dried.

- Business at the restaurant started to pick up.
- This happened when dinnertime began.
- The dishes came in faster and faster.

When dinnertime began,
business at the restaurant
started to pick up, and the
dishes came in faster and
faster.

- I tried to scrape and load the dishes as fast as I could.
- I couldn't keep up.

I tried to scrape and load the
dishes as fast as I could, but I
couldn't keep up.

- The counter was piled high with dishes.
- The busboys began to stack pans of them on the floor.

When the counter was piled high
with dishes, the busboys began
to stack pans of them on the
floor.

- I was hot and sweaty.
- My arms were spotted with bits of food.
- My fingertips were burned from grabbing the clean dishes out of the machine.

I was hot and sweaty, my arms were spotted with bits of food, <u>and</u> my fingertips were burned from grabbing the clean dishes out of the machine.

- Then my boss burst through the double doors of the kitchen.
- He told me to hurry up.
- He told me the dining room was almost out of clean dishes.

Then my boss burst through the double doors of the kitchen <u>and</u> told me to hurry up <u>because</u> the dining room was almost out of clean dishes.

- My back was aching.
- My head was splitting.
- I smelled like the garbage can next to me.
- This happened when the restaurant was ready to close.

<u>When</u> the restaurant was ready to close, my back was aching, my head was splitting, <u>and</u> I smelled like the garbage can next to me.

- It took all my courage to return to this job the next night.
- I stuck it out.
- I needed the money.

It took all my courage to return to this job the next night, <u>but</u> I stuck it out <u>since</u> I needed the money.

- I hope never to have to be a dishwasher again.
- I did become an expert one.
- I did this after I had been on the job for a few days.

<u>Although</u> I hope never to have to be a dishwasher again, I did become an expert one <u>after</u> I had been on the job for a few days.

8 Standard English Verbs

Answers are on page 570.

Introductory Activity

Underline what you think is the correct form of the verb in each pair of sentences below.

That radio station once (play, <u>played</u>) top-forty hits.
It now (play, <u>plays</u>) classical music.

When Sherry was a little girl, she (hope, <u>hoped</u>) to become a movie star.
Now she (hope, <u>hopes</u>) to be accepted at law school.

At first, my father (juggle, <u>juggled</u>) with balls of yarn.
Now that he is an expert, he (juggle, <u>juggles</u>) raw eggs.

On the basis of the above examples, see if you can complete the following statements.

1. The first sentence in each pair refers to an action in (<u>past time</u>, the present time), and the regular verb has an ___*-ed or -d*___ ending.

2. The second sentence in each pair refers to an action in (past time, <u>the present time</u>), and the regular verb has an ___*-s*___ ending.

Answers are on page 570.

Many people have grown up in communities where nonstandard verb forms are used in everyday life. Such nonstandard forms include *they be, it done, we has, you was, she don't,* and *it ain't.* Community dialects have richness and power but are a drawback in college and the world at large, where standard English verb forms must be used. Standard English helps ensure clear communication among English-speaking people everywhere, and it is especially important in the world of work.

This chapter compares the community dialect and the standard English forms of a regular verb and three common irregular verbs.

Regular Verbs: Dialect and Standard Forms

The chart below compares community dialect (nonstandard) and standard English forms of the regular verb *talk*.

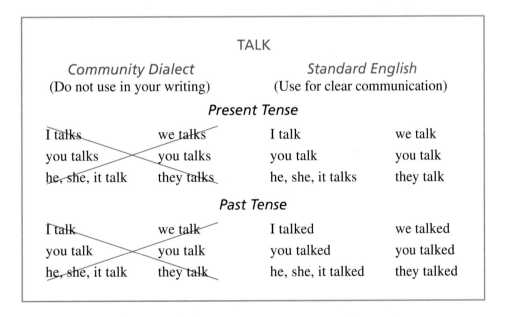

TALK

Community Dialect (Do not use in your writing)		*Standard English* (Use for clear communication)	
Present Tense			
I talks	we talks	I talk	we talk
you talks	you talks	you talk	you talk
he, she, it talk	they talks	he, she, it talks	they talk
Past Tense			
I talk	we talk	I talked	we talked
you talk	you talk	you talked	you talked
he, she, it talk	they talk	he, she, it talked	they talked

One of the most common nonstandard forms results from dropping the endings of regular verbs. For example, people might say "Rose work until ten o'clock tonight" instead of "Rose work*s* until ten o'clock tonight." Or they'll say "I work overtime yesterday" instead of "I work*ed* overtime yesterday." To avoid such nonstandard usage, memorize the forms shown above for the regular verb *talk.* Then do the activities that follow. These activities will help you make it a habit to include verb endings in your writing.

Present Tense Endings

ALLWRITE!
18.2a

The verb ending -*s* or -*es* is needed with a regular verb in the present tense when the subject is *he, she, it,* or any one person or thing.

He	He lifts weights.
She	She runs.
It	It amazes me.
One person	Their son Ted swims.
One person	Their daughter Terry dances.
One thing	Their house jumps at night with all the exercise.

Practice 1

All but one of the ten sentences that follow need -*s* or -*es* endings. Cross out the nonstandard verb forms and write the standard forms in the spaces provided. Mark the one sentence that needs no change with a *C*.

_____ends_____ Example   The sale ~~end~~ tomorrow.

_____wears_____ 1. Lucille ~~wear~~ a wig to cover up her thinning gray hair.

_____says_____ 2. My horoscope ~~say~~ that today is a good day for romance.

subscribes 3. Huang ~~subscribe~~ to three newsmagazines to keep up with current events.

believes 4. My mother ~~believe~~ in always trying her best.

_____sees_____ 5. A dog ~~see~~ only tones of gray, black, and white.

distributes 6. At Thanksgiving, our church ~~distribute~~ turkeys to the needy.

_____C_____ 7. Andrea breaks her cigarettes in half before smoking them.

_____feeds_____ 8. Chris ~~feed~~ chopped-up flies and mosquitoes to his tropical fish.

overcooks 9. That diner ~~overcook~~ all its food.

polishes 10. He ~~polish~~ his shoes using a melted wax crayon and an old towel.

Practice 2

Rewrite the short selection below, adding present tense *-s* verb endings wherever needed.

> Lou work for a company that deliver singing telegrams. Sometimes he put on a sequined tuxedo or wear a Cupid costume. He compose his own songs for birthdays, anniversaries, bachelor parties, and other occasions. Then he show up at a certain place and surprise the victim. He sing a song that include personal details, which he get in advance, about the recipient of the telegram. Lou love the astonished looks on other people's faces; he also enjoy earning money by making people happy on special days.

Lou works for a company that delivers singing telegrams. Sometimes he

puts on a sequined tuxedo or wears a Cupid costume. He composes his

own songs for birthdays, anniversaries, bachelor parties, and other occa-

sions. Then he shows up at a certain place and surprises the victim. He

sings a song that includes personal details, which he gets in advance,

about the recipient of the telegram. Lou loves the astonished looks on

other people's faces; he also enjoys earning money by making people happy

on special days.

_____

_____

_____

Past Tense Endings

ALLWRITE!
18.2b

The verb ending *-d* or *-ed* is needed with a regular verb in the past tense.

Yesterday we finished painting the house.
I completed the paper an hour before class.
Fred's car stalled on his way to work this morning.

Practice 1

All but one of the ten sentences that follow need -d or -ed endings. Cross out the nonstandard verb forms and write the standard forms in the spaces provided. Mark the one sentence that needs no change with a C.

jumped   Example   The cat ~~jump~~ on my lap when I sat down.

turned   1. The first time I baked a pound cake, it ~~turn~~ out to be a ton cake.

bounced   2. The line drive slammed into the fence and ~~bounce~~ into the stands for a ground-rule double.

paged   3. Ben ~~page~~ through the book, looking for the money he had hidden there.

crushed   4. Mario ~~crush~~ the sunglasses in his back pocket as he flopped on the sofa.

C   5. The sweating workers shoveled hot tar onto the road and then smoothed it out.

washed   6. The surgeons ~~wash~~ their hands before they entered the operating room.

cracked   7. The detective ~~crack~~ the case after finding a key witness.

collected 8. When she was a teenager, Rita ~~collect~~ pictures of her favorite rock stars.

pulled   9. As they struggled, the mugger ~~pull~~ the gold chain from Val's neck.

lacked   10. Ken knew he ~~lack~~ the ability to make the varsity team, but he tried out anyway.

Practice 2

Rewrite this selection, adding past tense -d or -ed verb endings where needed.

> Mrs. Bayne stroll across the street to her neighbor's yard sale. She examine the rack of used clothes, check the prices, and accidentally knock a blouse off its hanger. She poke through a box of children's toys, spilling a carton full of wooden blocks. She leaf through some old magazines, ripping a few of the brittle pages. At a table of kitchen equipment, she push down the buttons on a toaster and force them up again. Mrs. Bayne then wander off without buying anything.

Mrs. Bayne strolled across the street to her neighbor's yard sale.

She examined the rack of used clothes, checked the prices, and acciden-

tally knocked a blouse off its hanger. She poked through a box of children's

toys, spilling a carton full of wooden blocks. She leafed through some old

magazines, ripping a few of the brittle pages. At a table of kitchen

equipment, she pushed down the buttons on a toaster and forced them

up again. Mrs. Bayne then wandered off without buying anything.

Three Common Irregular Verbs: Dialect and Standard Forms

The following charts compare the nonstandard and standard dialects of the common irregular verbs *be, have,* and *do.* (For more on irregular verbs, see Chapter 9, beginning on page 161.)

BE

Community Dialect		*Standard English*	
(Do not use in your writing)		(Use for clear communication)	

Present Tense

I be (*or* is)	we be	I am	we are
you be	you be	you are	you are
he, she, it be	they be	he, she, it is	they are

Past Tense

I were	we was	I was	we were
you was	you was	you were	you were
he, she, it were	they was	he, she, it was	they were

HAVE

Community Dialect		*Standard English*	
(Do not use in your writing)		(Use for clear communication)	

Present Tense

I has	we has	I have	we have
you has	you has	you have	you have
he, she, it have	they has	he, she, it has	they have

Past Tense

I has	we has	I had	we had
you has	you has	you had	you had
he, she, it have	they has	he, she, it had	they had

DO

Community Dialect		Standard English	
(Do not use in your writing)		(Use for clear communication)	

Present Tense

I does	we does	I do	we do
you does	you does	you do	you do
he, she, it do	they does	he, she, it does	they do

Past Tense

I done	we done	I did	we did
you done	you done	you did	you did
he, she, it done	they done	he, she, it did	they did

Note   Many people have trouble with one negative form of *do*. They will say, for example, "She don't listen" instead of "She doesn't listen," or they will say "This pen don't work" instead of "This pen doesn't work." Be careful to avoid the common mistake of using *don't* instead of *doesn't*.

Practice 1

Underline the standard form of the irregular verb *be, have,* or *do.*

1. My brother Ronald (be, is) a normal, fun-loving person most of the time.
2. But he (have, has) a hobby that changes his personality.
3. He (be, is) an amateur actor with our community theater group.
4. When he (do, does) a part in a play, he turns into the character.
5. Once the company (done, did) a play about Sherlock Holmes, the detective.
6. In the show, Ronald (was, were) a frightened man stalked by a murderer.
7. The role (had, have) a strange effect on my brother.
8. At home, he (were, was) nervous and jittery.
9. I (done, did) my best to calm him.
10. However, he remained convinced that he (was, were) being followed.

Practice 2

Cross out the nonstandard verb form in each sentence. Then write the standard form of *be, have,* or *do* in the space provided.

_____is_____ 1. That music store, Platters, ~~be~~ the largest in the area.

_____has_____ 2. It ~~have~~ all the latest releases.

_____has_____ 3. In addition, a special section ~~have~~ classic CDs at reasonable prices.

_____are_____ 4. The salespeople ~~is~~ very knowledgeable about music.

_____are_____ 5. They ~~is~~ willing to help a customer find any CD in the store.

_____do_____ 6. They also ~~does~~ their best to order any CD available.

_____do_____ 7. The owners of Platters ~~does~~ a good job promoting local recording artists, too.

_____has_____ 8. The store ~~have~~ posters of local groups in the windows.

_____does_____ 9. It ~~do~~ special promotions of their performances.

_____are_____ 10. My friends and I ~~be~~ loyal and satisfied customers of Platters.

Practice 3

Fill in each blank with the standard form of *be, have,* or *do.*

My friend Tyrell _____is_____ a real bargain hunter. If any store _____has_____ a sale, he runs right over and buys two or three things, whether or not they _____are_____ things he needs. Tyrell _____does_____ his best, also, to get something for nothing. Last week, he _____was_____ reading the paper and saw that the First National Bank's new downtown offices _____were_____ offering gifts for new accounts. "Those freebies sure _____do_____ look good," Tyrell said. So he went downtown, opened an account, and _____had_____ the manager give him a Big Ben alarm clock. When he got back with the clock, he _____was_____ smiling. "I _____am_____ a very busy man," he told me, "and I really need the free time."

■ Review Test 1

Underline the standard verb form.

1. We (<u>pay</u>, pays) more for car insurance since the accident.
2. Two years ago, my brother and his wife (adopt, <u>adopted</u>) a handicapped child.
3. The baby (grasp, <u>grasps</u>) his mother's long hair in his tiny fist.
4. The original Frisbees (was, <u>were</u>) tin pie plates from a baking company.
5. Greta (don't, <u>doesn't</u>) approve of her brother's deer hunting.
6. My stepmother likes to work in the yard whenever the sun (be, <u>is</u>) shining.
7. Lorraine looks like a squirrel when she (<u>chews</u>, chew) a big wad of gum.
8. My little sister (<u>has</u>, have) an unusual ailment—an allergy to homework.
9. Louise (grease, <u>greases</u>) the casserole dish with melted chicken fat.
10. My brother (own, <u>owns</u>) a World War II flyer's leather jacket that belonged to our father.

■ Review Test 2

Cross out the nonstandard verb forms in the sentences that follow. Then write the standard English verb forms in the space above, as shown.

Example   For most of yesterday morning, the children ~~play~~ *played* quietly in the sandbox.

1. Sandra ~~dunk~~ *dunks (or dunked)* the chicken wings into the sweet-and-sour sauce.
2. My parents ~~locks~~ *lock (or locked)* themselves in the bathroom during an argument.
3. A suspicious-looking man ~~ask~~ *asked* if I wanted to buy a new microwave oven for fifty dollars.
4. My sister ~~bite~~ *bites* the erasers off her pencils.
5. Theo ~~ride~~ *rides (or rode)* a bicycle to work in order to save money on gas.
6. The school ~~don't~~ *doesn't* allow anyone to use the darkroom without an appointment.
7. For the third time in the movie, a car ~~bounce~~ *bounced* headlong down a cliff and burst into flames.
8. The mail carrier ~~give~~ *gives* us a pink slip when we have a package waiting at the post office.
9. The ceilings ~~was~~ *were* ringed with water marks from the leaky roof.
10. Instead of a keyhole, each hotel room door ~~have~~ *has(or had)* a slot for a magnetic card.

9 Irregular Verbs

Introductory Activity

You may already have a sense of which common English verbs are regular and which are not. To test yourself, fill in the past tense and past participle of the verbs below. Five are regular verbs and so take *-d* or *-ed* in the past tense and past participle. For these verbs, write *R* under *Verb Type* and then write their past tense and past participle verb forms. Five are irregular verbs and will probably not sound right when you try to add *-d* or *-ed*. For these verbs, write *I* under *Verb Type*. Also, see if you can write in their irregular verb forms.

Present	*Verb Type*	*Past*	*Past Participle*
fall	I	fell	fallen
1. scream	R	screamed	screamed
2. write	I	wrote	written
3. steal	I	stole	stolen
4. ask	R	asked	asked
5. kiss	R	kissed	kissed
6. choose	I	chose	chosen
7. ride	I	rode	ridden
8. chew	R	chewed	chewed
9. think	I	thought	thought
10. dance	R	danced	danced

Answers are on page 571.

161

A Brief Review of Regular Verbs

Every verb has four principal parts: present, past, past participle, and present participle. These parts can be used to build all the verb tenses (the times shown by a verb).

Most verbs in English are regular. The past and past participle of a regular verb are formed by adding -d or -ed to the present. The *past participle* is the form of the verb used with the helping verbs *have, has,* or *had* (or some form of *be* with passive verbs, which are explained on page 191). The *present participle* is formed by adding -ing to the present.

Here are the principal forms of some regular verbs:

Present	*Past*	*Past Participle*	*Present Participle*
laugh	laughed	laughed	laughing
ask	asked	asked	asking
touch	touched	touched	touching
decide	decided	decided	deciding
explode	exploded	exploded	exploding

List of Irregular Verbs

Irregular verbs have irregular forms in the past tense and past participle. For example, the past tense of the irregular verb *grow* is *grew*; the past participle is *grown*.

Almost everyone has some degree of trouble with irregular verbs. When you are unsure about the form of a verb, you can check the following list of irregular verbs. (The present participle is not shown on this list, because it is formed simply by adding -ing to the base form of the verb.) Or you can check a dictionary, which gives the principal parts of irregular verbs.

Present	Past	Past Participle
arise	arose	arisen
awake	awoke *or* awaked	awoke *or* awaked
be (am, are, is)	was (were)	been
become	became	become
begin	began	begun
bend	bent	bent
bite	bit	bitten
blow	blew	blown
break	broke	broken
bring	brought	brought
build	built	built
burst	burst	burst
buy	bought	bought
catch	caught	caught
choose	chose	chosen
come	came	come
cost	cost	cost
cut	cut	cut
do (does)	did	done
draw	drew	drawn
drink	drank	drunk
drive	drove	driven
eat	ate	eaten
fall	fell	fallen
feed	fed	fed
feel	felt	felt
fight	fought	fought
find	found	found
fly	flew	flown
freeze	froze	frozen
get	got	got *or* gotten
give	gave	given
go (goes)	went	gone
grow	grew	grown
have (has)	had	had
hear	heard	heard
hide	hid	hidden
hold	held	held
hurt	hurt	hurt
keep	kept	kept
know	knew	known

Present	Past	Past Participle
lay	laid	laid
lead	led	led
leave	left	left
lend	lent	lent
let	let	let
lie	lay	lain
light	lit	lit
lose	lost	lost
make	made	made
meet	met	met
pay	paid	paid
ride	rode	ridden
ring	rang	rung
rise	rose	risen
run	ran	run
say	said	said
see	saw	seen
sell	sold	sold
send	sent	sent
shake	shook	shaken
shrink	shrank	shrunk
shut	shut	shut
sing	sang	sung
sit	sat	sat
sleep	slept	slept
speak	spoke	spoken
spend	spent	spent
stand	stood	stood
steal	stole	stolen
stick	stuck	stuck
sting	stung	stung
swear	swore	sworn
swim	swam	swum
take	took	taken
teach	taught	taught
tear	tore	torn
tell	told	told
think	thought	thought
wake	woke *or* waked	woken *or* waked
wear	wore	worn
win	won	won
write	wrote	written

Practice 1

Cross out the incorrect verb form in each of the following sentences. Then write the correct form of the verb in the space provided.

began   Example   When the mud slide started, the whole neighborhood ~~begun~~ going downhill.

took   1. The boys ~~taked~~ cigarettes into the darkened theater.

chosen   2. The fire department has finally ~~chose~~ two women for its training program.

caught   3. The daredevil ~~catched~~ a bullet in his teeth.

stolen   4. Someone has ~~stole~~ the tape deck from my car.

saw   5. After I ~~seen~~ my new haircut, I cried.

gone   6. I have ~~went~~ to the lost-and-found office several times, but my leather gloves haven't turned up yet.

fallen   7. The stunt man has ~~fell~~ off hundreds of horses without injuring himself.

sworn   8. Steve has ~~swore~~ to control his temper.

shrunk   9. The bacon strips in the pan had ~~shrank~~ into blackened stubs.

spoken   10. Why haven't you ~~spoke~~ up about your problems?

Practice 2

For each of the italicized verbs in the following sentences, fill in the three missing forms in the order shown in the box:

> a. Present tense, which takes an -s ending when the subject is *he, she, it,* or any *one person or thing* (see page 154)
>
> b. Past tense
>
> c. Past participle—the form that goes with the helping verb *have, has,* or *had*

Example   My little nephew loves to *break* things. Every Christmas he (a) _____breaks_____ his new toys the minute they're unwrapped. Last year he (b) _____broke_____ five toys in seven minutes and then went on to smash his family's new china platter. His mother says he won't be happy until he has (c) _____broken_____ their hearts.

1. My husband always seems to *lose* things. He (a) _____loses_____ his eyeglasses about three times a day. Once he (b) _____lost_____ one of his running shoes while he was out jogging. He has (c) _____lost_____ so many car keys that we keep one taped inside the bumper of our Chevy.

2. Jamie is often asked to *bring* her gorgeous sister to parties. Poor Jamie (a) _____brings_____ Vanessa and then fades into the wallpaper. Last week she (b) _____brought_____ Vanessa to a pool party. Jamie felt as if she had (c) _____brought_____ a human magnet instead of a sister, since all the guys clustered around Vanessa the entire night.

3. Small babies can be taught to *swim*. They don't (a) _____swim_____ like adults, but they do float and keep their heads above water. Babies are accustomed to a watery environment, since they (b) _____swam_____ inside their mothers' bodies in a bath of fluid. Babies who have (c) _____swum_____ in pools shortly after birth seem to become more confident swimmers as children.

4. My brother actually likes to *go* to the dentist. He (a) _____goes_____ at least every three months for a checkup. He (b) _____went_____ last week just to have his teeth flossed. He has (c) _____gone_____ to his dentist so regularly that Dr. Ross has been able to afford a new sports car.

5. The vast crowd in the stadium waits for the rock concert to *begin*. The fans don't care if it (a) _____begins_____ late, since they are having a great time eating, drinking, and listening to cassette tapes. In fact, if the concert (b) _____began_____ on time, they would feel cheated. Once it has (c) _____begun_____, the stadium will vibrate from the screams of the fans and the roar of the music.

6. My little boy likes to *hide* from me. I usually find him, since he (a) _____ *hides* _____ in obvious places, like under the bed or inside the closet. Once, however, he (b) _____ *hid* _____ in an unusual place. I searched all over until I discovered that he had (c) _____ *hidden* _____ inside an empty garbage can.

7. I like to *choose* unusual items when I order from a restaurant menu. My friends always (a) _____ *choose* _____ something safe and familiar, but I'm more adventurous. Once I (b) _____ *chose* _____ stuffed calves' brains, which were delicious. I have (c) _____ *chosen* _____ items like squid, sea urchins, and pickled pigs' feet just to see how they would taste.

8. Last month I had to *speak* before the PTA members at my daughter's school. I can (a) _____ *speak* _____ comfortably to small groups, but this was a meeting of hundreds of people in an auditorium. Before I gave my report, I (b) _____ *spoke* _____ to the principal and told him how nervous I was. He assured me that even though he had (c) _____ *spoken* _____ in public many times over the years, he still got butterflies in his stomach.

9. Sheila has to *take* her dog to the veterinarian. Whenever she (a) _____ *takes* _____ him, though, he howls in the waiting room or lunges at the other pets. The last time Sheila (b) _____ *took* _____ Bruno, he had an accident on the linoleum floor. This time, however, Sheila has (c) _____ *taken* _____ the precaution of keeping Bruno away from his water bowl for several hours.

10. Greg hates to *wake* up. When he does (a) _____ *wake* _____ up, he is groggy and miserable. Once he (b) _____ *woke* _____ up and yelled at his pet hamster for looking at him the wrong way. He has (c) _____ *woken* _____ up this way so often that his family won't speak to him until noon.

Troublesome Irregular Verbs

Three common irregular verbs that often give people trouble are *be, have,* and *do.* See pages 157–158 for a discussion of these verbs. Three sets of other irregular verbs that can lead to difficulties are *lie-lay, sit-set,* and *rise-raise.*

Lie-Lay

The principal parts of *lie* and *lay* are as follows:

Present	Past	Past Participle
lie	lay	lain
lay	laid	laid

To lie means *to rest* or *recline. To lay* means *to put something down.*

To Lie	To Lay
Tony *lies* on the couch.	I *lay* the mail on the table.
This morning he *lay* in the tub.	Yesterday I *laid* the mail on the counter.
He has *lain* in bed all week with the flu.	I have *laid* the mail where everyone will see it.

Practice

Underline the correct verb. Use a form of *lie* if you can substitute *recline.* Use a form of *lay* if you can substitute *place.*

1. Unknowingly, I had (lain, <u>laid</u>) my coat down on a freshly varnished table.

2. Like a mini solar collector, the cat (<u>lay</u>, laid) in the warm rays of the sun.

3. He was certain he had (lain, <u>laid</u>) the tiles in a straight line until he stepped back to look.

4. (<u>Lying</u>, Laying) too long in bed in the morning can give me a headache.

5. I (<u>lay</u>, laid) on the doctor's examining table, staring into the bright bars of fluorescent light on the ceiling.

Sit-Set

The principal parts of *sit* and *set* are as follows:

Present	Past	Past Participle
sit	sat	sat
set	set	set

To sit means *to take a seat* or *to rest. To set* means *to put* or *to place.*

To Sit	To Set
I *sit* down during work breaks.	Tony *sets* out the knives, forks, and spoons.
I *sat* in the doctor's office for three hours.	His sister already *set* out the dishes.
I have always *sat* in the last desk.	They have just *set* out the dinnerware.

Practice

Underline the correct form of the verb. Use a form of *sit* if you can substitute *rest*. Use a form of *set* if you can substitute *place*.

1. Harriet (sat, set) the bowl of strawberries on the table, and four pairs of hands lunged for it.

2. The insurance agent (sat, set) down his briefcase and began his sales pitch.

3. You can't (sit, set) on my couch in those filthy jeans.

4. Marcus (sat, set) the heavy pumpkin on the front step.

5. I was (sitting, setting) my bag on the rack above my seat when the bus lurched away.

Rise-Raise

The principal parts of *rise* and *raise* are as follows:

Present	Past	Past Participle
rise	rose	risen
raise	raised	raised

To rise means *to get up* or *to move up*. *To raise* (which is a regular verb with simple *-ed* endings) means *to lift up* or *to increase in amount*.

To Rise	To Raise
The soldiers *rise* at dawn.	I'm going to *raise* the stakes in the card game.
The crowd *rose* to applaud the batter.	I *raised* the shades to let in the sun.
Dracula has *risen* from the grave.	I would have quit if the company had not *raised* my salary.

Practice

Underline the correct verb. Use a form of *rise* if you can substitute *get up* or *move up*. Use a form of *raise* if you can substitute *lift up* or *increase*.

1. When food prices (rise, raise), people living on Social Security suffer.

2. They have (risen, raised) their daughter to be a self-sufficient person.

3. As the crowd watched, the World War II veteran (rose, raised) the flag.

4. The reporters (rose, raised) as the president entered the room for the press conference.

5. The promising weather report (rose, raised) our hopes for an enjoyable camping trip.

■ **Review Test 1**

Cross out the incorrect verb form. Then write the correct form of the verb in the space provided.

sang   1. The famous recording star first ~~sung~~ in his hometown church choir.

bitten   2. After Lola was ~~bit~~ by the parrot, her finger was sore for a week.

took   3. Last August, Carmen ~~taked~~ her family to Yellowstone National Park.

run   4. The plane would have ~~ran~~ off the runway if the pilot hadn't been so skillful.

burst   5. He heard a frightening hissing sound before the pipes ~~bursted~~.

wrote   6. I couldn't believe I got a B on the first paper I ~~writed~~ in college.

lay   7. Stefano ~~laid~~ in a lounge chair, staring up at the moon through his new binoculars.

gone   8. The class clown had ~~went~~ too far, and the students waited to see what the teacher would do.

risen   9. The sun had already ~~rose~~ by the time I got home from the party.

swam   10. As we approached the quiet pond, a beaver slid into the water and ~~swum~~ toward its underwater lodge.

■ **Review Test 2**

Write short sentences that use the form requested for the following irregular verbs.

Example   Past of *ride:* _The Lone Ranger rode into the sunset._

Answers will vary, but these forms of the verbs should be used:

1. Past of *drink* _drank_

2. Present of *bring* _bring (or brings)_

3. Past participle of *grow* _grown_

4. Present of *swim* _swim (or swims)_

5. Past participle of *write* _written_

6. Past of *give* _gave_

7. Present of *do* _do (or does)_

8. Past participle of *begin* _begun_

9. Past of *go* _went_

10. Present of *know* _know (or knows)_

10 Subject-Verb Agreement

Introductory Activity

As you read each pair of sentences below, write a check mark beside the sentence that you think uses the underlined word correctly.

There <u>was</u> many applicants for the position. _____
There <u>were</u> many applicants for the position. ___✓___

The pictures in that magazine <u>is</u> very controversial. _____
The pictures in that magazine <u>are</u> very controversial. ___✓___

Everybody usually <u>watch</u> the lighted numbers in an elevator. _____
Everybody usually <u>watches</u> the lighted numbers in an elevator. ___✓___

On the basis of the above examples, see if you can complete the following statements.

1. In the first two pairs of sentences, the subjects are _____applicants_____
   and _____pictures_____. Since both these subjects are plural, the verb must be plural.

2. In the last pair of sentences, the subject, *Everybody,* is a word that is always (<u>singular</u>, plural), and so that verb must be (<u>singular</u>, plural).

Answers are on page 571.

A verb must agree with its subject in number. A *singular subject* (one person or thing) takes a singular verb. A *plural subject* (more than one person or thing) takes a plural verb. Mistakes in subject-verb agreement are sometimes made in the following situations:

1   When words come between the subject and the verb
2   When a verb comes before the subject
3   With indefinite pronouns
4   With compound subjects
5   With *who, which,* and *that*

Each situation is explained on the following pages.

Words between the Subject and the Verb

Words that come between the subject and the verb do not change subject-verb agreement. In the following sentence,

> The breakfast cereals in the pantry are made mostly of sugar.

the subject (*cereals*) is plural and so the verb (*are*) is plural. The words *in the pantry* that come between the subject and the verb do not affect subject-verb agreement. To help find the subject of certain sentences, you should cross out prepositional phrases (explained on page 93):

> One ~~of the crooked politicians~~ was jailed for a month.
>
> The posters ~~on my little brother's wall~~ included rock singers, monsters, and blond television stars.

Following is a list of common prepositions:

Common Prepositions				
about	before	by	inside	over
above	behind	during	into	through
across	below	except	of	to
among	beneath	for	off	toward
around	beside	from	on	under
at	between	in	onto	with

Practice

Draw one line under the subject. Then lightly cross out any words that come between the subject and the verb. Finally, draw two lines under the correct verb in parentheses.

Example   The price ~~of the stereo speakers~~ (is, are) too high for my wallet.

1. The leaders ~~of the union~~ (has, have) called for a strike.

2. One ~~of Omar's pencil sketches~~ (hangs, hang) in the art classroom.

3. Three days ~~of anxious waiting finally~~ (ends, end) with a phone call.

4. The members ~~of the car pool~~ (chips, chip) in for the driving expenses.

5. The woman ~~with the teased, sprayed hairdo~~ (looks, look) as if she were wearing a plastic helmet.

6. The addition ~~of heavy shades to my sunny windows~~ (allows, allow) me to sleep during the day.

7. Several houses ~~in the old whaling village~~ (has, have) been designated as historical landmarks.

8. The stack ~~of baseball cards in my little brother's bedroom~~ (is, are) two feet high.

9. Gooey puddles ~~of egg white~~ (spreads, spread) over the stove as Mike cracks the shells against the frying pan.

10. The giant-size box ~~of Raisinets~~ (sells, sell) for three dollars at the theater's candy counter.

Verb before the Subject

ALLWRITE!

17.3c,d

A verb agrees with its subject even when the verb comes *before* the subject. Words that may precede the subject include *there, here,* and, in questions, *who, which, what,* and *where.*

Inside the storage shed are the garden tools.

At the street corner were two panhandlers.

There are times I'm ready to quit my job.

Where are the instructions for the microwave oven?

If you are unsure about the subject, ask *who* or *what* of the verb. With the first sentence above, you might ask, "What are inside the storage shed?" The answer, garden *tools,* is the subject.

Practice

Draw one line under the subject in each sentence. Then draw two lines under the correct verb in parentheses.

1. Lumbering along the road (was, were) six heavy trucks.
2. There (is, are) now wild coyotes wandering the streets of many California suburbs.
3. Lining the country lanes (is, are) rows of tall, thin poplar trees.
4. At the back of my closet (is, are) the high platform boots I bought ten years ago.
5. Helping to unload the heavy sofa from the delivery truck (was, were) a skinny young boy.
6. Nosing through the garbage bags (was, were) a furry animal with a hairless tail.
7. Here (is, are) the rug shampooer I borrowed last month.
8. Along the side of the highway (was, were) a sluggish little stream.
9. Where (is, are) the box of kitchen trash bags?
10. On the door of his bedroom (is, are) a sign reading, "Authorized personnel only."

Indefinite Pronouns

17.5

The following words, known as *indefinite pronouns,* always take singular verbs.

<table>
<tr><td colspan="4" align="center">*Indefinite Pronouns*</td></tr>
<tr><td>*(-one* words)</td><td>*(-body* words)</td><td>*(-thing* words)</td><td></td></tr>
<tr><td>one</td><td>nobody</td><td>nothing</td><td>each</td></tr>
<tr><td>anyone</td><td>anybody</td><td>anything</td><td>either</td></tr>
<tr><td>everyone</td><td>everybody</td><td>everything</td><td>neither</td></tr>
<tr><td>someone</td><td>somebody</td><td>something</td><td></td></tr>
</table>

Note   *Both* always takes a plural verb.

Practice

Write the correct form of the verb in the space provided.

is, are 1. Neither of those last two books on the list _____is_____ required for the course.

remembers, remember 2. Nobody _____remembers_____ seeing a suspicious green car cruising the street.

fits, fit 3. Both of these belts no longer _____fit_____.

has, have 4. Somebody _____has_____ been playing my records.

wanders, wander 5. Nobody _____wanders_____ in those woods during hunting season without wearing bright-colored clothing.

needs, need 6. Each of those dogs _____needs_____ to be inoculated against rabies.

keeps, keep 7. One of my friends _____keeps_____ a pet iguana in her dorm room.

sneaks, sneak 8. Everyone _____sneaks_____ stationery and pens out of our office.

is, are 9. Either of those motels _____is_____ clean and reasonably priced.

eats, eat 10. One of my children _____eats_____ raw onions as if they were apples.

Compound Subjects

17.2

Subjects joined by *and* generally take a plural verb.

Yoga and biking are Lola's ways of staying in shape.
Ambition and good luck are the keys to his success.

When subjects are joined by *or, either . . . or, neither . . . nor, not only . . . but also,* the verb agrees with the subject closer to the verb.

Either the restaurant manager or his assistants deserve to be fired for the spoiled meat used in the stew.

The nearer subject, *assistants,* is plural, and so the verb is plural.

Practice

Write the correct form of the verb in the space provided.

looks, look   1. This coat and scarf _____ look _____ warm, but the wind seems to go right through them.

is, are   2. The bridge and the tunnel _____ are _____ closed for repairs.

confuses, confuse   3. The pitcher's unusual stance and strange grip _____ confuse _____ his opponents.

is, are   4. The footnotes and one picture in this book _____ are _____ printed upside down.

stars, star   5. Either a giant jellyfish or oversize lobsters _____ star _____ in this Japanese monster movie.

Who, Which, and That

17.3a

When *who, which,* and *that* are used as subjects, they take singular verbs if the word they stand for is singular and plural verbs if the word they stand for is plural. For example, in the sentence

Freddie is one of those people <u>who</u> <u>are</u> very private.

the verb is plural because *who* stands for *people,* which is plural. On the other hand, in the sentence

Freddie is a person <u>who</u> <u>is</u> very private.

the verb is singular because *who* stands for *person,* which is singular.

Practice

Write the correct form of the verb in the space provided.

roams, roam   1. The dogs which _____ roam _____ around this area are household pets abandoned by cruel owners.

begins, begin   2. A sharp pain that _____ begins _____ in the lower abdomen may signal appendicitis.

thunders, thunder   3. The heavy trucks that _____ thunder _____ past my Honda make me feel as though I'm being blown off the road.

fears, fear   4. The canyon tour isn't for people who _____*fear*_____ heights.

tastes, taste   5. This drink, which _____*tastes*_____ like pure sugar, is supposed to be 100 percent fruit juice.

Collaborative Activity

Part A: Editing and Rewriting

Working with a partner, read the short paragraph below and see if you can mark off the five mistakes in subject-verb agreement. Then use the space provided to correct the five agreement errors. Feel free to discuss the rewrite quietly with your partner and refer back to the chapter when necessary.

Sometimes I just don't understand people. For instance, my neighbors Adolfo and Janelle go to the gym almost every day. Adolfo rides an exercise bike, Janelle runs on the treadmill, and they both take aerobic classes. Neither of them like to pay for the gym membership. But, as Janelle says, "Fitness and good health is very important to us both." Now, I think it's great that anyone are trying to stay fit and healthy. But this is the part of their activities that don't make sense to me. In order to get to the gym, these fitness nuts drive half a mile. Then they come home and take the elevator three stories up to their apartment. Wouldn't plain old walking and climbing stairs burns calories as well as the exercise they do in an expensive gym?

Neither . . . likes	part . . . that doesn't
Fitness and good health are	walking and climbing . . . burn
anyone is	

Part B: Creating Sentences

Working with a partner, write sentences as directed. With each item, pay special attention to subject-verb agreement.

Answers will vary.

1. Write a sentence in which the words *in the cafeteria* or *on the table* come between the subject and verb. Underline the subject of your sentence and circle the verb.

Continued

2. Write a sentence that begins with the words *there is* or *there are*. Underline the subject of your sentence and circle the verb.

3. Write a sentence in which the indefinite pronoun *nobody* or *anything* is the subject.

4. Write a sentence with the compound subjects *manager* and *employees*. Underline the subject of your sentence and circle the verb.

Reflective Activity
Answers will vary.
1. Look at the paragraph about Adolfo and Janelle that you revised above. Which rule involving subject-verb agreement gave you the most trouble? How did you figure out the correct answer?

2. Explain which of the five subject-verb agreement situations discussed in this chapter is most likely to cause you problems.

■ Review Test 1

Complete each of the following sentences, using *is, are, was, were, have,* or *has.* Underline the subject of each of these verbs. In some cases you will need to provide that subject.

Example   The hot dogs in that luncheonette _are hazardous to your health._
Answers will vary.
1. Either of those small keys _____

_____

2. The practical joker in our office _____

_____

3. The rock star and his bodyguard _____

_____

4. He was the kind of customer who _____

   _____

5. Posted on the office door _____

   _____

6. There's always someone who _____

   _____

7. The old boiler, along with the rusty water tanks, _____

   _____

8. Hanging from her rearview mirror _____

   _____

9. The first few times that I tried to roller-skate _____

   _____

10. The spectators outside the courtroom _____

    _____

■ **Review Test 2**

Underline the correct word in the parentheses.

1. The number of commercials between television shows (is, are) increasing.

2. Lani and Paco (works, work) overnight at the motel's registration desk.

3. A report on either book (counts, count) as extra credit.

4. Both the mattress and the box spring on this bed (is, are) filled with rusty, uncoiling springs.

5. Nobody in that class ever (argues, argue) with the professor.

6. Remembering everyone's birthday and organizing family reunions (is, are) my sister's main hobbies.

7. Lying like limp little dolls on the bed (was, were) the exhausted children.

8. The woman from the telephone company who (empties, empty) the pay phones wears a photo ID tag around her neck.

9. The illegal dogfights which (occurs, occur) regularly in our town are being investigated by the SPCA.

10. Sewn into the sweater's seam (was, were) an extra button and a small hank of matching yarn for repairs.

■ Review Test 3

There are eight mistakes in subject-verb agreement in the following passage. Cross out each incorrect verb and write the correct form above it. In addition, underline the subject of each of the verbs that must be changed.

What are the <u>factors</u> that ~~makes~~ *make* a third-grade child aggressive and destructive? And, on the other hand, what experiences help a third-grader make friends easily and earn good grades in school? <u>Years</u> of research on a group of children from infancy through elementary school ~~has~~ *have* provided an answer, or at least a new theory. A <u>psychologist</u> from one of our leading universities ~~claim~~ *claims* that <u>success</u> in the early grades ~~are~~ *is* the direct result of a close relationship with the mother. <u>Babies</u> who have this relationship with a mother ~~seems~~ *seem* to gain the strength and self-esteem they need for future success in the classroom and in life. A strong, secure <u>bond</u> between a mother and child ~~are~~ *is* formed when mothers respond quickly and consistently to their babies' needs. Both the <u>speed</u> and the <u>attention</u> ~~is~~ *are* important in earning a baby's trust. The researcher points out that there ~~are~~ *is* no <u>evidence</u> of a link between day-care arrangements and weaker mother-baby attachments. It is the quality of the relationship, not the actual hours spent, that causes a child to feel secure.

11 Consistent Verb Tense

Keeping Tenses Consistent

18.5

Do not shift tenses unnecessarily. If you begin writing a paper in the present tense, don't shift suddenly to the past. If you begin in the past, don't shift without reason to the present. Notice the inconsistent verb tenses in the following example:

> Smoke <u>spilled</u> from the front of the overheated car. The driver <u>opens</u> up the hood, then <u>jumped</u> back as steam <u>billows</u> out.

The verbs must be consistently in the present tense:

> Smoke <u>spills</u> from the front of the overheated car. The driver <u>opens</u> up the hood, then <u>jumps</u> back as steam <u>billows</u> out.

Or the verbs must be consistently in the past tense:

> Smoke <u>spilled</u> from the front of the overheated car. The driver <u>opened</u> up the hood, then <u>jumped</u> back as steam <u>billowed</u> out.

Practice

In each item, one verb must be changed so that it agrees in tense with the other verbs. Cross out the incorrect verb and write the correct form in the space at the left.

looked

Example   I gave away my striped sweater after three people told me I ~~look~~ like a giant bee.

smeared

1. Kim swabbed the inside of her cheek with a Q-tip, ~~smears~~ the cells on a glass slide, and then looked at them through the microscope.

started

2. Debbie, a moody adolescent, threw the blouse down, shouted at her mother, and then ~~starts~~ to cry.

breathed

3. On the highway, one rescuer rolled the unconscious man onto his back, pinched his nostrils shut, and then ~~breathe~~ into his mouth.

saw

4. In this neighborhood, the kids play stickball in the street; they ~~sawed~~ off broom handles for bats and borrow garbage can lids for bases.

rolled

5. Unknowingly, Marvin picked a box of detergent with a hole in it. He left a thin trail of white powder as he ~~rolls~~ his cart around the store.

points

6. To get clearer reception, Vernon jiggles the radio tuning knob, adjusts the position of the radio, and ~~pointed~~ the antenna out the window.

swallows

7. While Dan searches for the pizza cutter in the kitchen drawer, Tony picks the pepperoni slices off the pie and quickly ~~swallowed~~ them.

pushed

8. Alfonso lunged for the child and ~~pushes~~ him to safety as the speeding cyclist whizzed by.

coat

9. Because the kitchen lacks an exhaust fan, cooking fumes fill the house and thin layers of grease ~~coated~~ the ceilings.

notices

10. As she unpacks the wall planking, Becky discovers large knotholes in some of the boards and ~~noticed~~ one piece with a long vertical crack.

■ **Review Test 1**

Change the verbs where needed in the following selection so that they are consistently in the past tense. Cross out each incorrect verb and write the correct form above it, as shown in the example. You will need to make ten corrections.

Making a foul shot that won a basketball game was a special moment for me. For most of the year, I sat on the bench. The coach put me on the team after the tryouts and then *forgot* ~~forgets~~ about me. Then my chance *appeared* ~~appears~~ near the end of the Rosemont High School game. The score was tied 65 to 65. Because of injuries and foul-outs, most of the substitutes, except me, were in the game. Then our last first-stringer, Larry Toner, got an elbow in the eye and *left* ~~leaves~~ the game. The coach looked at me and said, "Get in there, Watson." The clock showed ten seconds to go. Rosemont had the ball when, suddenly, one of their players *missed* ~~misses~~ a pass. People *scrambled* ~~scramble~~ for the ball; then our center, Kevin, grabbed it and *started* ~~starts~~ down the court. He looked around and saw me about twenty feet from the basket. I caught his pass, and before I could decide whether to shoot or pass, a Rosemont player *fouled* ~~fouls~~ me. The referee's whistle blew, and I had two free throws with two seconds left in the game. My stomach *churned* ~~churns~~ as I stepped to the foul line. I almost couldn't hold the ball because my hands were so damp with sweat. I shot and missed, and the Rosemont crowd *sighed* ~~sighs~~ with relief. My next shot would mean a win for us or overtime.

Continued

I looked at the hoop, shot, and waited for what seemed like forever. The ball

circled

~~circles~~ the rim and dropped in, and then the buzzer sounded. Everyone on the

smacked

team slapped me on the back and the coach ~~smacks~~ my rear end, saying, "All

right, Watson!" I'll always remember that moment.

■ **Review Test 2**

Change verbs as necessary in the following selection so that they are consistently in the past tense. Cross out each incorrect verb and write the correct form above it. You will need to make ten corrections in all.

According to an old Greek myth, the goddess of the harvest had one

child, a beautiful daughter. One day, as the daughter was gathering flowers,

saw

the god of the underworld drove by in his chariot. He ~~sees~~ her and fell madly

reached

in love with her. He ~~reaches~~ out, grabbed the frightened girl, and pulled her into

the chariot beside him. The daughter's screams were useless as the two drove

below the surface of the earth. Soon they reached the land of the dead, where

forced   *realized*

he ~~forces~~ her to become his wife. Not long afterward, the goddess ~~realizes~~ her

daughter was missing. She searched for her all over the world. When she

neglected

could not find the girl, she became so grief-stricken that she ~~neglects~~ her

duties, and all over the earth, the crops weakened and died. Finally she threat-

ened that nothing would grow until her daughter was returned to her. Zeus,

had

king of the gods, then commanded that the daughter ~~has~~ to be released—but

only if she had not eaten anything. The god of the underworld agreed to let

tricked   *left*

her go, but he ~~tricks~~ her into eating six seeds before she ~~leaves~~. Because the

girl had eaten the food of Death, she had to live in Death's kingdom six

months of the year, one for each of the seeds. In this way, the Greeks said,

the seasons came into being. When the daughter was permitted to rejoin her

began

mother, she brought spring and summer with her—and the crops ~~begin~~ to

was

grow. But when fall came, she ~~is~~ forced to return to the land of the dead, and

all growing things on earth died with her.

12 Additional Information about Verbs

The purpose of this special chapter is to provide additional information about verbs. Some people will find the grammatical terms here a helpful reminder of earlier school learning about verbs. For them, these terms will increase their understanding of how verbs function in English. Other people may welcome more detailed information about terms used elsewhere in the text. In either case, remember that the most common mistakes people make when writing verbs have been treated in earlier sections of the book.

Verb Tense

18.2

Verbs tell us the time of an action. The time that a verb shows is usually called *tense*. The most common tenses are the simple present, past, and future. In addition, there are nine other tenses that enable us to express more specific ideas about time than we could with the simple tenses alone. Following are the twelve verb tenses and examples of each tense. Read them to increase your sense of the many different ways of expressing time in English.

Tenses	Examples
Present	I *work.*
	Tanya *works.*
Past	Howard *worked* on the lawn.
Future	You *will work* overtime this week.
Present perfect	Gail *has worked* hard on the puzzle.
	They *have worked* well together.
Past perfect	They *had worked* eight hours before their shift ended.
Future perfect	The volunteers *will have worked* many unpaid hours.
Present progressive	I *am* not *working* today.
	You *are working* the second shift.
	The clothes dryer *is* not *working* properly.
Past progressive	She *was working* outside.
	The plumbers *were working* here this morning.
Future progressive	The sound system *will be working* by tonight.
Present perfect progressive	Married life *has* not *been working* out for that couple.
Past perfect progressive	I *had been working* overtime until recently.
Future perfect progressive	My sister *will have been working* at that store for eleven straight months by the time she takes a vacation next week.

The perfect tenses are formed by adding *have, has,* or *had* to the past participle (the form of the verb that ends, usually, in -*ed*). The progressive tenses are formed by adding *am, is, are, was,* or *were* to the present participle (the form of the verb that ends in -*ing*). The perfect progressive tenses are formed by adding *have been, has been,* or *had been* to the present participle.

Certain tenses are explained in more detail on the following pages.

Present Perfect
(*have* or *has* + past participle)

The present perfect tense expresses an action that began in the past and has recently been completed or is continuing in the present.

The city *has* just *agreed* on a contract with the sanitation workers.

Tony's parents *have lived* in that house for twenty years.

Lola *has watched* reruns of *Star Trek* since she was a little girl.

Past Perfect
(*had* + past participle)

The past perfect tense expresses a past action that was completed before another past action.

Lola *had learned* to dance by the time she was five.

The class *had* just *started* when the fire bell rang.

Bad weather *had* never *been* a problem on our vacations until last year.

Present Progressive
(*am, is,* or *are* + *-ing* form)

The present progressive tense expresses an action still in progress.

I *am taking* an early train into the city every day this week.

Karl *is playing* softball over at the field.

The vegetables *are growing* rapidly.

Past Progressive
(*was* or *were* + *-ing* form)

The past progressive expresses an action that was in progress in the past.

I *was spending* twenty dollars a week on cigarettes before I quit.

Last week, the store *was selling* many items at half price.

My friends *were driving* over to pick me up when the accident occurred.

Practice

For the sentences that follow, fill in the present or past perfect or the present or past progressive of the verb shown. Use the tense that seems to express the meaning of each sentence best.

Example   *park*   This summer, Mickey _____*is parking*_____ cars at a French restaurant.

watch   1. The police ____*had watched*____ the house for months before they made the arrests.

write   2. She ____*has written*____ to the newspaper several times, but the editors never publish her letters.

take   3. I ____*am taking*____ a course in adolescent psychology; maybe it will help me understand my teenagers.

lift   4. The fog ____*had lifted*____ well before the morning rush hour began.

improve   5. For the last two years, our community group ____*has improved*____ our street by cleaning up trash and planting trees.

protest   6. The waitresses ____*are protesting*____ against the skimpy new uniforms that they are being told to wear.

dread   7. I ____*have dreaded*____ heights ever since one of my brothers pushed me off a wall when I was six.

vow   8. This semester, he ____*has vowed*____ to stick to an organized study schedule.

peek   9. Some students ____*were peeking*____ into their notes when the professor entered the exam room.

get   10. You ____*are getting*____ some gray hairs; why don't you let me pull them out?

Verbals

ALLWRITE!
18.4

Verbals are words formed from verbs. Verbals, like verbs, often express action. They can add variety to your sentences and vigor to your writing style. The three kinds of verbals are *infinitives, participles,* and *gerunds.*

Infinitive

An infinitive is *to* plus the base form of the verb.

> I started *to practice.*
> Don't try *to lift* that table.
> I asked Russ *to drive* me home.

Participle

A participle is a verb form used as an adjective (a descriptive word). The present participle ends in -*ing.* The past participle ends in -*ed* or has an irregular ending.

> *Favoring* his *cramped* leg, the *screaming* boy waded out of the pool.
> The *laughing* child held up her *locked* piggy bank.
> *Using* a shovel and a bucket, I scooped water out of the *flooded* basement.

Gerund

A gerund is the -*ing* form of a verb used as a noun.

> *Studying* wears me out.
> *Playing* basketball is my main pleasure during the week.
> Through *jogging,* you can get yourself in shape.

Practice

In the space beside each sentence, identify the italicized word as a participle (*P*), an infinitive (*I*), or a gerund (*G*).

___P___ 1. In the cave, dozens of *grinning* skulls greeted the explorer.

___G___ 2. *Launching* a new business can be a risky proposition.

___I___ 3. Gwen likes *to rearrange* her living room furniture.

___G___ 4. *Fixing* minor car problems is one of the skills taught at the women's center.

___I___ 5. The children tried *to make* a tent by throwing a blanket over a clothesline.

___P___ 6. The little girl wore the *gleaming* patent leather shoes home from the store.

_____P_____   7. *Listening* intently, the students translated Spanish sentences into English.

_____P_____   8. I read the *gripping* spy novel until two o'clock in the morning.

_____G_____   9. *Writing* reports for the judge is part of Nina's job as a probation officer.

_____I_____   10. *To fasten* the buttons on the back of her dress, Connie twisted her arms.

Active and Passive Verbs

18.7

When the subject of a sentence performs the action of a verb, the verb is in the *active voice*. When the subject of a sentence receives the action of a verb, the verb is in the *passive voice*.

The passive form of a verb consists of a form of the verb *be* plus the past participle of the main verb. Look at the active and passive forms of the verbs below.

Active	*Passive*
Lola *ate* the vanilla pudding. (The subject, *Lola*, is the doer of the action.)	The vanilla pudding *was eaten by* Lola. (The subject, *pudding,* does not act. Instead, something happens to it.)
The plumber *replaced* the hot-water heater. (The subject, *plumber,* is the doer of the action.)	The hot-water heater *was replaced by* the plumber. (The subject, *heater,* does not act. Instead, something happens to it.)

In general, active verbs are more effective than passive ones. Active verbs give your writing a simpler and more vigorous style. The passive form of verbs is appropriate, however, when the performer of the action is unknown or is less important than the receiver of the action. For example:

My house was vandalized last night.
(The performer of the action is unknown.)

Troy was seriously injured as a result of your negligence.
(The receiver of the action, *Troy,* is being emphasized.)

Practice

Change the following sentences from the passive to the active voice. Note that you may have to add a subject in some cases.

Examples   The moped bicycle was ridden by Tony.

Tony rode the moped bicycle.

The basketball team was given a standing ovation.

The crowd gave the basketball team a standing ovation.

(Here a subject had to be added.)

Answers may vary.

1. Carla's long hair was snipped off by the beautician.

   The beautician snipped off Carla's long hair.

2. The teachers' strike was protested by the parents.

   The parents protested the teachers' strike.

3. The silent alarm was tripped by the alert bank teller.

   The alert bank teller tripped the silent alarm.

4. The escaped convicts were tracked by relentless bloodhounds.

   Relentless bloodhounds tracked the escaped convicts.

5. The new CAT scanner was donated to the hospital.

   A famous entertainer donated the new CAT scanner to the hospital.

6. A gallon glass jar of pickles was dropped in the supermarket aisle by a stock clerk.

   A stock clerk dropped a gallon glass jar of pickles in the supermarket aisle.

7. The deer was struck as it crossed the highway.

   A car struck the deer as it crossed the highway.

8. I was referred by my doctor to a specialist in hearing problems.

   My doctor referred me to a specialist in hearing problems.

9. One wall of my living room is covered by family photographs.

   Family photographs cover one wall of my living room.

10. The town was gripped by fear during the accident at the nuclear power plant.

    Fear gripped the town during the accident at the nuclear power plant.

■ Review Test

On separate paper, write three sentences apiece that use:

Answers will vary.

1. Present perfect tense

2. Past perfect tense

3. Present progressive tense

4. Past progressive tense

5. Infinitive

6. Participle

7. Gerund

8. Passive voice (when the subject is unknown or is less important than the receiver of an action—see page 191)

13 Pronoun Reference, Agreement, and Point of View

Introductory Activity

Read each pair of sentences below, noting the underlined pronouns. Then see if you can circle the correct letter in each of the statements that follow.

1. a. None of the nominees for "best actress" showed <u>their</u> anxiety as the names were being read.

   b. None of the nominees for "best actress" showed <u>her</u> anxiety as the names were being read.

2. a. At the mall, <u>they</u> are already putting up Christmas decorations.

   b. At the mall, <u>shop owners</u> are already putting up Christmas decorations.

3. a. I go to the steak house often because <u>you</u> can get inexpensive meals there.

   b. I go to the steak house often because <u>I</u> can get inexpensive meals there.

In the first pair, (a, b) uses the underlined pronoun correctly because the pronoun refers to *None*, which is a singular word.

In the second pair, (a, b) is correct because otherwise the pronoun reference would be unclear.

In the third pair, (a, b) is correct because the pronoun point of view should not be shifted unnecessarily.

Answers are on page 572.

Pronouns are words that take the place of nouns (words for persons, places, or things). In fact, the word *pronoun* means *for a noun.* Pronouns are shortcuts that keep you from unnecessarily repeating words in writing. Here are some examples of pronouns:

> Meena shampooed *her* dog. (*Her* is a pronoun that takes the place of *Meena's.*)
>
> As the door swung open, *it* creaked. (*It* replaces *door.*)
>
> When the motorcyclists arrived at McDonald's, *they* removed *their* helmets. (*They* replaces *motorcyclists; their* replaces *motorcyclists'.*)

This section presents rules that will help you avoid three common mistakes people make with pronouns. The rules are as follows:

1 A pronoun must refer clearly to the word it replaces.

2 A pronoun must agree in number with the word or words it replaces.

3 Pronouns should not shift unnecessarily in point of view.

Pronoun Reference

19.5

A sentence may be confusing and unclear if a pronoun appears to refer to more than one word, as in this sentence:

> I locked my suitcase in my car, and then it was stolen.

What was stolen? It is unclear whether the suitcase or the car was stolen.

> I locked my suitcase in my car, and then my car was stolen.

A sentence may also be confusing if the pronoun does not refer to any specific word. Look at this sentence:

> We never buy fresh vegetables at that store because they charge too much.

Who charges too much? There is no specific word that *they* refers to. Be clear.

> We never buy fresh vegetables at that store because the owners charge too much.

Here are additional sentences with unclear pronoun reference. Read the explanations of why they are unclear and look carefully at the ways they are corrected.

Unclear	Clear
Lola told Gina that she had gained weight.	Lola told Gina, "You've gained weight."
(*Who* had gained weight: Lola or Gina? Be clear.)	(Quotation marks, which can sometimes be used to correct an unclear reference, are explained in Chapter 25.)
My older brother is an electrician, but I'm not interested in it.	My older brother is an electrician, but I'm not interested in becoming one.
(There is no specific word that *it* refers to. It would not make sense to say, "I'm not interested in electrician.")	
Our instructor did not explain the assignment, which made me angry.	I was angry that our instructor did not explain the assignment.
(Does *which* mean that the instructor's failure to explain the assignment made you angry, or that the assignment itself made you angry. Be clear.)	

Practice

Rewrite each of the following sentences to make clear the vague pronoun reference. Add, change, or omit words as necessary.

Example   Lana thanked Denise for the gift, which was very thoughtful of her.
          <u>Lana thanked Denise for the thoughtful gift.</u>

Note: The practice sentences could be rewritten to have meanings other than the ones indicated below.

1. At the gas station, they told us one of our tires looked soft.

   <u>When we pulled into the gas station, the attendant told us one of our</u>

   <u>tires looked soft.</u>

2. Nora dropped the heavy ashtray on her foot and broke it.

   <u>Nora broke the heavy ashtray when she dropped it on her foot.</u>

   _____

3. Vicki asked for a grade transcript at the registrar's office, and they told her it would cost three dollars.

   <u>Vicki asked for a grade transcript at the registrar's office, and the clerk</u>

   <u>told her it would cost three dollars.</u>

4. Don't touch the freshly painted walls with your hands unless they're dry.

Don't touch the freshly painted walls with your hands unless the walls are dry.

5. Maurice stays up half the night watching *Chiller Theater,* which really annoys his wife.

Maurice's habit of staying up half the night watching <u>Chiller Theater</u> really annoys his wife.

6. Robin went to the store's personnel office, where they are interviewing for sales positions.

Robin went to the store's personnel office to be interviewed for a sales position.

7. Leon told his brother that he needed to lose some weight.

Leon told his brother, "You need to lose some weight."

8. I wrote to the insurance company, but they haven't answered my letters.

I wrote to the insurance company but haven't received an answer.

9. Because my eyes were itchy and bloodshot, I went to the doctor to see what he could do about it.

I went to the doctor to see what he could do about my itchy, bloodshot eyes.

10. I took the loose pillows off the chairs and sat on them.

I took the loose pillows off the chairs and sat on the pillows.

Pronoun Agreement

17.8

A pronoun must agree in number with the word or words it replaces. If the word a pronoun refers to is singular, the pronoun must be singular; if the word is plural, the pronoun must be plural. (Note that the word a pronoun refers to is known as the *antecedent.*)

Lola agreed to lend me her Billie Holiday albums.

The gravediggers sipped coffee during their break.

In the first example, the pronoun *her* refers to the singular word *Lola;* in the second example, the pronoun *their* refers to the plural word *gravediggers.*

Practice

Write the appropriate pronoun (*they, their, them, it*) in the blank space in each of the following sentences.

Example   My credit cards got me into debt, so I burned _____ *them* _____.

1. I peeled off my sweaty bandanna and dipped _____ *it* _____ into the cool stream.

2. Karen sanded the cabinets and coated _____ *them* _____ with clear varnish.

3. Since my parents retired, _____ *they* _____ have started to share the household chores.

4. Waiting in the stalled school bus, the children threw _____ *their* _____ books out the windows and lobbed potato chips at each other.

5. The dog pawed at the flower and pulled _____ *it* _____ out of the ground.

Indefinite Pronouns

ALLWRITE!

17.5

The following words, known as *indefinite pronouns,* are always singular.

Indefinite Pronouns		
(-one words)	**(-body words)**	
one	nobody	each
anyone	anybody	either
everyone	everybody	neither
someone	somebody	

Either of the apartments has *its* drawbacks.

One of the girls lost *her* skateboard.

Everyone in the class must hand in *his* paper tomorrow.

In each example, the pronoun is singular because it refers to one of the indefinite pronouns. There are two important points to remember about indefinite pronouns.

Point 1   The last example above suggests that everyone in the class is male. If the students were all female, the pronoun would be *her.* If the students were a mixed group of males and females, the pronoun form would be *his or her.*

Everyone in the class must hand in *his or her* paper tomorrow.

Some writers still follow the traditional practice of using *his* to refer to both men and women. Many now use *his or her* to avoid an implied sexual bias. Perhaps the best practice, though, is to avoid using either *his* or the somewhat awkward *his or her.* This can often be done by rewriting a sentence in the plural:

All students in the class must hand in *their* papers tomorrow.

Here are some examples of sentences that can be rewritten in the plural.

A young child is seldom willing to share her toys with others.
Young children are seldom willing to share their toys with others.

Anyone who does not wear his seat belt will be fined.
People who do not wear their seat belts will be fined.

A newly elected politician should not forget his or her campaign promises.
Newly elected politicians should not forget their campaign promises.

Point 2   In informal spoken English, *plural* pronouns are often used with indefinite pronouns. Instead of saying

Everybody has *his or her* own idea of an ideal vacation.

we are likely to say

Everybody has *their* own idea of an ideal vacation.

Here are other examples:

> Everyone in the class must pass in *their* papers.
> Everybody in our club has *their* own idea about how to raise money.
> No one in our family skips *their* chores.

In such cases, the indefinite pronouns are clearly plural in meaning. Also, the use of such plurals helps people avoid the awkward *his or her*. In time, the plural pronoun may be accepted in formal speech or writing. Until that happens, however, you should use the grammatically correct singular form in your writing.

Practice

Underline the correct pronoun.

Example   Neither of those houses has (its, their) own garage.

1. Girls! Did everyone remember to bring (her, their) insect repellent?

2. Anyone can pass our men's physical education course if (he, they) will laugh at all the instructor's jokes.

3. Each of the jockeys wore (his, their) own distinctive racing silks.

4. Neither of the Mets' relief pitchers was able to get (his, their) curve ball across.

5. If any student wants to apply for the scholarship offered by the women's college, (she, they) will need two recommendations.

6. Either type of video recording system has (its, their) drawbacks.

7. Each woman rushed to pick up (her, their) forms and secure a place in line.

8. Three boys were suspected, but nobody would confess to leaving (his, their) fingerprints all over the window.

9. All women leaving the room should pick up (her, their) lab reports.

10. During the fire, any one of those men could have lost (his, their) balance on that narrow ledge.

Pronoun Point of View

Pronouns should not shift their point of view unnecessarily. When writing a paper, be consistent in your use of first-, second-, or third-person pronouns.

Type of Pronoun	Singular	Plural
First-person pronouns	I (my, mine, me)	we (our, us)
Second-person pronouns	you (your)	you (your)
Third-person pronouns	he (his, him)	they (their, them)
	she (her)	
	it (its)	

Note   Any person, place, or thing, as well as any indefinite pronoun like *one, anyone, someone,* and so on (page 198), is a third-person word.

For instance, if you start writing in the first-person *I*, don't jump suddenly to the second-person *you*. Or if you are writing in the third-person *they*, don't shift unexpectedly to *you*. Look at the examples.

Inconsistent	*Consistent*
One reason that *I* like living in the city is that *you* always have a wide choice of sports events to attend.	One reason that *I* like living in the city is that *I* always have a wide choice of sports events to attend.
(The most common mistake people make is to let a *you* slip into their writing after they start with another pronoun.)	
Someone who is dieting should have the help of friends; *you* should also have plenty of willpower.	*Someone* who is dieting should have the help of friends; *he* or *she* should also have plenty of willpower.
Students who work while *they* are going to school face special problems. For one thing, *you* seldom have enough study time.	Students who work while *they* are going to school face special problems. For one thing, *they* seldom have enough study time.

Practice

Cross out inconsistent pronouns in the following sentences and write the correction above the error.

Example   I work much better when the boss doesn't hover over ~~you~~ *me* with instructions on what to do.

1. As we drove through the Pennsylvania countryside, ~~you~~ *we* saw some of the horse-drawn buggies used by the Amish people.

2. One of the things I like about the corner store is that ~~you~~ *I* can buy homemade sausage there.

3. In our family, we had to learn to keep our bedrooms neat before ~~you~~ *we* were given an allowance.

4. No matter how hard we may be working, the minute ~~you~~ *we* relax, the supervisor will be watching.

5. People shouldn't discuss cases outside of court if ~~you~~ *they* serve on a jury.

6. As I read the daily papers, ~~you~~ *I* get depressed by all the violent crime occurring in this country.

7. I never eat both halves of a hamburger bun, because ~~you~~ *I* save calories that way.

8. If someone started a bakery or doughnut shop in this town, ~~you~~ *he or she* could make a lot of money.

9. Fran likes to shop at the factory outlet because ~~you~~ *she* can buy discount clothing there.

10. I can't wait for summer, when ~~you~~ *I* can stop wearing heavy coats and itchy sweaters.

■ Review Test 1

Underline the correct word in the parentheses.

1. John spent all morning bird-watching and didn't see a single (one, <u>bird</u>).

2. Of the six men on the committee, no one was prepared to give (<u>his</u>, their) report, so the deadline was extended.

3. If a student in that women's college wants to get a good schedule, (<u>she</u>, you) must enroll as soon as possible.

4. Neither of the luncheonettes near our office has a very wide choice of sand-wiches on (its, their) menu.

5. My father has cut down on salt because it can give (you, him) high blood pressure.

6. Well, gentlemen, if anyone objects to the plan, (he, they) should speak up now.

7. I put my wet umbrella on the porch until (it, the umbrella) was dry.

8. I don't like that fast-food restaurant, because (they, the employees) are inefficient.

9. Doctors make large salaries, but (you, they) often face the pressure of deal-ing with life and death.

10. After eight hours in the cramped, stuffy car, I was glad (it, the trip) was over.

■ **Review Test 2**

Cross out the pronoun error in each sentence and write the correction in the space provided at the left. Then circle the letter that correctly describes the type of error that was made.

Examples   _**People**_   ~~Anyone~~ turning in their papers late will be penalized.

       Mistake in: a. pronoun reference   (b.) pronoun agreement

       **Paul**   When Clyde takes his son Paul to the park, ~~he~~ enjoys himself.

       Mistake in: (a.) pronoun reference   b. pronoun point of view

       _**we**_   From where we stood, ~~you~~ could see three states.

       Mistake in: a. pronoun agreement   (b.) pronoun point of view

_**we**_

1. In our company, ~~you~~ have to work for one year before getting vacation time.

    Mistake in: a. pronoun agreement   (b.) pronoun point of view

**word processors**

2. Amy signed up for a word processing course because she heard that ~~they~~ are in demand.

    Mistake in: (a.) pronoun reference   b. pronoun agreement

_**we**_

3. We did not eat much of the fruit, for ~~you~~ could tell that it was not fresh.

    Mistake in: a. pronoun agreement   (b.) pronoun point of view

**the counselors**

4. Eric visited the counseling center because ~~they~~ can help him straighten out his schedule.

    Mistake in: (a.) pronoun reference   b. pronoun agreement

<u>his or her</u>   5. Every student who was in the chemistry lab has ~~their~~ own memories of the fire.

Mistake in: a. pronoun reference   (b.) pronoun agreement

Hint   You may want to rewrite item 5 in the plural, using the lines below.

Students who were in the chemistry lab have their own memories of the fire.

_____

<u>the cheese slices (or the hamburgers)</u>   6. After LaTanya put cheese slices on the hamburgers, the dog ate ~~them~~.

Mistake in: (a.) pronoun agreement   b. pronoun point of view

<u>they</u>   7. If people feel that they are being discriminated against in jobs or housing, ~~you~~ should contact the appropriate federal agency.

Mistake in: a. pronoun agreement   (b.) pronoun point of view

<u>the neighbor's</u>   8. Norma told her neighbor that ~~her~~ house needed a new coat of paint.

Mistake in: (a.) pronoun reference   b. pronoun agreement

<u>his</u>   9. One of the actors forgot ~~their~~ lines and tried to ad-lib.

Mistake in: (a.) pronoun agreement   b. pronoun point of view

<u>he or she</u>   10. If anyone wants a tryout, ~~they~~ should be at the gym at four o'clock.

Mistake in: a. pronoun reference   (b.) pronoun agreement

Hint   You may want to rewrite item 10 in the plural, using the lines below.

If players want a tryout, they should be at the gym at four o'clock.

_____

14 Pronoun Types

Introductory Activity

In each pair, write a check beside the sentence that you think uses pronouns correctly.

Andi and *I* enrolled in a computer course. __✓__
Andi and *me* enrolled in a computer course. _____

The police officer pointed to my sister and *me*. __✓__
The police officer pointed to my sister and *I*. _____

Lola prefers men *whom* take pride in their bodies. _____
Lola prefers men *who* take pride in their bodies. __✓__

The players are confident that the league championship is *theirs'*.
_____
The players are confident that the league championship is *theirs*.
__✓__

Them concert tickets are too expensive. _____
Those concert tickets are too expensive. __✓__

Our parents should spend some money on *themself* for a change.
_____
Our parents should spend some money on *themselves* for a change.
__✓__

Answers are on page 573.

This chapter describes some common types of pronouns: subject and object pronouns, possessive pronouns, demonstrative pronouns, and reflexive pronouns.

Subject and Object Pronouns

Pronouns change their form depending on the place they occupy in a sentence. Here is a list of subject and object pronouns:

Subject Pronouns	Object Pronouns
I	me
you	you (no change)
he	him
she	her
it	it (no change)
we	us
they	them

Subject Pronouns

19.2a

Subject pronouns are subjects of verbs.

They are getting tired. (*They* is the subject of the verb *are getting*.)

She will decide tomorrow. (*She* is the subject of the verb *will decide*.)

We women organized the game. (*We* is the subject of the verb *organized*.)

Several rules for using subject pronouns, and mistakes people sometimes make, are explained starting below.

Rule 1   Use a subject pronoun in a sentence with a compound (more than one) subject.

Incorrect	Correct
Dwayne and *me* went shopping yesterday.	Dwayne and *I* went shopping yesterday.
Him and *me* spent lots of money.	*He* and *I* spent lots of money.

If you are not sure which pronoun to use, try each pronoun by itself in the sentence. The correct pronoun will be the one that sounds right. For example, "*Me* went shopping yesterday" does not sound right; "*I* went shopping yesterday" does.

Rule 2   Use a subject pronoun after forms of the verb *be*. Forms of *be* include *am, are, is, was, were, has been, have been,* and others.

> It was *I* who telephoned.
> It may be *they* at the door.
> It is *she.*

The sentences above may sound strange and stilted to you, since this rule is seldom actually followed in conversation. When we speak with one another, forms such as "It was me," "It may be them," and "It is her" are widely accepted. In formal writing, however, the grammatically correct forms are still preferred. You can avoid having to use a subject pronoun after *be* simply by rewording a sentence. Here is how the preceding examples could be reworded:

> *I* was the one who telephoned.
> *They* may be at the door.
> *She* is here.

Rule 3   Use subject pronouns after *than* or *as* when a verb is understood after the pronoun.

> You read faster than I (read). (The verb *read* is understood after *I*.)
> Tom is as stubborn as I (am). (The verb *am* is understood after *I*.)
> We don't go out as much as they (do). (The verb *do* is understood after *they*.)

Notes

a   Avoid mistakes by mentally adding the "missing" verb at the end of the sentence.

b   Use object pronouns after *as* or *than* when a verb is not understood after the pronoun.

> The law applies to you as well as me.
> Our boss paid Monica more than me.

Object Pronouns

19.2b

Object pronouns (*me, him, her, us, them*) are the objects of verbs or prepositions. (Prepositions are connecting words like *for, at, about, to, before, by, with,* and *of.* See also page 93.)

> Nika chose *me*. (*Me* is the object of the verb *chose.*)
> We met *them* at the ball park. (*Them* is the object of the verb *met.*)
> Don't mention UFOs to *us*. (*Us* is the object of the preposition *to.*)
> I live near *her.* (*Her* is the object of the preposition *near.*)

People are sometimes uncertain about what pronoun to use when two objects follow the verb.

Incorrect	*Correct*
I spoke to George and *he.*	I spoke to George and *him.*
She pointed at Hana and *I.*	She pointed at Hana and *me.*

Hint   If you are not sure what pronoun to use, try each pronoun by itself in the sentence. The correct pronoun will be the one that sounds right. For example, "I spoke to he" doesn't sound right; "I spoke to him" does.

Practice 1

Underline the correct subject or object pronoun in each of the following sentences. Then show whether your answer is a subject or an object pronoun by circling the *S* or *O* in the margin. The first one is done for you as an example.

S Ⓞ   1. I left the decision to (<u>him</u>, he).

Ⓢ O   2. At a sale, my mother and (<u>I</u>, me) get bargain-hunting fever.

S Ⓞ   3. As he gazed at (she, <u>her</u>) and the children, he knew he was happy.

S Ⓞ   4. The panhandler asked my brother and (I, <u>me</u>) for some change.

S Ⓞ   5. Without (she, <u>her</u>) and (he, <u>him</u>), this club would be a disaster.

Ⓢ O   6. Suki can change a tire faster than (<u>I</u>, me).

Ⓢ O   7. (<u>We</u>, Us) athletes always have to stay in shape.

Ⓢ O   8. It was (<u>she</u>, her) who noticed that the phone was off the hook.

S Ⓞ   9. The bad feelings between you and (I, <u>me</u>) have lasted too long.

Ⓢ O   10. Before the wedding, Romeo and (<u>he</u>, him) tried, without much luck, to put on the cummerbunds that came with the tuxedos.

Practice 2

For each sentence, in the space provided, write an appropriate subject or object pronoun. Try to use as many different pronouns as possible. The first one is done for you as an example.

Answers will vary; below are some possibilities.

1. Dina ran after Kris and _____ *me* _____ to return the keys she had borrowed.

2. That video equipment belongs to Barry and _____ *me (or him, or her, or them)* .

3. Sally and _____ *I (or he, etc.)* decided to open a bookstore together.

4. Herb has worked at the welding shop longer than _____ *I (or she, etc.)* .

5. Take that box of candy from the shelf and give it to _____ *me (or him, etc.)* .

6. Why do you and _____ *I (or she, etc.)* always get stuck with the cleaning up?

7. I really envy _____ *them* _____ for their ability to get along with people.

8. The police caught Val and _____ *him (or them, etc.)* as they were trying to break into the boarded-up store.

9. My neighbor and _____ *I (or she, etc.)* are soap-opera addicts.

10. Neither Ron nor _____ *I (or he, etc.)* is afraid of walking through the cemetery at night.

Relative Pronouns

19.3

Relative pronouns do two things at once. First, they refer to someone or something already mentioned in the sentence. Second, they start a short word group that gives additional information about this someone or something. Here is a list of relative pronouns, followed by some example sentences:

Relative Pronouns	
who	which
whose	that
whom	

The only friend *who* really understands me is moving away.

The child *whom* Ben and Arlene adopted is from Korea.

Chocolate, *which* is my favorite food, upsets my stomach.

I guessed at half the questions *that* were on the test.

In the example sentences, *who* refers to *friend,* *whom* refers to *child,* *which* refers to *chocolate,* and *that* refers to *questions.* In addition, each of these relative pronouns begins a group of words that describes the person or thing being referred to. For example, the words *whom Ben and Arlene adopted* tell which child the sentence is about, and the words *which is my favorite food* give added information about chocolate.

Points to Remember about Relative Pronouns

Point 1   *Whose* means *belonging to whom.* Be careful not to confuse *whose* with *who's,* which means *who is.*

Point 2   *Who, whose,* and *whom* all refer to people. *Which* refers to things. *That* can refer to either people or things.

> I don't know *whose* book this is.
>
> Don't sit on the chair *which* is broken.
>
> Let's elect a captain *that* cares about winning.

Point 3   *Who, whose, whom,* and *which* can also be used to ask questions. When they are used in this way, they are called *interrogative* pronouns:

> *Who* murdered the secret agent?
>
> *Whose* fingerprints were on the bloodstained knife?
>
> To *whom* have the detectives been talking?
>
> *Which* suspect is going to confess?

Note   In informal usage, *who* is generally used instead of *whom* as an interrogative pronoun. Informally, we can say or write, "*Who* are you rooting for in the game?" or "*Who* did the instructor fail?" More formal usage would use *whom:* "Whom are you rooting for in the game?" and "Whom did the instructor fail?"

Point 4   *Who* and *whom* are used differently. *Who* is a subject pronoun. Use *who* as the subject of a verb:

> Let's see *who* will be teaching the course.

Whom is an object pronoun. Use *whom* as the object of a verb or a preposition:

> Dr. Martinez is the instructor *whom* I like best.
>
> I haven't decided for *whom* I will vote.

You may want to review the material on subject and object pronouns on pages 206–208.

Here is an easy way to decide whether to use *who* or *whom.* Find the first verb after the place where the *who* or *whom* will go. See if it already has a subject. If it does have a subject, use the object pronoun *whom.* If there is no subject, give it one by using the subject pronoun *who.* Notice how *who* and *whom* are used in the sentences that follow:

> I don't know *who* sideswiped my car.
>
> The suspect *whom* the police arrested finally confessed.

In the first sentence, *who* is used to give the verb *sideswiped* a subject. In the second sentence, the verb *arrested* already has a subject, *police.* Therefore, *whom* is the correct pronoun.

Practice 1

Underline the correct pronoun in each of the following sentences.

1. Alexandre Dumas, (who, which) wrote *The Three Musketeers,* once fought a sword duel in which his pants fell down.

2. The power failure, (who, which) caused the stage to go black, happened during the singer's performance of "You Light Up My Life."

3. The football coach wasn't very encouraging toward Mark, (who, whom) he advised to get extra health insurance.

4. A national animal-protection society honored a high school student (who, whom) refused to dissect a frog in her biology class.

5. Several of the students (who, which) were taking College Survival Skills dropped out before the end of the semester.

Practice 2

Answers will vary.

On separate paper, write five sentences using *who, whose, whom, which,* and *that.*

Possessive Pronouns

ALLWRITE!
19.2c

Possessive pronouns show ownership or possession.

> Clyde shut off the engine of *his* motorcycle.
> The keys are *mine*.

Here is a list of possessive pronouns:

<table>
<tr><td colspan="2" align="center">Possessive Pronouns</td></tr>
<tr><td>my, mine</td><td>our, ours</td></tr>
<tr><td>your, yours</td><td>your, yours</td></tr>
<tr><td>his</td><td>their, theirs</td></tr>
<tr><td>her, hers</td><td></td></tr>
<tr><td>its</td><td></td></tr>
</table>

Points to Remember about Possessive Pronouns

Point 1   A possessive pronoun *never* uses an apostrophe. (See also pages 288–289.)

Incorrect	*Correct*
That coat is *hers'*.	That coat is *hers*.
The card table is *theirs'*.	The card table is *theirs*.

Point 2   Do not use any of the following nonstandard forms to show possession.

Incorrect	*Correct*
I met a friend of *him*.	I met a friend of *his*.
Can I use *you* car?	Can I use *your* car?
Me sister is in the hospital.	*My* sister is in the hospital.
That magazine is *mines*.	That magazine is *mine*.

Practice

Cross out the incorrect pronoun form in each of the sentences that follow. Write the correct form in the space at the left.

_____My_____   Example   ~~Me~~ car has broken down again.

_____hers_____   1. Is this pocketbook ~~hers'~~?

_____mine_____   2. That pile of books you knocked over is ~~mines~~.

_____ours_____   3. Those running shoes are ~~ours'~~.

_____its_____   4. It took that dog six months to learn ~~it's~~ name.

_____their_____   5. The store owners asked ~~they~~ employees to work until 9 P.M.

Demonstrative Pronouns

Demonstrative pronouns point to or single out a person or thing. There are four demonstrative pronouns:

Demonstrative Pronouns	
this	these
that	those

Generally speaking, *this* and *these* refer to things close at hand; *that* and *those* refer to things farther away.

> Is anyone using *this* spoon?
> I am going to throw away *these* magazines.
> I just bought *that* white Volvo at the curb.
> Pick up *those* toys in the corner.

Note   Do not use *them, this here, that there, these here,* or *those there* to point out. Use only *this, that, these,* or *those.*

	Incorrect	*Correct*

Incorrect

Them tires are badly worn.

This here book looks hard to read.

That there candy is delicious.

Those there squirrels are pests.

Correct

Those tires are badly worn.

This book looks hard to read.

That candy is delicious.

Those squirrels are pests.

Practice 1

Cross out the incorrect form of the demonstrative pronoun and write the correct form in the space provided.

Those   Example   ~~Them~~ clothes need washing.

This   1. ~~This here~~ waitress will take your order.

Those   2. ~~Them~~ sunglasses make you look really sharp.

These   3. ~~These here~~ phones are out of order.

Those   4. ~~Them~~ flash cubes won't fit my camera.

that   5. I didn't know ~~that there~~ gun was loaded.

Practice 2

Write four sentences using *this, that, these,* and *those*.

Answers will vary.

Reflexive Pronouns

Reflexive pronouns are pronouns that refer to the subject of a sentence. Here is a list of reflexive pronouns:

Reflexive Pronouns		
myself	herself	ourselves
yourself	itself	yourselves
himself		themselves

Sometimes the reflexive pronoun is used for emphasis:

> You will have to wash the dishes *yourself*.
> We *ourselves* are willing to forget the matter.
> The president *himself* turns down his living room thermostat.

Points to Remember about Reflexive Pronouns

Point 1   In the plural *-self* becomes *-selves*.

> Lola soaks *herself* in Calgon bath oil.
> They treated *themselves* to a vacation in Bermuda.

Point 2   Be careful that you do not use any of the following incorrect forms as reflexive pronouns.

Incorrect	Correct
He believes in *hisself*.	He believes in *himself*.
We drove the children *ourself*.	We drove the children *ourselves*.
They saw *themself* in the fun house mirror.	They saw *themselves* in the fun house mirror.
I'll do it *meself*.	I'll do it *myself*.

Practice

Cross out the incorrect form of the reflexive pronoun and write the correct form in the space at the left.

<u>themselves</u>   Example   She believes that God helps those who help ~~themself~~.

<u>ourselves</u>   1. We painted the kitchen ~~ourself~~.

<u>himself</u>   2. The mayor ~~hisself~~ spoke to the striking bus drivers.

<u>themselves</u>   3. Marian's sons don't like being left by ~~theirselves~~ in the house.

<u>yourself</u>   4. You must get the tickets ~~yourselfs~~.

<u>ourselves</u>   5. Bill and I cooked the dinner ~~ourself~~.

■ **Review Test 1**

Underline the correct word in the parentheses.

Example   Tomas and (I, me) have already seen the movie.

1. It looks as if (this, this here) tape recorder is out of order.

2. I exercise twice as much as (she, her), and I'm in worse shape.

3. The only thing for Jack and (I, me) to eat was cold rice.

4. That folding umbrella you just picked up is (our's, ours).

5. Since Paula and (he, him) are engaged, we should give them a party.

6. Why do our parents always embarrass (we, us) kids by showing those old home movies?

7. The manager (hisself, himself) plans to take a cut in salary.

8. They knew the stolen clock radios were (theirs, their's), but they couldn't prove it.

9. If you put (them, those) vegetables in the microwave oven, they'll defrost in a few minutes.

10. My nephews couldn't stop giggling after they saw (theirselves, themselves) in their Halloween costumes.

■ **Review Test 2**

Cross out the pronoun error in each sentence and write the correct form above it.

1. I asked the dentist's receptionist for appointments for my sister and (I, me).

2. I can't tell if (them, those) potatoes are cooked all the way through or not.

3. Since the fault is (yours, your's), you owe me the cost of the repairs.

4. When the will was read, my cousin and (me, I) had inherited a thousand dollars each.

5. After we finished figuring out our income taxes, we rewarded (ourself, ourselves) and the kids with a trip to the shopping mall.

6. Demetri's car had (its, it's) antenna broken off while it was parked outside the bowling alley.

7. Nothing bothers (he, him) more than having to make extra trips to the hardware store after he's started to fix something.

8. (This, This here) town needs a tough sheriff.

9. Since I take better notes than (he, him), we studied from mine for the exam.

10. In small claims court, the judges (themself, themselves) decide the cases and award the damages.

■ Review Test 3

On separate paper, write sentences that use correctly each of the following words or word groups.

Example   Peter and him *The coach suspended Peter and him.*

Answers will vary.

1. you and I

2. yours

3. Kathy and me

4. Leon and he

5. the neighbors and us

6. taller than I

7. yourselves

8. with Roberto and him

9. those

10. Lisa and them

15 Adjectives and Adverbs

Introductory Activity

Write in an appropriate word or words to complete each of the sentences below.

Answers will vary.

1. The teenage years were a _____ time for me.

2. The mechanic listened _____ while I described my car problem.

3. Basketball is a _____ game than football.

4. My brother is the _____ person in our family.

Now see if you can complete the following sentences.

The word inserted in the first sentence is an (<u>adjective</u>, adverb); it describes the word *time*.

The word inserted in the second sentence is an (adjective, <u>adverb</u>);

it probably ends in the two letters __*ly*__ and describes the word *listened*.

The word inserted in the third sentence is a comparative adjective;

it may be preceded by *more* or end in the two letters __*er*__.

The word inserted in the fourth sentence is a superlative adjective;

it may be preceded by *most* or end in the three letters __*est*__.

Answers are on page 574.

Adjectives and adverbs are descriptive words. Their purpose is to make the meaning of the words they describe more specific.

Adjectives

What Are Adjectives?

20.1

Adjectives describe nouns (names of persons, places, or things) or pronouns.

> Charlotte is a *kind* woman. (The adjective *kind* describes the noun *woman*.)
>
> He is *tired*. (The adjective *tired* describes the pronoun *he*.)

An adjective usually comes before the word it describes (as in *kind woman*). But it can also come after forms of the verb *be (is, are, was, were,* and so on). Less often, an adjective follows verbs such as *feel, look, smell, sound, taste, appear, become,* and *seem.*

> The bureau is *heavy*. (The adjective *heavy* describes the bureau.)
>
> These pants are *itchy*. (The adjective *itchy* describes the pants.)
>
> The children seem *restless*. (The adjective *restless* describes the children.)

Using Adjectives to Compare

ALLWRITE!
20.4

For most short adjectives, add *-er* when comparing two things and *-est* when comparing three or more things.

> I am *taller* than my brother, but my father is the *tallest* person in the house.
>
> The farm market sells *fresher* vegetables than the corner store, but the *freshest* vegetables are the ones grown in my own garden.

For most *longer* adjectives (two or more syllables), add *more* when comparing two things and *most* when comparing three or more things.

> Backgammon is *more enjoyable* to me than checkers, but chess is the *most enjoyable* game of all.
>
> My mother is *more talkative* than my father, but my grandfather is the *most talkative* person in the house.

Points to Remember about Adjectives

Point 1   Be careful not to use both an *-er* ending and *more*, or both an *-est* ending and *most*.

Incorrect	*Correct*
Football is a *more livelier* game than baseball.	Football is a *livelier* game than baseball.
Tod Traynor was voted the *most likeliest* to succeed in our high school class.	Tod Traynor was voted the *most likely* to succeed in our high school class.

Point 2   Pay special attention to the following words, each of which has irregular forms.

	Comparative (Two)	*Superlative (Three or More)*
bad	worse	worst
good, well	better	best
little	less	least
much, many	more	most

Practice 1

Fill in the comparative or superlative forms for the following adjectives. Two are done for you as examples.

	Comparative (Two)	*Superlative (Three or More)*
fast	faster	fastest
timid	more timid	most timid
kind	kinder	kindest
ambitious	more ambitious	most ambitious
generous	more generous	most generous
fine	finer	finest
likable	more likable	most likable

Practice 2

Add to each sentence the correct form of the word in the margin.

Example   *bad*   The _____*worst*_____ day of my life was the one when my house caught fire.

thick   1. I attempted to bite into the _____*thickest*_____ sandwich I had ever seen.

lazy   2. Each perfect summer day was _____*lazier*_____ than the last.

harsh   3. The judge pronounced the _____*harshest*_____ sentence possible on the convicted robber.

flexible   4. My new hairbrush is _____*more flexible*_____ than my old one and doesn't pull out as many hairs.

bad   5. I felt even _____*worse*_____ after I had taken the anti-motion sickness pills.

good   6. The _____*best*_____ seats in the stadium are completely sold out.

little   7. I'm looking for a cereal with _____*less*_____ sugar than "Candy Flakes."

vulnerable 8. The body's central trunk is _____*less vulnerable*_____ to frostbite than the hands and feet.

wasteful   9. Many people throughout the world feel that Americans are the _____*most wasteful*_____ people on earth.

shiny   10. My hair looked _____*shinier*_____ than usual after I began taking vitamins.

Adverbs

What Are Adverbs?

20.6

Adverbs describe verbs, adjectives, or other adverbs. An adverb usually ends in *-ly*.

Charlotte spoke *kindly* to the confused man. (The adverb *kindly* describes the verb *spoke*.)

The man said he was *completely* alone in the world. (The adverb *completely* describes the adjective *alone*.)

Charlotte listened *very* sympathetically to his story. (The adverb *very* describes the adverb *sympathetically*.)

A Common Mistake with Adjectives and Adverbs

Perhaps the most common mistake that people make with adjectives and adverbs is to use an adjective instead of an adverb after a verb.

Incorrect	*Correct*
Tony breathed *heavy.*	Tony breathed *heavily.*
I rest *comfortable* in that chair.	I rest *comfortably* in that chair.
She learned *quick.*	She learned *quickly.*

Practice

Underline the adjective or adverb needed.

1. She walked (hesitant, <u>hesitantly</u>) into the room.
2. I could have won the match (easy, <u>easily</u>) if I had concentrated more.
3. After turning the motorcycle (sharp, <u>sharply</u>), Marilyn tried to regain her balance.
4. The bus stopped (abrupt, <u>abruptly</u>), and the passengers were thrown forward.
5. The candidate waged an (<u>aggressive</u>, aggressively) campaign, and the voters turned against him.
6. The man talked (regretful, <u>regretfully</u>) about the chances he had missed.
7. The instructor spoke so (quick, <u>quickly</u>) that we gave up taking notes.
8. The students eat so (messy, <u>messily</u>) that the cafeteria must be cleaned twice a day.
9. The boy was (<u>envious</u>, enviously) of his brother's new cowboy boots.
10. Maureen worked (terrible, <u>terribly</u>) hard at her job, yet she managed to find time for her children.

Well and *Good*

Two words often confused are *well* and *good*. *Good* is an adjective; it describes nouns. *Well* is usually an adverb; it describes verbs. *Well* (rather than *good*) is also used when referring to a person's health.

Here are some examples:

I became a *good* swimmer. (*Good* is an adjective describing the noun *swimmer.*)

For a change, two-year-old Rodney was *good* during the church service. (*Good* is an adjective describing Rodney and comes after *was*, a form of the verb *be*.)

Maryann did *well* on that exam. (*Well* is an adverb describing the verb *did.*)

I explained that I wasn't feeling *well.* (*Well* is used in reference to health.)

Practice

Write *well* or *good* in the sentences that follow.

1. I think I've done _____*well*_____ on the first quiz.

2. Our young son is a _____*good*_____ chess player.

3. The neighbors said they knew the suspect _____*well*_____.

4. We need a _____*good*_____ quarterback for our team.

5. I knew I wasn't doing _____*well*_____ in math class.

■ Review Test 1

Cross out the adjective or adverb error in each sentence and write the correction in the space at the left.

frequently

harder

Examples   My boss ~~frequent~~ tells me to slow down.

   For me, the country is a ~~more harder~~ place to live than the city.

well

1. I knew she wasn't feeling ~~good~~ when I saw her put her head in her hands.

better

2. It is ~~best~~ for me now to be in school than to have a full-time job.

softly

3. The mother pressed the baby against her shoulder and sang ~~soft~~ in his ear.

gratefully

4. After the two-week camping trip, Donna gazed ~~grateful~~ at her warm bathroom and clean towels.

dullest

5. That show is the ~~most dullest~~ one on television.

restlessly

6. Squirming ~~restless~~ in the seat next to her date, Carol felt uneasy during the violent movie scene.

kindest

7. My sister Ella is the ~~kinder~~ of the four children in our family.

imploringly

8. Clutching a box of chocolate-flavored cereal, the boy stood in the supermarket aisle and looked ~~imploring~~ at his mother.

well

9. He had done ~~good~~ on the first test, so he decided not to study for the next one.

suspiciously

10. Peering ~~suspicious~~ at the can of corn, the woman peeled back the new price label that had been stuck over the old one.

■ **Review Test 2**

Write a sentence that uses each of the following adjectives and adverbs correctly.
Answers will vary.

1. nervous _____

2. nervously _____

3. good _____

4. well _____

5. carefully _____

6. most honest _____

7. easier _____

8. best _____

9. more useful _____

10. loudest _____

16 Misplaced Modifiers

Introductory Activity

Because of misplaced words, each of the sentences below has more than one possible meaning. In each case, see if you can explain both the intended meaning and the unintended meaning.

1. The farmers sprayed the apple trees wearing masks.

    Intended meaning: _The farmers were wearing masks._

    Unintended meaning: _The apple trees were wearing masks._

2. The woman reached out for the faith healer who had a terminal disease.

    Intended meaning: _The woman had a terminal disease._

    Unintended meaning: _The faith healer had a terminal disease._

Answers are on page 574.

225

What Misplaced Modifiers Are and How to Correct Them

16.2

Misplaced modifiers are words that, because of awkward placement, do not describe the words the writer intended them to describe. Misplaced modifiers often confuse the meaning of a sentence. To avoid them, place words as close as possible to what they describe.

Misplaced Words	*Correctly Placed Words*
They could see the Goodyear blimp *sitting on the front lawn.*	Sitting on the front lawn, they could see the Goodyear blimp.
(The *Goodyear blimp* was sitting on the front lawn?)	(The intended meaning—that the Goodyear blimp was visible from the front lawn—is now clear.)
We had a hamburger after the movie, *which was too greasy for my taste.*	After the movie, we had a hamburger, which was too greasy for my taste.
(The *movie* was too greasy for your taste?)	(The intended meaning—that the hamburger was greasy—is now clear.)
Our phone *almost rang* fifteen times last night.	Our phone rang almost fifteen times last night.
(The phone *almost rang* fifteen times, but in fact did not ring at all?)	(The intended meaning—that the phone rang a little under fifteen times—is now clear.)

Other single-word modifiers to watch out for include *only, even, hardly, nearly,* and *often.* Such words should be placed immediately before the word they modify.

Practice 1

Underline the misplaced word or words in each sentence. Then rewrite the sentence, placing related words together to make the meaning clear.

Example   Anita returned the hamburger to the supermarket <u>that was spoiled.</u>

Anita returned the hamburger that was spoiled to

the supermarket.

1. We noticed several dead animals <u>driving along the wooded road.</u>
   Driving along the wooded road, we noticed several dead animals.

2. Maya envisioned the flowers that would bloom <u>in her mind.</u>
   In her mind, Maya envisioned the flowers that would bloom.

3. I watched my closest friends being married <u>in my tuxedo.</u>
   In my tuxedo, I watched my closest friends being married.

4. Zoe carried her new coat on her arm <u>which was trimmed with fur.</u>
   Zoe carried her new coat, which was trimmed with fur, on her arm.

5. We just heard that all major highways were flooded <u>on the radio.</u>
   We just heard on the radio that all major highways were flooded.

6. Fresh-picked blueberries <u>almost</u> covered the entire kitchen counter.
   Fresh-picked blueberries covered almost the entire kitchen counter.

7. Betty licked the homemade peach ice cream <u>making sounds of contentment.</u>
   Making sounds of contentment, Betty licked the homemade peach ice cream.

8. The salesman confidently demonstrated the vacuum cleaner <u>with a grin.</u>
   With a grin, the salesman confidently demonstrated the vacuum cleaner.

9. Natasha is delivering singing telegrams <u>dressed in a top hat and tails.</u>
   Dressed in a top hat and tails, Natasha is delivering singing telegrams.

10. The local drama group needs people to build scenery <u>badly.</u>
    The local drama group badly needs people to build scenery.

Practice 2

Rewrite each sentence, adding the *italicized* words. Make sure that the intended meaning is clear and that two different interpretations are not possible.

Example   I borrowed a pen for the essay test. (Insert *that ran out of ink.*)
            For the essay test, I borrowed a pen that ran out of ink.

1. I opened my mouth for the dentist. (Insert *with a pounding heart.*)
   With a pounding heart, I opened my mouth for the dentist.

2. Newspapers announced that the fighter jets had landed. (Insert *all over the world.*)
   Newspapers all over the world announced that the fighter jets had landed.

3. Newborn kangaroos crawl into their mothers' pouches. (Insert *which resemble blind, naked worms.*)
   Newborn kangaroos, which resemble blind, naked worms, crawl into their
   mothers' pouches.

4. Bruce Springsteen's latest album has sold five million copies. (Insert *almost.*)
   Bruce Springsteen's latest album has sold almost five million copies.

5. Tanya proudly deposited the fifty dollars she had earned typing term papers. (Insert *in her savings account.*)
   Tanya proudly deposited in her savings account the fifty dollars she had
   earned typing term papers.

■ **Review Test 1**

Write *M* for *misplaced* or *C* for *correct* in the space to the left of each sentence.

M   1. Books don't sell well in the bookstores with hard covers.

C   2. Books with hard covers don't sell well in the bookstores.

M   3. Marilyn went to the door to let in the plumber wearing her nightgown.

C   4. Wearing her nightgown, Marilyn went to the door to let in the plumber.

C   5. Franco spent nearly three hours in the doctor's office.

M   6. Franco nearly spent three hours in the doctor's office.

M   7. I spent three days in a hospital watching TV reruns recovering from surgery.

C   8. Recovering from surgery, I spent three days in a hospital watching TV reruns.

C   9. Paula searched through the closet for something to wear on her date.

M   10. Paula searched for something to wear on her date through the closet.

M   11. Nick and Fran found six boxes of pictures of their vacation in the attic.

M   12. Nick and Fran found six boxes of pictures in the attic of their vacation.

C   13. In the attic, Nick and Fran found six boxes of pictures of their vacation.

C   14. Mrs. Liu mistakenly put the milk container which was leaking in the refrigerator.

M   15. Mrs. Liu mistakenly put the milk container in the refrigerator which was leaking.

M   16. Susie whispered a silent prayer before the exam began under her breath.

C   17. Susie whispered a silent prayer under her breath before the exam began.

C   18. Under her breath, Susie whispered a silent prayer before the exam began.

C   19. On the patio, we ate roast beef sandwiches dripping with gravy.

M   20. We ate roast beef sandwiches on the patio dripping with gravy.

■ **Review Test 2**

Underline the five misplaced modifiers in the passage below. Then, in the spaces
that follow, show how you would correct them.

> The tired hikers <u>almost</u> slept for ten hours in the trail shelter. Then Rick
> awakened and hurried out of his cot when he saw a black spider <u>looking out</u>
> <u>of the corner of his eye.</u> At this point, his brother Hal woke up with a start
> and sneezed several times. Because Hal was coming down with a cold, Rick
> agreed to prepare the breakfast. He first fetched a canteen of orange juice
> from a nearby stream <u>which had cooled overnight.</u> Next, he started a fire
> and set about boiling water for coffee and frying up some bacon and eggs.
> Meanwhile, Hal sniffled, sipped some orange juice, and waited by the fire
> for a cup of coffee <u>wearing a heavy sweatshirt and gloves.</u> After both had
> eaten, Rick was ready to plan another day's hiking. But Hal was interested
> only in hiking to the bus on the nearby highway <u>that could drop him a block</u>
> <u>from his house.</u>

1. The tired hikers slept for almost ten hours in the trail shelter.

2. Then Rick awakened and hurried out of his cot when, looking out of the
   corner of his eye, he saw a black spider.

3. He first fetched from a nearby stream a canteen of orange juice which
   had cooled overnight.

4. Meanwhile, wearing a heavy sweatshirt and gloves, Hal sniffled, sipped
   some orange juice, and waited by the fire for a cup of coffee.

5. But Hal was interested only in hiking on the nearby highway to the bus
   that could drop him a block from his house.

17 Dangling Modifiers

Note for the Introductory Activity below: Some instructors might consider the first example a misplaced modifier, since the subject of the phrase munching leaves from a tall tree—*the giraffe—does appear later in the sentence. However, correcting the error would involve changing words:*

Munching leaves from a tall tree, the eighteen-foot-tall giraffe fascinated the children.

or

The children were fascinated by the eighteen-foot-tall giraffe, *which was munching leaves from a tall tree.*

Thus this type of error is classified as a dangling modifier in Sentence Skills. *In general, if a word group is a participial phrase, and if the phrase occurs at the beginning of the sentence but modifies a subject that does not appear until later in the sentence, it is labeled a dangling rather than a misplaced modifier.*

Introductory Activity

Because of dangling words, each of the sentences below has more than one possible meaning. In each case, see if you can explain both the intended meaning and the unintended meaning.

1. Munching leaves from a tall tree, the children were fascinated by the eighteen-foot-tall giraffe.

   Intended meaning: *The giraffe was munching leaves.*

   Unintended meaning: *The children were munching leaves.*

2. Arriving home after ten months in the army, Michael's neighbors threw a block party for him.

   Intended meaning: *Michael was arriving home after ten months in the army.*

   Unintended meaning: *The neighbors were arriving home after ten months in the army.*

Answers are on page 575.

What Dangling Modifiers Are and How to Correct Them

16.4

A modifier that opens a sentence must be followed immediately by the word it is meant to describe. Otherwise, the modifier is said to be *dangling*, and the sentence takes on an unintended meaning. For example, look at this sentence:

> While sleeping in his backyard, a Frisbee hit Russ on the head.

The unintended meaning is that the *Frisbee* was sleeping in his backyard. What the writer meant, of course, was that *Russ* was sleeping in his backyard. The writer should have placed *Russ* right after the modifier, revising the rest of the sentence as necessary:

> While sleeping in his backyard, *Russ* was hit on the head by a Frisbee.

The sentence could also be corrected by adding the missing subject and verb to the opening word group:

> While *Russ* was sleeping in his backyard, a Frisbee hit him on the head.

Other sentences with dangling modifiers follow. Read the explanations of why they are dangling and look carefully at how they are corrected.

Dangling	*Correct*
Having almost no money, my survival depended on my parents.	Having almost no money, *I* depended on my parents for survival.
(*Who* has almost no money? The answer is not *survival* but *I*. The subject *I* must be added.)	*Or:* Since *I* had almost no money, I depended on my parents for survival.
Riding his bike, a German shepherd bit Tony on the ankle.	Riding his bike, *Tony* was bitten on the ankle by a German shepherd.
(*Who* is riding the bike? The answer is not *German shepherd*, as it unintentionally seems to be, but *Tony*. The subject *Tony* must be added.)	*Or:* While *Tony* was riding his bike, a German shepherd bit him on the ankle.

When trying to lose weight, all snacks are best avoided.	When trying to lose weight, *you* should avoid all snacks.
(*Who* is trying to lose weight? The answer is not *snacks* but *you.* The subject *you* must be added.)	*Or:* When *you* are trying to lose weight, avoid all snacks.

These examples make clear two ways of correcting a dangling modifier. Decide on a logical subject and do one of the following:

1   Place the subject *within* the opening word group:

Since *I* had almost no money, I depended on my parents for survival.

Note   In some cases an appropriate subordinating word such as *since* must be added, and the verb may have to be changed slightly as well.

2   Place the subject right *after* the opening word group:

Having almost no money, *I* depended on my parents for survival.

Sometimes even more rewriting is necessary to correct a dangling modifier. What is important to remember is that a modifier must be placed as close as possible to the word that it modifies.

Practice 1

Rewrite each sentence to correct the dangling modifier. Mark the one sentence that is correct with a *C.*

1.   Foaming at the mouth, the dog warden had the stray put to sleep.

   The dog warden had the stray, which was foaming at the mouth, put to sleep.

2.   Kicked carelessly under the bed, Marian finally found her slippers.

   Marian finally found her slippers, which had been kicked carelessly under the bed.

3.   Rusty with disuse, I tried out the old swing set.

   I tried out the old swing set, which was rusty with disuse.

4. Having given up four straight hits, the manager decided to replace his starting pitcher.

   The manager decided to replace his starting pitcher, who had given up four straight hits.

5. Having frozen on the vines, the farmers lost their entire tomato crop.

   The farmers lost their entire tomato crop, which had frozen on the vines.

6. While I was pouring out the cereal, a coupon fell into my bowl of milk.

   C

7. Dancing on their hind legs, the audience cheered wildly as the elephants paraded by.

   The audience cheered wildly as the elephants, which were dancing on their hind legs, paraded by.

8. Burned beyond all recognition, Marta took the overdone meat loaf from the oven.

   Marta took the overdone meat loaf, which was burned beyond all recognition, from the oven.

9. Tattered, faded, and hanging in shreds, we decided to replace the dining room wallpaper.

   We decided to replace the dining room wallpaper, which was tattered, faded, and hanging in shreds.

10. When sealed in plastic, a person can keep membership cards clean.

    A person can keep membership cards clean by sealing them in plastic.

Practice 2

Complete the following sentences. In each case, a logical subject should follow the opening words.

Example   Checking the oil stick, *I saw that my car was a quart low.*
Answers will vary.

1. Since going back to school, _____

2. After finishing an eight-hour shift, _____

3. While playing the radio, _____

4. Before learning how to drive, _____

5. At the age of eight, _____

■ Review Test 1

Write *D* for *dangling* or *C* for *correct* in front of each sentence. Remember that the opening words are a dangling modifier if they are not followed immediately by a logical subject.

_____D_____ 1. Yellowed with age, the young journalist could hardly read the old newspaper clipping.

_____C_____ 2. The young journalist could hardly read the old newspaper clipping that was yellowed with age.

_____D_____ 3. Tired and exasperated, the fight we had was inevitable.

_____C_____ 4. Since we were tired and exasperated, the fight we had was inevitable.

_____C_____ 5. After signing the repair contract, I had second thoughts.

_____D_____ 6. After signing the repair contract, second thoughts made me uneasy.

_____D_____ 7. At the age of twelve, several colleges had already accepted the boy genius.

_____C_____ 8. At the age of twelve, the boy genius had already been accepted by several colleges.

_____D_____ 9. While setting up the board, several game pieces were missing.

_____C_____ 10. While setting up the board, we noticed that several game pieces were missing.

_____D_____ 11. Walking to class, a gorgeous white Corvette sped by me at sixty miles an hour.

_____C_____ 12. As I was walking to class, a gorgeous white Corvette sped by me at sixty miles an hour.

_____C_____ 13. While waiting for the dentist to see her, Vicky became more nervous.

_____D_____ 14. While waiting for the dentist to see her, Vicky's nervousness increased.

_____C_____ 15. While she was waiting for the dentist to see her, Vicky became more nervous.

_____D_____ 16. Protected with slipcovers, my mother lets us put our feet on the living room furniture.

_____C_____ 17. My mother lets us put our feet on the living room furniture, since it is protected with slipcovers.

_____D_____ 18. Packed tightly in a tiny can, Fran had difficulty removing the anchovies.

_____C_____ 19. Since they were packed tightly in a tiny can, Fran had difficulty removing the anchovies.

_____C_____ 20. Packed tightly in a tiny can, the anchovies were difficult for Fran to remove.

■ **Review Test 2**

Underline the five dangling modifiers in this passage. Then correct them in the spaces provided.

   For years, students have been using the same methods of cheating on exams. One tried-and-true technique is the casual glance. <u>Pretending to stare thoughtfully out the window,</u> peripheral vision will be used to look at another student's paper. Another all-time favorite method, the pencil or pen drop, requires a helper. <u>Dropping a pen and then diving for it,</u> "Number seventeen" (or the number of some other question) is whispered. Then, <u>making a similar pen drop,</u> the answer is whispered by the helper. The most elaborate system, though, is writing up cheat sheets. <u>Tucked up a shirtsleeve,</u> pages of textbook material are condensed into tiny scraps of paper. No matter how smooth a cheater's style is, however, the time-tested methods are often ineffective. <u>Having been a student at one time,</u> the same ones are probably familiar to the instructor.

1. Pretending to stare thoughtfully out the window, a student will use peripheral vision to look at another student's paper.

2. Dropping a pen and then diving for it, a cheater whispers "Number seventeen" (or the number of some other question).

3. Then, making a similar pen drop, the helper whispers the answer.

4. Tucked up a shirtsleeve, tiny scraps of paper condense pages of textbook material.

5. Having been a student at one time, the instructor is probably familiar with the same ones.

18 Faulty Parallelism

Introductory Activity

Read aloud each pair of sentences below. Write a checkmark beside the sentence that reads more smoothly and clearly and sounds more natural.

Pair 1

_____ I use my computer to write papers, to search the Internet, and for playing video games.

_✓_ I use my computer to write papers, to search the Internet, and to play video games.

Pair 2

_____ One option the employees had was to take a cut in pay; the other was longer hours of work.

_✓_ One option the employees had was to take a cut in pay; the other was to work longer hours.

Pair 3

_____ Dad's favorite chair has a torn cushion, the armrest is stained, and a musty odor.

_✓_ Dad's favorite chair has a torn cushion, a stained armrest, and a musty odor.

Answers are on page 575.

Parallelism Explained

16.5

Words in a pair or a series should have parallel structure. By balancing the items in a pair or a series so that they have the same kind of structure, you will make the sentence clearer and easier to read. Notice how the parallel sentences that follow read more smoothly than the nonparallel ones.

Nonparallel (Not Balanced)	*Parallel (Balanced)*
Fran spends her free time reading, listening to music, and she works in the garden.	Fran spends her free time reading, listening to music, and working in the garden. (A balanced series of *-ing* words: *reading, listening, working.*)
After the camping trip I was exhausted, irritable, and wanted to eat.	After the camping trip I was exhausted, irritable, and hungry. (A balanced series of descriptive words: *exhausted, irritable, hungry.*)
My hope for retirement is to be healthy, to live in a comfortable house, and having plenty of money.	My hope for retirement is to be healthy, to live in a comfortable house, and to have plenty of money. (A balanced series of *to* verbs: *to be, to live, to have.*)
Nightly, Alexei puts out the trash, checks the locks on the doors, and the burglar alarm is turned on.	Nightly, Alexei puts out the trash, checks the locks on the doors, and turns on the burglar alarm. (Balanced verbs and word order: *puts out the trash, checks the locks, turns on the burglar alarm.*)

Balanced sentences are not a skill you need to worry about when you are writing first drafts. But when you rewrite, you should try to put matching words and ideas into matching structures. Such parallelism will improve your writing style.

Practice 1

The unbalanced part of each sentence is *italicized.* Rewrite this part so that it matches the rest of the sentence.

Example   In the afternoon, I changed two diapers, ironed several shirts, and *was watching* soap operas. ___watched___

1. As the home team scored the winning touchdown, the excited fans screamed, cheered, and *pennants were waved.*

   waved pennants

2. Would you prefer to go for a walk outside or *staying indoors?*

   to stay indoors

3. Before Pete could assemble the casserole, he had to brown the meat, dice the vegetables, and *a cream sauce had to be made.*

   make a cream sauce

4. Please feed the dog, *the heat must be turned down,* and lock the doors.

   turn down the heat

5. That restaurant specializes in *hamburgers that are overdone,* wilted salads, and stale pastries.

   overdone hamburgers

6. The old Ford sputtered, *was coughing,* and finally stopped altogether.

   coughed

7. The hospital patients can sometimes be cranky, *make a lot of demands,* and ungrateful.

   demanding

8. After eating a whole pizza, *two milk shakes,* and sampling a bag of chips, Ernest was still hungry.

   drinking two milk shakes

9. As soon as she gets up, she starts the coffee machine, turns on the radio, and *a frozen waffle is put into the toaster.*

   puts a frozen waffle into the toaster

10. The boss told Vern that he had only two options: to work harder or *leaving the company.*

    to leave the company

Practice 2

Complete the following statements. The first two parts of each statement are parallel in form; the part that you add should be parallel in form as well.

Example   Three things I like about myself are my sense of humor, my thought-

fulness, and *my self-discipline.*
_____

Answers will vary.

1. The movie was terrible: the scenery was fake, the plot was ridiculous, and

_____

2. My New Year's resolutions were to lose weight, to stop smoking, and

_____

3. The people in the long checkout line flipped through magazines, stared at the

cashier, or _____

4. During my first day as a waitress, I learned how to fold napkins, how to use

the coffee machine, and _____

5. My best friend is honest, dependable, and _____

Collaborative Activity

Part A: Editing and Rewriting

Working with a partner, read carefully the short paragraph below and mark the five instances of faulty parallelism. Then use the space provided to correct the instances of faulty parallelism. Feel free to discuss the rewrite quietly with your partner and refer back to the chapter when necessary.

¹For the 10 percent of the American population that is left-handed,
writing
life is not easy. ²Using a pair of scissors or ~~to write~~ in a spiral notebook

can be very difficult. ³The scissors and the notebook are two items

designed for right-handers. ⁴Also, have you ever seen a "southpaw"
write
take notes or ~~writing~~ an exam at one of those right-handed half-desks?

Continued

[delete]

⁵The poor "lefty" has to twist like a yoga devotee or ~~in the style of~~ a

circus acrobat in order to reach the paper. ⁶But a recent study proves

that being left-handed can be psychologically damaging as well as ~~tax~~

physically taxing.

~~a person physically.~~ ⁷A survey of 2,300 people showed that 20 percent

more left-handers than right-handers smoked. ⁸Perhaps left-handed

to forget

people smoke to relieve the tension or ~~they are forgetting~~ the

problems of living in a right-handed world.

_____

_____

_____

_____

_____

_____

_____

_____

_____

_____

_____

_____

_____

_____

_____

_____

Continued

Part B: Creating Sentences

Working with a partner, make up your own short test on faulty parallelism, as directed.

Answers will vary.

1. Write a sentence that includes three things you want to do tomorrow. One of those things should not be in parallel form. Then correct the faulty parallelism.

   Nonparallel _____

   _____

   Parallel _____

   _____

2. Write a sentence that names three positive or three negative qualities of a person you know.

   Nonparallel _____

   _____

   Parallel _____

   _____

3. Write a sentence that includes three everyday things that annoy you.

   Nonparallel _____

   _____

   Parallel _____

   _____

Reflective Activity

Answers will vary.

1. Look at the paragraph that you revised above. How does parallel form improve the paragraph?

2. How would you evaluate your use of parallel form in your writing? Do you use it almost never, at times, or often? How would you benefit from using it more?

■ **Review Test 1**

Cross out the unbalanced part of each sentence. Then rewrite the unbalanced part so that it matches the other item or items in the sentence.

Example   I enjoy watering the grass and ~~to work~~ in the garden.

working

1. The traffic cop blew his whistle, ~~was waving his hands,~~ and nodded to the driver to start moving.

   waved his hands

2. Mike's letter of application was smudged, improperly spaced, and ~~it had wrinkles.~~

   wrinkled

3. Kendra spoke vividly and ~~with force~~ at the student government meeting.

   forcefully

4. I like Mariah Carey; ~~Whitney Houston is preferred by my sister.~~

   my sister prefers Whitney Houston

5. Darkening skies, ~~branches that were waving,~~ and scurrying animals signaled the approaching storm.

   waving branches

6. The pitcher wiped his brow, straightened his cap, and ~~he was tugging at his sleeve.~~

   tugged at his sleeve

7. The driving instructor told me to keep my hands on the wheel, to drive defensively, and ~~the use of caution at all times.~~

   to use caution at all times

8. The customer made choking noises, turned red, and ~~was pointing to his throat~~.

   pointed to his throat

9. My sister eats spaghetti without sauce, cereal without milk, and ~~doesn't put mustard on hot dogs.~~

   hot dogs without mustard

10. The scratches on my car's hood were caused by rocks hitting it, ~~people who sat on it,~~ and cats jumping on it.

    people sitting on it

■ Review Test 2

Answers will vary.
On separate paper, write five sentences of your own that use parallel structure. Each sentence should contain three items in a series. Do not use the same format for each sentence.

■ Review Test 3

There are six nonparallel parts in the following passage. The first is corrected for you as an example. Underline and correct the other five.

Consumers have several sources of information they can use in the never-ending war against poor services and <u>merchandise that is shoddy.</u> For one thing, consumers can take advantage of the Better Business Bureau. If you plan to contract the Fly-By-Night Company to paint your house or <u>the replacement of siding,</u> you should first phone your local Better Business Bureau to learn about any complaints against that company. Second, consumers can refer to helpful information available from the U.S. Government Printing Office. You can learn, for instance, how to buy a house, <u>shopping for health insurance,</u> or protect yourself from auto repair rip-offs. Finally, careful buyers can turn to *Consumer Reports,* an independent magazine <u>and one which is nonprofit</u> that tests and rates a wide range of consumer products. For example, if you are thinking about buying a certain car, *Consumer Reports* will give you information on its comfort level, safety features, fuel economy, and <u>record for repair.</u> If consumers remember to look before they leap and <u>are taking</u> advantage of the above sources of information, they are more likely to get a fair return on their hard-earned dollars.

1. *shoddy merchandise*
2. *replace your siding*
3. *shop for health insurance*
4. *an independent nonprofit magazine*
5. *repair record*
6. *to take*

19 Sentence Variety II

Like Chapter 7, this chapter will show you several ways to write effective and varied sentences. You will increase your sense of the many ways available to you for expressing your ideas. The practices here will also reinforce much of what you have learned in this section about modifiers and the use of parallelism.

-ing Word Groups

Use an *-ing* word group at some point in a sentence. Here are examples:

The doctor, *hoping* for the best, examined the x-rays.

Jogging every day, I soon raised my energy level.

More information about *-ing* words, also known as *present participles,* appears on page 190.

Practice 1

Combine each pair of sentences below into one sentence by using an *-ing* word and omitting repeated words. Use a comma or commas to set off the *-ing* word group from the rest of the sentence.

Example   • The diesel truck chugged up the hill.
          • It spewed out smoke.

Spewing out smoke, the diesel truck chugged up the hill.

or   *The diesel truck, spewing out smoke, chugged up the hill.*

Answers will vary.

1. • The sparrow tried to keep warm.
   • It fluffed out its feathers.

Fluffing out its feathers, the sparrow tried to keep warm.

_____

2. • I managed to get enough toothpaste on my brush.
   • I squeezed the tube as hard as I could.

Squeezing the tube as hard as I could, I managed to get enough

toothpaste on my brush.

3. • The janitor started up the enormous boiler.
   • He checked the glass-faced gauges.

Checking the glass-faced gauges, the janitor started up the enormous

boiler.

4. • The runner set his feet into the starting blocks.
   • He stared straight ahead.

Staring straight ahead, the runner set his feet into the starting

blocks.

5. • The produce clerk cheerfully weighed bags of fruit and vegetables.
   • He chatted with each customer.

The produce clerk, chatting with each customer, cheerfully weighed

bags of fruit and vegtables.

Practice 2

Answers will vary.
On separate paper, write five sentences of your own that contain *-ing* word groups.

-ed Word Groups

Use an *-ed* word group at some point in a sentence. Here are examples:

> *Tired* of studying, I took a short break.
>
> Mary, *amused* by the joke, told it to a friend.
>
> I opened my eyes wide, *shocked* by the red "F" on my paper.

More information about *-ed* words, also known as *past participles,* appears on page 190.

Practice 1

Combine each of the following pairs of sentences into one sentence by using an *-ed* word and omitting repeated words. Use a comma or commas to set off the *-ed* word group from the rest of the sentence.

Example • Tim woke up with a start.
         • He was troubled by a dream.

Troubled by a dream, Tim woke up with a start.

or *Tim, troubled by a dream, woke up with a start.*

Answers may vary.

1. • I dozed off.
   • I was bored with the talk show.

   Bored with the talk show, I dozed off.

2. • The old dollar bill felt like tissue paper.
   • It was crinkled with age.

   Crinkled with age, the old dollar bill felt like tissue paper.

3. • The students acted nervous and edgy.
   • They were crowded into a tiny, windowless room.

   Crowded into a tiny, windowless room, the students acted nervous and

   edgy.

4. • I waited for someone to open the door.
   • I was loaded down with heavy bags of groceries.

   Loaded down with heavy bags of groceries, I waited for someone to

   open the door.

5. • Ron bought a green-striped suit.
   • He was tired of his conservative wardrobe.

   Tired of his conservative wardrobe, Ron bought a green-striped suit.

   _____

Practice 2

Answers will vary.
On separate paper, write five sentences of your own that contain -*ed* word groups.

-*ly* Openers

Use an -*ly* word to open a sentence. Here are examples:

Gently, he mixed the chemicals together.

Anxiously, the contestant looked at the game clock.

Skillfully, the quarterback rifled a pass to his receiver.

More information about -*ly* words, which are also known as *adverbs,* appears on page 221.

Practice 1

Combine each of the following pairs of sentences into one sentence by starting with an -*ly* word and omitting repeated words. Place a comma after the opening -*ly* word.

Example   • I gave several yanks to the starting cord of the lawn mower.
           • I was angry.

           Angrily, I gave several yanks to the starting cord of the lawn

           mower.

1. • Clarissa hung up on the telemarketer.
   • She was abrupt.

   Abruptly, Clarissa hung up on the telemarketer.

   _____

2. • The thief slipped one of the watches into her coat sleeve.
    • She was casual.

    Casually, the thief slipped one of the watches into her coat sleeve.

    _____

3. • I tugged on my shoes and pants as the doorbell rang.
    • I was swift.

    Swiftly, I tugged on my shoes and pants as the doorbell rang.

    _____

4. • The defense lawyer cross-examined the witnesses.
    • He was gruff.

    Gruffly, the defense lawyer cross-examined the witnesses.

    _____

5. • Estelle poked the corner of a handkerchief into her eye.
    • She was careful.

    Carefully, Estelle poked the corner of a handkerchief into her eye.

    _____

Practice 2
Answers will vary.
On separate paper, write five sentences of your own that begin with *-ly* words.

To Openers

Use a *to* word group to open a sentence. Here are examples.

To succeed in that course, you must attend every class.

To help me sleep better, I learned to quiet my mind through meditation.

To get good seats, we went to the game early.

The *to* in such a group is also known as an *infinitive,* as explained on page 190.

Practice 1

Combine each of the following pairs of sentences into one sentence by starting with a *to* word group and omitting repeated words. Use a comma after the opening *to* word group.

Example • I fertilize the grass every spring.
         • I want to make it greener.

To make the grass greener, I fertilize it every spring.

1. • We set bricks on the ends of the picnic table.
   • We did this to anchor the flapping tablecloth.

   To anchor the flapping tablecloth, we set bricks on the ends of the

   picnic table.

2. • Darryl scraped the windshield with a plastic credit card.
   • He did this to break up the coating of ice.

   To break up the coating of ice, Darryl scraped the windshield with a

   plastic credit card.

3. • We gave our opponents a ten-point advantage.
   • We wanted to make the basketball game more even.

   To make the basketball game more even, we gave our opponents a

   ten-point advantage.

4. • I offered to drive the next five hundred miles.
   • I wanted to give my wife a rest.

   To give my wife a rest, I offered to drive the next five hundred miles.

5. • Fran added Hamburger Helper to the ground beef.
   • She did this to feed the unexpected guests.

   To feed the unexpected guests, Fran added Hamburger Helper to the

   ground beef.

Practice 2

Answers will vary.
On separate paper, write five sentences of your own that begin with *to* word groups.

Prepositional Phrase Openers

Use prepositional phrase openers. Here are examples:

From the beginning, I disliked my boss.

In spite of her work, she failed the course.

After the game, we went to a movie.

Prepositional phrases include words like *in, from, of, at, by,* and *with.* A full list is on page 93.

Practice 1

Combine each of the following groups of sentences into one sentence, omitting repeated words. Start each sentence with a suitable prepositional phrase and put the other prepositional phrases in places that sound right. Generally, you should use a comma after the opening prepositional phrase.

Example
- A fire started.
- It did this at 5 A.M.
- It did this inside the garage.

At 5 A.M., a fire started inside the garage.

1.
- The old man wrote down my address.
- He did this on the bus.
- He did this with a stubby pencil.

On the bus, the old man wrote down my address with a stubby pencil.

2.
- Special bulletins interrupted regular programs.
- They did this during the day.
- The bulletins were about the election returns.

During the day, special bulletins about the election returns interrupted regular programs.

3.
- My clock radio turned itself on.
- It did this at 6:00 A.M.
- It did this with a loud blast.
- The loud blast was of rock music.

At 6:00 A.M., my clock radio turned itself on with a loud blast of rock music.

4. • The security guard looked.
   • He did this at the concert.
   • He did this in Sue's pocketbook.
   • He did this for concealed bottles.

   At the concert, the security guard looked in Sue's pocketbook for

   concealed bottles.

5. • A plodding turtle crawled.
   • It did this on the highway.
   • It did this toward the grassy shoulder of the road.

   On the highway, a plodding turtle crawled toward the grassy shoulder

   of the road.

Note: Other combinations are, of course, possible.

Practice 2

Answers will vary.
On separate paper, write five sentences of your own, each beginning with a prepositional phrase and containing at least one other prepositional phrase.

Series of Items

Use a series of items. Following are two of the many items that can be used in a series: adjectives and verbs.

Adjectives in Series

Adjectives are descriptive words. Here are examples:

The *husky young* man sanded the *chipped, weather-worn* paint off the fence.

Husky and *young* are adjectives that describe *man; chipped* and *weather-worn* are adjectives that describe *paint.* More information about adjectives appears on page 219.

Practice 1

Combine each of the following groups of sentences into one sentence by using adjectives in a series and omitting repeated words. Use a comma between adjectives only when *and* inserted between them sounds natural.

Example • I sewed a set of buttons onto my coat.
• The buttons were shiny.
• The buttons were black.
• The coat was old.
• The coat was green.

I sewed a set of shiny black buttons onto my old green coat.

1. • The child gazed at the gift box.
• The child was impatient.
• The child was excited.
• The gift box was large.
• The gift box was mysterious.

Impatient and excited, the child gazed at the large, mysterious gift box.

2. • Juice spurted out of the caterpillar.
• The juice was sticky.
• The caterpillar was fuzzy.
• The caterpillar was crushed.

Sticky juice squirted out of the fuzzy crushed caterpillar.

3. • The car dangled from the crane.
• The car was battered.
• The crane was gigantic.
• The crane was yellow.

The battered car dangled from the gigantic yellow crane.

4. • Patty squeezed her feet into the shoes.
• Patty's feet were swollen.
• Patty's feet were tender.
• Patty's feet were sunburned.
• The shoes were tight.

Patty squeezed her swollen, tender, sunburned feet into the tight shoes.

5. • The cook flipped the hamburgers on the grill.
   • The cook was tall.
   • The cook was white-aproned.
   • The hamburgers were thick.
   • The hamburgers were juicy.
   • The grill was grooved.
   • The grill was metal.

     The tall white-aproned cook flipped the thick, juicy hamburgers on the

     grooved metal grill.

Practice 2

Answers will vary.
On separate paper, write five sentences of your own that contain a series of adjectives.

Verbs in Series

Verbs are words that express action. Here are examples:

> In my job as a cook's helper, I *prepared* salads, *sliced* meat and cheese, and *made* all kinds of sandwiches.

Basic information about verbs appears on pages 90–91.

Practice 1

Combine each group of sentences below into one sentence by using verbs in a series and omitting repeated words. Use a comma between verbs in a series.

Examples • In the dingy bar Sam shelled peanuts.
         • He sipped a beer.
         • He talked up a storm with friends.

           In the dingy bar Sam shelled peanuts, sipped a beer, and talked

           up a storm with friends.

1. • The bank robber donned his gloves.
   • He twirled the lock.
   • He opened the door of the vault.

   The bank robber donned his gloves, twirled the lock, and opened the

   door of the vault.

2. • Fans at the rock concert popped balloons.
   • They set off firecrackers.
   • They dropped bottles from the balcony.

   Fans at the rock concert popped balloons, set off firecrackers, and

   dropped bottles from the balcony.

3. • The doctor slid the needle into Gordon's arm.
   • She missed the vein.
   • She tried again.

   The doctor slid the needle into Gordon's arm, missed the vein, and

   tried again.

4. • The magician walked over hot coals.
   • He lay on a bed of nails.
   • He stuck pins into his hands.

   The magician walked over hot coals, lay on a bed of nails, and stuck

   pins into his hands.

5. • The journalists surrounded the president.
   • They shouted questions.
   • They snapped pictures.

   The journalists surrounded the president, shouted questions, and

   snapped pictures.

Practice 2
Answers will vary.
On separate paper, write five sentences of your own that use verbs in a series.

Note   The section on faulty parallelism (pages 237–244) gives you practice in some of the other kinds of items that can be used in a series.

■   **Review Test 1**

Combine each group of short sentences into one sentence. Various combinations are possible. Choose the combination that reads most smoothly and clearly and that sounds most appropriate in the context of surrounding sentences.

Note   In combining short sentences into one sentence, omit repeated words where necessary. Use separate paper.

English Class

Possible answers:

- The teacher said, "Name three famous poets."
- She was looking at John.

<u>Looking</u> at John, the teacher said, "Name three famous poets."

- The teacher repeated the question when John didn't answer.
- She did this in an encouraging voice.

<u>In</u> an encouraging voice, the teacher repeated the question when John didn't answer.

- John sat up straight.
- He did this quickly.
- John named Shakespeare and Frost.
- He couldn't name a third poet.

John <u>quickly</u> sat up straight <u>and</u> named Shakespeare and Frost, <u>but</u> he couldn't name a third poet.

- The teacher was feeling sorry for John.
- The teacher decided to give him a hint.

<u>Feeling</u> sorry for John, the teacher decided to give him a hint.

- She was smiling warmly.
- She asked, "What's taking you so long, fellow?"

<u>Smiling</u> warmly, she asked, "What's taking you so long, fellow?"

- Many long seconds passed, and then John blurted, "Longfellow."
- John was happy.

Many long seconds passed, and then John <u>happily</u> blurted, "Longfellow."

- John heard the other students laughing.
- The students were behind him.
- The laughing was loud.

John heard the other students laughing <u>loudly</u> behind him.

- One student called out, "What took you so long, fellow?"
- The student did so in a teasing tone.

In a teasing tone, one student called out, "What took you so long, fellow?"

- John realized why everyone was laughing.
- He was embarrassed.

John, embarrassed, realized why everyone was laughing.

- But John joined in the laughter.
- He had a good sense of humor.

But, having a good sense of humor, John joined in the laughter.

■ ## Review Test 2

Combine each group of short sentences into one sentence. Various combinations are possible. Choose the combination that reads most smoothly and clearly and that sounds most appropriate in the context of surrounding sentences.

Note   In combining short sentences into one sentence, omit repeated words where necessary. Use separate paper.

Practical Joker

- My brother Mark was handing me what looked like a kaleidoscope.
- Mark is my older brother.
- He said to me, "Twist this tube and watch the patterns of glass."

Possible answers:

Handing me what looked like a kaleidoscope, my older brother Mark said to me, "Twist this tube and watch the patterns of glass."

- I twisted the tube.
- I said that I couldn't see anything.

Twisting the tube, I said that I couldn't see anything.

- Mark said, "You must be blind."
- As he said this, he was laughing loudly.

Laughing loudly, Mark said, "You must be blind."

- I knew that Mark was a practical joker.
- I looked in a mirror.
- I saw a black ring around my right eye.

Knowing that Mark was a practical joker, I looked in a mirror and saw a black ring around my right eye.

- However, Mark outsmarted himself.
- He did this on one Sunday evening.
- It was an evening when I took a shower to be ready for school the next day.

<u>On</u> one Sunday evening <u>when</u> I took a shower to be ready for school the next day, however, Mark outsmarted himself.

- Mark had unscrewed the showerhead.
- He had poured in a packet of dye.
- He replaced the showerhead.
- He waited for his victim to take a shower.

Mark had <u>unscrewed</u> the shower-head, <u>poured</u> in a packet of dye, <u>replaced</u> the showerhead, <u>and</u> <u>waited</u> for his victim to take a shower.

- While Mark was in the kitchen, my father headed for the bathroom.
- This was unfortunate.
- My father was wearing his robe.
- His robe was red-and-white striped.

<u>Unfortunately</u>, while Mark was in the kitchen, my father headed for the bathroom <u>wearing</u> his <u>red-and-white-striped</u> robe.

- Soon, a shout pierced the bathroom walls.
- The shout was deafening.
- The shout was angry.

Soon, an <u>angry</u>, <u>deafening</u> shout pierced the bathroom walls.

- My father burst through the door.
- He was splattered in navy blue.

My father, <u>splattered in navy blue</u>, burst through the door.

- Mark did the sensible thing.
- Mark took off through the back door.
- He ran till he was out of sight.
- He didn't return until my father cooled off.

<u>Doing</u> the sensible thing, Mark <u>took</u> <u>off</u> through the back door, <u>ran</u> till he was out of sight, <u>and</u> <u>didn't return</u> until my father cooled off.

20 Paper Format

Introductory Project

Which of the paper openings below seems clearer and easier to read?

✓*A*

	Finding Faces
	It takes just a little imagination to find faces in the
	objects around you. For instance, clouds are sometimes
	shaped like faces. If you lie on the ground on a partly

B

	"finding faces"
	It takes just a little imagination to find faces in the objects
	around you. For instance, clouds are sometimes shaped like
	faces. If you lie on the ground on a partly cloudy day, chan-
	ces are you will be able to spot many well-known faces

What are three reasons for your choice?

In "A," the title is capitalized and centered and has no quotation marks

around it; there is a blank line between the title and the body of the

paragraph; the first line is indented; there are left and right margins

around the body of the paper; no words are incorrectly hyphenated.

Answers are on page 577.

Guidelines for Preparing a Paper

Here are guidelines to follow in preparing a paper for an instructor.

1 Use full-size theme or typewriter paper, 8½ by 11 inches.

2 Leave wide margins (1 to 1½ inches) all around the paper. In particular, do not crowd the right-hand or bottom margin. This white space makes your paper more readable; also, the instructor has room for comments.

3 If you write by hand:

- Use a pen with blue or black ink (*not* a pencil).
- Be careful not to overlap letters and not to make decorative loops on letters.
- On narrow-ruled paper, write on every other line.
- Make all your letters distinct. Pay special attention to *a, e, i, o,* and *u*— five letters that people sometimes write illegibly.

4 Center the title of your paper on the first line of the first page. Do not put quotation marks around the title. Do not underline the title. Capitalize all the major words in a title, including the first word. Short connecting words within a title, such as *of, for, the, in,* and *to,* are not capitalized.

5 Skip a line between the title and the first line of your text. Indent the first line of each paragraph about five spaces (half an inch) from the left-hand margin.

6 Make commas, periods, and other punctuation marks firm and clear. Leave a slight space after each period. When you type, leave a double space after a period.

7 If you break a word at the end of a line, break only between syllables (see page 332). Do not break words of one syllable.

8 Put your name, date, and course number where your instructor asks for them.

Remember these points about the title and the first sentence of your paper.

9 The title should be several words that tell what the paper is about. It should usually *not* be a complete sentence. For example, if you are writing a paper about your jealous sister, the title could simply be: My Jealous Sister.

10 Do not rely on the title to help explain the first sentence of your paper. The first sentence must be independent of the title. For instance, if the title of your paper is the one shown above, the first sentence should *not* be, "She has been this way as long as I can remember." Rather, the first sentence might be, "My sister has always been a jealous person."

Practice 1

Identify the mistakes in format in the following lines from a student theme. Explain the mistakes in the spaces provided. One mistake is described for you as an example.

	"Too small to fight back"
	Until I was ten years old, I was at the mercy of my
	parents. Because they were bigger than I was, they cou-
	ld decide when we were going out, where we were going,
	and how long it would take to get there. I especially hated
	the long weekend trips that we would take even during

1. Do not break words of one syllable (could).
2. Do not use quotation marks around the title.
3. Capitalize the major words in the title (Too Small to Fight Back).
4. Skip a line between the title and the first line of the paper.
5. Indent the first line of the paper.
6. Keep margins on both sides of the paper.

Practice 2

As already stated, a title should tell in several words what a paper is about. Often a title can be based on the sentence that expresses the main idea of a paper.

Following are five main-idea sentences from student papers. Write a suitable and specific title for each paper, basing the title on the main idea.

Example   Title: _Aging Americans as Outcasts_
            Our society treats aging Americans as outcasts in many ways.

Answers will vary. Some possible titles are shown.

1. Title: _My First-Grade Teacher_
   I will never forget my first-grade teacher.
2. Title: _My Hardest Year_
   The first year of college was the hardest year of my life.

3. Title: <u>My Father's Sense of Humor</u>

My father has a wonderful sense of humor.

4. Title: <u>Ways to Conserve Energy</u>

There are several ways that Americans could conserve energy.

5. Title: <u>Violence in the Movies</u>

In the past few years I have become concerned about the amount of violence in movies.

Practice 3

In four of the five following sentences, the writer has mistakenly used the title to help explain the first sentence. But as has already been stated, you must *not* rely on the title to help explain your first sentence.

Rewrite the sentences so that they stand independent of the title. Write *Correct* under the one sentence that is independent of the title.

Example   Title: Flunking an Exam

First sentence: I managed to do this because of several bad habits.

Rewritten: <u>I managed to flunk an exam because of several bad</u>

<u>habits.</u>

1. Title: Lack of Communication

First sentence: This is often the reason why a relationship comes to an end.

Rewritten: <u>Lack of communication is often the reason why a relationship</u>

<u>comes to an end.</u>

2. Title: Educational TV Programs

First sentence: They are in trouble today for several reasons.

Rewritten: <u>Educational TV programs are in trouble today for several</u>

<u>reasons.</u>

3. Title: My First Day of College

First sentence: My first day of college was the most frustrating day of my life.

Rewritten: <u>Correct</u>

_____

4. Title: The Worst Vacation I Ever Had
   First sentence: It began when my brother suggested that we rent a large van and drive to Colorado.
   Rewritten: <u>The worst vacation I ever had began when my brother suggested that we rent a large van and drive to Colorado.</u>

5. Title: Professional Athletes
   First sentence: Most of them have been pampered since grade school days.
   Rewritten: <u>Most professional athletes have been pampered since grade school days.</u>

■ Review Test

Use the space provided below to rewrite the following sentences from a student paper, correcting the mistakes in format.

	"my first Blind Date"
	It is an occasion I will not easily forget. I was only thirt-
	een and had not gone out very much at all, but since I was
	so young, it hardly mattered. Then, one day, my mother
	came back from her appointment at the hairdresser's, smiling
	from ear to ear. She informed me that I was going out on

	My First Blind Date
	My first blind date is an occasion I will not easily forget.
	I was only thirteen and had not gone out very much at all,
	but since I was so young, it hardly mattered. Then one
	day, my mother came back from her appointment at the
	hairdresser's, smiling from ear to ear. She informed me that

21 Capital Letters

Introductory Activity

You probably know a good deal about the uses of capital letters. Answering the questions below will help you check your knowledge.

Answers will vary for 1–13.

1. Write the full name of a good friend: _____

2. In what city and state were you born? _____

3. What is your present street address? _____

4. Name a country where you would like to travel: _____

5. Name a school that you attended: _____

6. Give the name of a store where you buy food: _____

7. Name a company where you or anyone you know works:

   _____

8. Which day of the week gives you the best chance to relax? _____

9. What holiday is your favorite? _____

10. Which brand of toothpaste do you use? _____

11. Give the brand name of candy or chewing gum you like: _____

12. Name a song or a television show you enjoy: _____

13. Write the title of a magazine or newspaper you read:

    _____

Items 14–16 Three capital letters are needed in the example below. Underline the words you think should be capitalized. Then write them, capitalized, in the spaces provided.

on Super Bowl Sunday, my roommate said, "let's buy some snacks and invite a few friends over to watch the game." i knew my plans to write a term paper would have to be changed.

14. _____On_____   15. _____Let's_____   16. _____I_____

Answers are on page 577.

Main Uses of Capital Letters

25.1

Capital letters are used with:

1 First word in a sentence or direct quotation

2 Names of persons and the word *I*

3 Names of particular places

4 Names of days of the week, months, and holidays

5 Names of commercial products

6 Titles of books, magazines, articles, films, television shows, songs, poems, stories, papers that you write, and the like

7 Names of companies, associations, unions, clubs, religious and political groups, and other organizations

Each use is illustrated on the pages that follow.

First Word in a Sentence or Direct Quotation

Our company has begun laying people off.

The doctor said, "This may hurt a bit."

"My husband," said Sheryl, "is a light eater. When it's light, he starts to eat."

Note   In the third example above, *My* and *When* are capitalized because they start new sentences. But *is* is not capitalized, because it is part of the first sentence.

Names of Persons and the Word *I*

At the picnic, I met Tony Curry and Lola Morrison.

Names of Particular Places

After graduating from Gibbs High School in Houston, I worked for a summer at a nearby Holiday Inn on Clairmont Boulevard.

But   Use small letters if the specific name of a place is not given.

After graduating from high school in my hometown, I worked for a summer at a nearby hotel on one of the main shopping streets.

Names of Days of the Week, Months, and Holidays

This year, Memorial Day falls on the last Thursday in May.

But   Use small letters for the seasons—summer, fall, winter, spring.

In the early summer and fall, my hay fever bothers me.

Names of Commercial Products

The consumer magazine gave high ratings to Cheerios breakfast cereal, Breyer's ice cream, and Progresso chicken noodle soup.

But   Use small letters for the *type* of product (breakfast cereal, ice cream, chicken noodle soup, and the like).

Titles of Books, Magazines, Articles, Films, Television Shows, Songs, Poems, Stories, Papers That You Write, and the Like

My oral report was on *The Diary of a Young Girl,* by Anne Frank.
While watching *The Young and the Restless* on television, I thumbed through *Cosmopolitan* magazine and the *New York Times.*

Names of Companies, Associations, Unions, Clubs, Religious and Political Groups, and Other Organizations

A new bill before Congress is opposed by the National Rifle Association.

My wife is Jewish; I am Roman Catholic. We are both members of the Democratic Party.

My parents have life insurance with Prudential, auto insurance with Allstate, and medical insurance with Blue Cross and Blue Shield.

Practice

In the sentences that follow, cross out the words that need capitals. Then write the capitalized forms of the words in the space provided. The number of spaces tells you how many corrections to make in each case.

Example   Rhonda said, "~~why~~ should I bother to *eat* this ~~hershey~~ bar? I should just apply it directly to my hips."   _____Why_____   _____Hershey_____

1. My sister, a greeting card addict, sends cards on the ~~fourth~~ of ~~july~~ and ~~veterans' day~~.

   _____Fourth_____   _____July_____   _____Veterans'_____   _____Day_____

2. My lazy brother George said, "~~when~~ I get the urge to exercise, ~~I~~ lie down until it goes away."

   _____When_____   _____I_____

3. When Len's ~~toyota~~ ran out of gas on the ~~long island expressway~~, he hitched a ride to the nearest filling station.

   _____Toyota_____   _____Long_____   _____Island_____   _____Expressway_____

4. According to the latest issue of TV ~~guide~~, ~~sixty minutes~~ is still the most popular show in its time slot.

   _____Guide_____   _____Sixty_____   _____Minutes_____

5. Alberta opened an account at the First ~~national bank~~ in order to get the free ~~general electric~~ clock radio offered to new depositors.

   _____National_____   _____Bank_____   _____General_____   _____Electric_____

6. Teresa works part time at the ~~melrose diner~~ and takes courses at the Taylor ~~business institute~~.

   _____Melrose_____   _____Diner_____   _____Business_____   _____Institute_____

7. In a story by Ray Bradbury called "~~a sound~~ of ~~thunder~~," tourists of the future can travel back in time to observe living dinosaurs.

   _____A_____   _____Sound_____   _____Thunder_____

8. Stacy, whose ambition is to be a hairdresser, studies at the ~~pacific school~~ of ~~cosmetology~~.

   _____Pacific_____   _____School_____   _____Cosmetology_____

9. Last night there was a fire at the ~~sears~~ store on ~~ninth street~~.

   _____Sears_____   _____Ninth_____   _____Street_____

10. For breakfast, I mixed a glass of ~~tang~~ and fried some ~~swift's~~ bacon-flavored strips.

   _____Tang_____   _____Swift's_____

Other Uses of Capital Letters

Capital letters are also used with

1   Names that show family relationships
2   Titles of persons when used with their names
3   Specific school courses
4   Languages
5   Geographic locations
6   Historical periods and events
7   Races, nations, and nationalities
8   Opening and closing of a letter

Each use is illustrated on the pages that follow.

Names That Show Family Relationships

> Aunt Fern and Uncle Jack are selling their house.
> I asked Grandfather to start the fire.
> Is Mom feeling better?

But   Do not capitalize words like *mother, father, grandmother, grandfather, uncle, aunt,* and so on when they are preceded by *my* or another possessive word.

> My aunt and uncle are selling their house.
> I asked my grandfather to start the fire.
> Is my mom feeling better?

Titles of Persons When Used with Their Names

> I wrote an angry letter to Senator Blutt.
> Can you drive to Dr. Stein's office?
> We asked Professor Bushkin about his attendance policy.

But   Use small letters when titles appear by themselves, without specific names.

I wrote an angry letter to my senator.

Can you drive to the doctor's office?

We asked our professor about his attendance policy.

Specific School Courses

My courses this semester include Accounting I, Introduction to Data Processing, Business Law, General Psychology, and Basic Math.

But   Use small letters for general subject areas.

This semester I'm taking mostly business courses, but I have a psychology course and a math course as well.

Languages

Yasmin speaks English and Spanish equally well.

Geographic Locations

I lived in the South for many years and then moved to the West Coast.

But   Use small letters in giving directions.

Go south for about five miles and then bear west.

Historical Periods and Events

One essay question dealt with the Battle of the Bulge in World War II.

Races, Nations, Nationalities

The census form asked whether I was Caucasian, African American, Native American, Latino, or Asian.

Last summer I hitchhiked through Italy, France, and Germany.

The city is a melting pot for Koreans, Vietnamese, and Mexican Americans.

But   Use small letters when referring to *whites* or *blacks.*

Both whites and blacks supported our mayor in the election.

Opening and Closing of a Letter

Dear Sir: Sincerely yours,

Dear Madam: Truly yours,

Note   Capitalize only the first word in a closing.

Practice

Cross out the words that need capitals in the following sentences. Then write the capitalized forms of the words in the spaces provided. The number of spaces tells you how many corrections to make in each case.

1. Last year ~~uncle harry~~ had a hair transplant; the doctor inserted little plugs of real hair into his scalp.

   _____Uncle_____   _____Harry_____

2. Before school started this fall, my little boy begged for some new ~~bic~~ pens and a ~~snoopy~~ lunch box.

   _____Bic_____   _____Snoopy_____

3. I wrote to ~~congressman hughes~~ about my problem but received only a form letter in reply.

   _____Congressman_____   _____Hughes_____

4. A teenage ~~native~~ American girl guided the explorers Lewis and Clark on their journey to the ~~west coast.~~

   _____Native_____   _____West_____   _____Coast_____

5. I signed up for a course called ~~introduction~~ to ~~astronomy~~ after my original choice, ~~general biology,~~ closed out early.

   ___Introduction___   ___Astronomy___   ___General___   ___Biology___

Unnecessary Use of Capitals

Practice

Many errors in capitalization are caused by adding capitals where they are not needed. Cross out the incorrectly capitalized letters in the following sentences and write the correct forms in the spaces provided. The number of spaces tells you how many corrections to make in each sentence.

1. In our ~~High School~~, the vice-~~Principal~~ was in charge of ~~Discipline~~.

   _____high_____   _____school_____   _____principal_____   _____discipline_____

2. My ~~Father~~ settled in to watch his favorite *Twilight Zone* rerun, the one in which a man sitting in a plane sees a weird ~~Creature~~ out on the ~~Wing~~.

   _____father_____   _____creature_____   _____wing_____

3. A group called Project Bigfoot offers a thousand-dollar reward to anyone finding the ~~Skull~~, ~~Hair~~, or ~~Bones~~ of the legendary Bigfoot.

   _____skull_____   _____hair_____   _____bones_____

4. In Salt Lake City, Utah, there is a ~~Monument~~ to the sea gulls that saved the first ~~Settlers'~~ crops by eating a ~~Plague~~ of ~~Locusts~~.

   _____monument_____   _____settlers'_____   _____plague_____   _____locusts_____

5. "My brand-new ~~Motorcycle~~ was crushed by a ~~Tractor-Trailer~~ in the ~~Motel~~ parking lot," moaned Gene.

   _____motorcycle_____   _____tractor_____   _____trailer_____   _____motel_____

Collaborative Activity

Part A: Editing and Rewriting

Working with a partner, read the short paragraph that follows and mark the ten spots where capital letters are needed. Then use the space provided to rewrite the passage, adding the necessary capital letters. Feel free to discuss the rewrite quietly with your partner and refer back to the chapter when necessary.

Continued

¹Some seventh-graders in a ~~pittsburgh~~ *Pittsburgh* school have gone into the candy-making business. ²It all started one ~~january~~ *January* when a parent showed the children how to make chocolates. ³~~the~~ *The* first week, the children made 775 chocolate-covered pretzels and sold the entire batch. ⁴Then the ~~frick foundation~~ *Frick Foundation*, a charitable organization, donated $2,100. ⁵With this money, the students bought candy molds and began taking orders for $800 worth of ~~easter~~ *Easter* candy. ⁶They also produced red heart lollipops for Valentine's ~~day~~ *Day*. ⁷The children have even gotten good at packaging their products. ⁸They proudly tell their parents, "~~we~~ *We* are learning how to keep our own financial records!" ⁹They are now planning a line of candies for Christmas, to be delivered by their own Santa ~~claus~~ *Claus*. ¹⁰It is good to hear that one school in ~~america~~ *America* has experienced the sweet smell of success.

_____

_____

_____

_____

_____

_____

_____

_____

_____

_____

Continued

_____

_____

_____

_____

Part B: Creating Sentences

Working with a partner, write a sentence (or two) as directed. Pay special attention to capital letters.

Answers will vary.

1. Write about a place you like (or want) to visit. Be sure to include the name of the place, including the city, state, or country where it is located.

2. Write a sentence (or two) in which you state the name of your elementary school, your favorite teacher or subject, and your least favorite teacher or subject.

3. Write a sentence (or two) which mentions three brand-name products that you often use. You may begin the sentence with the words, "Three brand-name products I use every day are . . . "

4. Think of the name of your favorite musical artist or performer. Then write a sentence in which you include the musician's name and the title of one of his or her songs.

5. Write a sentence in which you describe something you plan to do two days from now. Be sure to include the date and day of the week in your sentence.

Reflective Activity

Answers will vary.

1. What would writing be like without capital letters? Use an example or two to help show how capital letters are important to writing.

2. What three uses of capital letters are most difficult for you to remember? Explain, giving examples.

■ Review Test 1

Cross out the words that need capitals in the following sentences. Then write the capitalized forms of the words in the spaces provided. The number of spaces tells you how many corrections to make in each sentence.

Example   During halftime of the ~~saturday~~ afternoon football game, my sister said, "~~let's~~ get some hamburgers from ~~wendy's~~ or put a pizza in the oven."

__Saturday__   __Let's__   __Wendy's__

1. Tracy put on a ~~johnny mathis~~ CD, and the outside world faded away.

   __Johnny__   __Mathis__

2. After ~~uncle~~ Bruce returned from his trip to ~~florida~~, he showed us endless slides of the ~~everglades~~ and ~~miami~~ Zoo.

   __Uncle__   __Florida__   __Everglades__   __Miami__

3. As ~~grandma~~ turned on the ~~wheel~~ of ~~fortune~~ show, we slipped out of the living room and began a serious game of ~~monopoly~~ in the den.

   __Grandma__   __Wheel__   __Fortune__   __Monopoly__

4. This ~~saint patrick's day~~, the local school band is going to march down ~~fifth avenue~~.

   __Saint__   __Patrick's__   __Day__   __Fifth__   __Avenue__

5. Jackie yelled, "~~you~~ kids have seen that episode of ~~star trek~~ at least fifteen times!"

   __You__   __Star__   __Trek__

6. Last spring, in my ~~introduction~~ to ~~anthropology~~ course, we had to start fires without using matches or flints.

   __Introduction__   __Anthropology__

7. After he watched the ~~miss america~~ contest on television, Norman dreamed that ~~miss texas~~ wanted to make him king for a day.

   __Miss__   __America__   __Miss__   __Texas__

8. In ~~namibia~~, a country in ~~africa~~, a small herd of elephants survives in an area where it hasn't rained for five years.

   __Namibia__   __Africa__

9. During our visit to the ~~west coast~~, we ate dinner on the *~~queen~~ Mary,* the old ~~british~~ luxury liner docked in Long Beach.

West	Coast	Queen	British

10. "Since last ~~september~~," said Dmitri, "~~i've~~ been repossessing cars for a collection agency. I've had to collect everything from a small ~~toyota~~ to a ~~rolls-royce~~."

September	I've	Toyota	Rolls	Royce

■ Review Test 2

On separate paper, write:

Answers will vary.

- Seven sentences demonstrating the seven main uses of capital letters.
- Eight sentences demonstrating the eight other uses of capital letters.

22 Numbers and Abbreviations

Introductory Activity

Write a check mark beside the item in each pair that you think uses numbers correctly.

I finished the exam by 8:55, but my grade was only 65 percent. __✓__

I finished the exam by eight-fifty-five, but my grade was only sixty-five percent. _____

9 people are in my biology lab, but there are 45 in my lecture group. _____

Nine people are in my biology lab, but there are forty-five in my lecture group. __✓__

Write a check mark beside the item in each pair that you think uses abbreviations correctly.

Both of my bros. were treated by Dr. Lewis after the mt. climbing accident. _____

Both of my brothers were treated by Dr. Lewis after the mountain climbing accident. __✓__

I spent two hrs. finishing my Eng. paper and handed it to my teacher, Ms. Peters, right at the deadline. _____

I spent two hours finishing my English paper and handed it to my teacher, Ms. Peters, right at the deadline. __✓__

Answers are on page 577.

Numbers

25.2

Rule 1 Spell out numbers that take no more than two words. Otherwise, use numerals—the numbers themselves.

> Last year Tina bought nine new records.
>
> Ray struck out fifteen batters in Sunday's softball game.

But

> Tina now has 114 records in her collection.
>
> Already this season Ray has recorded 168 strikeouts.

You should also spell out a number that begins a sentence:

> One hundred fifty first-graders throughout the city showed flu symptoms today.

Rule 2 Be consistent when you use a series of numbers. If some numbers in a sentence or paragraph require more than two words, then use numerals throughout the selection.

> This past spring, we planted 5 rhodos, 15 azaleas, 50 summersweet, and 120 myrtle around our house.

Rule 3 Use numbers to show dates, times, addresses, percentages, exact sums of money, and parts of a book.

> John Kennedy was killed on November 22, 1963.
>
> My job interview was set for 10:15. (*But:* Spell out numbers before *o'clock.* For example: The time was then changed to eleven o'clock.)
>
> Lee's new address is 118 North 35th Street.
>
> Almost 40 percent of my meals are eaten at fast-food restaurants.
>
> The cashier rang up a total of $18.35. (*But:* Round amounts may be expressed as words. For example: The movie has a five-dollar admission charge.)
>
> Read Chapter 6 in your math textbook and answer questions 1 to 5 on page 250.

Practice

Use the three rules to make the corrections needed in these sentences.

1. Vince's new girlfriend lives only *five* ~~5~~ blocks away from him.
2. My dog is *eight* ~~8~~ years old—that's *fifty-six* ~~56~~ in people years.
3. The box office opens at *10:30* ~~ten-thirty~~ in the morning.
4. However, some people have been waiting in line since *five* ~~5~~ o'clock.
5. About *65* ~~sixty-five~~ percent of the typical human body is water.
6. In order to speak one word, a human being uses *seventy-two* ~~72~~ muscles.
7. I liked the good old days when Lincoln's Birthday always fell on February *12* ~~twelfth~~.
8. At the firefighters' fund-raising breakfast, *600* ~~six hundred~~ sausages, 450 fried eggs, 900 pancakes, and *80* ~~eighty~~ packets of Alka-Seltzer were sold.
9. Two weeks after she died on November *3* ~~third~~, *1992* ~~nineteen-ninety-two~~, we heard that Mrs. Miller had left $2,500 to her pet canary.
10. My little brother got a notice from the library that his copy of *The* *Three* ~~3~~ *Musketeers* was *two* ~~2~~ weeks overdue.

Abbreviations

While abbreviations are a helpful time-saver in note-taking, you should avoid most abbreviations in formal writing. Listed below are some of the few abbreviations that can acceptably be used in compositions. Note that a period is used after most abbreviations.

1 Mr., Mrs., Ms., Jr., Sr., and Dr. when used with proper names:

   Mr. Rollin   Ms. Peters   Dr. Coleman

2 Time references:

   A.M., or A.M., or a.m.   P.M., or P.M., or p.m.   B.C., or B.C.; A.D. or A.D.

3 First or middle initial in a signature:

   T. Alan Parker   Linda M. Evans

4   Organizations, technical words, and trade names known primarily by their initials:

ABC   CIA   UNESCO   GM   AIDS   DNA

Practice

Cross out the words that should not be abbreviated and correct them in the spaces provided.

1. My mother can't go into a ~~dept.~~ store without making an impulse ~~purch.~~
   ___department___   ___purchase___

2. Driving along ~~Rt.~~ 90 in ~~Fla.~~, we saw armadillos along the roadside.
   ___Route___   ___Florida___

3. The fattest man who ever lived in ~~Amer.~~ weighed over nine hundred ~~lbs.~~ and was buried in a piano crate.
   ___America___   ___pounds___

4. This Swiss army knife has everything from a ~~pr.~~ of scissors to a six-~~in.~~ ruler.
   ___pair___   ___inch___

5. The first ~~appt.~~ my eye ~~dr.~~, Dr. C.I. Glass, could give me was for early next ~~mo.~~
   ___appointment___   ___doctor___   ___month___

6. After I study in the ~~lib.~~ for fifteen ~~min.~~, I get bored and open a ~~mag.~~
   ___library___   ___minutes___   ___magazine___

7. Only a ~~tsp.~~ of watery ~~Fr.~~ dressing was sprinkled over the limp lettuce salad.
   ___teaspoon___   ___French___

8. Mandy lost her ~~lic.~~ when she was arrested for ~~driv.~~ on the wrong side of the ~~rd.~~
   ___license___   ___driving___   ___road___

9. How can I be expected to ~~fin.~~ my ~~assign.~~ by 9 P.M. if there isn't one ball-~~pt.~~ pen in the house?
   ___finish___   ___assignment___   ___point___

10. The CBS Evening News suggested that if we don't approve of the new speed ~~lim.~~, we should let our state ~~sen.~~ or ~~rep.~~ know.
    ___limit___   ___senator___   ___representative___

■ **Review Test**

Cross out the mistake or mistakes in numbers and abbreviations and correct them in the spaces provided.

1. The Liberty Bell cracked several ~~yrs.~~ after the ~~Amer.~~ Revolution.

   _____years_____   _____American_____

2. The power failure happened at exactly ~~five-twenty~~ A.M. and lasted for almost ~~2~~ hours.

   _____5:20_____   _____two_____

3. I mailed my letter at the ~~p.o.~~ on Grant and Carter ~~Sts.~~

   _____post office_____   _____Streets_____

4. Little Juan's insect collection includes ~~seventeen~~ grasshoppers, ~~eight~~ moths, and 148 fireflies.

   _____17_____   _____8_____

5. I didn't have time to study for my ~~chem.~~ test because I had to study for my ~~Span.~~ final.

   _____chemistry_____   _____Spanish_____

6. I arrive at the Hartford ~~Ins.~~ ~~Build.~~ at ~~8~~ o'clock every morning.

   _____Insurance_____   _____Building_____   _____eight_____

7. How can I write a ~~3~~-page paper on a poem that's only ~~14~~ lines along?

   _____three_____   _____fourteen_____

8. Every ~~Mon.~~ morning I wake up wishing it were ~~Fri.~~

   _____Monday_____   _____Friday_____

9. Tom found a great bargain today—a wool jacket and ~~2~~ pairs of pants for ~~ninety dollars and ninety-nine cents.~~

   _____two_____   _____$90.99_____

10. This is the ~~3rd~~ time since New Year's that I've tried to lose ~~10 lbs.~~

   _____third_____   _____ten_____   _____pounds_____

23 End Marks

Introductory Activity

Add the end mark needed in each of the following sentences.

1. All week I have been feeling depressed.
2. What is the deadline for handing in the paper?
3. The man at the door wants to know whose car is double-parked.
4. That truck ahead of us is out of control!

Answers are on page 578.

A sentence always begins with a capital letter. It always ends with a period, a question mark, or an exclamation point.

Period (.)

23.1a

Use a period after a sentence that makes a statement.

More single parents are adopting children.
It has rained for most of the week.

Use a period after most abbreviations.

Mr. Sanchez   B.A.   Dr. Patel
Ms. Peters   A.M.   Tom Ricci, Jr.

Question Mark (?)

23.1b

Use a question mark after a *direct* question.

When is your paper due?
How is your cold?
Tom asked, "When are you leaving?"
"Why doesn't everyone take a break?" Lara suggested.

Do not use a question mark after an *indirect* question (a question not in the speaker's exact words).

She asked when the paper was due.
He asked how my cold was.
Tom asked when I was leaving.
Lara suggested that everyone take a break.

Exclamation Point (!)

ALLWRITE!
23.1d

Use an exclamation point after a word or sentence that expresses strong feeling.

Come here!

Ouch! This pizza is hot!

That truck just missed us!

Note   Be careful not to overuse exclamation points.

Practice

Add a period, a question mark, or an exclamation point, as needed, to each of the following sentences.

1. Why do shoelaces always snap when there are no spares in the house?
2. My father throws out most of his mail without even opening it.
3. Look out for the escaped tiger!
4. Is $47.50 your absolutely final offer for the lawn mower?
5. After working in the sun all day, Jerry felt as dry as a potato chip.
6. The ad read, "Do you want to be a millionaire without working?"
7. For a prank, the boys ran out of the water yelling, "Shark!"
8. Eduardo had the nerve to ask if my blond hair came out of a bottle.
9. While Marian was rinsing the dishes, her class ring fell down the drain.
10. "The end is near," said the wild-eyed man in the street as he passed out leaflets.

■ Review Test

Add a period, question mark, or exclamation point as needed to each of the following sentences.

1. Why do these mashed potatoes look green?

2. The group which donates the most blood wins free T-shirts.

3. Watch out so you don't step in that broken glass!

4. The artist throws buckets of paint at a huge canvas on the wall.

5. Did you know that Trina has a twin brother?

6. There's the man who stole my wallet!

7. The dinosaurs in that movie looked like overgrown lizards.

8. Have you read the new book by Stephen King?

9. All that remained after the car accident was a bloodstain.

10. Be careful not to run over that turtle on the highway!

24 Apostrophe

Introductory Activity

Look over carefully the three items below. Then see if you can answer the questions that follow each item.

1. the desk of the editor   =   the editor's desk

   the car of Giovanni   =   Giovanni's car

   the teeth of my cat   =   my cat's teeth

   the smile of the child   =   the child's smile

   the briefcase of my mother   =   my mother's briefcase

What is the purpose of the apostrophe in the examples above?

To show ownership or possession
_____

2. She is my best friend.   =   She's my best friend.

   I am afraid of snakes.   =   I'm afraid of snakes.

   Do not watch too much TV. =   Don't watch too much TV.

   They are a perfect match.   =   They're a perfect match.

   It is a terrible movie.   =   It's a terrible movie.

What is the purpose of the apostrophe in the examples above?

To indicate missing letters and shortened spellings
_____

3. Several families were affected by the flood. One family's car floated away and was found in a field more than a mile away.

Why does the apostrophe belong in the second sentence but not the first?

Because families signals a plural noun, while family's indicates ownership

or possession.

Answers are on page 578.

The two main uses of the apostrophe are

24.6

1   To show the omission of one or more letters in a contraction.

2   To show ownership or possession.

Each use is explained on the pages that follow.

Apostrophe in Contractions

A contraction is formed when two words are combined to make one word. An apostrophe is used to show where letters are omitted in forming the contraction. Here are two contractions:

> have + not = haven't (the *o* in *not* has been omitted)
>
>   I + will = I'll (the *wi* in *will* has been omitted)

The following are some other common contractions:

I + am	= I'm			it + is	= it's	
I + have	= I've			it + has	= it's	
I + had	= I'd			is + not	= isn't	
who + is	= who's			could + not	= couldn't	
do + not	= don't			I + would	= I'd	
did + not	= didn't			they + are	= they're	
let + us	= let's			there + is	= there's	

Note   The combination *will* + *not* has an unusual contraction: *won't*.

Practice 1

Combine the following words into contractions. One is done for you.

they + will	=	*they'll*	they + are	=	*they're*
should + not	=	*shouldn't*	can + not	=	*can't*
does + not	=	*doesn't*	who + is	=	*who's*
is + not	=	*isn't*	would + not	=	*wouldn't*
will + not	=	*won't*	are + not	=	*aren't*

Practice 2

Write the contraction for the words in parentheses.

Example   He (could not) _____couldn't_____ come.

1. When you hear the whistle blow, (you will) _____you'll_____ know (it is) _____it's_____ quitting time.

2. Because he (had not) _____hadn't_____ studied the owner's manual, he (could not) _____couldn't_____ figure out how to start the power mower.

3. There (is not) _____isn't_____ a rug in this house that (does not) _____doesn't_____ have stains on it.

4. (I am) _____I'm_____ fine in the morning if (I am) _____I'm_____ left alone.

5. (Where is) _____Where's_____ the idiot (who is) _____who's_____ responsible for leaving the front door wide open?

Note   Even though contractions are common in everyday speech and in written dialogue, usually it is best to avoid them in formal writing.

Practice 3
Answers will vary.
Write five sentences using the apostrophe in different contractions.

1. _____
2. _____
3. _____
4. _____
5. _____

Four Contractions to Note Carefully

Four contractions that deserve special attention are *they're, it's, you're,* and *who's.* Sometimes these contractions are confused with the possessive words *their, its, your,* and *whose.* The following chart shows the difference in meaning between the contractions and the possessive words.

Contractions	Possessive Words
they're (means *they are*)	their (means *belonging to them*)
it's (means *it is* or *it has*)	its (means *belonging to it*)
you're (means *you are*)	your (means *belonging to you*)
who's (means *who is*)	whose (means *belonging to whom*)

Note   Possessive words are explained further on page 291.

Practice

Underline the correct form (the contraction or the possessive word) in each of the following sentences. Use the contraction whenever the two words of the contraction (*they are, it is, you are, who is*) would also fit.

1. (It's, Its) the rare guest who knows when (it's, its) time to go home.

2. If (they're, their) going to bring (they're, their) vacation pictures, I'm leaving.

3. (You're, Your) a difficult kind of person because you always want (you're, your) own way.

4. I don't know (who's, whose) fault it was that the window got broken, but I know (who's, whose) going to pay for it.

5. Unless (it's, its) too much trouble, could you make it (you're, your) business to find out (who's, whose) been throwing garbage into my yard?

Apostrophe to Show Ownership or Possession

To show ownership or possession, we can use such words as *belongs to, owned by,* or (most commonly) *of.*

the knapsack *that belongs to* Lola

the grades *possessed by* Travis

the house *owned by* my mother

the sore arm *of* the pitcher

But the apostrophe plus *s* (if the word does not end in *-s*) is often the quickest and easiest way to show possession. Thus we can say:

Lola's knapsack
Travis's grades
my mother's house
the pitcher's sore arm

Points to Remember

1 The *'s* goes with the owner or possessor (in the examples given, *Lola, Travis, mother,* and *pitcher*). What follows is the person or thing possessed (in the examples given, *knapsack, grades, house,* and *sore arm*). An easy way to determine the owner or possessor is to ask the question "Who owns it?" In the first example, the answer to the question "Who owns the knapsack?" is *Lola*. Therefore, the *'s* goes with *Lola*.

2 In handwriting, there should always be a break between the word and the *'s*.

Lola's   not   Lola's
Yes   No

3 A singular word ending in *-s* (such as *Travis*) also shows possession by adding an apostrophe plus *s* (Travis's).

Practice 1

Rewrite the italicized part of each of the sentences below, using the *'s* to show possession. Remember that the *'s* goes with the owner or possessor.

Examples   *The motorcycle owned by Clyde* is a frightening machine.
                 Clyde's motorcycle

                 The roommate of my brother is a sweet and friendly person.
                 My brother's roommate

1. The *rifle of the assassin* failed to fire.
   The assassin's rifle

2. The playboy spent *the inheritance of his mother* within six months.
   his mother's inheritance

3. *The throat of Ali* tightened when the doorbell rang.
   Ali's throat

4. The new salesman took *the parking space of Sam.*
   Sam's parking space

5. *The hat of the chef* fell into the pea soup.
   The chef's hat

6. A big man wearing sunglasses stayed near *the wife of the president.*
   the president's wife

7. *The hand of the mugger* closed over the victim's mouth.
   The mugger's hand

8. The *briefcase of Harry* was still there, but the documents were gone.
   Harry's briefcase

9. *The shoulder bag of Sandy* had vanished from her locker.
   Sandy's shoulder bag

10. *The leash of the dog* was tangled around a fire hydrant.
    The dog's leash

Practice 2

Underline the word in each sentence that needs an ʼs. Then write the word correctly in the space at the left. One is done for you as an example.

ex-husband's   1. Julie is always upset after one of her <u>ex-husband</u> visits.

instructor's   2. My <u>instructor</u> worst habit is leaving her sentences unfinished.

astrologer's   3. The <u>astrologer</u> predictions were all wrong.

Ellen's   4. <u>Ellen</u> jeans were so tight that she had to lie flat in order to zip them.

lemonade's   5. The <u>lemonade</u> bitter flavor assaulted my taste buds.

sister's   6. My <u>sister</u> life is like a soap opera.

Brian's   7. <u>Brian</u> gold wedding band slid into the garbage disposal.

Nita's   8. <u>Nita</u> ten-year-old Volvo is still dependable.

Ted's   9. We didn't believe any of Uncle <u>Ted</u> stories.

hypnotist's 10. The <u>hypnotist</u> piercing eyes frightened Kelly.

Practice 3

Add an *'s* to each of the following words to make it the possessor or owner of something. Then write sentences using the words. Your sentences can be serious or playful. One is done for you as an example.

Sentences will vary.

1. Cary _____ *Cary's* _____

    Cary's hair is bright red. _____

2. friend _____ *friend's* _____

    _____

3. cashier _____ *cashier's* _____

    _____

4. teammate _____ *teammate's* _____

    _____

5. brother _____ *brother's* _____

    _____

Apostrophe versus Possessive Pronouns

Do not use an apostrophe with possessive pronouns. They already show ownership. Possessive pronouns include *his, hers, its, yours, ours,* and *theirs.*

Incorrect	*Correct*
The bookstore lost its' lease.	The bookstore lost its lease.
The racing bikes were theirs'.	The racing bikes were theirs.
The change is yours'.	The change is yours.
His' problems are ours', too.	His problems are ours, too.
His' skin is more tanned than hers'.	His skin is more tanned than hers.

Apostrophe versus Simple Plurals

When you want to make a word plural, just add an *s* at the end of the word. Do *not* add an apostrophe. For example, the plural of the word *movie* is *movies,* not *movie's* or *movies'.* Look at this sentence:

When Korie's cat began catching birds, the neighbors called the police.

The words *birds* and *neighbors* are simple plurals, meaning more than one bird, more than one neighbor. The plural is shown by adding *-s* only. (More information about plurals starts on page 342.) On the other hand, the *'s* after *Korie* shows possession—that Korie owns the cat.

Practice

In the spaces provided under each sentence, add the one apostrophe needed and explain why the other words ending in *s* are simple plurals.

Example   Originally, the cuffs of mens pants were meant for cigar ashes.

cuffs: *simple plural meaning more than one cuff*

mens: *men's, meaning "belonging to men"*

ashes: *simple plural meaning more than one ash*

1. Phil thinks that the diners hamburgers taste better than sirloin steaks.

diners: *diner's, meaning "the hamburgers of the diner"*

hamburgers: *simple plural meaning more than one hamburger*

steaks: *simple plural meaning more than one steak*

2. San Franciscos cable cars can go up hills at a sixty-degree angle.

San Franciscos: *San Francisco's, meaning "the cable cars of San Francisco"*

cars: *simple plural meaning more than one car*

hills: *simple plural meaning more than one hill*

3. My twelve-year-old brothers collection of baseball cards is in six shoe boxes.

brothers: *brother's, meaning "the collection of my brother"*

cards: *simple plural meaning more than one card*

boxes: *simple plural meaning more than one box*

4. Only women shaped like toothpicks look decent in this years fashions.

toothpicks: *simple plural meaning more than one toothpick*

years: *year's, meaning "the fashions of this year"*

fashions: *simple plural meaning more than one fashion*

5. Pedros blood pressure rose when he drove around the mall for twenty minutes and saw that there were no parking spaces.

Pedros: *Pedro's, meaning "the blood pressure of Pedro"*

minutes: *simple plural meaning more than one minute*

spaces: *simple plural meaning more than one space*

6. The write-ups of Rubys promotion made her coworkers jealous.

write-ups: *simple plural meaning more than one write-up*

Rubys: *Ruby's, meaning "the promotion of Ruby"*

coworkers: *simple plural meaning more than one coworker*

7. My sons backyard fort is made from pieces of scrap lumber, old nails, and spare roof shingles.

sons: *son's, meaning "the fort of my son"*

pieces: *simple plural meaning more than one piece*

nails: *simple plural meaning more than one nail*

shingles: *simple plural meaning more than one shingle*

8. The mayors double-talk had reporters scratching their heads and scribbling in their notebooks.

mayors: *mayor's, meaning "the double-talk of the mayor"*

reporters: *simple plural meaning more than one reporter*

heads: *simple plural meaning more than one head*

notebooks: *simple plural meaning more than one notebook*

9. Two cuts over the boxers left eye prompted the referee to stop the fight after six rounds.

cuts: *simple plural meaning more than one cut*

boxers: *boxer's, meaning "the left eye of the boxer"*

rounds: *simple plural meaning more than one round*

10. As rock music blared over the cafeterias loudspeakers, Theresa tried to study for her exams.

cafeterias: _cafeteria's, meaning "the loudspeakers of the cafeteria"_

loudspeakers: _simple plural meaning more than one loudspeaker_

exams: _simple plural meaning more than one exam_

Apostrophe with Plural Words Ending in -s

Plurals that end in -s show possession simply by adding the apostrophe, rather than an apostrophe plus s.

Both of my *neighbors'* homes have been burglarized recently.

The many *workers'* complaints were ignored by the company.

All the *campers'* tents were damaged by the hailstorm.

Practice

In each sentence, cross out the one plural word that needs an apostrophe. Then write the word correctly, with the apostrophe, in the space provided.

Example _bosses'_ My two ~~bosses~~ tempers are much the same: explosive.

stores' 1. Little Bobby wanted to look in all the mall ~~stores~~ windows.

friends' 2. Why are all my ~~friends~~ problems easier to solve than my own?

Cowboys' 3. Dad hopes that the Dallas ~~Cowboys~~ new quarterback will get them into the Super Bowl.

students' 4. The ~~students~~ insect collections were displayed in a glass case.

voters' 5. The poll showed that the ~~voters~~ wish was to replace all the politicians in office.

Collaborative Activity

Part A: Editing and Rewriting

Working with a partner, read carefully the short paragraph below. Then use the space provided to rewrite the paragraph, adding ten apostrophes where needed to indicate contractions and possessives. Feel free to discuss the rewrite quietly with your partner and refer back to the chapter when necessary.

¹If ~~youre~~ *you're* going to visit someone in the hospital, ~~dont~~ *don't* be gloomy. ²Other ~~peoples~~ *people's* problems ~~wont~~ *won't* help someone ~~whos~~ *who's* sick to feel better. ³But you ~~dont~~ *don't* have to limit yourself to "safe" topics like ~~todays~~ *today's* weather. ⁴You can even discuss the ~~patients~~ *patient's* condition, as long as neither of you gets upset. ⁵Also, ~~dont~~ *don't* stay too long. ⁶Patients are usually weak and ~~cant~~ *can't* talk for long periods. ⁷Leave before the patient gets tired.

_____

_____

_____

_____

_____

_____

_____

_____

_____

_____

_____

_____

Continued

Part B: Creating Sentences

Working with a partner, write sentences that use apostrophes as directed.
Answers will vary.

1. Write a sentence describing something a friend owns. For instance, you might mention a pet or a material possession.

   _____

2. Using an apostrophe to show a contraction, write a sentence about something at school or work that you feel is wrong and needs to be changed.

   _____

3. Write a sentence that correctly uses the word *teachers*. Then write a second sentence that correctly uses the word *teacher's*.

   _____

   _____

Reflective Activity
Answers will vary.

1. Look at the paragraph about the hospital visit that you revised above. How has adding apostrophes affected the reading of the paragraph?

2. Explain what it is about apostrophes that you find most difficult to remember and apply. Use an example to make your point clear.

■ Review Test 1

In each sentence cross out the two words that need apostrophes. Then write the words correctly in the spaces provided.

1. That ~~restaurants~~ menu ~~hasnt~~ changed its selections since ten years ago.

   _____restaurant's_____   _____hasn't_____

2. Steve ~~doesnt~~ begin writing his papers until the day before ~~theyre~~ due.

   _____doesn't_____   _____they're_____

3. My ~~fathers~~ habit is never to root for a team until he thinks ~~its~~ going to lose.

    __father's__   __it's__

4. The toddler knocked his ~~mothers~~ sewing box onto the floor; then, he dropped her calculator into the ~~dogs~~ water bowl.

    __mother's__   __dog's__

5. Part of ~~Colins~~ nursing training consists of a stint in the local ~~hospitals~~ trauma center.

    __Colin's__   __hospital's__

6. "~~Youre~~ daring someone to steal that camera if you carry it to the rock concert," warned ~~Tinas~~ dad.

    __You're__   __Tina's__

7. Ever since my sister passed her ~~drivers~~ test, she keeps asking for the keys to our ~~parents~~ car.

    __driver's__   __parents'__

8. The department store ~~wouldnt~~ exchange ~~Carols~~ birthday gift, since pierced earrings cannot be returned.

    __wouldn't__   __Carol's__

9. I use ~~Sids~~ dry-cleaning service because he will clean ~~anyones~~ American flag free.

    __Sid's__   __anyone's__

10. When little ~~Dannys~~ cut was being stitched up, he asked the doctor why he ~~didnt~~ use a sewing machine.

    __Danny's__   __didn't__

■ **Review Test 2**

Rewrite the following sentences, changing the underlined words into either (1) a contraction or (2) a possessive.

1. I wanted to buy the house of my uncle but could not get a mortgage.

    __my uncle's house__

    __couldn't__

2. The issue of this week of the *National Enquirer* features the diet of a Hollywood starlet on which she lost fifteen pounds in three days.

This week's issue

a Hollywood starlet's diet

3. The programs of next week always look better than what is on now.

Next week's programs

what's

4. The tires of the car are as smooth as the eggs of a hen.

The car's tires

hen's eggs

5. The voice of the instructor boomed in the ears of Marie as she sat in the front row.

The instructor's voice

Marie's ears

25 Quotation Marks

Introductory Activity

Read the following scene and underline all the words enclosed within quotation marks. Your instructor may also have you dramatize the scene, with one person reading the narration and three persons acting the speaking parts—Tray, Tina, and Mario. The two speakers should imagine the scene as part of a stage play and try to make their words seem as real and true-to-life as possible.

At a party that Tray and his wife Tina hosted recently, Tray got angry at a guy named Mario who kept bothering Tina. "Listen, man," Tray said, "what's this thing you have for my wife? There are lots of other women at this party."

"Relax," Mario replied. "Tina is very attractive, and I like talking with her."

"Listen, Mario," Tina said. "I've already told you three times that I don't want to talk to you anymore. Please leave me alone."

"Look, there's no law that says I can't talk to you if I want to," Mario challenged.

"Mario, I'm only going to say this once," Tray warned. "Lay off my wife, or leave this party *now.*"

Mario grinned at Tray smugly. "You've got good liquor here. Why should I leave? Besides, I'm not done talking with Tina."

Tray went to his basement and was back a minute later holding a two-by-four. "I'm giving you a choice," Tray said. "Leave by the door or I'll slam you out the window."

Mario left by the door.

1. On the basis of the above selection, what is the purpose of quotation marks?

   Quotation marks set off the exact words of a speaker.

2. Do commas and periods that come after a quotation go inside or outside the quotation marks?

   They go inside the quotation marks.

Answers are on page 579.

299

The two main uses of quotation marks are:

1   To set off the exact words of a speaker or writer
2   To set off the titles of short works

Each use is explained on the pages that follow.

Quotation Marks to Set Off the Words of a Speaker or Writer

Use quotation marks when you want to show the exact words of a speaker or writer:

> "Who left the cap off the toothpaste?" Lola demanded.
> (Quotation marks set off the exact words that Lola spoke.)
>
> Ben Franklin wrote, "Keep your eyes wide open before marriage, half shut afterward."
> (Quotation marks set off the exact words that Ben Franklin wrote.)
>
> "You're never too young," my Aunt Fern often tells me, "to have a heart attack."
> (Two pairs of quotation marks are used to enclose the aunt's exact words.)
>
> Maria complained, "I look so old some days. Even makeup doesn't help. I feel as though I'm painting a corpse!"
> (Note that the end quotes do not come until the end of Maria's speech. Place quotation marks before the first quoted word of a speech and after the last quoted word. As long as no interruption occurs in the speech, do not use quotation marks for each new sentence.)

Punctuation Hint   In the four examples above, notice that a comma sets off the quoted part from the rest of the sentence. Also observe that commas and periods at the end of a quotation always go *inside* quotation marks.

Complete the following statements that explain how capital letters, commas, and periods are used in quotations. Refer to the four examples as guides.

• Every quotation begins with a _____*capital*_____ letter.

• When a quotation is split (as in the sentence about Aunt Fern), the second part does not begin with a capital letter unless it is a _____*new*_____ sentence.

- _____*Commas*_____ are used to separate the quoted part of a sentence from the rest of the sentence.
- Commas and periods that come at the end of a quotation go _____*inside*_____ quotation marks.

The answers are *capital, new, Commas,* and *inside.*

Practice 1

Insert quotation marks where needed in the sentences that follow.

1. "This is the tenth commercial in a row," complained Niko.
2. The police officer said sleepily, "I could really use a cup of coffee."
3. My boss asked me to step into his office and said, "Joanne, how would you like a raise?"
4. "I'm out of work again," Miriam sighed.
5. "I didn't know this movie was R-rated!" Lorraine gasped.
6. "Why does my dog always wait until it rains before he wants to go out?" Donovon asked.
7. A sign over the box office read, "Please form a single line and be patient."
8. "Unless I run three miles a day," Marty said, "my legs feel like lumpy oatmeal."
9. "I had an uncle who knew when he was going to die," claimed Dan. "He saw the date in a dream."
10. The unusual notice in the newspaper read, "Young farmer would be pleased to hear from young lady with tractor. Send photograph of tractor."

Practice 2

Rewrite the following sentences, adding quotation marks where needed. Use a capital letter to begin a quotation, and use a comma to set off a quoted part from the rest of the sentence.

Example   I'm getting tired Theo said.

           "I'm getting tired," Theo said. _____

1. The officer said I'm giving you a ticket.

   The officer said, "I'm giving you a ticket."

2. Please wait your turn the frantic clerk begged.

   "Please wait your turn," the frantic clerk begged.

3. Phil yelled where's the Drano?

   Phil yelled, "Where's the Drano?"

4. These directions don't make any sense Lin muttered.

   "These directions don't make any sense," Lin muttered.

5. Inside every fat person, someone once said, is a thin person struggling to get out.

   "Inside every fat person," someone once said, "is a thin person struggling

   to get out."

Practice 3

1. Write three quotations that appear in the first part of a sentence.

   Example   *"Let's go shopping," I suggested.*

   a.   *Answers will vary.*

   b.   _____

   c.   _____

2. Write three quotations that appear at the end of a sentence.

   Example   *Bob asked, "Have you had lunch yet?"*

   a.   *Answers will vary*

   b.   _____

   c.   _____

3. Write three quotations that appear at the beginning and end of a sentence.

   Example   *"If the bus doesn't come soon," Mary said, "we'll freeze."*

   a.   *Answers will vary.*

   b.   _____

   c.   _____

Indirect Quotations

An indirect quotation is a rewording of someone else's comments rather than a word-for-word direct quotation. The word *that* often signals an indirect quotation.

Direct Quotation	Indirect Quotation
George said, "My son is a daredevil."	George said that his son is a daredevil.
(George's exact spoken words are given, so quotation marks are used.)	(We learn George's words *indirectly*, so no quotation marks are used.)
Carol's note to Arnie read, "I'm at the neighbors' house. Give me a call."	Carol left a note for Arnie that said she would be at the neighbors' house and he should give her a call.
(The exact words that Carol wrote in the note are given, so quotation marks are used.)	(We learn Carol's words *indirectly*, so no quotation marks are used.)

Practice 1

Rewrite the following sentences, changing words as necessary to convert the sentences into direct quotations. The first one is done for you as an example.

1. Lew asked Marian if she had had a bad day at work.
   Lew asked Marian, "Did you have a bad day at work?"

2. Marian exclaimed that it was the worst day of her life.
   Marian exclaimed, "It was the worst day of my life."

3. Lew said to tell him all about it.
   Lew said, "Tell me all about it."

4. Marian insisted that he wouldn't understand her job problems.
   Marian insisted, "You wouldn't understand my job problems."

5. Lew said he would certainly try.
   Lew said, "I will certainly try."

Practice 2

Rewrite the following sentences, converting each direct quotation into an indirect statement. In each case you will have to add the word *that* or *if* and change other words as well.

Example   The barber asked Reggie, "Have you noticed how your hair is thinning?"
           The barber asked Reggie if he had noticed how his hair was thinning.

1. He said, "I need a vacation."

   <u>He said that he needed a vacation.</u>

2. Gretchen said, "Purple is my favorite color."

   <u>Gretchen said that purple was her favorite color.</u>

3. She asked the handsome stranger, "Could I buy you a drink?"

   <u>She asked the handsome stranger if she could buy him a drink.</u>

4. My brother asked, "Has anyone seen my frog?"

   <u>My brother asked if anyone had seen his frog.</u>

5. Fran complained, "I married a man who falls asleep during horror movies."

   <u>Fran complained that she married a man who falls asleep during horror movies.</u>

Quotation Marks to Set Off the Titles of Short Works

24.3c

Titles of short works are usually set off by quotation marks, while titles of long works are underlined. Use quotation marks to set off the titles of such short works as articles in books, newspapers, or magazines; chapters in a book; short stories; poems; and songs. On the other hand, you should underline the titles of books, newspapers, magazines, plays, movies, compact disk titles, and television shows. See the following examples.

Quotation Marks	*Underlines*
the article "The Toxic Tragedy"	in the book <u>Who's Poisoning America</u>
the article "New Cures for Headaches"	in the newspaper <u>The New York Times</u>
the article "When the Patient Plays Doctor"	in the magazine <u>Family Health</u>
the chapter "Connecting with Kids"	in the book <u>Straight Talk</u>
the story "The Dead"	in the book <u>Dubliners</u>
the poem "Birches"	in the book <u>The Complete Poems of Robert Frost</u>
the song "Some Enchanted Evening"	in the album <u>South Pacific</u>
	the television show <u>Jeopardy</u>
	the movie <u>Rear Window</u>

Note   In printed form, the titles of long works are set off by italics—slanted type that looks *like this.*

Practice

Use quotation marks or underlines as needed.

1. My recently divorced sister refused to be in the talent show when she was told she'd have to sing "Love Is a Many-Splendored Thing."

2. Disgusted by the constant dripping noise, Brian opened his copy of <u>Handy Home Repairs</u> to the chapter entitled "Everything about the Kitchen Sink."

3. My little brother has seen the movie <u>Star Wars</u> at least eight times.

4. Before they bought new car tires, Nick and Fran studied the article "Testing Tires" in the February, 2003, issue of <u>Consumer Reports</u>.

5. Many people mistakenly think that <u>Huckleberry Finn</u> and <u>The Adventures of Tom Sawyer</u> are children's books only.

6. I just found out that the musical <u>My Fair Lady</u> is taken from a play by George Bernard Shaw called <u>Pygmalion</u>.

7. The ending of Shirley Jackson's story "The Lottery" really surprised me.

8. I sang the song "Mack the Knife" in our high school production of <u>The Threepenny Opera</u>.

9. Unless he's studied the <u>TV Guide</u> listings thoroughly, my father won't turn on his television.

10. Stanley dreamed that both <u>Time</u> and <u>Newsweek</u> had decided to use him in their feature article "Man of the Year. "

Other Uses of Quotation Marks

1 To set off special words or phrases from the rest of a sentence:

Many people spell the words "all right" as one word, "alright," instead of correctly spelling them as two words.

I have trouble telling the difference between "principal" and "principle."

2 To mark off a quote within a quote. For this purpose, single quotes (' ') are used:

Ben Franklin said, "The noblest question in the world is, 'What good may I do in it?'"

"If you want to have a scary experience," Eric told Lynn, "read Stephen King's story 'The Mangler' in his book *Night Shift*."

Collaborative Activity

Part A: Editing and Rewriting

Working with a partner, read the short passage below and circle the ten sets of mistakes involving quotation marks. Then use the space provided to rewrite the passage, adding the ten sets of quotation marks. Feel free to discuss the rewrite quietly with your partner and refer back to the chapter when necessary.

[1] Fran put aside her books to answer the phone. [2] "Hello," she said.

[3] "Hey, Fran, take a break," said Nick. [4] "There's a great party going on here. [5] Why don't you come over?"

[6] Fran hesitated. [7] She was tired and bored; the party was tempting. [8] She felt like a cartoon character with a devil perched on one shoulder and an angel on the other.

[9] "Go to the party," the devil said. [10] "Forget this studying."

[11] "Stay home," the angel whispered, "or you'll regret it tomorrow."

[12] Interrupting Fran's thoughts, Nick urged, "Oh, come on, you can cram when you get home."

[13] Fran felt an imaginary stab from the devil's pitchfork. [14] "I want to, Nick," she said.

[15] Then she gave in to the imaginary angel. [16] "But I can't. [17] I really have to pass this test."

_____

_____

_____

_____

_____

_____

_____

_____

_____

_____

_____

_____

_____

Part B: Creating Sentences

Working with a partner, write sentences that use quotation marks as directed.

Answers will vary.

1. Write a sentence in which you quote a favorite expression of some-one you know. Identify the person's relationship to you.

   Example   My brother Sam often says after a meal, "That wasn't bad at all."

   _____

   _____

   _____

2. Write a quotation that contains the words *Tony asked Lola*. Write a second quotation that includes the words *Lola replied*.

   _____

   _____

   _____

3. Write a sentence that interests or amuses you from a book, magazine, or newspaper. Identify the title and author of the book, magazine, or newspaper article.

   Example   In her book <u>At Wit's End</u>, Erma Bombeck advises, "Never go to a doctor whose office plants have died."

   _____

   _____

   _____

Reflective Activity

Answers will vary.

1. Look at the paragraph about Fran and Nick that you revised above. How has adding quotation marks affected the reading of the para-graph?

Continued

2. What would writing be like without quotation marks? Explain, using an example, how quotation marks are important to understanding writing.

3. Explain what it is about quotation marks that is most difficult for you to remember and apply. Use an example to make your point clear. Feel free to refer back to anything in this chapter.

■ Review Test 1

Place quotation marks around the exact words of a speaker or writer in the sentences that follow.

1. "Look at the dent in my car!" André cried.

2. My mother always says to me, "When in doubt, don't."

3. Franklin Roosevelt said, "The only thing we have to fear is fear itself."

4. "It's much too quiet in here," whispered Vince as he entered the library.

5. The sign on the manager's desk reads: "I'd like to help you out. Which way did you come in?"

6. Clutching his partner's hands in midair, the trapeze artist murmured, "We've got to stop meeting like this."

7. "I've got two tickets on the fifty-yard line!" the scalper shouted as the fans filed into the stadium.

8. Looking at the fanatic football fan who had removed his shirt in subzero weather, Lonnie said, "There's a guy whose elevator doesn't go to the top."

9. "I can't believe it," he muttered. "I put the hammer right there a minute ago, and now it's gone."

10. "Why doesn't anyone ever get hungry at the beach?" Dad asked. When we didn't answer, he explained, "Because of all the sand which is there."

■ Review Test 2

Answers will vary.
Go through the comics section of a newspaper to find a comic strip that amuses you. Be sure to choose a strip where two or more characters are speaking to each other. Write a full description that will enable people who have not read the comic strip to visualize it clearly and appreciate its humor. Describe the setting and action in each panel and enclose the words of the speakers in quotation marks.

26 Comma

Introductory Activity

Commas often (though not always) signal a minor break or pause in a sentence. Each of the six pairs of sentences below illustrates one of six main uses of the comma. Read each pair of sentences aloud and place a comma wherever you feel a slight pause occurs. Then refer to the box at the bottom of the page, choose the rule that applies, and write its letter on the line provided.

a   1. Joel watched the eleven o'clock news, a movie, a *Honeymooners* rerun, and the station sign-off.
           Please endorse your check, write your account number on the back, and fill out a deposit slip.

b   2. Even though I was safe indoors, I shivered at the thought of the bitter cold outside.
           To start the car, press the accelerator and then turn the ignition key.

c   3. The opossum, like the kangaroo, carries its young in a pouch.
           George Derek, who was arrested, was a classmate of mine.

d   4. I enrolled in the course, but my name was not on the class list.
           A police cruiser blocked the busy intersection, and an ambulance pulled up on the sidewalk near the motionless victims.

e   5. Emily said, "Why is it so hard to remember your dreams the next day?"
           "After I left the interview," said David "I couldn't remember a word I had said."

f   6. Mike has driven over 1,500,000 accident-free miles in his job as a long-distance trucker.
           The Gates Trucking Company of 1800 Industrial Highway, Jersey City, New Jersey, gave Mike an award on January 26, 1998, for his superior safety record.

> a. *separate items in a list*
> b. *separate introductory material from the sentence*
> c. *separate words that interrupt the sentence*
> d. *separate complete thoughts in a sentence*
> e. *separate direct quotations from the rest of the sentence*
> f. *separate numbers, addresses, and dates in everyday writing*

Answers are on page 580.

Six Main Uses of the Comma

23.2

Commas are used mainly as follows:

1   To separate items in a series
2   To set off introductory material
3   On both sides of words that interrupt the flow of thought in a sentence
4   Between two complete thoughts connected by *and, but, for, or, nor, so, yet*
5   To set off a direct quotation from the rest of a sentence
6   For certain everyday material

You may find it helpful to remember that the comma often marks a slight pause, or break, in a sentence. These pauses or breaks occur at the points where the six main comma rules apply. Read aloud the sentence examples given on the following pages for each of the comma rules and listen for the minor pauses or breaks that are signaled by commas.

At the same time, you should keep in mind that commas are far more often overused than underused. As a general rule, you should *not* use a comma unless a given comma rule applies or unless a comma is otherwise needed to help a sentence read clearly. A good rule of thumb is that "when in doubt" about whether to use a comma, it is often best to "leave it out."

After reviewing each of the comma rules that follow, you will practice adding commas that are needed and omitting commas that are not needed.

1 Comma between Items in a Series

Use a comma to separate items in a series.

Magazines, paperback novels, and textbooks crowded the shelves.
Hard-luck Harold needs a loan, a good-paying job, and a close friend.
Pat sat in the doctor's office, checked her watch, and chewed gum nervously.
Lola bit into the ripe, juicy apple.
More and more people entered the crowded, noisy stadium.

Note   A comma is used between two descriptive words in a series only if *and* inserted between the words sounds natural. You could say:

Lola bit into the ripe *and* juicy apple.
More and more people entered the crowded *and* noisy stadium.

But notice in the following sentences that the descriptive words do not sound natural when *and* is inserted between them. In such cases, no comma is used.

> The model wore a light sleeveless blouse. ("A light *and* sleeveless blouse" doesn't sound right, so no comma is used.)
>
> Dr. Van Helsing noticed two tiny puncture marks on his patient's neck. ("Two *and* tiny puncture marks" doesn't sound right, so no comma is used.)

Practice 1

Place commas between items in a series.

1. Jin-Mae packed tennis rackets, a volleyball, and a first-aid kit in the car.
2. Marty never reads anything in the paper except the comics, the sports page, and the personals.
3. On the Johnsons' lawn are a cement birdbath, two stone deer, a flagpole, and a plastic daisy.

Practice 2

For each item, cross out the one comma that is not needed. Add the one comma that is needed between items in a series.

1. A metal tape measure, a pencil, a ruler, and a hammer dangled, from the carpenter's pockets.
2. The fortune-teller uncovered the crystal ball, peered into it, and began, to predict my future.
3. That hairdresser is well known, for her frizzy perms, butchered haircuts, and brassy hair colorings.

2 Comma after Introductory Material

Use a comma to set off introductory material.

> Fearlessly, Lola picked up the slimy slug.
>
> Just to annoy Tony, she let it crawl along her arm.
>
> Although I have a black belt in karate, I decided to go easy on the demented bully who had kicked sand in my face.
>
> Mumbling under her breath, the woman picked over the tomatoes.

Notes

a If the introductory material is brief, the comma is sometimes omitted. In the activities here, you should include the comma.

b A comma is also used to set off extra material placed at the end of a sentence. Here are two sentences where this comma rule applies:

I spent all day at the employment office, trying to find a job that suited me.

Tony has trouble accepting criticism, except from Lola.

Practice 1

Place commas after introductory material.

1. With shaking hands, the frightened baby-sitter dialed the police emergency number.

2. During the storm, snow drifted through cracks in the roof of the cabin.

3. Ashamed to ask for help, Betty glanced around nervously at the other students to see how they were filling out the computer questionnaire.

Practice 2

In each sentence, cross out the one comma that is not needed. Add the one comma that is needed after introductory material.

1. In order to work at that fast-food restaurant, you have to wear a cowboy hat and six-guns. In addition, you have to shout "Yippee!" every time, someone orders the special Western-style double burger.

2. Barely awake, the woman slowly rocked, her crying infant. While the baby softly cooed, the woman fell asleep.

3. When I painted the kitchen, I remembered to cover the floor with newspapers. Therefore, I was able to save the floor from looking, as if someone had thrown confetti on it.

3 Comma around Words Interrupting the Flow of Thought

Use a comma before and after words that interrupt the flow of thought in a sentence.

The car, cleaned and repaired, is ready to be sold.

Joanne, our new neighbor, used to work as a bouncer at Rexy's Tavern.

Taking long walks, especially after dark, helps me sort out my thoughts.

Usually you can "hear" words that interrupt the flow of thought in a sentence. However, when you are not sure if certain words are interrupters, remove them from the sentence. If it still makes sense without the words, you know the words are interrupters and that the information they give is nonessential. Such nonessential information is set off with commas. In the following sentence,

> Susie Hall, who is my best friend, won a new car in the *Reader's Digest* sweepstakes.

the words *who is my best friend* are extra information, not needed to identify the subject of the sentence, *Susie Hall.* Put commas around such nonessential information. On the other hand, in the sentence

> The woman who is my best friend won a new car in the *Reader's Digest* sweepstakes.

the words *who is my best friend* supply essential information needed for us to identify the woman. If the words were removed from the sentence, we would no longer know which woman won the sweepstakes. Commas are not used around such essential information.

Here is another example:

> *The Shining,* a novel by Stephen King, is the scariest book I've ever read.

Here the words *a novel by Stephen King* are extra information, not needed to identify the subject of the sentence, *The Shining.* Commas go around such nonessential information. On the other hand, in the sentence

> Stephen King's novel *The Shining* is the scariest book I've ever read.

the words *The Shining* are needed to identify the novel. Commas are not used around such essential information.

Most of the time you will be able to "hear" words that interrupt the flow of thoughts in a sentence and will not have to think about whether the words are essential or nonessential.*

---

*Some instructors refer to nonessential or extra information that is set off by commas as a *nonrestrictive* clause. Essential information that interrupts the flow of thought is called a *restrictive* clause. No commas are used to set off a restrictive clause.

Practice 1

Add commas to set off interrupting words.

1. This all-purpose kitchen gadget,ladies and gentlemen,sells for only $19.98!

2. Tigers,because they eat people,do not make good house pets.

3. A practical joker had laid a dummy,its straw-filled "hands" tied with rope,across the railroad tracks.

Practice 2

For each item, cross out the one comma that is not needed. Add the comma that is needed to completely set off interrupting words.

1. My brother, who likes only natural foods,would rather eat a soybean patty$_x$ than a cheeseburger.

2. That room,with its filthy rug$_x$ and broken dishwasher, is the nicest one in the building.

3. My aunt,who claims she is an artist, painted her living room ceiling$_x$ to look like the sky at midnight.

4 Comma between Complete Thoughts Connected by a Joining Word

Use a comma between two complete thoughts connected by *and, but, for, or, nor, so, yet.*

My parents threatened to throw me out of the house, so I had to stop playing the drums.

The polyester bedsheets had a gorgeous design on them, but they didn't feel as comfortable as plain cotton sheets.

The teenage girls walked the hot summer streets, and the teenage boys drove by in their shined-up cars.

Notes

a The comma is optional when the complete thoughts are short:

Calvin relaxed but Robert kept working.

The soda was flat so I poured it away.

b Be careful not to use a comma in sentences having *one* subject and a *double* verb. The comma is used only in sentences made up of two complete thoughts (two subjects and two verbs). In the sentence

Dawn lay awake that stormy night and listened to the thunder crashing.

there is only one subject (*Dawn*) and a double verb (*lay* and *listened*). No comma is needed. Likewise, the sentence

The quarterback kept the ball and plunged across the goal line for a touch-down.

has only one subject (*quarterback*) and a double verb (*kept* and *plunged*); therefore, no comma is needed.

Practice

Place a comma before a joining word that connects two complete thoughts (two subjects and two verbs). Remember, do *not* place a comma within sentences that have only one subject and a double verb. If a sentence is correct, mark it with a *C*.

1. Vince has to make sixty sandwiches an hour, or he'll lose his job at Burgerland.

2. The doctor assured me that my back was fine, but it still felt as rigid as an iron rod.

3. That new video store gets the latest releases, and it provides free popcorn for customers who rent two or more movies.

4. My new toaster is more hi-tech than my old one, but it burns toast just as often.

C 5. Carol and Barbara pulled the volleyball net as tight as they could and then lashed it to a convenient pair of trees.

C 6. Ralph refuses to pay rent to his parents and will not do any chores at home.

7. Frieda wore a pair of wooden clogs while housecleaning, and the people in the apartment next door could hear her clomping up and down the stairs.

8. William kept the cookie in his mouth until its chocolate coating melted, and then he crunched the naked wafer into bits.

9. My little sister loves to call strangers on the telephone, but she hangs up as soon as anyone answers.

C 10. Ronnie plans to make a million dollars by the time he's twenty-five and then write a book about his experiences.

5 Comma with Direct Quotations

Use a comma to set off a direct quotation from the rest of a sentence.

> "Please take a number," said the deli clerk.
>
> Fred told Martha, "I've just signed up for a knitting class."
>
> "Those who sling mud," a famous politician once said, "usually lose ground."
>
> "Reading this book," complained Stan, "is about as interesting as watching paint dry."

Note   A comma or a period at the end of a quotation goes inside quotation marks. See also page 300.

Practice 1

In each sentence, add the one or more commas needed to set off the quoted material.

1. Frowning, the clerk asked, "Do you have a driver's license and two major credit cards for identification?"

2. In my high school yearbook, my best friend wrote, "2 Good 2 B 4 Gotten."

3. "The only thing that man couldn't talk his way out of," said Richie, "is a coffin."

Practice 2

In each sentence, cross out the one comma that is not needed. Add the comma that is needed to set off a quotation from the rest of the sentence.

1. "Could you spare a quarter," the boy asked passersby~x~ in the mall, "for a video game?"

2. "Man does not live by words alone," wrote Adlai Stevenson, "despite the fact~x~ that sometimes he has to eat them."

3. "That actress," said Velma, "has promoted everything~x~ from denture cleaner to shoelaces."

6 Comma with Everyday Material

Use a comma with certain everyday material as shown in the following sections.

Persons Spoken To

Sally, I think that you should go to bed.

Please turn down the stereo, Jo.

Please, sir, can you spare a dollar?

Dates

Our house was burglarized on October 28, 2003, and two weeks later on November 11, 2003.

Addresses

Lola's sister lives at Greenway Village, 342 Red Oak Drive, Los Angeles, California 90057.

Note   No comma is used before the ZIP code.

Openings and Closings of Letters

Dear Vanessa,	Sincerely,
Dear John,	Truly yours,

Note   In formal letters, a colon is used after the opening:

Dear Sir:

Dear Madam:

Numbers

Government officials estimate that Americans spend about 785,000,000 hours a year filling out federal forms.

Practice

Place commas where needed.

1. I am sorry, sir, but you cannot sit at this table.

2. On May 6, 1954, Roger Bannister became the first person to run a mile in under four minutes.

3. Redeeming the savings certificate before June 30, 2004, will result in a substantial penalty.

4. A cash refund of one dollar can be obtained by sending proof of purchase to Seven Seas, P.O. Box 760, El Paso, Texas 79972.

5. Leo, turn off that TV set this minute!

Unnecessary Use of Commas

Remember that if no clear rule applies for using a comma, it is usually better not to use a comma. As stated earlier, "When in doubt, leave it out." Following are some typical examples of unnecessary commas.

Incorrect

Sharon told me, that my socks were different colors.

(A comma is not used before *that* unless the flow of thought is interrupted.)

The union negotiations, dragged on for three days.

(Do not use a comma between a simple subject and verb.)

I waxed all the furniture, and cleaned the windows.

(Use a comma before *and* only with more than two items in a series or when *and* joins two complete thoughts.)

Sharon carried, the baby into the house.

(Do not use a comma between a verb and its object.)

I had a clear view, of the entire robbery.

(Do not use a comma before a prepositional phrase.)

Practice

Cross out the one comma that does not belong in each sentence. Do not add any commas.

1. A new bulletproof material has been developed, that is very lightweight.

2. The vet's bill included charges, for a distemper shot.

3. Since the firehouse, is directly behind Ken's home, the sound of its siren pierces his walls.

4. Hard sausages, and net-covered hams hung above the delicatessen counter.

5. The students in the dance class, were dressed in a variety of bright tights, baggy sweatshirts, and woolly leg warmers.

6. A woman in the ladies' room asked me, if she could borrow a safety pin.

7. Telephone books, broken pencils, and scraps of paper, littered the reporter's desk.

8. The frenzied crowd at the game cheered, and whistled.

9. Splitting along the seams, the old mattress spilled its stuffing, on the ground.

10. To satisfy his hunger, Enrique chewed on a piece of dry, rye bread.

Collaborative Activity

Part A: Editing and Rewriting

Working with a partner, read carefully the short paragraph below and mark the ten places where commas are missing. Then, in the space between the lines, insert the ten additional commas needed. Feel free to discuss the rewrite quietly with your partner and refer back to the chapter when necessary.

[1] You may have heard of Robinson ~~Crusoe but~~ *Crusoe, but* there is an even stranger story of shipwreck and survival. [2] In ~~1757 a~~ *1757, a* Scottish whaling ship sank in the icy polar seas of the Arctic. [3] Only one ~~man Bruce~~ *man, Bruce*

Continued

Gordon, survived   shelter, Gordon
~~Gordon survived.~~ 4Without food or ~~shelter Gordon~~ spent his lonely

                                    day, the
first night huddled on the ice. 5The next ~~day the~~ whaling ship—upside-

down—rose to the surface of the sea and lodged tightly in the ice

            Gordon, using   debris, managed
floes. 6~~Gordon using~~ some of the shipwreck ~~debris managed~~ to break

into a cabin window. 7He survived for a year in the freezing world of

the upside-down ship by using some stored coal to build a fire.

        Eventually, Bruce
8~~Eventually Bruce~~ Gordon was rescued by a band of Eskimo hunters.

                                            village, the
9After living for more than five years in the native ~~village the~~

shipwrecked sailor finally made it back to Scotland.

Part B: Creating Sentences

Working with a partner, write sentences that use commas as directed.
Answers will vary.

1. Write a sentence mentioning three items you want to get the next
    time you go to the store.

    _____

    _____

2. Write two sentences describing how you relax after getting home
    from school or work. Start the first sentence with *After* or *When*.
    Start the second sentence with *Next*.

    _____

    _____

3. Write a sentence that tells something about your favorite movie,
    book, television show, or song. Use the words *which is my favorite
    movie* (or *book, television show,* or *song*) after the name of the
    movie, book, television show, or song.

    _____

    _____

Continued

4. Write two complete thoughts about a person you know. The first thought should mention something that you like about the person. The second thought should mention something you don't like. Join the two thoughts with *but*.

_____

_____

5. Invent a line that Lola might say to Tony. Use the words *Lola said* in the sentence. Then include Tony's reply, using the words *Tony responded*.

_____

_____

6. Write a sentence about an important event in your life. Include in your sentence the day, month, and year of the event.

_____

_____

Reflective Activity

Answers will vary.

1. Look at the paragraph about Bruce Gordon that you revised above. Explain how adding commas has affected the reading of the paragraph.

2. What would writing be like without the comma? How do commas help writing?

3. What comma rule is the most difficult for you to remember and apply? Explain, giving an example.

■ Review Test 1

Insert commas where needed. In the space provided under each sentence, summarize briefly the rule that explains the use of the comma or commas.

1. During the sudden downpour, people covered their heads with folded newspapers.

   Comma after introductory material

2. Helen's sister always stopped her from buying expensive items by saying, "You have champagne taste and a beer budget."

   Set off a direct quotation

3. The damp, musty, shadowy cellar was our favorite playground.

   Separate items in a series

4. My favorite pillow, a sad specimen leaking chunks of foam, is over ten years old.

   Set off words interrupting the flow of thought

5. Mary Ann started work as a file clerk on June 21, 2002, and quit on June 22.

   Set off everyday material

6. Phan agreed to sit in the window seat, but he kept his eyes tightly shut during the takeoff and landing.

   Separate two complete thoughts

7. The massive fullback, his uniform torn and bloodied, hobbled back to the huddle.

   Set off words interrupting the flow of thought

8. Martin Luther King wrote, "A man can't ride on your back unless it's bent."

   Set off a direct quotation

9. If you want to avoid that run-down feeling, you should look both ways before crossing the street.

   Comma after introductory material

10. My brother, who is a practical joker, once put a plastic shark in our bathtub.

    Set off words interrupting the flow of thought

■ **Review Test 2**

Insert commas where needed. One sentence does not need commas; mark this sentence *C* for "correct."

1. Thelma and Louise, a corn snake who lived at the San Diego Zoo, was popular with visitors.

2. Her popularity wasn't because corn snakes, which are harmless, are at all rare.

3. In fact, corn snakes are among the most common North American snakes.

4. Thelma and Louise was a perfectly ordinary snake, except for one little thing.

5. She had, believe it or not, two heads.

6. Scientists say that two-headed snakes are born fairly often, but they usually don't survive long.

7. Because their two heads often want to go in different directions, such snakes are slow and clumsy.

8. The two-headed babies are quickly caught and eaten by hawks, raccoons, skunks, and other animals.

9. But in the safety of the zoo, Thelma and Louise lived a long life.

C 10. She even gave birth to fifteen normal babies.

■ **Review Test 3**

Answers will vary.
On separate paper, write six sentences, each demonstrating one of the six main comma rules.

27 Other Punctuation Marks

Introductory Activity

Each of the sentences below needs one of the following punctuation marks.

;   —   -   ( )   :

See if you can insert the correct mark in each case.

1. The following items were on Ted's grocery list: soda, potato chips, chocolate chip cookies, ice cream, and carrots.

2. A life-size statue of her cat adorns the living room of Diana's penthouse.

3. Sigmund Freud, the pioneer of psychoanalysis (1856–1939) was a habitual cocaine user.

4. As children, we would put pennies on the railroad track, we wanted to see what they would look like after being run over by a train.

5. The stuntwoman was battered, broken, and barely breathing but alive.

Answers are on page 581.

Colon (:)

The colon is a mark of introduction. Use the colon at the end of a complete statement to do the following:

1 Introduce a list.

My little brother has three hobbies: playing video games, racing his Hot Wheels cars all over the floor, and driving me crazy.

2 Introduce a long quotation.

Janet's paper was based on a passage from George Eliot's novel *Middlemarch:* "If we had a keen vision and feeling of all ordinary human life, it would be like hearing the grass grow and the squirrel's heart beat, and we should die of that roar which lies on the other side of silence. As it is, the quickest of us walk about well wadded with stupidity."

3 Introduce an explanation.

There are two ways to do this job: the easy way and the right way.

Two minor uses of the colon are after the opening in a formal letter (*Dear Sir or Madam:*) and between the hour and the minute when writing the time (*The bus will leave for the game at 11:45*).

Practice

Place colons where needed.

1. A comedian once defined mummies as follows:Egyptians who are pressed for time.

2. The manager boasted that his restaurant was full of good things:good food, good selections, and good prices.

3. In her book *The Plug-In Drug,* Marie Winn describes the effect of television on family life:"By its domination of the time families spend together, it destroys the special quality that distinguishes one family from another, a quality that depends to a great extent on what a family *does,* what special rituals, games, recurrent jokes, familiar songs, and shared activities it accumulates."

Semicolon (;)

ALLWRITE!

24.1

The semicolon signals more of a pause than the comma alone but not quite the full pause of a period. Use a semicolon to do the following:

1 Join two complete thoughts that are not already connected by a joining word such as *and, but, for,* or *so.*

> The chemistry lab blew up; Professor Thomas was fired.
>
> I once stabbed myself with a pencil; a black mark has been under my skin ever since.

2 Join two complete thoughts that include a transitional word such as *however, otherwise, moreover, furthermore, therefore,* or *consequently.*

> I cut and raked the grass; moreover, I weeded the lawn.
>
> Sally finished typing the paper; however, she forgot to bring it to class.

Note   The first two uses of the semicolon are treated in more detail on pages 126–128.

3 Mark off items in a series when the items themselves contain commas.

> This fall I won't have to work on Labor Day, September 7; Veterans' Day, November 11; or Thanksgiving Day, November 26.
>
> At the final Weight Watchers' meeting, prizes were awarded to Teri Johnson, for losing 20 pounds; Irving Ross, for losing 26 pounds; and Betty Mills, the champion loser, who lost 102 pounds.

Practice

Place semicolons where needed.

1. Be sure to plug up all unused electrical outlets;otherwise, your toddler might get a severe shock.

2. In the old horror movie, the incredible shrinking man battled a black widow spider;he finally speared it with a straight pin.

3. Having nothing better to do, Laurie watched the *Today* show from 7:00 to 9:00 A.M.;a rerun of *Good Morning, Miami,* from 9:00 to 10:00;and soap operas from 12:30 to 4:00 A.M.

Dash (—)

ALLWRITE!

24.4

A dash signals a degree of pause longer than a comma but not as complete as a period. Use the dash to set off words for dramatic effect.

I suggest—no, I insist—that you stay for dinner.

The prisoner walked toward the electric chair—grinning.

A meaningful job, a loving wife, and a car that wouldn't break down all the time—these are the things he wanted in life.

Practice

Place dashes where needed.

1. Our dishwasher doesn't dry very well‾the glasses look as if they're crying.

2. After I saw two museums, three monuments, and the governor's mansion, there was only one other place I wanted to see‾my hotel room.

3. I hoped‾no, I prayed‾that the operation would be successful.

Hyphen (-)

Use a hyphen in the following ways:

1   With two or more words that act as a single unit describing a noun.

The society ladies nibbled at the deep-fried grasshoppers.

A white-gloved waiter then put some snails on their table.

Your dictionary will often help when you are unsure about whether to use a hyphen between words.

2   To divide a word at the end of a line of writing or typing.

Although it had begun to drizzle, the teams decided to play the champion-ship game that day.

Notes

a   Divide a word between syllables. Use your dictionary (see page 332) to be sure of correct syllable divisions.

b   Do not divide words of one syllable.

c   Do not divide a word if you can avoid dividing it.

Practice

Place hyphens where needed.

1. Al's Auto Agency is a first-rate place to buy a brand-new car.

2. Nick and Fran dream of someday replacing their worn-out rugs with wall-to-wall carpeting in every room.

3. "What's a great-looking guy like you doing in a two-bit place like this?" she asked.

Parentheses ( )

24.5

Use parentheses to do the following:

1   Set off extra or incidental information from the rest of a sentence.

The chapter on drugs in our textbook (pages 142–178) contains some frightening statistics.

The normal body temperature of a cat (101 to 102 degrees) is 3 degrees higher than the temperature of its owner.

2   Enclose letters or numbers that signal items in a series.

Three steps to follow in previewing a textbook are to (1) study the title, (2) read the first and last paragraphs, and (3) study the headings and subheadings.

Note   Do not use parentheses too often in your writing.

Practice

Add parentheses where needed.

1. The high ticket prices (fifty to ninety dollars) made Rodney think twice about going to the rap concert.

2. In the last election (the April primary), only 20 percent of the eligible voters showed up at the polls.

3. When you come to take the placement test, please bring with you (1) two sharpened pencils and (2) an eraser.

■ Review Test 1

At the appropriate spot or spots, place the punctuation mark shown in the margin.

Example   **;**   The singles dance was a success; I met several people I wanted to
                    see again.

:   1. Fascinated, Corey read two unusual recipes in *The Joy of Cooking*:roasted
               saddle of moose and woodchuck smothered with onions.

—   2. Sam's Pizza Heaven is advertising a Friday-night special on lasagna‿all you
               can eat for $2.99.

-   3. Very few older cars have front-wheel drive.

( )   4. The sign on my instructor's office door read, "Available only during office
               hours (2 to 4 P.M.)"

:   5. In *Walden,* Thoreau wrote:"I went to the woods because I wished to live
               deliberately, to front only the essential facts of life, and see if I could not learn
               what it had to teach, and not, when I came to die, discover that I had not
               lived."

;   6. Mosquitoes prefer to bite children rather than adults;they are also more
               attracted to blonds than to brunettes.

—   7. Please‿go to the Seven-Eleven‿it's that little store in the middle of the next
               block‿and get a carton of milk.

-   8. We can't afford to see first-run movies anymore.

( )   9. Four hints for success in taking exams are (1)review your notes the night
               before, (2)be on time for the exam, (3)sit in a quiet place, and (4)read all
               directions carefully before you begin to write.

;   10. My neighbor's boxer, Dempsey, is a great watchdog;in fact, he can sit on
               my porch and watch me for hours.

■ Review Test 2

Answers will vary.
On separate paper, write two sentences for each of the following punctuation
marks: colon, semicolon, dash, hyphen, parentheses.

28 Dictionary Use

Introductory Activity

The dictionary is an indispensable tool, as will be apparent if you try to answer the following questions *without* using the dictionary.

1. Which one of the following words is spelled incorrectly?

   fortuitous
   <u>fortutious</u>   macrobiotics   stratagem

2. If you wanted to hyphenate the following word correctly, at which points would you place the syllable divisions?

   h i/e r/o/g l y p h/i c s

3. What common word has the sound of the first *e* in the word *chameleon*? __*be*__

4. Where is the primary accent in the following word?

   o c/t o/g e/<u>n a r</u>/i/a n

5. What are the two separate meanings of the word *earmark*?
   (1) Identifying mark on the ear of a domestic animal

   (2) Identifying feature or characteristic

Your dictionary is a quick and sure authority on all these matters: spelling, syllabication, pronunciation, and word meanings. And as this chapter will show, it is also a source for many other kinds of information.

Answers are on page 582.

The dictionary is a valuable tool. To take advantage of it, you need to understand the main kinds of information that a dictionary gives about a word. Look at the information provided for the word *dictate* in the following entry from the *American Heritage Dictionary,* paperback edition.*

Spelling and syllabication   *Pronunciation*   *Part of speech*

dic•tate (dĭk′tāt′, dĭk-tāt′) *v.* **-tat•ed, -tat•ing.**
1. To say or read aloud for transcription.
2. To prescribe or command with authority.
—*n.* (dĭk′tāt′). An order; directive. [< Lat.
dictare.] —**dic•ta′tion** *n.*

Meanings

Etymology

Other form of the word

Spelling

The first bit of information, in the boldface (heavy type) entry itself, is the spelling of *dictate.* You probably already know the spelling of *dictate,* but if you didn't, you could find it by pronouncing the syllables in the word carefully and then looking it up in the dictionary.

Use your dictionary to correct the spelling of the following words:

responsable	responsible	delite	delight
thorogh	thorough	duble	double
akselerate	accelerate	carefull	careful
finaly	finally	luckyer	luckier
refiree	referee	dangrous	dangerous
shizophrenic	schizophrenic	accomodate	accommodate
prescripshun	prescription	envalope	envelope
hankercheif	handkerchief	prenatel	prenatal
marryed	married	progres	progress
alright	all right	jeneric	generic
fotographer	photographer	excelent	excellent
krucial	crucial	persue	pursue

Syllabication

The second bit of information that the dictionary gives, also within the boldface entry, is the syllabication of *dic•tate*. Note that a dot separates each syllable (or part) of the word. Use your dictionary to mark the syllable divisions in the following words. Also indicate how many syllables are in each word.

c o n•t a c t   (___2___ syllables)

m a g•n e t•i c   (___3___ syllables)

d e•h u•m a n•i z e   (___4___ syllables)

s e n•t i•m e n•t a l•i z e   (___5___ syllables)

Noting syllable divisions will enable you to *hyphenate* a word: divide it at the end of one line of writing and complete it at the beginning of the next line. You can correctly hyphenate a word only at a syllable division, and you may have to check your dictionary to make sure of the syllable divisions for a particular word.

Pronunciation

The third bit of information in the dictionary entry is the pronunciation of *dictate:* (dik′tat′) or (dik-tat′). You already know how to pronounce *dictate,* but if you did not, the information within the parentheses would serve as your guide. Use your dictionary to complete the pronunciation exercises on page 334.

Vowel Sounds

You will probably use the pronunciation key in your dictionary mainly as a guide to pronouncing different vowel sounds (*vowels* are the letters *a, e, i, o,* and *u*). Here is the pronunciation key that appears on every other page of the paperback *American Heritage Dictionary:*

ă pat ā pay â care ä father ě pet ē be ǐ pit ī tie î pier ŏ pot ō toe
ô paw, for oi noise o͝o took o͞o boot ou out th thin *th* this ŭ cut
û urge yo͞o abuse zh vision ə about, item, edible, gallop, circus

This key tells you, for example, that the short *a* is pronounced like the *a* in *pat,* the long *a* is like the *a* in *pay,* and the short *i* is like the *i* in *pit.*

Now look at the pronunciation key in your own dictionary. The key is probably located in the front of the dictionary or at the bottom of every page. What common word in the key tells you how to pronounce each of the following sounds?

Answers may vary.

ĕ	pet		ō	toe
ī	pie		ŭ	cut
ŏ	pot		o͞o	boot

(Note that a long vowel always has the sound of its own name.)

The Schwa (ə)

The symbol ə looks like an upside-down *e*. It is called a *schwa,* and it stands for the unaccented sound in such words as *about, item, edible, gallop,* and *circus.* More approximately, it stands for the sound *uh*—like the *uh* that speakers sometimes make when they hesitate. Perhaps it would help to remember that *uh,* as well as ə, could be used to represent the schwa sound.

Here are three of the many words in which the schwa sound appears: *socialize* (sō'shə līz or sō'shuh līz); *legitimate* (lə jĭt'ə mĭt or luh jĭt'uh mĭt); *oblivious* (ə blĭv'ē əs or uh blĭv'ē uhs). Open your dictionary to any page, and you will almost surely be able to find three words that make use of the schwa in the pronunciation in parentheses after the main entry. Write three such words and their pronunciations in the following spaces:

Answers will vary.

1. _____

2. _____

3. _____

Accent Marks

Some words contain both a primary accent, shown by a heavy stroke ('), and a secondary accent, shown by a lighter stroke ('). For example, in the word *vicissitude* (vĭ sĭs'ĭ to͞od'), the stress, or accent, goes chiefly on the second syllable (sĭs'), and, to a lesser extent, on the last syllable (to͞od').

Use your dictionary to add stress marks to the following words:

soliloquy (sə lĭl'ə kwē)   inventory (in' vən tôr' ĕ)

diatribe (dī'ə trīb)   marmalade (mär' mə lād')

rheumatism (ro͞o'mə tīz' əm)   recognition (rek' eg nish' ən)

representation (rĕp'rĭ zĕn tā'shən)   monumental (mŏn' yə men' tl)

Full Pronunciation

Use your dictionary to write out the full pronunciation (the information given in parentheses) for each of the following words:

1. germane __jər-mān′__
2. jettison __jĕt′ĭ-sən__
3. juxtapose __jŭk′stə-pōz′__
4. catastrophic __kăt′ə-strŏf′ĭk__
5. alacrity __ə-lăk′rĭ-tē__
6. exacerbate __ĭg-zăs′ər-bāt__
7. sporadic __spə-răd′ĭk__
8. cacophony __kə-kŏf′ə-nē__

9. intrepid __ĭn-trĕp′ĭd__
10. oligarchy __ŏl′ĭ-gär′kē__
11. raucous __rô′kəs__
12. temerity __tə-mĕr′ĭ-tē__
13. forensic __fə-rĕn′sĭk__
14. megalomania __meg′ə-lō-mā′nē-ə__
15. perpetuity __pûr′pĭ-tōō′ĭ-tē__

Now practice pronouncing each word. Use the pronunciation key in your dictionary as an aid to sounding out each syllable. Do *not* try to pronounce a word all at once; instead, work on mastering *one syllable at a time.* When you can pronounce each of the syllables in a word successfully, then say them in sequence, add the accent, and pronounce the entire word.

Other Information about Words

Parts of Speech

The dictionary entry for *dictate* includes the abbreviation *v.* This means that the meanings of *dictate* as a verb will follow. The abbreviation *n.* is then followed by the meaning of *dictate* as a noun.

At the front of your dictionary, you will probably find a key that will explain the meanings of abbreviations used in the dictionary. Use the key to fill in the meanings of the following abbreviations:

pl. = __plural__   adj. = __adjective__

sing. = __singular__   adv. = __adverb__

Principal Parts of Irregular Verbs

Dictate is a regular verb and forms its principal parts by adding *-d, -d,* and *-ing* to the stem of the verb. When a verb is irregular, the dictionary lists its principal parts. For example, with *begin* the present tense comes first (the entry itself, *begin*). Next comes the past tense (*began*), and then the past participle (*begun*)— the form of the verb used with such helping words as *have, had,* and *was.* Then comes the present participle (*beginning*)—the *-ing* form of the word.

Look up the principal parts of the following irregular verbs and write them in the spaces provided. The first one has been done for you.

Present	Past	Past Participle	Present Participle
see	saw	seen	seeing
go	went	gone	going
ride	rode	ridden	riding
speak	spoke	spoken	speaking

Plural Forms of Irregular Nouns

The dictionary supplies the plural forms of all irregular nouns (regular nouns form the plural by adding *-s* or *-es*). Give the plurals of the following nouns:

crisis	crises
library	libraries
phenomenon	phenomena
variety	varieties

Note   See page 342 for more information about plurals.

Meanings

When a word has more than one meaning, the meanings are numbered in the dictionary, as with the verb *dictate*. In many dictionaries, the most common meanings are presented first. The introductory pages of your dictionary will explain the order in which meanings are presented.

Use the sentence context to try to explain the meaning of the underlined word in each of the following sentences. Write your definition in the space provided. Then look up and record the dictionary meaning of the word. Be sure you pick out the meaning that fits the word as it is used in the sentence.

Answers will vary for the students' definitions.

1. The insurance company <u>compensated</u> Jean for the two weeks she missed work.

   Your definition: _____

   Dictionary definition: *made a payment to* _____

2. Howard is in excellent <u>condition</u> from running two miles a day.

   Your definition: _____

   Dictionary definition: *state of health* _____

3. The underworld chief attained power by <u>liquidating</u> his competitors.

   Your definition: _____

   Dictionary definition: *killing* _____

Etymology

Etymology refers to the history of a word. Many words have origins in foreign languages, such as Greek (abbreviated Gk in the dictionary) or Latin (L). Such information is usually enclosed in brackets and is more likely to be present in a hardbound desk dictionary than in a paperback one. A good desk dictionary will tell you, for example, that the word *cannibal* derives from the name of the man-eating tribe, the Caribs, that Christopher Columbus discovered on Cuba and Haiti.

The following are good desk dictionaries:

The American Heritage Dictionary

Random House College Dictionary

Webster's New Collegiate Dictionary

Webster's New World Dictionary

See if your dictionary says anything about the origins of the following words.
Students' answers may vary somewhat.

derrick   *from Derrick, a seventeenth-century English hangman* ___

_____

berserk *from an Old Norse word meaning "a wild man"*

boycott *after Charles C. Boycott, a landlord who was isolated from public services because he opposed land reform*

chauvinism *after Chauvin, a legendary French soldier famous for his devotion to Napoleon*

Usage Labels

As a general rule, use only standard English words in your writing. If a word is not standard English, your dictionary will probably give it a usage label such as *informal, nonstandard, slang, vulgar, obsolete, archaic,* or *rare.*

Look up the following words and record how your dictionary labels them. Remember that a recent hardbound desk dictionary will always be the best source of information about usage.

Students' answers may vary.

messed up *slang*

peppy *informal*

techie *informal*

ain't *nonstandard*

gross out (meaning *to fill with disgust*) *slang*

Synonyms

A *synonym* is a word that is close in meaning to another word. Using synonyms helps you avoid unnecessary repetition of the same word in a paper. A paperback dictionary is not likely to give you synonyms for words, but a good desk dictionary will. (You might also want to own a *thesaurus,* a book that lists synonyms and antonyms. An *antonym* is a word approximately opposite in meaning to another word.)

Consult a desk dictionary that gives synonyms for the following words, and write some of the synonyms in the spaces provided.

Student's answers may vary.

frighten *alarm, panic, scare, startle, terrify*

giant *colossal, enormous, huge, immense, tremendous*

insane *batty, crazy, cuckoo, deranged, lunatic, mad*

■ **Review Test**

Items 1–5   Use your dictionary to answer the following questions.

1. How many syllables are in the word *magnanimous?* <u>four</u>

2. Where is the primary accent in the word *detrimental?* <u>third syllable</u>

3. In the word *tractable,* the second *a* is pronounced like

   a. short *a.*

   b. long *a.*

   c. short *i.*

   ⓓ schwa.

4. In the word *officiate,* the second *i* is pronounced like

   a. short *i.*

   b. long *i.*

   ⓒ long *e.*

   d. schwa.

5. In the word *sedentary,* the first *e* is pronounced like

   ⓐ short *e.*

   b. long *e.*

   c. short *i.*

   d. schwa.

Items 6–10   There are five misspelled words in the following sentence. Cross out each misspelled word and write the correct spelling in the spaces provided.

   Our ~~physicle~~ education ~~instructer,~~ Mrs. Stevens, ~~constently~~ tells us that people who ~~exersize~~ every day have a more positive ~~atitude~~ toward life than people who never work out.

6. <u>physical</u>

7. <u>instructor</u>

8. <u>constantly</u>

9. <u>exercise</u>

10. <u>attitude</u>

29 Spelling Improvement

Introductory Activity

See if you can circle the word that is misspelled in each of the following pairs:

(akward)	*or*	awkward
exercise	*or*	(exercize)
business	*or*	(buisness)
worried	*or*	(worryed)
(shamful)	*or*	shameful
(begining)	*or*	beginning
(partys)	*or*	parties
(sandwichs)	*or*	sandwiches
heroes	*or*	(heros)

Answers are on page 582.

26.1

Poor spelling often results from bad habits developed in the early school years. With work, such habits can be corrected. If you can write your name without misspelling it, there is no reason why you can't do the same with almost any word in the English language. Following are seven steps you can take to improve your spelling.

Step 1: Using the Dictionary

Get into the habit of using the dictionary. When you write a paper, allow yourself time to look up the spelling of all the words you are unsure about. Do not underestimate the value of this step just because it is such a simple one. By using the dictionary, you can probably make yourself a 95 percent better speller.

Step 2: Keeping a Personal Spelling List

Keep a list of words you misspell, and study those words regularly. Use the chart on the inside front cover of this book as a starter. When you accumulate additional words, you may want to use a back page of your English notebook.

Hint   When you have trouble spelling long words, try to break each word into syllables and see whether you can spell the syllables. For example, *misdemeanor* can be spelled easily if you can hear and spell in turn its four syllables: *mis-de-mean-or.* The word *formidable* can be spelled easily if you hear and spell in turn its four syllables: *for-mi-da-ble.* Remember, then: try to see, hear, and spell long words in terms of their syllables.

Step 3: Mastering Commonly Confused Words

Master the meanings and spellings of the commonly confused words on pages 353–368. Your instructor may assign twenty words for you to study at a time and give you a series of quizzes until you have mastered all the words.

Step 4: Using Electronic Aids

There are two electronic aids that may help your spelling. First, a *computer with a spell-checker* will identify incorrect words and suggest correct spellings. If you know how to write on a computer, you will have no trouble learning how to use the spell-check feature.

Second, *electronic spell-checkers* are pocket-size devices that look much like the pocket calculator you may carry to your math class. They are a good example of how technology can help the learning process. Electronic spellers can be found in the typewriter or computer section of any discount store, at prices in the $100 range. The checker has a tiny keyboard. You type out the word the way you think it is spelled, and the checker quickly provides you with the correct spelling of related words. Some of these checkers even *pronounce* the word aloud for you.

Step 5: Understanding Basic Spelling Rules

Explained briefly here are three rules that may improve your spelling. While exceptions sometimes occur, these rules hold true most of the time.

1 **Changing y to i.** When a word ends in a consonant plus *y,* change *y* to *i* when you add an ending.

try + ed = tried	marry + es = marries
worry + es = worries	lazy + ness = laziness
lucky + ly = luckily	silly + est = silliest

2 **Final silent e.** Drop a final *e* before an ending that starts with a vowel (the vowels are *a, e, i, o,* and *u*).

hope + ing = hoping	sense + ible = sensible
fine + est = finest	hide + ing = hiding

Keep the final *e* before an ending that starts with a consonant.

use + ful = useful	care + less = careless
life + like = lifelike	settle + ment = settlement

3 **Doubling a final consonant.** Double the final consonant of a word when all the following are true:

a The word is one syllable or is accented on the last syllable.

b The word ends in a single consonant preceded by a single vowel.

c The ending you are adding starts with a vowel.

sob   + ing = sobbing   big   + est = biggest
drop + ed = dropped   omit + ed = omitted
admit + ing = admitting   begin + ing = beginning

Practice

Combine the following words and endings by applying the three rules above.

1. carry + ed = _carried_   6. permit + ed = _permitted_
2. revise + ing = _revising_   7. glide + ing = _gliding_
3. study + es = _studies_   8. angry + ly = _angrily_
4. wrap   + ing = _wrapping_   9. rebel + ing = _rebelling_
5. horrify + ed = _horrified_   10. grudge + es = _grudges_

Step 6: Understanding Plurals

Most words form their plurals by adding *-s* to the singular.

Singular	*Plural*
blanket	blankets
pencil	pencils
street	streets

Some words, however, form their plurals in special ways, as shown in the rules that follow.

1   Words ending in *-s, -ss, -z, -x, -sh,* or *-ch* usually form the plural by adding *-es.*

kiss	kisses	inch	inches
box	boxes	dish	dishes

2   Words ending in a consonant plus *y* form the plural by changing *y* to *i* and adding *-es.*

party	parties	county	counties
baby	babies	city	cities

3   Some words ending in *f* change the *f* to *v* and add *-es* in the plural.

leaf	leaves	life	lives
wife	wives	yourself	yourselves

4   Some words ending in *o* form their plurals by adding *-es*.

potato	potatoes	mosquito	mosquitoes
hero	heroes	tomato	tomatoes

5   Some words of foreign origin have irregular plurals. When in doubt, check your dictionary.

antenna	antennae	crisis	crises
criterion	criteria	medium	media

6   Some words form their plurals by changing letters within the word.

man	men	foot	feet
tooth	teeth	goose	geese

7   Combined words (words made up of two or more words) form their plurals by adding *-s* to the main word.

brother-in-law	brothers-in-law
passerby	passersby

Practice

Complete these sentences by filling in the plural of the word at the left.

crash   1. In driver training school, Bea covered her eyes during the film showing bloody car _____*crashes*_____.

match   2. Leon collects packs of _____*matches*_____ from hotels and restaurants.

doily   3. Lace _____*doilies*_____ are pinned to the arms of Aunt Agatha's chairs.

cross   4. The jeweled _____*crosses*_____ in the museum display case were priceless.

dozen   5. At the base of the rotten oak were _____*dozens*_____ of sucker shoots.

potato   6. Sherry tossed five _____*potatoes*_____ into the pot.

twenty   7. I dug deep in my pocket and pulled out two ___twenties___ to pay for the groceries.

wife   8. Three of the sheik's ___wives___ emerged from the long limousine.

passerby   9. Several ___passersby___ stopped to listen to the street musician.

medium   10. The candidate said that the print and electronic ___media___ had not paid enough attention to his campaign.

Step 7: Mastering a Basic Word List

Make sure you can spell all the words in the following list. They are some of the words used most often in English. Your instructor may assign twenty words for you to study at a time and give you a series of quizzes until you have mastered the words.

ability	another		being		
absent	answer	**20**	believe		
accident	anxious		between		
across	apply		bottom	**40**	
address	approve		breathe		
advertise	argue		building		
advice	around		business		
after	attempt		careful		
again	attention		careless		
against	awful		cereal		
all right	awkward		certain		
almost	balance		change		
a lot	bargain		cheap		
although	beautiful		chief		
always	because		children		
among	become		church		
angry	before		cigarette		
animal	begin		clothing		

collect	flower	loneliness
color	foreign	making **120**
comfortable	friend	marry
company	garden	match
condition	general	matter
conversation **60**	grocery	measure
daily	guess	medicine
danger	happy	middle
daughter	heard	might
death	heavy	million
decide	height	minute
deposit	himself	mistake
describe	holiday	money
different	house **100**	month
direction	however	morning
distance	hundred	mountain
doubt	hungry	much
dozen	important	needle
during	instead	neglect
each	intelligence	newspaper
early	interest	noise
earth	interfere	none **140**
education	kitchen	nothing
either	knowledge	number
English	labor	ocean
enough **80**	language	offer
entrance	laugh	often
everything	leave	omit
examine	length	only
exercise	lesson	operate
expect	letter	opportunity
family	listen	original

ought	restaurant	through
pain	ridiculous	ticket
paper	said	tired
pencil	same	today
people	sandwich	together
perfect	send	tomorrow
period	sentence	tongue
personal	several	tonight
picture	shoes	touch
place **160**	should	travel **220**
pocket	since	truly
possible	sleep	understand
potato	smoke	unity
president	something	until
pretty	soul	upon
problem	started	usual
promise	state	value
property	straight	vegetable
psychology	street	view
public	strong **200**	visitor
question	student	voice
quick	studying	warning
raise	success	watch
ready	suffer	welcome
really	surprise	window
reason	teach	would
receive	telephone	writing
recognize	theory	written
remember	thought	year
repeat **180**	thousand	yesterday **240**

■ **Review Test**

Items 1–8   Use the three spelling rules to spell the following words.

1. date   + ing   = _dating_
2. hurry   + ed   = _hurried_
3. drive   + able   = _drivable_
4. try   + es   = _tries_
5. swim   + ing   = _swimming_
6. guide   + ed   = _guided_
7. happy   + est   = _happiest_
8. bare   + ly   = _barely_

Items 9–14   Circle the correctly spelled plural in each pair.

9. gooses   (geese)
10. richs   (riches)
11. heros   (heroes)
12. wolfs   (wolves)
13. (pantries)   pantrys
14. lifes   (lives)

Items 15–20   Circle the correctly spelled word (from the basic word list) in each pair.

15. dout   (doubt)
16. (written)   writen
17. (a lot)   alot
18. exercize   (exercise)
19. origenal   (original)
20. anser   (answer)

30 Omitted Words and Letters

Introductory Activity

Some people drop small connecting words such as *of, and,* or *in* when they write. They may also drop the *-s* endings of plural nouns. See if you can find the six places in the passage below where letters or words have been dropped. Supply whatever is missing.

Two glass bottle*s* of apple juice lie broken *in* the supermarket aisle.

Suddenly, a toddler who has gotten away from his parents appears at

the head of the aisle. He spots the broken bottles and begins to run

toward them. His chubby body lurches along like *a* windup toy, and his

arm*s* move excitedly up and down. Luckily, *an* alert shopper quickly reacts

to the impending disaster and blocks the toddler's path. Then the shop-

per waits with *the* crying, frustrated little boy until his parents show up.

Answers are on page 582.

Be careful not to leave out words or letters when you write. The omission of words like *a, an, of, to,* or *the* or the *-s* ending needed on nouns or verbs may confuse and irritate your readers. They may not want to read what they regard as careless work.

Finding Omitted Words and Letters

Finding omitted words and letters, like finding many other sentence-skills mistakes, is a matter of careful proofreading. You must develop your ability to look carefully at a page to find places where mistakes may exist.

The exercises here will give you practice in finding omitted words and omitted *-s* endings on nouns. Another section of this book (pages 154–155) gives you practice in finding omitted *-s* endings on verbs.

Practice

Add the missing word (*a, an, the, of,* or *to*) as needed.

Example   Some people regard television as *a* tranquilizer that provides temporary relief from *the* pain and anxiety *of* modern life.

1. In the rest room, Jeff impatiently rubbed his hands under *the* mechanical dryer, which blew out feeble puffs *of* cool air.

2. On February 10, 1935, *The New York Times* reported that *an* eight-foot alligator had been dragged out of *a* city sewer by three teenage boys.

3. Dave dressed up as *a* stuffed olive for Halloween by wearing *a* green plastic garbage bag and a red knitted cap.

4. Mrs. Chan nearly fainted when she opened *the* health insurance bill and saw *an* enormous rate increase.

5. At 4 A.M., *the* all-night supermarket where I work hosts *an* assortment of strange shoppers.

6. With *a* loud hiss, *the* inflated beach ball suddenly shrank to *the* size of *an* orange.

7. The boiling milk bubbled over the sides *of* the pot, leaving a gluey white film on *the* stove top.

8. Susan turned *to* the answer page of the crossword book, pretended *to* herself that she hadn't, and turned back to her puzzle.

9. In order *to* ^ avoid stepping on the hot blacktop of *the* ^ parking lot, the barefoot boy tiptoed along the cooler white lines.

10. The messy roommates used hubcaps for ashtrays *and* ^ scribbled graffiti on their own bathroom walls.

The Omitted *-s* Ending

The plural form of regular nouns usually ends in *-s*. One common mistake that some people make with plurals is to omit this *-s* ending. People who drop the ending from plurals when speaking also tend to do it when writing. This tendency is especially noticeable when the meaning of the sentence shows that a word is plural.

> Ed and Mary pay four hundred dollar a month for an apartment that has only two room.

The *-s* ending has been omitted from *dollars* and *rooms*.

The activities that follow will help you correct the habit of omitting the *-s* endings from plurals.

Practice 1

Add *-s* endings where needed.

Example   Kyle beat me at several game*s* of darts.

1. Can you really get fifteen shave*s* from one of those razor blade*s*?

2. With perfect timing, the runner's powerful leg*s* glided smoothly over a dozen hurdle*s*.

3. One of the strangest fad*s* of the 1950s was the promotion of chocolate-covered ant*s* by candy manufacturers.

4. Because pet owner*s* abandoned them, small bands of monkey*s* are now living in southern Florida.

5. The photographer*s* locked themselves in steel cages in order to film great white shark*s* in their underwater environment.

6. The breeze blew dandelion spore*s* and dry brown leave*s* through the air.

7. Jim made twelve circular cage^s from chicken wire and set them around his growing tomato plant^s.

8. The special this week is three pound^s of grape^s for eighty-nine cent^s.

9. The rope sole^s on my summer shoe^s have begun to disintegrate.

10. The skinny man ordered two double cheeseburger^s and three vanilla shake^s.

Practice 2

Write sentences that use plural forms of the following pairs of words.

Answers will vary.

Example   girl, bike   *The little girls raced their bikes down the street.*

1. paper, grade _____

_____

2. pillow, bed _____

_____

3. sock, shoe _____

_____

4. day, night _____

_____

5. game, ball _____

_____

Note   People who drop the *-s* ending on nouns also tend to omit endings on verbs. Pages 154–155 will help you correct the habit of dropping endings on verbs.

■ Review Test 1

In each of the following sentences, two small connecting words are needed. Write them in the spaces provided, and write a caret (^) at each place in the sentence where a connecting word should appear.

_____a_____   1. Suffering from^ horrible head cold, Susan felt as though she were trying^ breathe
_____to_____   under water.

_____to_____   2. Because he forgot the key^ his padlock, Al asked^ gym attendant to saw the lock
_____the_____   off his locker.

_____a_____   3. The store made mistake when it sent me a letter saying that I hadn't paid
_____of_____   any my bills for six months.

_____the____   4. The children laughed with delight when small dog jumped on circus clown's
_____the____   back.

_____of_____   5. Dr. Marini recommends that my grandfather drink one glass wine every day
_____his____   to stimulate appetite and improve his circulation.

■ Review Test 2

Add the two -s endings needed in each sentence.

vessels   1. The whites of Sam's eyes were red from broken blood vessel, and his forehead
bruises   was a mass of purple bruise.

jobs   2. Ray has held five different job in four different cities in the past two year.
years

specialists   3. I've been to several specialist, but I still don't know what's causing these
headaches   terrible headache.

trees   4. Lian watched with dread as a bulldozer began knocking down tree and shrub
shrubs   in the patch of woods next door.

miles   5. Vance was driving eighty mile an hour when two police car stopped him.
cars

31 Commonly Confused Words

Introductory Activity

Circle the five words that are misspelled in the following passage. Then write their correct spellings in the spaces provided.

If (your) a resident of a temperate climate, you may suffer from feelings of depression in the winter and early spring. Scientists are now studying people (who's) moods seem to worsen in winter, and (there) findings show that the amount of daylight a person receives is an important factor in "seasonal depression." When a person gets (to) little sunlight, his or her mood darkens. (Its) fairly easy to treat severe cases of seasonal depression; the cure involves spending a few hours a day in front of full-spectrum fluorescent lights that contain all the components of natural light.

1. _you're_
2. _whose_
3. _their_
4. _too_
5. _It's_

Answers are on page 582.

Homonyms

The commonly confused words shown below are known as *homonyms;* they have the same sounds but different meanings and spellings. Complete the activities for each set of words, and check off and study the words that give you trouble.

Common Homonyms

all ready	pair	threw
already	pear	through
brake	passed	to
break	past	too
coarse	peace	two
course	piece	wear
hear	plain	where
here	plane	weather
hole	principal	whether
whole	principle	whose
its	right	who's
it's	write	your
knew	than	you're
new	then	
know	their	
no	there	
	they're	

---

all ready   completely prepared
already   previously, before

We were *all ready* to go, for we had eaten and packed *already* that morning.

Fill in the blanks: Eliza has _____*already*_____ phoned them twice to ask if they'll be _____*all ready*_____ to go by nine o'clock.

Write sentences using *all ready* and *already.*

Answers will vary for students' sentences throughout this section.

_____

brake   stop
break   come apart

Dot slams the *brake* pedal so hard that I'm afraid I'll *break* my neck in her car.

Fill in the blanks: I hit the _____brake_____ pedal so hard that my car spun around on the slick highway; luckily, there was a _____break_____ in the traffic at that point.

Write sentences using *brake* and *break.*

_____

_____

coarse   rough
course   part of a meal; a school subject; direction; certainly (with *of*)

During the *course* of my career as a waitress, I've dealt with some very *coarse* customers.

Fill in the blanks: As her final project in the weaving _____course_____, Maria made a tablecloth out of _____coarse_____ fibers in shades of blue.

Write sentences using *coarse* and *course.*

_____

_____

hear   perceive with the ear
here   in this place

If I *hear* another insulting ethnic joke *here,* I'll leave.

Fill in the blanks: Do you want to _____hear_____ about what happened to the last visitors who stayed _____here_____ at the count's castle?

Write sentences using *hear* and *here.*

_____

_____

hole   an empty spot
whole entire

If there is a *hole* in the tailpipe, I'm afraid we will have to replace the *whole* exhaust assembly.

Fill in the blanks: He walked the ____whole____ way, despite the ____hole____ in the sole of his right shoe.

Write sentences using *hole* and *whole*.

_____

_____

its   belonging to it
it's shortened form for *it is* or *it has*

The kitchen floor has lost *its* shine because *it's* been used as a roller skating rink by the children.

Fill in the blanks: ____It's____ foolish to wear your flimsy jacket with ____its____ thin hood in this downpour.

Write sentences using *its* and *it's*.

_____

_____

knew past tense of *know*
new   not old

We *knew* that the *new* television comedy would be canceled quickly.

Fill in the blanks: Georgia ____knew____ that a ____new____ color set would tempt the children to spend more hours parked in front of the TV.

Write sentences using *knew* and *new*.

_____

_____

know   to understand
no   a negative

I never *know* who might drop in even though *no* one is expected.

Fill in the blanks: Now that we _____ *know* _____ how the movie ends—thanks to you—there will be _____ *no* _____ pleasure in watching it.

Write sentences using *know* and *no.*

_____

_____

pair   a set of two
pear   a fruit

The dessert consisted of a *pair* of thin biscuits topped with vanilla ice cream and poached *pear* halves.

Fill in the blanks: The _____ *pair* _____ of infant overalls has a _____ *pear* _____ embroidered on the bib.

Write sentences using *pair* and *pear.*

_____

_____

passed   went by; succeeded in; handed to
past   a time before the present; by, as in "I drove past the house"

After Trina *passed* the driver's test, she drove *past* all her friends' houses and honked the horn.

Fill in the blanks: As his mother _____ *passed* _____ around her traditional Christmas cookies, Terry remembered all the times in the _____ *past* _____ when he had left some of those very cookies on a plate for Santa Claus.

Write sentences using *passed* and *past.*

_____

_____

peace   calm
piece   a part

The *peace* of the little town was shattered when a *piece* of a human body was found in the town dump.

Fill in the blanks: I won't give you any _____peace_____ unless you share that _____piece_____ of coconut cake with me.

Write sentences using *peace* and *piece*.

_____

_____

plain   simple
plane   aircraft

The *plain* box contained a very expensive model *plane* kit.

Fill in the blanks: The black-and-silver _____plane_____ on the runway looked exotic next to the _____plain_____ ones surrounding it.

Write sentences using *plain* and *plane.*

_____

_____

principal   main; a person in charge of a school; amount of money borrowed
principle   a law or standard

My *principal* goal in child rearing is to give my daughter strong *principles* to live by.

Fill in the blanks: The _____principal_____ sport at our high school, basketball, was coached by a man whose guiding _____principle_____ was team play.

Write sentences using *principal* and *principle.*

_____

_____

Note   It might help to remember that the *le* in *principle* is also in *rule*—the meaning of *principle.*

right   correct; opposite of *left;* privilege
write   what you do in English

It is my *right* to refuse to *write* my name on your petition.

Fill in the blanks: As I rested my fractured _____*right*_____ arm on his desk,

I asked the doctor to _____*write*_____ out a prescription for a painkiller.

Write sentences using *right* and *write.*

_____

_____

than   used in comparisons
then   at that time

I glared angrily at my boss, and *then* I told him our problems were more serious *than* he suspected.

Fill in the blanks: Frankenstein's monster played peacefully with the little girl;
_____*then*_____ he was chased by the villagers, who were more hysterical
_____*than*_____ stampeding turkeys.

Write sentences using *than* and *then.*

_____

_____

Note   It might help to remember that *then* (the word spelled with an *e*) is a tim*e* signal (time also has an *e*).

their   belonging to them
there   at that place; a neutral word used with verbs like *is, are, was, were, have,* and *had*
they're   shortened form of *they are*

The tenants *there* are complaining because *they're* being cheated by *their* landlords.

Fill in the blanks: _____*There*_____ has been an increase in burglaries in

_____*their*_____ neighborhood, so _____*they're*_____ planning to install an alarm.

Write sentences using *their, there,* and *they're.*

_____

_____

_____

threw   past tense of *throw*
through   from one side to the other; finished

> When a character in a movie *threw* a cat *through* the window, I had to close my eyes.

Fill in the blanks: As Darryl picked _____*through*_____ the clothes in the dryer, he _____*threw*_____ the still-damp towels aside.

Write sentences using *threw* and *through.*

_____

_____

to   a verb part, as in *to smile;* toward, as in "I'm going to heaven."
too   overly, as in "The pizza was too hot"; also, as in "The coffee was hot, too."
two   the number 2

> Lola drove *to* the store *to* get some ginger ale. (The first *to* means *toward;* the second *to* is a verb part that goes with *get.*)
>
> The sport jacket is *too* tight; the pants are tight, *too.* (The first *too* means *overly;* the second *too* means *also.*)
>
> The *two* basketball players leaped for the jump ball. (2)

Fill in the blanks: I don't know how _____*two*_____ such different people were attracted _____*to*_____ each other and made a happy marriage, _____*too*_____.

Write sentences using *to, too,* and *two.*

_____

_____

_____

wear   to have on
where in what place

I work at a nuclear reactor, *where* one must *wear* a radiation-detection badge at all times.

Fill in the blanks: At the restaurant _____*where*_____ I work, the waiters _____*wear*_____ cowboy hats and Western snap-front shirts.

Write sentences using *wear* and *where.*

_____

_____

weather atmospheric conditions
whether if it happens that; in case; if

Because of the threatening *weather,* it's not certain *whether* or not the game will be played.

Fill in the blanks: The _____*weather*_____ vane was once a valuable agricultural tool, indicating _____*whether*_____ the wind was coming from the north, south, east, or west.

Write sentences using *weather* and *whether.*

_____

_____

whose belonging to whom
who's shortened form for *who is* and *who has*

The man *who's* the author of the latest diet book is a man *whose* ability to cash in on the latest craze is well known.

Fill in the blanks: The substitute teacher, _____*whose*_____ lack of experience was obvious, asked, " _____*Who's*_____ the person who threw that spitball?"

Write sentences using *whose* and *who's.*

_____

_____

your   belonging to you
you're   shortened form of *you are*

Since *your* family has a history of heart disease, *you're* the kind of person who should take extra health precautions.

Fill in the blanks: I may not like _____your_____ opinion, but _____you're_____ certainly entitled to express it in this class.

Write sentences using *your* and *you're.*

_____

_____

Other Words Frequently Confused

Following is a list of other words that people frequently confuse. Complete the activities for each set of words, and check off and study the ones that give you trouble.

21.6

Commonly Confused Words

a	among	desert	learn
an	between	dessert	teach
accept	beside	does	loose
except	besides	dose	lose
advice	can	fewer	quiet
advise	may	less	quite
affect	clothes	former	though
effect	cloths	latter	thought

---

a   Both *a* and *an* are used before other words to mean, approximately, *one.*
an

Generally you should use *an* before words starting with a vowel (*a, e, i, o, u*):

an absence   an exhibit   an idol   an offer   an upgrade

Generally you should use *a* before words starting with a consonant (all other letters):

    a pen   a ride   a digital clock   a movie   a neighbor

Fill in the blanks: In _____*an*_____ instant, he realized that _____*a*_____ diamond-patterned snake was slithering over his shoe.

Write sentences using *a* and *an*.

Answers will vary for students' sentences throughout this section.

_____

accept   receive; agree to
except   exclude; but

    If I *accept* your advice, I'll lose all my friends *except* you.

Fill in the blanks: The crowd couldn't _____*accept*_____ the judges' decision; _____*except*_____ for some minor mistakes, Jones had clearly won the fight.

Write sentences using *accept* and *except*.

_____

_____

advice   noun meaning *an opinion*
advise   verb meaning *to counsel, to give advice*

    Jake never listened to his parents' *advice,* and he ended up listening to a cop *advise* him of his rights.

Fill in the blanks: I asked a plumber to _____*advise*_____ me, since the _____*advice*_____ in the do-it-yourself book had been disastrous.

Write sentences using *advice* and *advise*.

_____

_____

affect   verb meaning *to influence*
effect   verb meaning *to bring about something;* noun meaning *result*

My sister Nicole cries for *effect,* but my parents caught on and her act no longer *affects* them.

Fill in the blanks: A dangerous flooding _____*effect*_____ is created when the full moon _____*affect*_____ s the tides in the spring.

Write sentences using *affect* and *effect.*

_____

_____

among   implies three or more
between   implies only two

We selfishly divided the box of candy *between* the two of us rather than *among* all the members of the family.

Fill in the blanks: _____*Among*_____ the heads of lettuce in the bin was one with a large insect nestled _____*between*_____ the wrapper and the outer leaf.

Write sentences using *among* and *between.*

_____

_____

beside   along the side of
besides   in addition to

Fred sat *beside* Teresa. *Besides* them, there were ten other people at the Tupperware party.

Fill in the blanks: _____*Besides*_____ the broken leg, he suffered a deep cut _____*beside*_____ his mouth.

Write sentences using *beside* and *besides.*

_____

_____

can refers to the ability to do something
may refers to permission or possibility

If you *can* work overtime on Saturday, you *may* take Monday off.

Fill in the blanks: Although that mole _____*can*_____ be removed, it _____*may*_____ be better to leave it alone.

Write sentences using *can* and *may*.

_____

_____

clothes articles of dress
cloths pieces of fabric

I tore up some old *clothes* to use as polishing *cloths.*

Fill in the blanks: Maxine used inexpensive dust _____*cloths*_____ to make _____*clothes*_____ for her daughter's doll.

Write sentences using *clothes* and *cloths.*

_____

_____

desert noun meaning *a stretch of dry land;*
verb meaning *to abandon one's post or duty*
dessert noun meaning *last part of a meal*

Don't *desert* us now; order a sinful *dessert* along with us.

Fill in the blanks: Guests began to _____*desert*_____ the banquet room after the strawberry shortcake _____*dessert*_____ had been cleared away.

Write sentences using *desert* and *dessert.*

_____

_____

does   form of the verb *do*
dose   an amount of medicine

> Elena *does* not realize that a *dose* of brandy is not the best medicine for the flu.

Fill in the blanks: If this _____*dose*_____ of cough syrup _____*does*_____ its work, I'll be able to give my speech.

Write sentences using *does* and *dose.*

_____

_____

fewer   used with things that can be counted
less   refers to amount, value, or degree

> I missed *fewer* classes than Rafael, but I wrote *less* effectively than he did.

Fill in the blanks: Larry took _____*fewer*_____ chances after the accident; he was _____*less*_____ sure of his driving ability.

Write sentences using *fewer* and *less.*

_____

_____

former   refers to the first of two items named
latter   refers to the second of two items named

> I turned down both the service station job and the shipping clerk job; the *former* involved irregular hours and the *latter* offered very low pay.

Fill in the blanks: She eats lots of raisins and strawberries; the _____*former*_____ contain iron and the _____*latter*_____ are rich in vitamin C.

Write sentences using *former* and *latter.*

_____

_____

Note   Be sure to distinguish *latter* from *later* (meaning *after some time*).

learn   to gain knowledge
teach   to give knowledge

After Keisha *learns* the new dance, she is going to *teach* it to me.

Fill in the blanks: If little Beth can _____learn_____ sign language, we can _____teach_____ her parents how to communicate with her.

Write sentences using *learn* and *teach.*

_____

_____

loose   not fastened; not tight-fitting
lose   misplace; fail to win

I am afraid I'll *lose* my ring: it's too *loose* on my finger.

Fill in the blanks: When he discovered that his pet turtles had gotten _____loose_____ he worried that he might _____lose_____ some of them.

Write sentences using *loose* and *lose.*

_____

_____

quiet   peaceful
quite   entirely; really; rather

After a busy day, the children were still not *quiet,* and their parents were *quite* tired.

Fill in the blanks: Chuck couldn't keep _____quiet_____ about the scholarship his daughter had won; it was really _____quite_____ an honor.

Write sentences using *quiet* and *quite.*

_____

_____

though   despite the fact that
thought   past tense of *think*

> *Though* I enjoyed the dance, I *thought* the cover charge of $5 was too high.

Fill in the blanks: _____Though_____ everyone claimed the silvery object was an airplane, I _____thought_____ it was a UFO.

Write sentences using *though* and *thought*.

_____

_____

Incorrect Word Forms

Following is a list of incorrect word forms that people sometimes use in their writing. Complete the activities for each word, and check off and study the words that give you trouble.

Incorrect Word Forms

being that	could of	would of
can't hardly	must of	irregardless
couldn't hardly	should of	

---

being that   Incorrect! Use *because* or *since*.

                             because
I'm going to bed now ~~being that~~ I must get up early tomorrow.

Correct the following sentences.

      Because
1. ~~Being that~~ the boss heard my remark, I doubt if I'll get the promotion.
                because
2. I'll have more cake, ~~being that~~ my diet is officially over.
                           since
3. Peter knows a lot about cars, ~~being that~~ his dad is a mechanic.

can't hardly   Incorrect! Use *can hardly* or *could hardly*.
couldn't hardly

                      can
Small store owners ~~can't~~ hardly afford to offer large discounts.

Correct the following sentences.

          could
1. They ~~couldn't~~ hardly see the drive-in movie screen through the fog.
     can
2. I ~~can't~~ hardly keep from laughing when I watch that show.
      could
3. We ~~couldn't~~ hardly wait to see her face when she walked into the surprise party.

could of   Incorrect! Use *could have, must have, should have, would have.*
must of
should of
would of

              have
I should ~~of~~ applied for a loan when my credit was good.

Correct the following sentences.

            have
1. Thelma must ~~of~~ painted the walls by herself.
           have
2. You should ~~of~~ left the tip on the table.
        have
3. I would ~~of~~ been glad to help if you had asked politely.
             have
4. No one could ~~of~~ predicted that accident.

irregardless   Incorrect! Use *regardless.*

    Regardless
~~Irregardless~~ of what anyone says, he will not change his mind.

Correct the following sentences.

    Regardless
1. ~~Irregardless~~ of what anybody else does, I'm wearing jeans to the meeting.
    Regardless
2. ~~Irregardless~~ of the weather, the parade will go on as scheduled.
    Regardless
3. ~~Irregardless~~ of what my parents say, I will continue to see Elena.

■ Review Test 1

These sentences check your understanding of *its, it's; there, their, they're; to, too, two;* and *your, you're.* Underline the correct word in the parentheses. Rather than guess, look back at the explanations of the words when necessary.

1. As I walked (<u>to</u>, too, two) the car, I stepped in the freshly laid cement that (to, too, <u>two</u>) workers had just smoothed over.

2. (Its, <u>It's</u>) safe (<u>to</u>, too, two) park (<u>your</u>, you're) car over (<u>there</u>, their, they're).

3. "(Your, <u>You're</u>) wearing (<u>your</u>, you're) shoes on the wrong feet," Carla whispered to her little sister.

4. (<u>There</u>, Their, They're) are more secrets about (there, <u>their</u>, they're) past than (there, their, <u>they're</u>) willing to share.

5. The (to, too, <u>two</u>) of us plan to go to (<u>your</u>, you're) party, (to, <u>too</u>, two).

6. (Its, <u>It's</u>) been a long time since (<u>your</u>, you're) car has had (<u>its</u>, it's) carburetor checked.

7. (<u>To</u>, Too, Two) get into the dance, (<u>your</u>, you're) friend will have to pay (to, too, <u>two</u>) dollars.

8. (Its, <u>It's</u>) a shame that (your, <u>you're</u>) being laid off from your job (<u>there</u>, their, they're).

9. (Its, <u>It's</u>) rumored that the team has lost (<u>its</u>, it's) best pitcher for the rest of the season.

10. (<u>There</u>, Their, They're) is a mistake on (there, <u>their</u>, they're) check, so they are speaking (<u>to</u>, too, two) the manager.

■ Review Test 2

The sentences that follow check your understanding of a variety of commonly confused words. Underline the correct word in the parentheses. Rather than guess, look back at the explanations of the words when necessary.

1. My sister is better at math (<u>than</u>, then) I am, but I (right, <u>write</u>) more easily.

2. I was (<u>all ready</u>, already) (<u>to</u>, too, two) sign up for (<u>your</u>, you're) (coarse, <u>course</u>) when I discovered it had (all ready, <u>already</u>) closed.

3. He is the kind of person who (<u>accepts</u>, excepts) any (<u>advice</u>, advise) he is given, even if (its, <u>it's</u>) bad.

4. I (<u>know</u>, no) you want to (<u>hear</u>, here) the (hole, <u>whole</u>) story.

5. (There, Their, They're) is no (plain, plane) paper in the house, only a (pair, pear) of lined pads.

6. Our team got a real (brake, break) when Pete's pop fly fell (among, between) (to, too, two) infielders for a base hit.

7. I (can't hardly, can hardly) (hear, here) the instructor in that (coarse, course) without making (a, an) effort.

8. If (your, you're) going to have (desert, dessert), pick something with (fewer, less) calories than chocolate cheesecake.

9. Looking (threw, through) his front window, Felipe could see a (pair, pear) of squirrels getting (there, their, they're) food ready for the cold (weather, whether) to come.

10. When I (learn, teach) you to drive a stick-shift car, we'll go (to, too, two) a (quiet, quite) country road where (there, their, they're) won't be much traffic.

■ **Review Test 3**
Answers will vary.
On separate paper, write short sentences using the ten words shown below.

there	too (meaning *also*)
past	affect
then	its
advise	who's
you're	break

32 Effective Word Choice

Introductory Activity

Put a check mark beside the sentence in each pair that makes more effective and appropriate use of words.

1. After a bummer of a movie, we pigged out on a pizza. _____

   After a disappointing movie, we devoured a pizza. _✓_

2. Feeling blue about the death of his best buddy, Tennyson wrote the tearjerker "In Memoriam." _____

   Mourning the death of his best friend, Tennyson wrote the moving poem "In Memoriam." _✓_

3. The personality adjustment inventories will be administered on Wednesday in the Student Center. _____

   Psychological tests will be given on Wednesday in the Student Center. _✓_

4. The referee in the game, in my personal opinion, made the right decision in the situation. _____

   I think the referee made the right decision. _✓_

Now see if you can circle the correct number in each case:

Pair (1), 2, 3, 4) contains a sentence with slang; pair (1, (2), 3, 4) contains a sentence with a cliché; pair (1, 2, (3), 4) contains a sentence with pretentious words; and pair (1, 2, 3, (4)) contains a wordy sentence.

Answers are on page 583.

Choose your words carefully when you write. Always take the time to think about your word choices, rather than simply using the first word that comes to mind. You want to develop the habit of selecting words that are appropriate and exact for your purposes. One way you can show sensitivity to language is by avoiding slang, clichés, pretentious words, and wordiness.

Slang

21.3a

We often use slang expressions when we talk because they are so vivid and colorful. However, slang is usually out of place in formal writing. Here are some examples of slang expressions:

The party was a *real horror show.*

I don't want to *lay a guilt trip* on you.

Our boss is not *playing with a full deck.*

Dad *flipped out* when he learned that Jan had *totaled* the car.

Someone *ripped off* Jay's new Adidas running shoes from his locker.

After the game, we *stuffed our faces* at the diner.

I finally told my parents to *get off my case.*

The movie really *grossed me out.*

Slang expressions have a number of drawbacks. They go out of date quickly, they become tiresome if used excessively in writing, and they may communicate clearly to some readers but not to others. Also, the use of slang can be an evasion of the specific details that are often needed to make one's meaning clear in writing. For example, in "The party was a real horror show," the writer has not provided the specific details about the party necessary for us to understand the statement clearly. Was it the setting, the food and drink (or lack of them), the guests, the music, or the hosts that made the party such a dreadful experience? In general, then, you should avoid slang in your writing. If you are in doubt about whether an expression is slang, it may help to check a recently published hardbound dictionary.

Practice

Rewrite the following sentences, replacing the italicized slang words with more formal ones.

Example   I was *so beat* Friday night that I decided *to ditch* the birthday party.

I was so exhausted Friday night that I decided not to go to the

birthday party.

Answers will vary.

1. The scene in the *flick* where Rocky ate six raw eggs *grossed me out.*

   The scene in the movie where Rocky ate six raw eggs made me sick.

2. *Ex-cons* have a hard time adjusting after leaving the *slammer.*

   Ex-offenders have a hard time adjusting after leaving prison.

3. Manny *whipped right through* the multiple-choice questions, but the essay section *threw him for a loop.*

   Manny went through the multiple-choice questions quickly but had trouble

   with the essay section.

4. The professional assassin *wasted* over twenty victims before someone *ratted* on him.

   The professional assassin killed over twenty victims before someone

   informed on him.

5. That book on suicide is *heavy;* it really *bent me out of shape.*

   That book on suicide is depressing; it really bothered me.

Clichés

ALLWRITE!
21.5

Clichés are expressions that have been worn out through constant use. Some typical clichés are listed on the following page.

Common Clichés

all work and no play	sad but true
at a loss for words	saw the light
better late than never	short and sweet
drop in the bucket	sigh of relief
easier said than done	singing the blues
had a hard time of it	taking a big chance
in the nick of time	time and time again
in this day and age	too close for comfort
it dawned on me	too little, too late
it goes without saying	took a turn for the worse
last but not least	under the weather
make ends meet	where he (*or* she) is coming from
needless to say	word to the wise
on top of the world	work like a dog

Clichés are common in speech but make your writing seem tired and stale. Also, they are often an evasion of the specific details that you must work to provide in your writing. You should, then, avoid clichés and try to express your meaning in fresh, original ways.

Practice 1

Underline the cliché in each of the following sentences. Then substitute specific, fresh words for the trite expression.

Example   My parents supported me through some <u>trying times</u>.

rough years

Answer will vary.

1. Salespeople who are rude <u>make my blood boil</u>.

   make me very angry

2. Doug has been <u>down in the dumps</u> ever since his girlfriend broke up with him.

   depressed

3. That new secretary is <u>one in a million</u>.

   wonderful

4. We decided to hire a hall and <u>roll out the red carpet</u> in honor of our parents' silver wedding anniversary.

have a celebration

5. The minute classes let out for the summer, I feel <u>free as a bird</u>.

free

Practice 2

Answers may vary.

Write a short paragraph describing the kind of day you had. Try to put as many clichés as possible into your writing. For example, "I had a long hard day. I had a lot to get done, and I kept my nose to the grindstone." By making yourself aware of clichés in this way, you should lessen the chance that they will appear in your writing.

Pretentious Words

Some people feel they can improve their writing by using fancy, elevated words rather than more simple, natural words. They use artificial and stilted language that more often obscures their meaning than communicates it clearly. Here are some unnatural-sounding sentences:

The football combatants left the gridiron.

His instructional technique is a very positive one.

At the counter, we inquired about the arrival time of the aircraft.

I observed the perpetrator of the robbery depart from the retail establishment.

The same thoughts can be expressed more clearly and effectively by using plain, natural language, as below:

The football players left the field.

He is a good instructor.

At the counter, we asked when the plane would arrive.

I saw the robber leave the store.

Following is a list of some other inflated words and the simple words that could replace them.

Inflated Words	Simpler Words
component	part
delineate	describe
facilitate	help
finalize	finish
initiate	begin
manifested	shown
subsequent to	after
to endeavor	to try
transmit	send

Practice

Cross out the two pretentious words in each sentence. Then substitute clear, simple language for the pretentious words.

Example   Tessa was ~~terminated~~ from her ~~employment~~.

Tessa was fired from her job.

Answers may vary.

1. I do not ~~comprehend~~ that ~~individual's~~ behavior.

   I do not understand that person's behavior.

2. He ~~eradicated~~ all the ~~imperfections~~ in his notes.

   He erased all the mistakes in his notes.

3. She ~~contemplated~~ his ~~utterance~~.

   She thought about what he said.

4. The police officer ~~halted~~ the ~~vehicle~~.

   The police officer stopped the car.

5. Inez told the counselor about her ~~vocational~~ ~~aspirations~~.

   Inez told the counselor about her career hopes.

Wordiness

22

Wordiness—using more words than necessary to express a meaning—is often a sign of lazy or careless writing. Your readers may resent the extra time and energy they must spend when you have not done the work needed to make your writing direct and concise.

Here is a list of some wordy expressions that could be reduced to single words.

Wordy Form	Short Form
a large number of	many
a period of a week	a week
arrive at an agreement	agree
at an earlier point in time	before
at the present time	now
big in size	big
due to the fact that	because
during the time that	while
five in number	five
for the reason that	because
good benefit	benefit
in every instance	always
in my opinion	I think
in the event that	if
in the near future	soon
in this day and age	today
is able to	can
large in size	large
plan ahead for the future	plan
postponed until later	postponed
red in color	red
return back	return

Here are examples of wordy sentences:

> At this point in time in our country, the amount of violence seems to be increasing every day.
>
> I called to the children repeatedly to get their attention, but my shouts did not get any response from them.

Omitting needless words improves these sentences:

> Violence is increasing in our country.
>
> I called to the children repeatedly, but they didn't respond.

Practice

Rewrite the following sentences, omitting needless words.

Example   Starting as of the month of June, I will be working at the store on a full-time basis.

As of June, I will be working at the store full time.

Answers may vary.

1. In light of the fact that I am a vegetarian, I don't eat meat.

   I am a vegetarian.

2. On Tuesday of last week, I started going to college classes on a full-time basis.

   Last Tuesday, I started going to college full time.

3. On account of the fact that all my money is gone and I am broke, I can't go to the movies.

   Since I'm broke, I can't go to the movies.

4. I repeated over and over again that I refused to go under any circumstances, no matter what.

   I repeated that I wouldn't go.

5. Regardless of what I say, regardless of what I do, my father is annoyed by my words and behavior.

   Everything I say and do annoys my father.

■ **Review Test 1**

Certain words are italicized in the following sentences. In the space provided, identify whether the words are slang (*S*), clichés (*C*), or pretentious words (*PW*). Then replace them with more effective words.

Answers may vary.

_C_   1. The sight of the car crash *sent chills down my spine.*
      frightened me greatly

_PW_   2. That garbage *receptacle is at maximum capacity.*
      can ... full

_S_   3. The *old geezer* kept his *choppers* in a glass on the nightstand.
      elderly man ... false teeth

_S_   4. The town *cheapskate* finally *cashed in his chips* and left all his money to charity.
      miser ... died

_C_   5. I left work ten minutes early and made it home *in no time flat.*
      very quickly

_PW_   6. Phyllis *lamented* her grandmother's *demise.*
      mourned ... death

_PW_   7. The pitcher *hurled* the *sphere* toward the batter.
      threw ... ball

_C_   8. When she got her first paycheck, Kwan was *sitting on top of the world.*
      extremely proud

_S_   9. After studying for three hours, we *packed it in* and *cruised over* to the pizza parlor.
      stopped ... went

_C_   10. Last year's popular television star turned out to be *a flash in the pan.*
      short-lived

■ **Review Test 2**

Rewrite the following sentences, omitting needless words.

Answers will vary; possible answers are shown.

1. Before I woke up this morning, while I was still asleep, I had a dream about an airline disaster in which a plane crashed.

   Before I woke up this morning, I dreamed about a plane crash.

2. Tamika lifted up the empty suitcase, which had nothing in it, and tossed it onto the unmade bed covered with messy sheets and blankets.

   Tamika lifted the empty suitcase and tossed it onto the unmade bed.

3. While he glared at me with an unfriendly face, I just sat there silently, not saying a word.

   While he glared at me, I sat silently.

4. Whereas some people feel that athletes are worth their salaries, I feel that the value of professional sports players in this country is vastly overrated moneywise.

   I feel that professional athletes are overpaid.

5. I don't like reading the historical type of novel because this kind of book is much too long and, in addition, tends to be boring and uninteresting.

   I find historical novels long and boring.

Part Three

Reinforcement of the Skills

Introduction

To reinforce the sentence skills presented in Part Two, this part of the book—Part Three—provides mastery tests, combined mastery tests, proofreading tests, and editing tests. There are four *mastery tests* for each of the skills where errors occur most frequently and two *mastery tests* for each of the remaining skills. A series of *combined mastery tests* will reassure your understanding of important related skills. *Editing and proofreading tests* offer practice in finding and correcting one kind of error in a brief passage. *Combined editing tests* then offer similar practice—except that each of these passages contains a variety of mistakes. Both the editing and the proofreading tests will help you become a skilled editor and proofreader. All too often, students can correct mistakes in practice sentences but are unable to do so in their own writing. You must learn to look carefully for sentence-skills errors and to make close checking a habit.

Appendix F at the end of the book provides progress charts that will help you keep track of your performance on these tests.

Mastery Tests

Subjects and Verbs

■ Mastery Test 1

Draw one line under subjects and two lines under verbs. Cross out prepositional phrases as necessary to help find subjects. (Be sure to underline all the parts of a verb. Also, remember that you may find more than one subject and one verb in a sentence.)

1. My cat sleeps ~~on the radiator~~.
2. An opened bag ~~of lemon cookies~~ hung ~~over the edge of the shelf~~.
3. Margie and Paul walked hand in hand ~~into the haunted house~~.
4. Those early Beatles records have become collectors' items.
5. Twenty people crammed themselves ~~into the tiny elevator~~.
6. The truck driver got out his jumper cables and attached them ~~to the battery of my car~~.
7. The man ~~in the gorilla suit~~ is my brother.
8. Vince always watches football ~~on television~~ but almost never goes ~~to a game~~.
9. Unable to find his parents ~~in the supermarket~~, Billy sat down and cried.
10. She opened the book, placed her finger ~~at the top of the page~~, and began to speed-read.

| Score | Number correct _____ × 10 = _____ % |

Subjects and Verbs

■ Mastery Test 2

Draw one line under subjects and two lines under verbs. Cross out prepositional phrases as necessary to help find subjects. (Be sure to underline all the parts of a verb. Also, remember that you may find more than one subject and one verb in a sentence.)

1. Nancy burned her arm ~~on the charcoal grill~~.

2. I always keep a first-aid kit ~~in the trunk of my car~~.

3. He has been looking ~~for that book for at least a week~~.

4. The new office manager was hired ~~on Tuesday~~ and fired ~~on Wednesday~~.

5. My grandfather is often troubled ~~by arthritis~~.

6. Cheryl and her sister found a ten-dollar bill ~~in the wastebasket~~.

7. Fred ran ~~across the porch~~ and tripped ~~on a loose board~~.

8. Those violent cartoons ~~on Saturday morning television~~ are too scary ~~for small children~~.

9. All ~~of the leftover Christmas decorations~~ just went ~~on sale at half price~~.

10. Bonnie and Clyde strode ~~into the bank~~, waved their guns, and told everyone to lie down ~~on the floor~~.

Score   Number correct _____ × 10 = _____ %

Subjects and Verbs

■ Mastery Test 3

Draw one line under subjects and two lines under verbs. Cross out prepositional phrases as necessary to help find subjects. (Be sure to underline all the parts of a verb. Also, remember that you may find more than one subject and one verb in a sentence.)

1. Tom reads the sports pages every morning.
2. The name ~~of that woman~~ just flew ~~out of my head~~.
3. Our dog whined pitifully ~~during the violent thunderstorm~~.
4. That screen has at least twenty holes and needs to be replaced.
5. Her problems are starting to sound ~~like TV reruns~~.
6. Three copies ~~of that book~~ have been stolen ~~from the library~~.
7. The little girl ~~with pigtails~~ did graceful cartwheels ~~in the yard~~.
8. My sixth-grade teacher never could understand my questions.
9. We bought a broken floor lamp ~~at our neighbor's garage sale~~ and then could not decide what to do ~~with it~~.
10. The mud slides, flooded roads, and washed-out bridges were caused ~~by last week's heavy rains~~.

Score   Number correct _____ × 10 = _____ %

Subjects and Verbs

■ **Mastery Test 4**

Draw one line under subjects and two lines under verbs. Cross out prepositional phrases as necessary to help find subjects. (Be sure to underline all the parts of a verb. Also, remember that you may find more than one subject and one verb in a sentence.)

1. A low whistle suddenly pierced the silence.

2. Liz had spread her beach towel over the hot sand.

3. At the health food bar, Bob was sipping a strawberry-coconut milk shake.

4. Our old car has been repaired only three times in the last four years.

5. Annabelle's skin turned bright orange from the indoor tanning lotion.

6. Marsha and Ann begged their parents for permission to go to the rock concert.

7. The officer dismounted from his motorcycle, walked over to me, and asked for my license and registration.

8. Bananas, skim milk, and bran buds were the ingredients in the breakfast drink.

9. I listened to all the candidate's promises but did not believe a single one.

10. A doctor and nurse walked into the room, pulled down Mike's covers, and ordered him to roll over.

Fragments

■ **Mastery Test 1**

Each word group in the student paragraph below is numbered. In the space provided, write *C* if a word group is a complete sentence; write *frag* if it is a fragment. You will find ten fragments in the paragraph.

1. _C_
2. _frag_
3. _C_
4. _frag_
5. _C_
6. _frag_
7. _frag_
8. _C_
9. _frag_
10. _C_
11. _frag_
12. _frag_
13. _C_
14. _C_
15. _frag_
16. _C_
17. _C_
18. _frag_
19. _C_
20. _frag_

[1]One of my favorite dishes to cook and eat is chili. [2]The hotter the better. [3]First, I chop onion, garlic, and sweet red and green peppers into small cubes. [4]While I fry the vegetables in one pan. [5]I brown some lean ground beef in another pan. [6]Then combine the two mixtures. [7]And add a can of shiny red kidney beans. [8]Next, I decide what kind of seasonings to use. [9]In addition to chili powder, hot pepper flakes, and Tabasco sauce. [10]I sometimes add unusual ingredients. [11]Like molasses, cinnamon, chocolate, beer, red wine, or raisins. [12]Stirring the bubbling pot and inhaling the spicy aromas. [13]I occasionally taste the mixture to make sure it's good. [14]I cook the chili over a low flame for as long as possible. [15]To give the flavors time to mellow and blend together. [16]Also, longer cooking time produces spicier chili. [17]My chili has been known to burn people's tongues and cause beads of perspiration to form on their brows. [18]And has made friends reach desperately for a glass of water. [19]However, no one has ever complained. [20]Or forgotten to ask for a second helping.

Score   Number correct _____ × 5 = _____ %

Fragments

■ Mastery Test 2

Underline the fragment in each item. Then make whatever changes are needed to turn the fragment into a sentence.

Example   In grade school, I didn't want to wear glasses.ₓ And avoided having to
get them by memorizing the Snellen eye chart.

1. Nita's sons kept opening and closing the refrigerator door.ₓ To see just when the little light inside went out.

2. Even though there are a million pigeons in the city,ₓ You never see a baby pigeon. It makes you wonder where they are hiding out.

3. Frank likes to get to work early,ₓ And spread papers all over his desk. Then he looks too busy to be given any more work.

4. Brenda's doctor warned her to cut out sweets,ₓ Especially ice cream and candy.

5. Dragging her feet in the paper slippers,ₓ The patient shuffled along the corridor. She hugged the wall closely as nurses and visitors bustled past her.

6. The children ignored the sign,ₓ That the lifeguard had posted. They raced around on the slick cement bordering the pool.

7. Pete flunked out of college,ₓ After only two semesters. The only thing he could pass was a football.

8. My neighbors' dog likes to borrow things. Today, I saw him trotting away from my back steps,ₓ Carrying one of my gardening shoes in his mouth.

9. Since cooking with a small toaster oven saves energy,ₓ I bought one to use for small meals and snacks.

10. My cousin sends me funny cards,ₓ Such as one with a picture of a lion hanging on to a parachute. It says, "Just thought I'd drop you a lion."

> *Score*   Number correct _____ × 10 = _____ %

Fragments

■ Mastery Test 3

Underline the fragment in each item. Then make whatever changes are needed to turn the fragment into a sentence.

1. As Robert twisted the front doorknob, *i*It came off in his hand. He regretted the day he had bought the house as a "do-it-yourself special."

2. Large, spiky plants called *Spanish spears* bordered the path. The leaves brushed against my legs, *a*And left little slash marks on my ankles.

3. Tim stockpiles canned and dried foods in his basement, *i*In case of emergency. Some of his Campbell's soup is eight years old.

4. At the amusement park, we piled into a boat shaped like a hollowed-out log. Then, gripping the boat's sides and screaming in fear, *W*We plunged through clouds of spray down a water-filled chute.

5. At the lumberyard, Clarence loaded his compact car, *W*With ten-foot planks of raw pine. The car's open hatchback bounced and vibrated as he drove away.

6. Before the newly painted parking stripes had dried, *c*Cars had begun driving over them. As a result, the lot was crisscrossed with pale white lines.

7. My father used to take me to ball games. He would always bring along a newspaper, *t*To read between innings.

8. When Lucas goes on vacation, he fills the bathtub with an inch of water, *and* *t*Then puts his houseplants in the tub. This way, they don't die of thirst.

9. Terry carries her portable tape player everywhere she goes. For example, *she takes it* to the bookstore. She can't survive for ten minutes without her favorite songs.

10. The perfect shell glittered on the ocean bottom. The diver lifted it off the sand, *a*And placed it in the bag hanging from his shoulder.

Score   Number correct _____ × 10 = _____ %

Fragments

■ Mastery Test 4

Underline and then correct the ten fragments in the following passage.

This summer, I discovered that nature offers some surprises to people. <u>Who take the</u> ^w
<u>time to look and listen.</u> After I began an exercise program of walking quickly a half hour
a day, I soon slowed down because the world around me was so interesting. <u>For one thing,</u>
<u>~~becoming~~ aware of the richness of the bird and animal life around me.</u> ^{I became} I saw a robin with
<u>strands of newspaper in his mouth. And realized it was building a nest in a nearby tree.</u> ^a A
family of quail exploded from hiding as I skirted a brushy field. I began to connect the
birdsongs I heard with individual birds. For instance, I now know the lonely call of a
mourning dove. <u>And the happy buzz of a chickadee.</u> ^a <u>After it rained, I discovered that</u>
creatures I have never seen before live in my neighborhood. In the mud beside my walking
paths were various tracks. <u>Among them, paws, hooves, and scaly feet.</u> ^{, a} I also found that
little dramas were taking place all the time. <u>And that there are some grim moments in</u> ^a
<u>nature.</u> I saw a swarm of maggots covering a dead mouse. I also came upon a fat snake
spread across the path. I prodded it with a stick. <u>To see if it would move.</u> ^t It shocked me
by coughing up an entire frog. My walks have taught me that there is a great deal to
discover. <u>When I open my eyes and ears.</u> ^w

Score   Number correct _____ × 10 = _____ %

Run-Ons

■ Mastery Test 1

In the space provided, write *R-O* beside run-on sentences and *C* for sentences that are punctuated correctly. Some of the run-ons have no punctuation between the two complete thoughts; others have only a comma.

Correct each run-on by using (1) a period and a capital letter, (2) a comma and a joining word, or (3) a semicolon. Do not use the same method of correction in every sentence.

Examples

____R-O____ I applied for the job, but I never got called in for an interview.

____R-O____ Carla's toothache is getting worse, she should go to a dentist soon.

Methods of correction will vary.

____R-O____ 1. This year's company picnic was not a success, for it attracted more bears than people.

____R-O____ 2. Chang is allergic to anything green, even houseplants make him sneeze.

____R-O____ 3. I was falling asleep in a hurry, I couldn't keep my eyes open any longer.

____R-O____ 4. Don't try to hand-feed the sharks, you could end up feeding them more than your hand.

____C____ 5. These days, getting married is a risky business, for over half of all marriages end in divorce.

____R-O____ 6. We quickly switched from one news program to another, but each one had the same story.

____R-O____ 7. An accident had happened on the bridge, traffic was backed up in both directions.

____R-O____ 8. On long car trips, my little brother drives me crazy, he insists on reading all the road signs out loud.

____R-O____ 9. Harold always finishes the ice cream, and then he puts the empty carton back in the freezer.

____C____ 10. It was too hot indoors to read, so I took my book onto the front porch.

> ***Score*** Number correct _____ × 10 = _____ %

Run-Ons

■ Mastery Test 2

In the space provided, write *R-O* beside run-on sentences. Write *C* beside the one sentence that is punctuated correctly. Some of the run-ons have no punctuation between the two complete thoughts; others have only a comma.

Correct each run-on by using (1) a period and capital letter, (2) a comma and joining word, or (3) a semicolon. Do not use the same method of correction for every sentence.

Methods of correction will vary.

R-O 1. I work for about two hours on my homework; I then spend about an hour watching television.

R-O 2. Sheets of heavy rain were pounding against my car windshield, so I pulled over to the side of the road.

R-O 3. A bus pulled away slowly from the curb. An elderly women ran after it, waving her hand for it to stop.

R-O 4. Our apartment gets really cold at night; the landlord refuses to turn up the heat.

R-O 5. The little boy was struggling with the top of the candy bag. It suddenly tore open and spilled M&Ms all over the floor.

R-O 6. Dozens of restaurants open in the city every year, but almost that many go out of business.

C 7. I got out of the shower to answer the telephone, but it stopped ringing as soon as I touched it.

R-O 8. The breakfast cereal is "new and improved"; it doesn't taste any different to me.

R-O 9. The line at the cash register wasn't moving. The cashier seemed to have gone home.

R-O 10. Several homeless men live under the bridge, so their sleeping bags and shopping carts are always there.

Score Number correct ______ × 10 = ______ %

Run-Ons

■ Mastery Test 3

In the space provided, write *R-O* for run-on sentences and *C* for sentences that are punctuated correctly. Some of the run-ons have no punctuation between the two complete thoughts; others have only a comma.

Correct each run-on by using (1) a period and capital letter, (2) a comma and a joining word, or (3) a semicolon. Do not use the same method of correction in every sentence.

Methods of correction will vary.

R-O   1. Stanley waited in the long bank line,ₓ₍.E₎ȅvery minute seemed like an hour.

R-O   2. Vandals had stripped the abandoned Buick₍, and₎ then they set it on fire.

R-O   3. The little boy stared at his empty cone₍.T₎ there was a puddle of mint chocolate chips at his feet.

R-O   4. Bored, Rita sat at her desk₍.S₎ she made a necklace out of paper clips and a tepee out of pencils.

C   5. I made sure not to put any syrup in Herbie's sundae, for his mother had mentioned that he was allergic to chocolate.

R-O   6. Using a handkerchief, the detective picked up the telephone receiver₍.H₎ he was being careful not to smudge the fingerprints.

R-O   7. Kareem ordered metallic paint for his new Chevette,ₓ₍.A₎ȁlso, he had a racing stripe painted along each side.

R-O   8. Ray's horoscope for last Monday said he would rise to great heights,ₓ₍.T₎ that was the day he began work as an elevator operator.

C   9. The line outside the movie theater was wrapped around the corner, so we walked along the line hoping to see someone we knew.

R-O   10. Lana tossed the trumpet case into the backseat,ₓ₍.S₎ she had twenty minutes to get to rehearsal.

Score Number correct _____ × 10 = _____ %

Run-Ons

■ Mastery Test 4

In the space provided, write *R-O* beside run-on sentences. Write *C* beside the one sentence that is punctuated correctly. Some of the run-ons have no punctuation between the two complete thoughts; others have only a comma.

Correct each run-on by using (1) a period and capital letter, (2) a comma and joining word, or (3) a semicolon. Do not use the same method of correction for every sentence.

Methods of correction will vary.

__R-O__ 1. Flora carried heavy trays all day long$\overset{;}{\wedge}$her feet felt like hundred-pound lead weights.

__C__ 2. The young woman paced anxiously while the laundry circled lazily in the dryer.

__R-O__ 3. The musician strummed his most popular song$\overset{,and}{\wedge}$the crowd waved cigarette lighters and chanted the words along with him.

__R-O__ 4. That man has a million-dollar company$\overset{,but}{\wedge}$he prefers to wear a stained T-shirt and torn jeans.

__R-O__ 5. I finished writing the paper for my English class$\overset{,so}{\wedge}$I started reading and taking notes on a chapter in my psychology text.

__R-O__ 6. The detective burst into the crowded party$\overset{;}{\wedge}$he announced that he knew the murderer's identity.

__R-O__ 7. Chicken and dumplings were cooking on the stove$\overset{.W}{\wedge}$we set the table for dinner.

__R-O__ 8. Sid is trying to smoke less$\overset{;}{\wedge}$he cut all his cigarettes in half and can smoke only one of those an hour.

__R-O__ 9. It was a beautiful springtime day full of sunshine and soft breezes$\overset{,but}{\wedge}$the park was strangely empty.

__R-O__ 10. Raoul sat on his sofa staring out at the cold gray snow$\overset{.H}{\wedge}$he wondered what it would be like to live in Hawaii.

Score Number correct _____	× 10 =	_____	%

Sentence Variety I

■ **Mastery Test 1**

Combine each group of short sentences into one sentence. Various combinations are possible. Choose the combination that reads most smoothly and clearly and that sounds most appropriate in the context of surrounding sentences.

Note In combining short sentences into one sentence, omit repeated words where necessary. Use separate paper.

Kids and Mud

Possible answers:

- Two toddlers sit on the ground.
- They play in the wet and gooey mud.

Two toddlers sit on the ground <u>where</u> they play in the wet and gooey mud.

- They keep busy for hours.
- They build all sorts of things.

They keep busy for hours, <u>and</u> they build all sorts of things.

- Kids can turn mud into cakes.
- They can turn twigs into candles.
- They do so when they are allowed to use their imagination.

<u>When</u> they are allowed to use their imagination, kids can turn mud into cakes, <u>and</u> they can turn twigs into candles.

- They don't need expensive toys.
- They don't even need a television set.

They don't need expensive toys, <u>and</u> they don't even need a television set.

- What they need is some wet dirt.
- They also need patient parents.
- Patient parents won't yell about their muddy clothes.

What they need is some wet dirt <u>and</u> patient parents <u>who</u> won't yell about their muddy clothes.

Score   Number correct _____ × 20 = _____ %

Sentence Variety I

■ Mastery Test 2

Combine each group of short sentences into one sentence. Various combinations are possible. Choose the combination that reads most smoothly and clearly and that sounds most appropriate in the context of surrounding sentences.

Note   In combining short sentences into one sentence, omit repeated words where necessary. Use separate paper.

Possible answers:

The Do-It-Yourself Special

- Kevin and Tyra decided to move out of their cramped apartment.
- They went to a real estate agent.
- The real estate agent was Kevin's high-school friend.

Kevin and Tyra decided to move out of their cramped apartment, so they went to a real estate agent who was Kevin's high-school friend.

- They looked at lots of houses.
- All the houses were too expensive.

They looked at lots of houses, but all the houses were too expensive.

- Finally, they found a house.
- They could afford the house.
- The house needed a lot of work.

Finally, they found a house that they could afford, but the house needed a lot of work.

- For example, the front steps had a railing.
- The railing was made of rusty pipes.
- The floors tilted a bit.
- The kitchen walls were covered in a crazy pattern of multicolored tiles.

For example, the front steps had a railing that was made of rusty pipes, the floors tilted a bit, and the kitchen walls were covered in a crazy pattern of multicolored tiles.

- There was a great deal of work to be done.
- Kevin and Tyra bought the do-it-yourself special.
- They knew it was a place they could call home.

Although there was a great deal of work to be done, Kevin and Tyra bought the do-it-yourself special because they knew it was a place they could call home.

Score   Number correct _____ × 20 = _____ %

Standard English Verbs

■ **Mastery Test 1**

Underline the correct words in the parentheses.

1. "Jim doesn't work," my father (claim, <u>claims</u>). "He just (push, <u>pushes</u>) pencils."

2. Because my engine (leak, <u>leaks</u>) oil, I (<u>park</u>, parks) my car in the street rather than in the driveway.

3. Perspiration (drip, <u>dripped</u>) off Tom's forehead as he (mix, <u>mixed</u>) sand into the new cement.

4. Every time our upstairs neighbor (do, <u>does</u>) his workout, we hear him grunt as he (lift, <u>lifts</u>) his barbells.

5. Lee (were, <u>was</u>) so famished that she (swallow, <u>swallowed</u>) the mouthful of hamburger without chewing it.

6. Uncle Arthur, who (<u>is</u>, be) as bald as a grapefruit, buys every new hair-growing tonic he (have, <u>has</u>) heard about on television.

7. You (frighten, <u>frightened</u>) me to death a minute ago when I (turn, <u>turned</u>) around and saw you standing in the doorway.

8. Before Sharon (take, <u>takes</u>) a bath, she (unplug, <u>unplugs</u>) the phone.

9. Why is it that whenever I (<u>drop</u>, drops) my toast, it (fall, <u>falls</u>) on the buttered side?

10. I just (finish, <u>finished</u>) reading a horror story about some creatures from outer space who (<u>invade</u>, invades) earth disguised as video games.

Score Number correct _____ × 10 = _____ %	

Standard English Verbs

■ Mastery Test 2

Cross out the nonstandard verb form and write the correct form in the space provided.

seems   Example   The job offer ~~seem~~ too good to be true.

breaks   1. Chung ~~break~~ into a rash when he eats strawberries.

feels   2. It ~~feel~~ strange to get up before the sun rises.

threaded   3. Before he showed the movie, Carlos ~~thread~~ the film through the reels of the projector.

did   4. The driver of the huge moving van ~~do~~ a double take as a tiny VW passed him on the turnpike.

asked   5. The bartender flattered my aunt when he ~~ask~~ her to prove she was of drinking age.

unbuttoned   6. As Lonnie strolled casually into the singles bar, he ~~unbutton~~ the top three buttons of his sports shirt.

intend   7. I ~~intends~~ to pay all my bills the minute I obtain some extra cash.

knocked   8. He's so lazy that if opportunity ~~knock~~, he'd say no one was at home.

pretend   9. Whenever we see my sister and her family coming down the front walk, we ~~pretends~~ we aren't at home.

has   10. Kenny ~~have~~ an antique car that looks like an overturned bathtub.

Score   Number correct _____ × 10 = _____ %

Standard English Verbs

■ Mastery Test 3

Part 1 Fill in each blank with the appropriate standard verb form of *be, have,* or *do* in the present or past tense.

A small town in New England _____*has*_____ the best kind of dogcatcher—
1

the kind who _____*does*_____ not want to hurt an animal. In this town, it
2

_____*is*_____ the law to shoot on sight dogs that _____*are*_____
3   4

running loose. It turned out that the local police _____*did*_____ not want to
5

enforce this law, so they asked the dogcatcher. He answered, "I _____*have*_____
6

never shot a dog in my life, and I _____*am*_____ not going to start shooting them
7

now." Instead, he _____*was*_____ seen on several occasions picking up stray
8

dogs and putting them in his car to return them to their homes. He _____*has*_____
9

often taken dogs to his own house until he can find their owners. This man

_____*is*_____ certainly worthy of being called a dog's best friend.
10

Part 2 Fill in each blank with the appropriate form of the regular verb shown in parentheses. Use the present or past tense as needed.

Ed's mother always (*clip*) _____*clips*_____ the cents-off coupons from the
11

newspaper and (*save*) _____*saves*_____ them for him. Every time he (*visit*)
12

_____*visits*_____, his mother (*refuse*) _____*refuses*_____ to let him go without
13   14

those little pieces of paper that advertise "12¢ off on 3 cans" or "Save 35¢ on large

economy size." Last week, she even (*hand*) _____*handed*_____ him some coupons for
15

dog food, although he has never (*own*) _____*owned*_____ a dog in his life. Whenever
16

he (*remember*) _____*remembers*_____ to take some of her coupons to the market,
17

they have usually already (*expire*) _____*expired*_____. But he never (*turn*)
18

_____*turns*_____ them down, because he (*know*) _____*knows*_____ that his
19   20

mother's coupons are her way of saying, "I love you."

Score Number correct _____ × 5 = _____ %

Standard English Verbs

■ Mastery Test 4

Part 1   Fill in each blank with the appropriate standard verb form of *be, have,* or *do* in the present or past tense.

My   grandmother   _____*was*_____   an   eccentric   character.   She
_____*had*_____ the idea that my name was Joe (which it _____*was*_____
not), and she insisted on calling me that. She_____*was*_____ also a miser; she
_____*did*_____ not hide money, though, only candy. Under her bed
_____*was*_____ a suitcase full of spearmint leaves and licorice. Once, when she
thought she _____*was*_____ alone, I saw her count the candy pieces and then put
them back. I'll never forget one thing she _____*did*_____. When I brought my
girlfriend home for the first time, Grandma _____*was*_____ sure we were married;
she kept asking us if we _____*had*_____ any children yet.

Part 2   Fill in each blank with the appropriate form of the regular verb shown in parentheses. Use the present or past tense as needed.

A funny thing (*happen*) _____*happened*_____ recently at the Port Authority Bus
Terminal in New York City. This terminal (*serve*) _____*serves*_____ 168,000 riders
every day, so commuters (*expect*) _____*expect*_____ all sorts of delays. In fact,
someone who (*ride*) _____*rides*_____ a bus can spend the first twenty minutes of
the trip just waiting in line to buy a ticket. To reward these long-suffering commuters, the
Port Authority (*ask*) _____*asked*_____ a sculptor to create a statue in their honor.
When the statue (*arrive*) _____*arrived*_____, it (*turn*) _____*turned*_____ out to
be three cast bronze commuters waiting in line. Then the statues were (*place*)
_____*placed*_____ in front of a gate, and a few commuters actually (*line*)
_____*lined*_____ up behind the bronze figures. "The line (*seem*)
_____*seemed*_____ to be moving about as fast as usual," one commuter said.

| Score   Number correct _____ × 5 = _____ % |

Irregular Verbs

■ **Mastery Test 1**

Underline the correct word in the parentheses.

1. My girlfriend and I (<u>saw</u>, seen) a bad car accident yesterday.
2. Tina (weared, <u>wore</u>) her favorite jeans until the patches were paper-thin.
3. Fran (<u>hurt</u>, hurted) her hand when she tried to open the mayonnaise jar.
4. That new Cutlass (<u>cost</u>, costed) more than I was willing to pay.
5. We should have (took, <u>taken</u>) the dog to the vet sooner.
6. Ralph has (drawed, <u>drawn</u>) blueprints for the cabin he hopes to build.
7. Simone (sended, <u>sent</u>) Mike their divorce papers in the mail.
8. Ever since Nicole (<u>became</u>, become) a supervisor, she hasn't talked to us.
9. Art (catched, <u>caught</u>) pneumonia when he went camping in the mountains.
10. I (<u>knew</u>, knowed) the answer—I just couldn't think of it.
11. I must have (drove, <u>driven</u>) around the development for half an hour looking for my brother's new house.
12. Within a month, the baby had (grew, <u>grown</u>) two inches and gained three pounds.
13. Before my grandfather died, he (<u>gave</u>, given) me his gold pocket watch and Army medals.
14. That gray-haired lumberjack has (arose, <u>arisen</u>) every day at dawn for the past fifty years.
15. When I heard that my car still hadn't been repaired, I (<u>lost</u>, losted) my temper.
16. As soon as you have (ate, <u>eaten</u>) all your ice cream, you may have some spinach.
17. Sarita (choose, <u>chose</u>) soft pink shag carpeting for her bedroom.
18. After raking the leaves, Julio (<u>lay</u>, laid) down under a tree and fell sound asleep.
19. The dummy (<u>sang</u>, sung) in a clear voice, but the ventriloquist's lips never moved.
20. Valerie had (rode, <u>ridden</u>) the roller coaster five times before she started complaining that everything was going around in circles.

Score   Number correct _____ × 5 = _____ %

Irregular Verbs

■ Mastery Test 2

Cross out the incorrect verb form. Write the correct form in the space provided.

swore   1. Paul ~~sweared~~ loudly when the wasp stung him.

bit   2. I ~~bited~~ down hard on a caramel and lost a filling.

driven   3. As the car groaned and lurched from side to side, we realized that Lamont had never ~~drove~~ with a manual shift before.

thrown   4. Because Fran had ~~throwed~~ away the receipt, she couldn't return the frying pan.

slid   5. Though the runner ~~slided~~ head first, he was still tagged out at home plate.

rang   6. Barry ~~rung~~ the bell for fifteen minutes and then decided that no one was home.

drank   7. After I ran three miles in ninety-degree heat, I ~~drunk~~ a whole quart of iced tea.

hid   8. Lenny ~~hided~~ his daughter's Christmas present so well that he couldn't find it.

known   9. If I had ~~knew~~ better, I would never have left my car door unlocked.

kept   10. Maria broke her engagement but ~~keeped~~ all the wedding presents.

caught   11. I stayed away from sick people and took extra vitamin C all winter, but I ~~catched~~ a cold anyway.

slept   12. On his first day of summer vacation, Danny ~~sleeped~~ until two in the afternoon.

shrank   13. My new cotton sweater ~~shrinked~~ so much that it now fits my kid sister.

written   14. Mac was instantly sorry he had ~~writed~~ such an angry e-mail, but there was no way to get it back.

lit   15. The hostess turned on soft music and ~~lighted~~ candles on the table before her guests arrived.

run   16. I had ~~runned~~ out of cash before payday, so I had to ask my parents for a loan.

made   17. Nobody believed the criminal's claim that Martians had ~~maked~~ him rob the bank.

spoke   18. After the politician was invited to say a few words, he ~~speaked~~ for half an hour.

shut   19. Something private must be going on in the meeting, because a committee member just got up and ~~shutted~~ the door.

left   20. The group of diners ordered the most expensive steaks, drank the best champagne, kept two waitresses busy all night, and then ~~leaved~~ only a two-dollar tip.

> **Score**   Number correct _____ × 5 = _____ %

Irregular Verbs

■ **Mastery Test 3**

Write in the space provided the correct form of the verb shown in the margin.

teach

1. When I was little, my parents ___taught___ me how to find my way home if I got lost.

lend

2. My best friend ___lent___ me ten dollars so I could buy Dad a birthday gift.

build

3. It took eight months before Andy's garage was finally ___built___.

wear

4. I used to fidget in class so much that I ___wore___ a hole in my trousers.

write

5. Susie has read every romance novel Barbara Cartland has ___written___.

fall

6. Frowning, the building inspector stood where the grocery store's sign had ___fallen___.

see

7. We ___saw___ the other car coming, but we couldn't stop in time.

send

8. Rina and Marvin ___sent___ telegrams to their families saying that they were eloping.

speak

9. I don't think he's heard a single word I have ___spoken___.

sleep

10. I must have ___slept___ twelve hours before I finally woke up.

Score Number correct _____ × 10 = _____ %

Irregular Verbs

■ **Mastery Test 4**

Write in the space provided the correct form of the verb shown in the margin.

burst   1. As soon as little Davy stuck a pin in it, the balloon _____burst_____.

go   2. When the alarm rang, Fred shut it off and _____went_____ back to sleep.

bring   3. Yesterday, my cousin _____brought_____ over his entire baseball card collection.

hurt   4. You really _____hurt_____ my feelings when you told me you didn't like my new outfit.

keep   5. Whenever she rode in a car, my mother _____kept_____ reminding the driver when a turn was coming up or a light was changing.

shake   6. After the collision, we were badly _____shaken_____ up, but we had no broken bones.

spend   7. Stanley _____spent_____ a fortune on fishing equipment, but all he ever caught was a cold.

shrink   8. When she saw the giant tomato reaching for her in her dream, Amy _____shrank_____ back in horror.

buy   9. Because stick shifts made her nervous, Mei Lin _____bought_____ a car with an automatic transmission.

stick   10. Why do I always get _____stuck_____ with taking the car for its inspection?

Score Number correct _____ × 10 = _____ %

Subject-Verb Agreement

■ Mastery Test 1

Underline the correct verb in the parentheses. Note that you will first have to determine the subject in each sentence. To help find subjects in certain sentences, you may find it helpful to cross out prepositional phrases.

1. The shelves in my bedroom closet (is, <u>are</u>) jammed with my sister's leftover belongings.

2. The toy trucks and Lincoln logs on the kitchen floor (belongs, <u>belong</u>) to my four-year-old niece.

3. Each of those custard pies (<u>looks</u>, look) gooey.

4. There (<u>goes</u>, go) Mario on his way to the bowling alley.

5. Annabelle and her sister (intends, <u>intend</u>) to compete in the next Miss America pageant.

6. Everyone in my family (<u>plans</u>, plan) to be at my parents' fiftieth wedding anniversary celebration.

7. Mary and her mother (is, <u>are</u>) going to Weight Watchers.

8. (<u>Does</u>, Do) your roof leak when it rains hard?

9. Either Elaine or Ray (<u>is</u>, are) working overtime this week.

10. Anything (<u>is</u>, are) likely to happen at one of Harold's parties.

11. The carton filled with roofing tiles (<u>was</u>, were) too heavy for me to lift.

12. Most of the game show hosts on television (looks, <u>look</u>) alike.

13. Not only loud talking but also loud clothes (gives, <u>give</u>) me a headache.

14. Here (is, <u>are</u>) the questions that will be on next week's assignment.

15. Sleeping in the doorway of the run-down building (was, <u>were</u>) two homeless women.

16. All the letters on that poster (glows, <u>glow</u>) in the dark.

17. One of my sisters (<u>plans</u>, plan) to learn karate this summer.

18. Neither the plumber nor his helpers (works, <u>work</u>) on weekends.

19. When (is, <u>are</u>) your sister and her four children coming for a visit?

20. Everyone watching a cowboy movie (<u>knows</u>, know) who the good guys are.

Score Number correct _____ × 5 = _____ %

Subject-Verb Agreement

■ Mastery Test 2

In the space provided, write the correct form of the verb shown in the margin.

comes, come   1. All the wrinkles in a drip-dry shirt _____ come _____ out with a cool iron.

Is, Are   2. _____ Are _____ all the bracelets Toshiko wears made of real gold?

does, do   3. Alcoholic beverages and allergy pills _____ do _____ not make a good combination.

was, were   4. No one _____ was _____ willing to take the blame for the spilled paint.

is, are   5. Under the sofa _____ is _____ a year's supply of dust.

was, were   6. Neither of the jackets I was looking for _____ was _____ in the closet.

sees, see   7. Krista and Eve _____ see _____ better with contact lenses than they saw with glasses.

is, are   8. Three of the books Sandy borrowed from the library _____ are _____ overdue.

was, were   9. A complete list of complaints and demands _____ was _____ read at the beginning of the tenants' meeting.

is, are   10. At the intersection of Pleasant Grove Lane and Valley View Road _____ is _____ the future location of the new shopping mall.

Score   Number correct _____ × 10 = _____ %

Subject-Verb Agreement

■ **Mastery Test 3**

Cross out the incorrect form of the verb. In addition, underline the subject that goes with the verb. Then write the correct form of the verb in the space provided. Mark the one sentence that is correct with a *C*.

_____are_____ 1. There ~~is~~ some unpleasant <u>surprises</u> among this month's bills.

_____do_____ 2. Those <u>piles</u> of dirty laundry ~~does~~ not belong to me.

_____have_____ 3. The <u>lilies</u> that we planted last year ~~has~~ grown to over six feet tall.

_____have_____ 4. My <u>counselor</u> and my English <u>instructor</u> ~~has~~ agreed to write job recommendations for me.

_____believes_____ 5. <u>Everyone</u> in my neighborhood under the age of ten ~~believe~~ in Santa Claus.

_____C_____ 6. Neither Gale nor Jerry plans to look for a job this summer.

_____stay_____ 7. Many gas <u>stations</u> on that highway ~~stays~~ open all night.

_____is_____ 8. The <u>mayor</u>, along with the council members, ~~are~~ helping carry sandbags for flood control.

_____was_____ 9. Lying across all the lanes of the highway ~~were~~ a jackknifed <u>tractor-trailer</u>.

_____have_____ 10. Emil's <u>parents</u>, who have been seeing a marriage counselor, ~~has~~ decided to get a divorce.

Score   Number correct _____ × 10 = _____ %

Subject-Verb Agreement

■ Mastery Test 4

Cross out the incorrect form of the verb. In addition, underline the subject that goes with the verb. Then write the correct form of the verb in the space provided. Mark the one sentence that is correct with a *C*.

hangs — 1. At the back of my mother's closet ~~hang~~ an old-fashioned muskrat fur <u>coat</u> with padded shoulders.

gets — 2. Anyone who <u>punches</u> in late more than once ~~get~~ an official warning from the personnel department.

contain — 3. Many <u>pages</u> of Naomi's diary ~~contains~~ R-rated material.

are — 4. His toy soldiers and stamp collection ~~is~~ the only <u>things</u> that mean anything to him.

was — 5. Leaning against the lamppost with his hands in his pockets ~~were~~ a dangerous-looking <u>character</u>.

C — 6. When I was seven, being alone in the house and hearing the walls creak in the wind were the scariest things in my life.

seems — 7. <u>Something</u> ~~seem~~ odd about Uncle Rico this evening; he's remembering everything people are saying.

burst — 8. The plastic trash <u>bags</u> that never ~~bursts~~ on TV always break in my kitchen.

act — 9. Thick white <u>fur</u> and black <u>skin</u> ~~acts~~ like a greenhouse, trapping heat and keeping a polar bear warm in the coldest weather.

are — 10. When ~~is~~ <u>Lew</u> and <u>Marian</u> going to return the camping equipment they borrowed from us?

Score   Number correct _____ × 10 = _____ %

Consistent Verb Tense

■ **Mastery Test 1**

In each item, one verb must be changed so that it agrees in tense with the other verbs. Cross out the inconsistent verb and write the correct form in the space provided.

wiped   1. Before the toothbrush was invented, people ~~wipe~~ their teeth with a rag that had chalk on it.

stop   2. When I drive to my 8:30 A.M. class, I always ~~stopped~~ at Ben's Bagel Bakery and get an onion bagel with cream cheese.

discovered   3. I stepped on a horseshoe crab at the beach and ~~discover~~ it had sky-blue blood.

washed   4. Sally ~~washes~~ her permanent-press curtains and hung them on the rods while they were still wet.

turns   5. While Miguel is dieting, he avoids submarine sandwiches, ~~turned~~ down Danish pastry, and passes up chocolate milk shakes.

frightened   6. Leo enjoyed his first airplane flight, although the trip ~~frightens~~ him so much at first that he held onto the armrests.

smoke   7. Whenever I ~~smoked~~ more than ten cigarettes a day, my eyes burn and my hands start to shake.

found   8. Lidia reached for the economy brand of ketchup but ~~finds~~ that it cost as much as the national brand.

observed   9. For my sociology project, I went to a laundromat, ~~observe~~ the people there, and took notes on their behavior.

pulled   10. Mrs. Frank sat wearily on her suitcase and stared off into space as the bus ~~pulls~~ into the station.

Score   Number correct _____ × 10 = _____ %

Consistent Verb Tense

■ Mastery Test 2

In each item, one verb must be changed so that it agrees in tense with the other verbs. Cross out the inconsistent verb and write the correct form in the space provided.

collected

1. After I got my promotion, my friends ~~collect~~ a hundred dollars, rented a hall, and threw a party in my honor.

argue

2. Every year when Christmas comes and we trim the tree, we ~~argued~~ about who gets to put the silver angel at the top.

ended

3. When the strike finally ~~ends~~ and the teachers went back to work, everyone rejoiced except the students.

pokes

4. Aunt Charlotte, who collects antique bottles, visits every garage sale in the neighborhood and ~~poked~~ around in people's attics for hidden treasures.

purchased

5. Leon decided to become a CIA agent, so he ~~purchases~~ a trench coat and began speaking in whispers whenever he was in public.

was

6. Everything was strangely peaceful on our street; not a person was in sight and not a car ~~is~~ moving.

look

7. When I wake up with a hangover, my head pounds, my eyes ~~looked~~ like road maps, and my teeth itch.

combed

8. I was really nervous before my first date. I ~~comb~~ my hair a dozen times and looked in the mirror over and over to make sure my false eyelashes hadn't come unglued.

collapses

9. At Thanksgiving, we consume a twenty-pound turkey and three kinds of pie for dessert. Then, everyone ~~collapsed~~ on the floor and moans in agony.

fixed

10. My little brother borrowed my dad's toolbox so he could play home repairman. Then he ~~fixes~~ all the kitchen chairs by removing the screws that held them together.

Score   Number correct _____ × 10 = _____ %

Pronoun Reference, Agreement, and Point of View

■ **Mastery Test 1**

Underline the correct word in the parentheses.

1. Each of my daughters had to get (her, their) own lunch before leaving for school.

2. Lonnell needed his writing folder from the file cabinet, but he couldn't find (it, the folder).

3. In our office we have to work for six months before (we, you) get a raise.

4. Shoppers seem to like the new store because (you, they) rarely have to wait in line.

5. Although I liked my math teacher, I never really understood (it, math).

6. The bellhop discovered that someone had left (his, their) expensive suit in one of the hotel closets.

7. If you want to lose weight by exercising, (one, you) should begin with a sensible program of light workouts.

8. Every player on the Rangers' bench pulled on (his, their) helmet and jumped onto the ice as soon as the fight broke out.

9. John's neighbor called to tell him that someone had parked in (his, John's) spot.

10. Whenever I go to that post office, (they, the clerks) act as if I'm troubling them when I ask for stamps.

11. On the first day of school, students spend most of the time getting (your, their) schedule in order and finding classrooms.

12. The cat sat staring at the bird in the cage, and (the bird, it) was very upset.

13. Elise treated Ariana to lunch at the restaurant that (she, Elise) likes best.

14. As we walked toward the accident site, (they, police officers) told us to stay out of the way.

15. Steve watches movies of all kinds, because he's interested in (it, making movies) as a possible career.

16. A person has to be self-confident to go to a party where (you, he or she) doesn't know anyone.

17. Felice stopped at the bakery to pick up the cake she'd ordered, but (he, the baker) was not finished decorating it.

18. I don't know anybody who has (their, his or her) report finished yet.

19. When I got my bike out of the garage, I noticed that (it, the garage) really needed cleaning.

20. There was a pretty bow on my present, but I threw (it, the bow) into the trash.

Score Number correct _____ × 5 = _____ %

Pronoun Reference, Agreement, and Point of View

■ Mastery Test 2

In the space provided, write *PE* for sentences that contain pronoun errors. Write *C* for the three sentences that use pronouns correctly. Then cross out each pronoun error and write a correction above it.

___PE___   Example   Each of the boys explained ~~their~~ *his* project.

Corrections may vary.

___PE___   1. Drew told his boss, ~~that he needed more time to finish the report~~. "I need more time to finish the report."

___C___   2. Each musician carried his or her own instrument onto the bus.

___C___   3. In this course, people can sit in class for weeks before the instructor calls on them.

___PE___   4. Harold refuses to take his children to amusement parks because he doesn't like ~~them~~. *amusement parks*

___PE___   5. Everyone who parks on that street has had ~~their~~ *his (or her)* car windows smashed.

___PE___   6. Carl says he has problems taking lecture notes because ~~they~~ *the instructors* all talk too fast.

___PE___   7. I hate standing in bakery lines where ~~you~~ *I* have to take a number.

___C___   8. "Anyone even suspected of cheating," warned the instructor at the boys' school, "forfeits his chance of passing this test."

___PE___   9. ~~The ace pilots flew in formation over the crowded stadium, which was breathtaking~~. *The ace pilots' flight in formation over the crowded stadium was breathtaking.*

___PE___   10. He avoids foods that might give ~~you~~ *him* heartburn.

Score   Number correct _____ × 10 = _____ %

Pronoun Reference, Agreement, and Point of View

■ Mastery Test 3

In the space provided, write *PE* for sentences that contain pronoun errors. Write *C* for the two sentences that use pronouns correctly. Then cross out each pronoun error and write a correction above it.
Some corrections may vary.

_PE_ 1. Pam called Ellen to tell her that the instructor had read ~~her~~ *Ellen's* paper to the class.

_PE_ 2. Danny's favorite Christmas toy is the robot ~~you~~ *he* must wind up.

_C_ 3. Neither contestant answered her bonus question about the Civil War battles correctly.

_PE_ 4. Jesse won't go for the job interview because he says ~~they~~ *the employers* hire only college graduates.

_PE_ 5. If you send in your ticket order in advance, ~~one~~ *you* can be sure of getting good seats.

_PE_ 6. With rain in the forecast, just about everybody in the stadium had an umbrella by ~~their~~ *his or her* side.

_PE_ 7. The old man asked me to move my suitcase off the bench so he could sit on ~~it~~ *the bench*.

_PE_ 8. Hana is really a generous person, but she keeps ~~it~~ *her generosity* hidden.

_C_ 9. Whenever we take our children on a trip, we have to remember to bring snacks and toys to keep them occupied.

_PE_ 10. One of the men in our cab company just got ~~their~~ *his* license revoked.

Score   Number correct _____ × 10 = _____ %

Pronoun Reference, Agreement, and Point of View

■ **Mastery Test 4**

In the space provided, write *PE* for sentences that contain pronoun errors. Write *C* for the sentence that uses pronouns correctly. Then cross out each pronoun error and write a correction above it.

Answers may vary.

_____PE_____   1. After Erica put the candles on her twin sons' birthday cakes, the dog ate ~~them~~. *the candles*

_____PE_____   2. None of the women in the class was eager to have ~~their~~ presentation put on *her* videotape.

_____PE_____   3. The cheeseburgers we were served were so thick that ~~you~~ could hardly bite *we* into them.

_____PE_____   4. The citizens protested at City Hall because ~~they~~ had raised taxes for the second *the legislators* year in a row.

_____PE_____   5. Tina knew Ed was still angry, but he wouldn't talk about ~~it~~. *his anger*

_____PE_____   6. Devon asked Spencer ~~to try out his new motorbike~~. *, "Why don't you try out my new motorbike?"*

_____PE_____   7. Carol was told to sign on the dotted line with her ballpoint pen, but she couldn't find ~~it~~. *her pen*

_____C_____   8. Either the dog or the cat had spilled water from its dish all over the kitchen floor.

_____PE_____   9. Davy complained to his brother that ~~he~~ always got asked to walk the puppy. *Davy*

_____PE_____   10. The grounder took a bad hop and bounced over the shortstop's head; ~~this~~ *this accident* resulted in two runs scoring.

Score   Number correct _____ × 10 = _____ %

Pronoun Types

■ Mastery Test 1

Underline the correct word in parentheses.

1. (Them, <u>Those</u>) doves nest in our cedar tree every year.

2. I suspect that those dirty dishes are (<u>yours</u>, your's).

3. Horror movies don't scare my friends and (I, <u>me</u>) one bit.

4. The four boys finally had the house all to (themself, <u>themselves</u>).

5. Laura and (<u>I</u>, me) have been engaged for over three years.

6. (<u>That</u>, That there) woman is a helicopter pilot.

7. Without asking for permission, (<u>he</u>, him) and Nelson began cutting up the cake.

8. My new Buick got (<u>its</u>, it's) first scratch when I parked too close to a fence.

9. Bernie decided to buy (hisself, <u>himself</u>) a reward for sticking to his diet for one solid month.

10. The plumber showed Elaine and (I, <u>me</u>) the corroded lead pipes under the sink.

11. Terry's foul-shooting percentage isn't as good as (<u>mine</u>, mines).

12. Lonnie needs some sleep right now more than he needs (we, <u>us</u>).

13. Marla is taking more courses this semester than (<u>I</u>, me).

14. I don't understand how (<u>this</u>, this here) formula is used.

15. Does anyone know how (<u>those</u>, them) screens got torn?

16. Any friend of the Newtons is a friend of (our's, <u>ours</u>).

17. The team members (theirselves, <u>themselves</u>) are selling candy door to door.

18. I wish (<u>those</u>, those there) babies would stop crying.

19. When you're finished with the radio, return it to either Roberta or (I, <u>me</u>).

20. Those power tools are (<u>hers</u>, hers').

Score   Number correct _____ × 5 = _____ %

Pronoun Types

■ Mastery Test 2

Cross out the incorrect pronoun in each sentence and write the correct form in the space provided at the left.

her	1. If we offered Michael and ~~she~~ some money, would they accept it?
those	2. Every one of ~~those there~~ courses is filled.
they	3. We caught a lot more fish than ~~them~~.
Those	4. ~~Them~~ mountains in the distance are the Catskills.
himself	5. Lenny ~~hisself~~ decided to confess to the robbery.
_I_	6. My dog and ~~me~~ usually eat our meals at the same time.
theirs	7. Our station wagon can hold more people than ~~their's~~.
These	8. ~~These here~~ boots will hurt you until they're fully broken in.
ourselves	9. This will be the first time in weeks we've had dinner by ~~ourself~~.
yours	10. Those garden tools of ~~your's~~ are getting rusty.
_me_	11. The sweaters Gloria knitted for Ron and ~~I~~ came out two sizes too small.
_me_	12. Every girl at the party wore jeans except Michelle and ~~I~~.
_us_	13. The chief showed ~~we~~ rookie firefighters what to do when an alarm sounded.
this	14. You can't park here, because ~~this here~~ space is reserved for the supervisor.
hers	15. Are these binoculars ~~her's~~?
_he_	16. Matina and ~~him~~ have nothing to discuss.
_he_	17. Of all my grandchildren, Chris and ~~him~~ wear me out the fastest.
that	18. Check the pockets of ~~that there~~ bathrobe for your glasses.
its	19. His bicycle had ~~its'~~ tires slashed overnight.
themselves	20. They've decided to repair the engine by ~~themselfs~~.

Score Number correct _____ × 5 = _____ %

Adjectives and Adverbs

■ **Mastery Test 1**

Part 1   Cross out the incorrect adjectival or adverbial form in each sentence. Then write the correct form in the space provided.

<u>well</u>   1. Clark runs ~~good~~ for a person who's thirty pounds overweight.

<u>strangely</u>   2. The car's brakes were acting ~~strange~~, so the mechanic checked the fluid.

<u>beautifully</u> 3. The girls sang ~~beautiful~~, but the faulty microphones spoiled the show.

<u>really</u>   4. That actor's inexperience is ~~real~~ obvious.

<u>carefully</u>   5. Janelle tiptoed ~~careful~~ past the guest room, not wanting to wake the sleeping children.

Part 2   Cross out the error in comparison in each sentence. Then write the correct form in the space provided.

<u>glossiest</u>   6. The ad tried to prove which model's hair was the ~~most glossiest~~ by using a light meter.

<u>better</u>   7. My sister does ~~more well~~ on standardized tests than I do.
~~more~~

<u>impatient</u>   8. The longer Luis waited in line at the bank, the ~~impatienter~~ he got.
~~most~~

<u>awkward</u>   9. My ~~awkwardest~~ moment came when I tried to introduce my wife to my boss and forgot both their names.

~~most~~
<u>productive</u> 10. This has been the ~~most productivest~~ session we've had yet.

Score   Number correct _____ × 10 = _____ %

Adjective and Adverbs

■ Mastery Test 2

Part 1   Cross out the incorrect adjectival and adverbial form in each sentence. Then write the correct form in the space provided.

quickly   1. Sherry ate ~~quick~~ so she wouldn't miss the beginning of the early show.

well   2. Xavier decided he wasn't feeling ~~good~~ enough to bowl for the team.

terribly   3. I had a ~~terrible~~ high fever and a deep cough.

easily   4. Hakim makes friends ~~easy~~ because he is so sure of himself.

tightly   5. Paul gripped the handle ~~tight~~ and told the barman to let the mechanical bull loose.

Part 2   Add to each sentence the correct form of the word in the margin.

loud   6. During the spring thunderstorm, each booming clap of thunder was ___louder___ than the preceding one.

tired   7. After doing fifty push-ups, I was ___more tired___ than I had been in years.

cheap   8. You'll need binoculars if you sit in the ___cheapest___ seats in the stadium.

bad   9. The ___worst___ clashes of the war occurred in the hot jungles of some small South Pacific islands.

little   10. This semester, I'm making ___less___ money at my after-school job, but I have more free time.

Score   Number correct _____ × 10 = _____ %

Misplaced Modifiers

■ Mastery Test 1

Underline the misplaced word or words in each sentence. Then rewrite the sentence, placing related words together and making the meaning clear.

Wording of answers may vary.

1. Leroy stepped on the worm <u>without shoes on.</u>

   Without shoes on, Leroy stepped on the worm.

2. Scott purchased an expensive ticket from a scalper <u>that turned out to be a fake.</u>

   Scott purchased from a scalper an expensive ticket that turned out to
   be a fake.

3. I watched a woman board a bus <u>wearing a dress that was several sizes too small.</u>

   I watched a woman wearing a dress that was several sizes too small
   board a bus.

4. A tray of doughnuts had been placed on the counter <u>which smelled delicious.</u>

   A tray of doughnuts, which smelled delicious, had been placed on the
   counter.

5. The student tried to study in the noisy library <u>with great concentration.</u>

   With great concentration, the student tried to study in the noisy library.

6. Craig was spotted by a teacher <u>cheating on an examination.</u>

   Craig was spotted cheating on an examination by a teacher.

7. I stayed at the cabin window watching the bear <u>in my pajamas.</u>

   In my pajamas, I stayed at the cabin window watching the bear.

8. Tri Lee <u>almost</u> read the whole psychology assignment in two hours.

   Tri Lee read almost the whole psychology assignment in two hours.

Score   Number correct _____ × 12.5 = _____ %

Misplaced Modifiers

■ Mastery Test 2

Underline the misplaced word or words in each sentence. Then rewrite the sentence, placing related words together and making the meaning clear.

Wording of answers may vary.

1. I bought the used car from a friend <u>with a bad exhaust system.</u>

   I bought the used car with a bad exhaust system from a friend.

2. The news featured a handicapped man who played basketball in a wheelchair <u>with no legs</u>.

   The news featured a handicapped man with no legs who played basketball in a wheelchair.

3. Our neighbor received a reward for returning the puppy to its family <u>that had been missing for a week</u>.

   Our neighbor received a reward for returning the puppy that had been missing for a week to its family.

4. We saw a commercial for a company that promises to remodel any bathroom <u>on television</u>.

   We saw on television a commercial for a company that promises to remodel any bathroom.

5. The hungry lions crept up behind the big game hunter who had fallen asleep <u>without making a sound.</u>

   Without making a sound, the hungry lions crept up behind the big game hunter who had fallen asleep.

6. Larissa watched her sons toss a baseball back and forth <u>through her living room picture window.</u>

   Through her living room picture window, Larissa watched her sons toss a baseball back and forth.

7. We were notified that we had won a trip to Disney World <u>by telegram.</u>

   We were notified by telegram that we had won a trip to Disney World.

8. I woke up this morning thinking I had a paper due <u>in a cold sweat.</u>

   I woke up in a cold sweat this morning thinking I had a paper due.

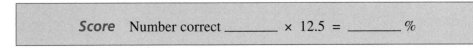

Score   Number correct _____ × 12.5 = _____ %

Dangling Modifiers

■ Mastery Test 1

Underline the dangling modifier in each sentence. Then rewrite the sentence, correcting the dangling modifier.

Wording of answers may vary.

1. Being made of clear glass, the children kept bumping into the sliding door.

   Since it was made of clear glass, the children kept bumping into the

   sliding door.

2. Still green, Helen put the tomato in sunlight to ripen.

   Since it was still green, Helen put the tomato in sunlight to ripen.

3. Though somewhat warped, my grandfather still enjoys playing his record collection from the forties.

   Though it is somewhat warped, my grandfather still enjoys playing his

   record collection from the forties.

4. Having turned crispy and golden, I removed the chicken from the pan.

   I removed the chicken, which had turned crispy and golden, from the pan.

5. Bigger than ever, Aunt Clara predicted that this year's watermelon entry would win first prize at the county fair.

   Aunt Clara predicted that this year's watermelon entry, which was bigger

   than ever, would win first prize at the county fair.

6. After changing the bait, the fish started to bite.

   After we changed the bait, the fish started to bite.

7. Coming home without a job, the comedies on television only made Helen feel depressed.

   Since she was coming home without a job, the comedies on television only

   made Helen feel depressed.

8. Having rehearsed his speech several times, Amal's presentation to the staff went smoothly.

   Since he had rehearsed his speech several times, Amal's presentation to

   the staff went smoothly.

Score   Number correct _____ × 12.5 = _____ %

Dangling Modifiers

■ Mastery Test 2

Underline the dangling modifier in each sentence. Then rewrite the sentence, correcting the dangling modifier.

Rewritten sentences may vary.

1. Being too heavy to lift, Jo asked Bob to help her move the sofa.

   Since it was too heavy to lift, Jo asked Bob to help her move the sofa.

2. Parched and dry, the ice-cold Coke soothed my throat.

   The ice-cold Coke soothed my throat, which was parched and dry.

3. Clutching a handful of silver and a portable TV set, our neighbor's watchdog surprised a burglar.

   Our neighbor's watchdog surprised a burglar, who was clutching a handful

   of silver and a portable TV set.

4. Living in a tent for two weeks, the camping trip made us appreciate hot showers and dry towels.

   After we had lived in a tent for two weeks, the camping trip made us

   appreciate hot showers and dry towels.

5. Thrown on the floor in a heap, we could not tell if the clothes were clean or dirty.

   We could not tell if the clothes that were thrown on the floor in a heap

   were clean or dirty.

6. Afraid to look his father in the eye, Danny's head remained bowed.

   Afraid to look his father in the eye, Danny kept his head bowed.

7. Straining at the leash, I could see my neighbor's Great Dane getting ready for his walk.

   I could see my neighbor's Great Dane, which was straining at the leash,

   getting ready for his walk.

8. While lying in bed with a cold, my cat jumped on me and curled up on my stomach.

   While I was lying in bed with a cold, my cat jumped on me and curled up on

   my stomach.

Score   Number correct _____ × 12.5 = _____ %

Faulty Parallelism

■ Mastery Test 1

The unbalanced part of each sentence is italicized. Rewrite this part so that it matches the rest of the sentence.

1. The bus squealed, grunted, and then *there was a hiss* as it shifted gears.
   hissed

2. *With grace* and skillfully, Charles took aim and tossed a quarter into the basket at the toll booth.
   Gracefully

3. Sue beats the blues by taking a hot bubble bath, cuddling up in a cozy quilt, and *eats her favorite snack.*
   eating her favorite snack

4. They didn't want a black-and-white set, but *a color set couldn't be afforded.*
   they couldn't afford a color set

5. We stayed at a country inn and dined on tender steak, baked Idaho potatoes, and *vegetables that were homegrown.*
   homegrown vegetables

6. When she learned she had won the gymnastic contest, Nikki gasped, screamed, and *all teammates were kissed by her.*
   kissed all her teammates

7. I avoid camping because I don't like to eat half-cooked food, sleep on rocks and twigs, or *the biting of insects.*
   get bitten by insects

8. Make sure you have proofread your paper, stapled it, and *there are numbers on the pages* before you turn it in.
   numbered the pages

9. Unless you are either very noisy or *persist,* you won't wake me up.
   persistent

10. Kerry uses his roller skates to get to school, to go to the store, and *for going to football practice.*
    to go to football practice

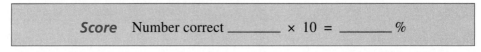

Score   Number correct _____ × 10 = _____ %

Faulty Parallelism

■ Mastery Test 2

Draw a line under the unbalanced part of each sentence. Then rewrite the unbalanced part so that it matches the other items in the sentence.

Rewritten parts may vary somewhat.

1. Stanley was so hungry he could have eaten a horse—roasted, broiled, or <u>in a stew.</u>

   stewed

2. In the last game, Julio had one single, <u>a two-base hit,</u> and one triple.

   one double

3. Bill told us to help ourselves from the buffet and <u>that we could fix our own drinks in the kitchen.</u>

   to fix our own drinks in the kitchen

4. My grandfather must have foods that are easy to cook and <u>digestible.</u>

   easy to digest

5. The awards show was filled with splashy dance numbers, <u>film clips that were boring,</u> and long-winded speeches.

   boring film clips

6. My driving instructor told me to keep both hands on the wheel, to use caution at all times, and <u>don't take my eyes off the road.</u>

   not to take my eyes off the road

7. Jackie sucked in her stomach, stopped breathing, and <u>was trying to pull the zipper up again.</u>

   tried to pull the zipper up again

8. Phil was so sick that all he was good for was lying in bed and <u>to look up at the ceiling.</u>

   looking up at the ceiling

9. When she gets very angry, Gale works off her anger by cleaning out her desk drawers, <u>windows getting washed,</u> or scrubbing the bathtub.

   washing the windows

10. The movie about the "mad slasher" was violent, <u>it caused shock,</u> and demeaning to women.

    shocking

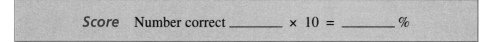

Score Number correct _____ × 10 = _____ %

Sentence Variety II

■ **Mastery Test 1**

Combine each group of short sentences into one sentence. A variety of combinations is possible. Choose the combination that reads most smoothly and clearly and that sounds most appropriate in the context of surrounding sentences.

Note   In combining short sentences into one sentence, omit repeated words where necessary. Use separate paper. The story continues in the next mastery test.

Bargain Flight

Possible answers:

- Ramon missed his grandparents.
- He decided to visit them.
- His grandparents are in Florida.
- He decided to do this during the semester break.

<u>Since</u> Ramon missed his grandparents, he decided to visit them in Florida during the semester break.

- Ramon needed to save money and time.
- He looked for a flight to Miami.
- He looked for a cheap flight.
- He looked for a direct flight.

<u>Needing</u> to save money and time, he looked for a <u>cheap</u>, <u>direct</u> flight to Miami.

- Florida Express Airline offered a fare.
- It was a no-frills fare.
- It was a non-stop fare.
- It was a hundred-dollar fare.

Florida Express Airline offered a <u>no-frills</u>, <u>nonstop</u>, <u>hundred-dollar</u> fare.

- Ramon was excited about the good deal.
- He bought a ticket.
- He packed his bags.

<u>Excited</u> about the good deal, he bought a ticket <u>and</u> packed his bags.

- However, Ramon began to have doubts about his bargain flight.
- He did this as he entered the terminal.
- The terminal was dingy.
- The terminal was little-used.

<u>As</u> he entered the <u>dingy</u>, <u>little-used</u> terminal, however, Ramon began to have doubts about his bargain flight.

Score   Number correct _____ × 20 = _____ %

Sentence Variety II

■ **Mastery Test 2**

Combine each group of short sentences into one sentence. A variety of combinations is possible. Choose the combination that reads most smoothly and clearly and that sounds most appropriate in the context of surrounding sentences.

Note   In combining short sentences into one sentence, omit repeated words where necessary. Use separate paper. The story continues from the previous mastery test.

Bargain Flight (Continued)

Possible answers:

- An airline clerk charged Ramon ten dollars to check in his suitcase.
- The clerk was rude.
- The suitcase was small.
- This happened at the Florida Express counter.

At the Florida Express counter, a <u>rude</u> *airline clerk charged Ramon ten dollars to check in his* <u>small</u> *suitcase.*

- Ramon and the other passengers had to sprint onto the runway.
- This was unexpected.
- They did this to board the plane.
- They did this when the boarding announcement was yelled out.

<u>When</u> *the boarding announcement was yelled out, Ramon and the other passengers* <u>unexpectedly</u> *had to sprint onto the runway to board the plane.*

- Ramon was sweaty and annoyed.
- He wedged himself into a seat.
- The seat was worn.
- The seat was narrow.
- He did this after pushing his way down the crowded aisle.

<u>Sweaty and annoyed</u>*, Ramon wedged himself into a* <u>worn</u>*,* <u>narrow</u> *seat* <u>after</u> *pushing his way down the crowded aisle.*

- The flight attendant sold Ramon a snack and a soda.
- This happened once the plane took off.
- The snack was five dollars.
- The snack was stale.
- The soda was two dollars.
- The soda was flat.

<u>Once</u> *the plane took off, the flight attendant sold Ramon a* <u>stale</u> <u>five-dollar</u> *snack and a* <u>flat</u> <u>two-dollar</u> *soda.*

- Ramon calculated that he had spent more money on the flight than planned.
- He swore to himself he'd never take a bargain flight again.
- This happened by the time the plane landed in Miami.

<u>By</u> *the time the plane landed in Miami, Ramon calculated that he had spent more money on the flight than planned,* <u>and</u> *he swore to himself he'd never take a bargain flight again.*

Score   Number correct _____ × 20 = _____ %

Capital Letters

■ Mastery Test 1

Cross out the two capitalization errors in each of the following sentences. Then write the corrections in the spaces provided.

sister

French

1. My ~~Sister~~ Tanya is studying ~~french~~ this semester.

Philadelphia

University

2. Bill Cosby's comedy routine focused on his childhood in ~~philadelphia~~ and his exploits at Temple ~~university~~.

You're

King

3. I ordered a Big Mac, and the cashier said, "~~you're~~ at Burger ~~king~~, you know."

Milky

Way

4. Alice found two ~~milky way~~ wrappers and a peach pit in the shag rug.

_My_

Way

5. The Frank Sinatra version of "~~my way~~" was blasting from the diner's jukebox.

Kodak

Olympus

6. I traded in my ~~kodak~~ for an ~~olympus~~ camera with a telephoto lens.

Mrs.

Pepsi

7. As soon as ~~mrs.~~ Werner pulled into the gas station, the children headed for the ~~pepsi~~ machine.

Year's

Day

8. Rita always breaks her New ~~year's~~ resolutions long before Valentine's ~~day~~.

Did

attic

9. Terry said, "~~did~~ you read the *National Enquirer* story about the woman who was locked in an ~~Attic~~ for forty-seven years?"

_Dr._

malpractice

10. My little brother really annoyed ~~dr.~~ Thompson by asking, "Is your ~~Malpractice~~ insurance paid up?"

Score   Number correct _____ × 5 = _____ %

Capital Letters

■ Mastery Test 2

Cross out the two capitalization errors in each of the following sentences. Then write the corrections in the spaces provided.

Miracle Gro	1. I fed my plants with ~~miracle-gro~~ so often that they died from overeating.
Chicago Inn	2. It would take eighteen hours to drive to ~~chicago,~~ so Brad suggested that we stay one night in a Holiday ~~inn.~~
Fourth July	3. Every ~~fourth~~ of ~~july,~~ my dog howls when he hears the fireworks.
It's Shoprite	4. "~~it's~~ so dull in this town," said Joe, "that sometimes we go down to the ~~shoprite~~ store just to watch them restock the toothpaste."
Tigers Detroit	5. The ~~tigers~~ played well in Florida but started losing when they got back to ~~detroit.~~
Visa Penney	6. To curb her impulse buying, Toni cut up her ~~visa~~ and J. C. ~~penney~~ charge cards.
Scope Right	7. During the argument, my brother accused me of needing ~~scope~~ mouthwash and I told him to buy some ~~right~~ Guard deodorant.
California Ford	8. On his way to ~~california,~~ the hitchhiker rode in a moving van, a 1972 ~~ford,~~ and a 1993 Cadillac.
Guide Monday	9. Because I hadn't gotten the new *TV* ~~*guide,*~~ I didn't know whether there was anything on ~~monday~~ night I wanted to watch.
Red Have	10. The ~~red~~ Cross poster urged, "~~have~~ a heart and give blood."

Score   Number correct _____ × 5 = _____ %

Capital Letters

■ **Mastery Test 3**

Cross out the two capitalization errors in each of the following sentences. Then write the corrections in the spaces provided.

With
enemies

1. "~~with~~ friends like you, George," said Pat, "a person doesn't need ~~Enemies~~."

steak
Baltimore

2. Every payday, we treat ourselves to dinner at a ~~Steak~~ house on ~~baltimore~~ Pike.

lottery
Marv's

3. Bill bought three ~~Lottery~~ tickets and a pack of gum at ~~marv's~~ News.

aunt
peppers

4. When my ~~Aunt~~ was pregnant, she craved raw green ~~Peppers~~ sprinkled with salt.

German
mosquito

5. Next to my neighbor's ~~german~~ shepherd, my toy poodle looks like a ~~Mosquito~~.

Wheat
Thins

6. Every time I buy a box of ~~wheat thins~~, the price goes up three cents.

Empire
State

7. Kelly almost fell over backward trying to see the top of the ~~empire state~~ Building.

Time
_I_

8. When my issue of _~~time~~_ arrives, ~~i~~ turn to the "Entertainment" section first.

Mets
triple

9. An infielder for the terrible New York ~~mets~~ team of 1962 once hit a ~~Triple~~ and was called out because he forgot to touch first base.

Prentices
apartment

10. The ~~prentices~~, who live in the next ~~Apartment~~, have a new baby that cries all the time.

Score Number correct _____ × 5 = _____ %

Capital Letters

■ Mastery Test 4

Cross out the two capitalization errors in each of the following sentences. Then write the corrections in the spaces provided.

University   1. Maxine begins classes at the ~~university~~ of ~~miami~~ this fall.
Miami

grandmother   2. My ~~Grandmother~~ starts buying Christmas presents in ~~august.~~
August

networks   3. The press conference was carried live on all three ~~Networks~~ the evening
Thanksgiving   before ~~thanksgiving~~.

Abbey   4. The disk jockey promised to play a track from the Beatles' album *~~abbey road~~*
Road   after the commercial.

Revolutionary 5. The history professor announced that there would be a quiz on Friday about
War   the ~~revolutionary war~~.

Elton   6. "I've just gotten a request," said the disk jockey, "to play some ~~elton john~~ for
John   the night crew at McNeil Industries."

English   7. I suddenly realized that my lunch consisted of an ~~english~~ muffin, ~~swiss~~ cheese,
Swiss   and German potato salad.

summer   8. Last ~~Summer~~, we drove to San Francisco in our ~~chevy~~ van.
Chevy

chemicals   9. A tractor-trailer loaded with ~~Chemicals~~ had flipped over at the intersection
Streets   of Oakdale and Cherry ~~streets~~.

cole   10. I ordered two corned beef sandwiches and a pound of ~~Cole~~ slaw from the
Dee-lish   ~~dee-lish~~ Delicatessen.

Score   Number correct _____ × 5 = _____ %

Numbers and Abbreviations

■ Mastery Test 1

Cross out the mistake in numbers or abbreviations in each sentence and correct it in the space provided.

_____two_____ 1. *Consumer Reports* rated 2 of twelve brands of bacon it tested as "unacceptable."

conditioner 2. When the air cond. broke down, the supermarket employees packed shaved ice around the dairy products.

_____1861_____ 3. After her husband died in eighteen-sixty-one, Queen Victoria went into mourning for twenty-five years.

_____page_____ 4. One pg. of the science textbook showed the stone tools of prehistoric people.

apartment 5. I managed to fit the entire contents of my apt. into the back of my brother's station wagon.

one thousand 6. The team of six bank robbers got away with less than 1,000 dollars.

_____109_____ 7. The telephone book lists one hundred and nine Richard Browns and 41 Dick Browns.

_____Florida_____ 8. The six of us left Cleveland in a camper and headed for Daytona Beach, Fla.

_____four_____ 9. On page 122 of the tax guide is a sample form showing a typical joint return filed by a couple with 4 dependents.

_____room_____ 10. By 9:30, every student in my ten o'clock psychology class was already in the examination rm.

Score   Number correct _____ × 10 = _____ %

Numbers and Abbreviations

■ Mastery Test 2

Cross out the mistake in numbers or abbreviations in each sentence and correct it in the space provided. Mark the one sentence that is correct with a *C*.

_____six_____   1. As soon as Karina finishes ~~6~~ months of work, she will get one week's paid vacation.

_____chapters_____   2. Tonight, I have to read two ~~chaps.~~ in my English textbook.

_____room_____   3. The new puppy chewed the wooden legs on our dining ~~rm.~~ chairs.

_____sixteen_____   4. Sherry answered ~~16~~ of the twenty test questions correctly.

_____73_____   5. There's a smudge on page ~~seventy-three~~ that looks like chocolate syrup and one on page 90 that looks like coffee.

_____president_____   6. The ~~pres.~~ waved to the crowd as he left on the flight to California.

_____1969_____   7. When the astronauts landed on the moon in ~~nineteen sixty-nine~~, they had traveled over 244,000 miles.

_____hours_____   8. If I go without a cigarette for several ~~hrs.~~, I begin to feel nervous.

_____C_____   9. Half of all the people in the United States live in just eight of the fifty states.

_____New York_____   10. The flight from San Juan, Puerto Rico, to ~~N. Y.~~ was delayed for more than three hours.

Score   Number correct _____ × 10 = _____ %

End Marks

■ **Mastery Test 1**

Add a period, question mark, or exclamation point, as needed, to each of the following sentences.

Note   End marks always go *inside* the quotation marks that appear in some sentences.

1. Andy wondered whether he would look better if he shaved off his beard.
2. "My hand's as swollen as a baseball glove," moaned Flora.
3. Suddenly, someone yelled, "Get off that wet cement!"
4. During the electrical storm, the nervous mother asked all her children to put on their rubber sneakers.
5. When Rob woke up, his tongue felt as though it were wearing a woolly sock.
6. "How many people here believe in ESP?" the speaker asked.
7. If I pay for the gas, will you do all the driving?
8. Hurry, grab the fire extinguisher!
9. Darlene slammed the phone down and yelled, "Don't call me again!"
10. Audrey asked, "Is the dinosaur the biggest animal that ever lived?"
11. Sylvia wondered if she would ever see Sam again.
12. On a bet, Pasquale drank a glassful of horseradish.
13. I yelled as my spoon touched something squishy in the coffee cup.
14. The TV evangelist exclaimed to his audience, "If you've been born again, raise your hand!"
15. Why does the same pair of jeans cost more in the women's department than in the men's?
16. Does a snake really shed its skin all in one piece?
17. Would someone give me a hand with this window?
18. Three people have asked me for a match already.
19. Will you please save my seat for me?
20. In the movies, it seems that only two minutes after a woman goes into labor, someone shouts, "It's a boy!"

> *Score*   Number correct _____ × 5 = _____ %

End Marks

■ **Mastery Test 2**

Add a period, question mark, or exclamation point, as needed, to each of the following sentences.

Note   End marks always go *inside* the quotation marks that appear in some sentences.

1. The coach screamed, "That runner was safe!"
2. "For someone so wrapped up in himself," Dora snapped, "Steve makes a pretty small package."
3. The stereo ad asked, "Are you ready for wall-to-wall sound?"
4. When she goes out, Edith worries about what her children are watching on TV.
5. The teenagers in the back row threw Milk Duds at the people in front.
6. The headline in the yellowing old newspaper read, "Horsecar Strikes Pedestrian."
7. "I can't believe you gave my favorite jacket to the Salvation Army!" Nick yelled.
8. When did our instructor say the paper would be due?
9. Please fill up the tank and check the oil.
10. It's strange that no one has ever told Vince that he needs to use mouthwash.
11. Ken put the money in a safe place and then couldn't find it.
12. Little Debbie asked her mother, "If I don't keep my dentist appointment, will my teeth fall out?"
13. I was told I could pick up this suit on Wednesday afternoon.
14. Can we stop for lunch soon?
15. The zookeeper yelled, "Close the cage!"
16. He wondered whether the mail had arrived yet.
17. I wish my boss would stop looking over my shoulder and asking when the project will be done.
18. Emmet remarked, "Can this be the same hotel we stayed at five years ago?"
19. Jan, expecting the glass door to open automatically, got a painful surprise.
20. He is afraid of only two things: snakes and the IRS.

Score   Number correct _____ × 5 = _____ %

Apostrophe

■ **Mastery Test 1**

In each sentence, cross out the word that needs an apostrophe. Then write the word correctly in the space provided.

nobody's 1. She is ~~nobodys~~ fool when money is involved.

duck's 2. The ~~ducks~~ beak had been taped shut.

Ronnie's 3. That was ~~Ronnies~~ third car accident this year.

hawk's 4. A ~~hawks~~ wings beat faster when it is about to dive at its prey.

safecracker's 5. The ~~safecrackers~~ eyes gleamed as the lock clicked open.

dentist's 6. My ~~dentists~~ worst habit is asking me questions when my mouth is stuffed with cotton.

_It's_ 7. ~~Its~~ been estimated that the typical American consumes one hundred pounds of white sugar a year.

company's 8. When the insurance ~~companys~~ check arrived, I ran to the bank.

doctor's (or doctors') 9. The ~~doctors~~ waiting room was stuffy and crowded.

resort's 10. The ~~resorts~~ policy is to give a partial refund if the weather is poor.

Score Number correct _____ × 10 = _____ %

Apostrophe

■ Mastery Test 2

In the space provided under each sentence, add the one apostrophe needed and explain why the other word ending in *s* is a simple plural.

Example   Joans hair began to fall out two days after she dyed it.

Joans: *Joan's, meaning "the hair belonging to Joan"*

days: *simple plural meaning more than one day*

1. The elderly womans long, knotty fingers show a lifetime of wear.

    womans: *woman's, meaning "the fingers of the woman"*

    fingers: *simple plural meaning more than one finger*

2. Studies show that a rooms color can affect our moods.

    rooms: *room's, meaning "the color of the room"*

    moods: *simple plural meaning more than one mood*

3. Kens homework is not yet done because of the two football games on TV today.

    Kens: *Ken's, meaning "the homework of Ken"*

    games: *simple plural meaning more than one game*

4. The raccoons tracks led from a hole in the backyard fence to our garbage can.

    raccoons: *raccoon's, meaning "the tracks of a raccoon"*

    tracks: *simple plural meaning more than one track*

5. In my mothers picture collection, my grandparents posed against a backdrop of painted scenery.

    mothers: *mother's, meaning "the picture collection belonging to my mother"*

    grandparents: *simple plural meaning more than one grandparent*

Score   Number correct _____ × 10 = _____ %

Apostrophe

■ Mastery Test 3

In each sentence two apostrophes are missing or are used incorrectly. Cross out the two errors and write the corrections in the spaces provided.

can't
evening's

1. I ~~cant~~ understand why our neighbors disturb the ~~evenings~~ quiet with their electronic bug zapper.

sister's
hours

2. My ~~sisters~~ habit of tying up the phone for ~~hours'~~ drives my parents crazy.

who's
children's

3. I wonder ~~whos~~ responsible for making ~~childrens~~ clothes so expensive.

saloon's
doors

4. The gunslinger barged through the ~~saloons~~ swinging ~~door's~~.

Olympics
athlete's

5. Qualifying for the ~~Olympic's~~ is an amateur ~~athletes~~ crowning achievement.

store's
antics

6. The ~~stores~~ photographer used a variety of ~~antics'~~ to get the children to smile.

supermarket's
machines

7. While her mother paid the clerk, Michelle wandered over to the ~~supermarkets~~ gum-ball ~~machine's~~.

couldn't
burglar's

8. The suspect ~~couldnt~~ have committed the crime, for his shoe size did not match the ~~burglars~~ footprints.

o'clock
factory's

9. At twelve ~~oclock~~, the ~~factorys~~ whistle blows, and the shift changes.

Dewdrops
bicycle's

10. ~~Dewdrops'~~ glistened on the ~~bicycles~~ vinyl seat.

Score Number correct _____	× 5 = _____	%

Apostrophe

■ **Mastery Test 4**

In each sentence two apostrophes are missing or are used incorrectly. Cross out the two errors and write the corrections in the spaces provided.

Sandy's
Jim's

1. ~~Sandys~~ brown eyes filled with tears as she listened to ~~Jims~~ explanation.

son's
Greenfields'

2. My ~~sons~~ toys were strewn all over the ~~Greenfields~~ driveway.

Mike's
child's

3. ~~Mikes~~ Saint Bernard has a custom-built shelter as big as a ~~childs~~ playhouse.

morning's
strips

4. Monday ~~mornings~~ *Press* omitted several popular comic ~~strip's~~.

Stan's
Bradleys'

5. ~~Stans~~ behavior at the ~~Bradleys~~ party surprised everyone.

jury's
defendants

6. When the ~~jurys~~ verdict was announced, both ~~defendants'~~ looked stunned.

Frank's
_he's_

7. When ~~Franks~~ phone bill comes in, ~~hes~~ likely to rip it into little pieces.

Helen's
father's

8. ~~Helens~~ mistake was to trust the strength of the fraying hammock in her ~~fathers~~ yard.

firefighters
family's

9. Two ~~firefighter's~~ rushed into the burning building to rescue the ~~familys~~ pet dog.

can't
mother's

10. When she ~~cant~~ handle her two toddlers, Madge takes them to her ~~mothers~~ house.

Score   Number correct _____ × 5 = _____ %

Quotation Marks

■ **Mastery Test 1**

Place quotation marks or underlines where needed.

1. The lifeguard shouted,"No ball playing in the water!"

2. Kathy insisted in a loud voice,"I'm not really overweight. I'm just six inches too short."

3. "If today were a blackboard," Terrence said,"I'd erase it and start over."

4. In her diet book, Miss Piggy advises,"Never eat anything at one sitting that you can't lift."

5. "Something is wrong with my radio," Fred said to the mechanic."It won't work unless the windshield wipers are turned on."

6. "You creep!"Zella yelled to the tailgater behind her."I've got small children in this car!"

7. The first chapter in the book How to Train Your Dog is entitled "Training the Master."

8. "Why do I skydive?"the elderly man repeated to the news reporter."Well, I guess because I'm terrible at checkers."

9. "I'll only warn you this time," said the officer."But next time you'd better drive more slowly or be prepared to open your wallet."

10. "When I was a child," said Cindy,"I thought that if you swallowed a watermelon seed, a watermelon would grow in your stomach."

Score   Number correct _____ × 10 = _____ %

Quotation Marks

■ Mastery Test 2

Place quotation marks or underlines where needed.

1. Darla said,"To err is human. That's why I do it so much."

2. At breakfast, Terry said,"I'll trade the sports section and a piece of bacon for the comics."

3. Danny's second-grade teacher asked,"How many months have twenty-eight days?"

4. "All twelve of them,"Danny answered.

5. "And the winner,"announced the host,"is Miss Mexico!"

6. "I'm not hungry,"said Bertha."I'm starved."

7. The bumper sticker on the car ahead of us read,"If you get any closer, introduce yourself."

8. "Where are you going?"asked Carrie sarcastically."A Halloween party?"

9. "If you guys don't start hustling,"warned the coach,"you're going to see football scholarships start vanishing into thin air."

10. The episode entitled"Finding a Voice"on the television series Nova describes how some people with cerebral palsy are now speaking through the use of computers that have artificial voices.

Score   Number correct _____ × 10 = _____ %

Quotation Marks

■ Mastery Test 3

Place quotation marks or underlines where needed.

1. "Minds are like parachutes," the teacher said. "They work only when they're open."

2. "If you refrigerate candles before using them," said the household hints book, "they'll last longer and won't drip."

3. In Psychology Today magazine, the author of the article called "The Techniques of the Artful Salesman" suggests that successful salespeople almost hypnotize their customers.

4. "When I wake up in the morning," said Fran, "I sometimes have dream hangovers. For several hours, I can't shake the emotions I felt in my dream."

5. "My insomnia is terrible these days," said Stan. "I can't even sleep on the job."

6. I turned the radio up when Elvis Presley's classic song "Blue Suede Shoes" came on.

7. I read a horror story entitled "Children of the Kingdom," in which giant slugs that eat people live in the sewers of New York City.

8. As the miser was taking a walk, a robber pressed a gun into his ribs and demanded, "Your money or your life!"

9. "Take my life," said the miser. "I'm saving my money for my old age."

10. The sign on Toshio's desk reads, "In the rat race, only the rats win."

Score   Number correct _____ × 10 = _____ %

Quotation Marks

■ Mastery Test 4

Place quotation marks or underlines where needed.

1. "When I saw Raiders of the Lost Ark," my grandfather said, "it reminded me of the old adventure serials we watched in the thirties and forties."

2. Before she asked her boss for a raise, Nadine said timidly, "Are you in a good mood, Mr. Huff?"

3. The newspaper headline read, "Good Humor Man Slays Ten."

4. The driver leaned out and handed two dollars to the toll collector, saying, "I'm paying for the car behind me, too."

5. "Did you know," he said to the expectant mother, "that it now costs $85,000 to raise a child to the age of eighteen?"

6. The TV announcer warned, "The latest figures indicate there will be a billion cars on the road by the year 2010. So if you want to cross the street, you'd better do it now."

7. My six-year-old nephew stared at me and asked, "How did you break your kneecap with that big, heavy cast on your leg?"

8. "I never go back on my word," he promised. "I might just go around it a little, though."

9. After Kay read a book called Chocolate: The Consuming Passion, she ran out and bought six Hershey bars.

10. Reassuring me that my diseased elm would recover, the tree surgeon said, "Don't worry. Its bark is worse than its blight."

Score Number correct _____ × 10 = _____ %

Comma

■ **Mastery Test 1**

Add commas where needed. Then refer to the box below and write, in the space provided, the letter of the comma rule that applies in each sentence.

a. Between items in a series	d. Between complete thoughts
b. After introductory material	e. With direct quotations
c. Around interrupters	f. With everyday material

_____a_____   1. Tasha makes her studying more bearable by having plenty of Triscuits, pretzels, and peanut-filled M&Ms close by.

_____b_____   2. Because Jim is the company's top salesperson, he receives special attention from the boss.

_____e_____   3. "You look different," said Lily. "Have you lost weight?"

_____c_____   4. My Uncle Al, who is hard of hearing, always asks me to repeat what I just said.

_____e_____   5. "I really appreciate the ride," the hitchhiker said. "A hundred cars must have passed me."

_____d_____   6. My little sister loves to ride on the back of my motorcycle, but my parents worry about her falling off.

_____f_____   7. I have to pay $8,250 by June 30, 1999, before I officially own my car.

_____a_____   8. Little Will emptied his piggy bank and sorted the nickels, dimes, and quarters into three shiny piles.

_____b_____   9. Huddled under a large piece of plastic, we waited out the rain delay in the ball game.

_____d_____ 10. The vacationing boys slept in the car that night, for they'd spent too much on meals and souvenirs.

Score Number correct _____ × 10 = _____ %	

Comma

■ Mastery Test 2

Add commas where needed. Then refer to the box below and write, in the space provided, the letter of the comma rule that applies in each sentence.

a. Between items in a series	d. Between complete thoughts
b. After introductory material	e. With direct quotations
c. Around interrupters	

___*b*___   1. As the noisy jet flew directly overhead, the framed photographs on the wall jumped and rattled.

___*a*___   2. Joe marinated the mild, sweet, purple-tinged onions in oil, vinegar, and parsley flakes.

___*d*___   3. Cecil's college expenses and dormitory rent both increased this semester, so he works nights at a pizza parlor.

___*a*___   4. The photo contest offered a prize for the best picture of a family pet, a baby, or a flower.

___*c*___   5. Boris, a man I didn't trust, had a smile as hard and cold as a car grille.

___*b*___   6. Trailing a cloud of choking perfume, the teenage girls arrived at the school dance.

___*e*___   7. "I've decided to get married," Teresa announced.

___*a*___   8. Lisa stopped in her tracks, turned around, and screamed when she realized she was being followed.

___*b*___   9. Despite the two cheeseburgers already under his belt, Mike ordered a fried chicken platter and a chocolate shake.

___*c*___   10. An industrious janitor, heedless of the lecture still in progress, began disconnecting the microphones.

Score   Number correct _____ × 10 = _____ %

Comma

■ Mastery Test 3

Add commas where needed. Then refer to the box below and write, in the space provided, the letter of the comma rule that applies in each sentence.

a. Between items in a series	d. Between complete thoughts
b. After introductory material	e. With direct quotations
c. Around interrupters	f. With everyday material

_____f_____ 1. My friend Tina lives at 333 Virginia Avenue, Atlantic City.

_____d_____ 2. I went to her house one night recently, and the two of us watched television for several hours.

_____c_____ 3. Tina, who is always hungry, suggested we go to Tony's Grill for a pizza.

_____b_____ 4. Along with about a dozen other cars, I parked in a tiny lot with a "No Parking" sign.

_____c_____ 5. I believed, foolishly enough, that my car would be safe there.

_____a_____ 6. We had our pizza, left the restaurant, and returned to the lot.

_____d_____ 7. A 1975 Chevy and a tow truck were parked in the lot, but my Honda and all the other cars had vanished.

_____b_____ 8. After walking twenty blocks back to Tina's house, I called the towing company.

_____e_____ 9. A recorded voice said, "Come to 26 Texas Avenue tomorrow morning with seventy-five dollars in cash."

_____b_____ 10. Whenever Tina craves pizza, I now buy a frozen pie at the local Seven-Eleven store.

Score Number correct _____ × 10 = _____ %	

Comma

■ Mastery Test 4

Add commas where needed. Then refer to the box below and write, in the space provided, the letter of the comma rule that applies in each sentence.

a. Between items in a series	d. Between complete thoughts
b. After introductory material	e. With direct quotations
c. Around interrupters	

_c_ 1. Matt's first car, a 1960 Chevy Impala, had enormous tail fins.

_e_ 2. Kia called from upstairs, "Could you turn the TV down?"

_a_ 3. The broken-down farm housed a swaybacked horse, a blind cow, and two lame chickens.

_b_ 4. In Phil's job as toll collector, he takes quarters from over 5,500 drivers every day.

_b_ 5. In the middle of the love scene, two little boys in the audience began to giggle.

_a_ 6. The combination of milk stains, peanut butter splotches, and jelly smears made the toddler's face look like a finger painting.

_b_ 7. Though public transportation saves her money, Dotty prefers driving to work.

_e_ 8. "Better to keep your mouth shut and be thought a fool," my father always says, "than to open it and remove all doubt."

_c_ 9. The fried eggs, as they sizzled in the rusty iron skillet, began to turn red.

_d_ 10. The road map must have been out of date, for the highway it showed no longer existed.

Score Number correct _____ × 10 = _____ %

Other Punctuation Marks

■ **Mastery Test 1**

At the appropriate spot (or spots), place the punctuation mark shown in the margin.

;   1. There are several ways to save money on your grocery bills;for example, never go shopping on an empty stomach.

:   2. There are only two ways to get there;hike or hitch a ride.

—   3. "The cooking at this restaurant," said the dissatisfied customer, "lacks just one thing good taste."

-      4. Pete's over the shoulder catch brought the crowd to its feet.

( )   5. Call your local office of the IRS(Internal Revenue Service)if you think you're entitled to a refund.

—   6. Annabelle gave Harold back his engagement ring without the diamond.

:   7. That new ice cream place has the great flavors:blueberry cheesecake, pineapple, bubble gum, and Oreo cookie.

—   8. Some teenage boys there they go around the corner just stole that man's wallet.

-      9. I'm waiting for the day when someone invents low calorie junk food.

;   10. In a study, people were asked who in their family got the most smiles and touches;44 percent said the family pet.

Score   Number correct _____ × 10 = _____ %

Other Punctuation Marks

■ Mastery Test 2

Add colons, semicolons, dashes, hyphens, or parentheses as needed. Each sentence requires only one of the five kinds of punctuation marks.

1. It's impossible for two blue-eyed parents to have a brown-eyed child.

2. People watch more television than most of us realize; the average set is on for more than six hours a day.

3. My aunt loves giving blow-by-blow accounts of all her operations.

4. Electrical storms, inflation, and my little brother's jokes—these are the things that bother me the most.

5. My car was losing power; I asked a gas station attendant to check the battery.

6. To cure hiccups, try one of the following methods: put a paper bag over your head, hold your breath, or eat a teaspoonful of sugar.

7. A portion of the sociology text (pages 150–158) deals with the changing roles of women.

8. My mother likes to listen to talk shows; she feels less lonely if there's a conversation going on.

9. Our math instructor said: "Standard units of measurement used to be set by parts of the body; for example, King Henry I of England defined a yard as the distance from his nose to his outstretched thumb."

10. From my second-row seat at the movies, I could count the leading lady's eyelashes.

Score   Number correct _____ × 10 = _____ %

Dictionary Use

■ Mastery Test 1

Items 1–5   Use your dictionary to answer the following questions.

1. How many syllables are in the word *incongruous?* _____ four _____

2. Where is the primary accent in the word *culmination?* _____ cul mi na´ tion _____

3. In the word *periphery,* the *i* is pronounced like
   a.   long *i.*
   b.   short *i.*
   c.   long *e.*
   d.   short *e.*

4. In the word *acquiesce,* the *i* is pronounced like
   a.   long *i.*
   b.   short *i.*
   c.   long *e.*
   d.   short *e.*

5. In the word *apostasy,* the first *a* is pronounced like
   a.   long *a.*
   b.   short *a.*
   c.   short *o.*
   d.   schwa.

Items 6–10   There are five misspelled words in the following sentence. Cross out each misspelled word and write in the correct spelling in the spaces provided.

~~Altho~~ there were legal suits filed against him, the ~~mayer~~ decided to run for reelection, but the ~~citizans~~ of our town were not ~~anxous~~ to give him a second ~~oportunity~~ at public office.

6. _____ Although _____   8. _____ citizens _____   10. _____ opportunity _____

7. _____ mayor _____   9. _____ anxious _____

Score   Number correct _____ × 10 = _____ %

Dictionary Use

■ Mastery Test 2

Items 1–5   Use your dictionary to answer the following questions.

1. How many syllables are in the word *pandemonium?* _____*five*_____

2. Where is the primary accent in the word *unremitting?* _____*un re mit´ ting*_____

3. In the word *expatriate,* the *i* is pronounced like a
    a. long *i.*
    b. short *i.*
    c. long *e.*
    d. short *e.*

4. In the word *recapitulate,* the *i* is pronounced like a
    a. long *i.*
    b. short *i.*
    c. long *e.*
    d. short *e.*

5. In the word *frivolous,* the first *o* is pronounced like a
    a. long *o.*
    b. short *o.*
    c. short *u.*
    d. schwa.

Items 6–10   There are five misspelled words in the following sentence. Cross out each misspelled word and write the correct spelling in the space provided.

We ~~regreted~~ that we could not attend your ~~anniversery~~ ~~celabration~~. Our station wagon broke down on the freeway, ~~leaveing~~ us with no means of ~~transpertation~~.

6. _____*regretted*_____   8. _____*celebration*_____   10. _____*transportation*_____

7. _____*anniversary*_____   9. _____*leaving*_____

Score   Number correct _____ × 10 = _____ %

Spelling Improvement

■ Mastery Test 1

Use the three spelling rules to spell the following words.

1. palate + able = _palatable_
2. silly   + est   = _silliest_
3. fate   + ful   = _fateful_
4. drag   + ing   = _dragging_
5. plan   + er   = _planner_
6. healthy + ly   = _healthily_
7. cause   + ing   = _causing_
8. prefer + ed   = _preferred_

Circle the correctly spelled plural in each pair.

9. (chiefs)   chievs   12. candys   (candies)
10. sandwichs   (sandwiches)   13. (vetoes)   vetos
11. yourselfs   (yourselves)   14. supplys   (supplies)

Circle the correctly spelled word (from the basic word list) in each pair.

15. compeny   (company)   18. (opportunity)   oppertunity
16. hieght   (height)   19. (restaurant)   restarant
17. (loneliness) lonliness   20. importent   (important)

| *Score* Number correct _____ × 5 = _____ % |

Spelling Improvement

■ Mastery Test 2

Use the three spelling rules to spell the following words.

1. drip   + ed   = *dripped*
2. merry   + ment = *merriment*
3. escape + ing   = *escaping*
4. expel   + ed   = *expelled*
5. finance + ing   = *financing*
6. accuse + er   = *accuser*
7. happy   + ness = *happiness*
8. spite   + ful   = *spiteful*

Circle the correctly spelled plural in each pair.

9. indexs   (indexes)   12. (babies)   babys
10. echos   (echoes)   13. lifes   (lives)
11. (gifts)   giftes   14. scratchs   (scratches)

Circle the correctly spelled word (from the basic word list) in each pair.

15. temorrow   (tomorrow)   18. straght   (straight)
16. truely   (truly)   19. (ready)   readdy
17. (vegetable) vegtable   20. (condition) condishun

Score Number correct _____ × 5 = _____ %

Omitted Words and Letters

■ **Mastery Test 1**

Part 1 In the spaces provided, write in the two short connecting words needed in each sentence. Use carets (∧) within the sentences to show where these words belong.

<u>to</u>

<u>in</u>
1. Returning her car, Sarah found she'd left the keys ∧ the ignition.

<u>a</u>

<u>a</u>
2. Tony has ∧ superstitious habit of dribbling the ball exactly six times before he shoots ∧ free throw.

<u>of</u>

<u>the</u>
3. Carefully, Joanne pasted small strips ∧ correction tape over each typing mistake on ∧ page.

<u>an</u>

<u>the</u>
4. I know ∧ easy way to get an A in that course—just agree with everything ∧ instructor says.

<u>the</u>

<u>the</u>
5. Andy dreaded ∧ tests he would have to undergo even more than ∧ operation itself.

Part 2 Add the two *-s* endings needed in each sentence.

<u>olives</u>

<u>pits</u>
6. Marcy ate an entire jar of olive and left a pile of pit on the coffee table.

<u>teenagers</u>

<u>bottles</u>
7. Shards of green glass glittered on the pavement where those teenager had smashed a whole six-pack of empty beer bottle.

<u>trays</u>

<u>cuts</u>
8. Our supermarket's deli section sells tray of party cold cut.

<u>holes</u>

<u>socks</u>
9. Hector's tight-fitting new shoes have worn hole in all his sock.

<u>rainstorms</u>

<u>plants</u>
10. Those heavy rainstorm have flattened all my tomato plant.

Score Number correct _____ × 5 = _____ %

Omitted Words and Letters

■ Mastery Test 2

Part 1   In the spaces provided, write in the two short connecting words needed in each sentence. Use carets (∧) within the sentences to show where these words belong.

_____to_____   1. This weekend, we're going ∧ replace all the shingles that have fallen off ∧ roof.

_____the_____

__at (or in)__   2. My favorite snacks ∧ this restaurant are the crispy baked-potato skins ∧ the

_____and_____   marinated mushrooms.

_____the_____   3. The eyes of ∧ woman on ∧ billboard seemed to follow me as I drove by.

_____the_____

_____my_____   4. When I sat down, three quarters fell out of ∧ pants pocket and rolled under ∧ sofa.

_____the_____

_____a_____   5. My pet turtles live in ∧ large, galvanized tin tub in ∧ garage.

_____the_____

Part 2   Add the two -s endings needed in each sentence.

_____books_____   6. After I had read several horror book, I began listening for weird sound.

_____sounds_____

___desserts___   7. I love to eat exotic dessert, but my husband likes only vanilla ice cream cone.

_____cones_____

___neighbors___   8. All the neighbor comment on my mother's garden of roses and daffodil.

___daffodils___

_____chairs_____ 9. I slowed the car when I noticed a pair of kitchen chair that had been set out

_____cans_____   along with three garbage can.

_____bags_____   10. The old man sold me two bag of cookie from a homemade stand in front of

___cookies___   his house.

Score   Number correct _____ × 5 = _____ %

Commonly Confused Words

■ **Mastery Test 1**

For each sentence, choose the correct words and write them in the spaces provided.

____you're____
____right____

1. When (you're, your) looking for the (right, write) career, it's helpful to talk to other people about their jobs.

____pair____
____loose____

2. Carol keeps a special (pair, pear) of (lose, loose) trousers with tough patches on the knees to wear while gardening.

____They're____
____right____

3. (There, Their, They're) the (right, write) size, but these screws still don't fit.

____principle____
____whole____

4. "It's a matter of (principal, principle)," the editor said. "I won't print anything unless it's the (hole, whole) truth."

____past____
____all ready____

5. By twenty (passed, past) eight o'clock, I was (all ready, already) for my ten o'clock interview.

____through____
____two____

6. We went (through, threw) the entrance to the amusement park's haunted house and were met by (to, too, two) scary-looking creatures.

____passed____
____except____

7. We all (past, passed) the midterm exam, (accept, except) for the student who had shown up for only three classes.

____can hardly____
____through____

8. I (can hardly, can't hardly) see (through, threw) my windshield, since it's covered with squashed bugs and grit.

____Whether____
____loses____

9. (Weather, Whether) or not Duane (loses, looses) his license depends on the outcome of the court hearing.

____effect____
____brakes____

10. The tragic (affect, effect) of one car's faulty (brakes, breaks) was a six-car pileup.

Score Number correct _____ × 5 = _____ %

Commonly Confused Words

■ **Mastery Test 2**

For each sentence, choose the correct words and write them in the spaces provided.

know

principles

1. We were expected to (know, no) the (principals, principles) of photosynthesis for the biology test.

You're

write

2. (You're, Your) the first professor to ask me to (right, write) a sixty-page term paper.

course

two

3. I took a (coarse, course) in speed-reading and can now read (to, too, two) books in the time it once took to read one.

already

here

4. "It's (all ready, already) eight o'clock, and nobody's (hear, here) yet," Fran complained.

quite

dessert

5. I ate so much that I was (quiet, quite) full before (desert, dessert) arrived.

Among

thought

6. (Among, Between) the three of us, we (though, thought) we could scrape up enough money for a large pizza.

should have

piece

7. You (should of, should have) saved the last (peace, piece) of chicken for me.

clothes

pair

8. At the back of my (cloths, clothes) closet, I discovered a (pair, pear) of old, mildewed sneakers.

Who's

beside

9. (Whose, Who's) willing to sit (beside, besides) me in the back seat?

plain

fewer

10. The (plain, plane) truth is that (fewer, less) Americans feel financially secure these days.

Score   Number correct _____ × 5 = _____ %

Commonly Confused Words

■ **Mastery Test 3**

Cross out the two mistakes in usage in each sentence. Then write the correct words in the spaces provided.

_____Does_____

_____whose_____   1. ~~Dose~~ anyone know ~~who's~~ glasses these are?

_____You're_____

_____than_____   2. ~~Your~~ a lot taller ~~then~~ I was when I was your age.

_____to_____

_____an_____   3. Monica went ~~too~~ the mall for one item but came home with ~~a~~ armful of
                      packages.

_____accept_____

_____advice_____   4. I told my brother that he should ~~except~~ my ~~advise~~ on all matters.

_____break_____

_____coarse_____   5. With his fingers, Gene attempted to ~~brake~~ off a piece of the crusty, ~~course~~ bread.

_____plane_____

_____Then_____   6. In August 1945, a lone ~~plain~~ passed over the city of Hiroshima. ~~Than~~ a living
                      hell began for the city's inhabitants.

_____who's_____

_____accepted_____ 7. Marilyn, a housewife ~~whose~~ returning to college, has been ~~excepted~~ in the
                      medical technicians' program.

_____its_____

_____among_____   8. We divided the huge hero sandwich, with ~~it's~~ layers of salami and cheese,
                      ~~between~~ the three of us.

_____Regardless_____

_____could have_____ 9. ~~Irregardless~~ of the rumors, nobody ~~could of~~ guessed that the business would
                      close.

_____There_____

_____threw_____   10. ~~Their~~ go the obnoxious fans who ~~through~~ bottles onto the field.

Score Number correct _____ × 5 = _____ %

Commonly Confused Words

■ Mastery Test 4

Cross out the two mistakes in usage in each sentence. Then write the correct words in the spaces provided.

<u>too</u>
<u>it's</u>

1. As soon as my jeans get ~~to~~ tight, I know ~~its~~ time to cut out junk food.

<u>must have</u>
<u>could</u>

2. I ~~must of~~ read the assignment five times, but I ~~couldn't~~ hardly make any sense out of it.

<u>past</u>
<u>knew</u>

3. After we drove ~~passed~~ the same diner for the third time, we ~~new~~ we were lost.

<u>since</u>
<u>lose</u>

4. I put my paycheck under my pillow, ~~being that~~ I was afraid I was going to ~~loose~~ it.

<u>through</u>
<u>whether</u>

5. As the wind blew ~~threw~~ the rafters, we wondered ~~weather~~ or not the old boathouse would survive the storm.

<u>two</u>
<u>wear</u>

6. I couldn't decide on which of the ~~too~~ costumes to ~~where~~ to the party.

<u>New</u>
<u>deserts</u>

7. ~~Knew deserts~~ are being created all over the world by the careless destruction of trees.

<u>plain</u>
<u>than</u>

8. The ~~plane~~ brown pears in the fruit bowl are sweeter ~~then~~ they look.

<u>hear</u>
<u>its</u>

9. Although I could ~~here it's~~ pitiful cries, I couldn't reach the animal caught under the caved-in shed.

<u>course</u>
<u>break</u>

10. Before I took this writing ~~coarse,~~ I would ~~brake~~ into a cold sweat every time I picked up a pen.

Score Number correct _____ × 5 = _____ %

Effective Word Choice

■ **Mastery Test 1**

Certain words are italicized in the following sentences. In the spaces at the left, identify whether these words are slang (*S*), clichés (*C*), or pretentious words (*PW*). Then, in the spaces below, replace the words with more effective diction.
Answers may vary for rewritten portions.

_C_ 1. After she received an A, Barbara was *walking on air* for the rest of the day.
happy

_S_ 2. A *wheeler-dealer* salesman sold Jim a *lemon*.
fast-talking   unreliable car

_PW_ 3. Robert's *rain garment was saturated*.
raincoat   soaked

_PW_ 4. He is inhumane to *members of the animal kingdom*.
animals

_S_ 5. I have a lot of studying to do, but *my brain is out to lunch*.
I can't keep my mind on my work

_C_ 6. After moving the furniture, James lay down on the couch and *went out like a light*.
fell asleep immediately

_S_ 7. My parents *hit the roof* when they saw the dented car.
became angry

_S_ 8. If I had known you were *broke*, I would have lent you the *dough*.
lacking funds   money

_PW_ 9. I *extinguished my smoking material* before boarding the *aircraft*.
put out my cigarette   plane

_S_ 10. Darlene gave the collection agency a *buzz* and asked to speak to the *head honcho*.
call   person in charge

| **Score** | Number correct _____ × 10 = _____ % |

Effective Word Choice

■ **Mastery Test 2**

Certain words are italicized in the following sentences. In the spaces at the left, identify whether these words are slang (*S*), clichés (*C*), or pretentious words (*PW*). Then, in the spaces below, replace the words with more effective diction.

Answers may vary for rewritten portions.

___PW___ 1. The professor *perceived* that the students *had a negative response to the idea.*

    realized   disagreed

___S___ 2. The movie was *a total downer.*

    depressing

___PW___ 3. At nursery school, my child is learning to *interact in a positive manner* with her *peers.*

    get along   age group

___C___ 4. Carlos felt *like a fish out of water* at the party.

    out of place

___C___ 5. I talked to my daughter until I was *blue in the face,* but my words *went in one ear and out the other.*

    exhausted   were ignored

___S___ 6. Leon *stuffed his face with* so many *munchies* that he felt sick.

    ate   snacks

___PW___ 7. Charlene *asserted* that her story was not a *fabrication.*

    said   lie

___S___ 8. I tried to *sack out* for a while, but some *yo-yo* kept calling my number by mistake.

    sleep   stupid person

___C___ 9. Teresa grabbed the rolls out of the oven *in the nick of time.*

    just in time

___S___ 10. *Keep your mitts off me* or you'll get a *knuckle sandwich.*

    Don't touch me   fist in your mouth

Score   Number correct _____ × 10 = _____ %

Effective Word Choice

■ **Mastery Test 3**

The following sentences include examples of wordiness. Rewrite the sentences in the space provided, omitting needless words.

Answers may vary.

1. Because of the fact that a time span of only five seconds separates the lightning from the thunder, we may safely conclude that the storm is directly overhead.

    Since the lightning and the thunder are only five seconds apart, the

    storm must be overhead.

2. After his long twelve-mile hike, Ruben was so exhausted that when he walked into his living room, he staggered.

    After the twelve-mile hike, Ruben staggered into his living room.

3. My mouth dropped open in amazement when I heard the startling news that Tim had just had a nervous breakdown last month.

    The news that Tim had a nervous breakdown last month surprised me.

4. Julia was convinced in her heart that she was doing the very best thing for both of them when she returned Clark's ring.

    Julia felt she was doing the right thing when she returned Clark's ring.

5. A sad-eyed mournful-looking little dog, no bigger than a puppy, followed my son home and walked behind him into the house.

    A small, sad-eyed dog followed my son home.

Score   Number correct _____ × 20 = _____ %

Effective Word Choice

■ Mastery Test 4

The following sentences include examples of wordiness. Rewrite the sentences in the space provided, omitting needless words.

Answers may vary.

1. My outgrown closet is filled to bursting with piles of useless junk that I no longer need.

   My closet is filled with junk.

   _____

2. The leaky faucet that wouldn't stop dripping annoyed and bothered me all night long.

   The dripping faucet annoyed me all night.

   _____

3. If you are having difficulties with your schoolwork and are not keeping up with your assignments, you should budget your time so that you stick to a schedule.

   If you are having trouble keeping up with your studies, you should budget

   your time.

4. The main idea that I am trying to get across in this essay is that no driver of a motor vehicle should be permitted to drive in excess of the speed limit of fifty-five miles per hour.

   Drivers should obey the fifty-five-miles-per-hour speed limit.

   _____

5. When we looked as if we didn't believe him, Frank got upset and indignant and insisted that his story was a true incident that had really happened.

   When we looked skeptical, Frank insisted that his story was true.

   _____

   _____

Score   Number correct _____ × 20 = _____ %

Combined Mastery Tests

Fragments and Run-Ons

■ Combined Mastery Test 1

Each of the word groups below is numbered. In the space provided, write *C* if a word group is a complete sentence, write *F* if it is a fragment, and write *R-O* if it is a run-on.

1. _C_
2. _F_
3. _R-O_
4. _F_
5. _C_
6. _F_
7. _C_
8. _F_
9. _R-O_
10. _C_
11. _F_
12. _C_
13. _R-O_
14. _F_
15. _C_
16. _C_
17. _F_
18. _R-O_
19. _C_
20. _F_

[1]A few years ago, an experiment was conducted in Germany. [2]To determine how dependent people are on their television sets. [3]The researchers chose 184 volunteers these people were paid to give up watching television for one year. [4]During the first months of the experiment. [5]Most of the subjects did not suffer any ill effects. [6]Or complain that they were missing anything important. [7]The volunteers said they had more free time, and they were grateful for the extra hours. [8]Spending them on reading, paying attention to their children, or visiting friends. [9]Another month went by, suddenly things took a turn for the worse. [10]The subjects became tense and restless. [11]In addition, quarreled frequently with other family members. [12]Their tension continued until the subjects were permitted to watch television again. [13]Nobody in the experiment survived an entire year without television, in fact, the longest anyone lasted was five months. [14]As soon as the television sets were turned on again. [15]The symptoms of anxiety disappeared. [16]This experiment suggests a conclusion. [17]Which would be dangerous to ignore. [18]Television is habit-forming it may be even more habit-forming than cigarettes or drugs. [19]Perhaps the little screen should carry a warning label. [20]Which says, "Caution—This Product May Be Hazardous to Your Health."

Score Number correct _____ × 5 = _____ %	

465

Fragments and Run-Ons

■ Combined Mastery Test 2

In the space provided, indicate whether each item below contains a fragment (*F*) or a run-on (*R-O*). Then correct the error.

___F___ 1. With mounting horror, Eleni looked at the anxiously awaited snapshots,ₓ ᵂ͟Which had just been developed. Not one picture had turned out.

___R-O___ 2. Doug tried to grasp his new soft contact lens;it was like trying to pick up a drop of water. The slippery little lens escaped from his fingers again and again.

___F___ 3. Wearing huge, bright-blue sunglasses with gold wires,ₓ ᵗ͟The new instructor strolled into class. One student whispered that she looked like a human dragonfly.

___F___ 4. Because Sandy carried a large shoulder bag when she went shopping,ₓ ˢ͟Store security guards regarded her with suspicion. They had been trained to watch out for shoplifters with extra-large purses.

___R-O___ 5. I watched my sister, a cleanliness fanatic, put away the produce. First she washed all the bananas and oranges, ͟ᵃⁿᵈ then she rubbed the onions with a towel.

___F___ 6. The crowd became silent. Then, while the drums rolled,ₓ ᵗ͟The acrobat attempted a triple somersault in midair.

___R-O___ 7. Irene peeled off the itchy wool knee socks,ₓ ͟; she stared at the vertical red ridges the tight socks had left on the tender skin. With a sigh, she massaged her sore shins.

___F___ 8. Although they sip nectar for energy,ₓ ᵇ͟Butterflies never eat anything substantial. They have no need to because their bodies don't grow. Their only function is to mate.

___R-O___ 9. When he smelled the acrid odor, Lee rushed to the kitchen. He popped up the smoking bread ͟, ᵇᵘᵗ something was still aflame in the toaster's crumb tray.

___F___ 10. Joanne painted her fingernails with pale-pink nail polish,ₓ ᵃ͟And put a slightly deeper shade of pink on her toenails. Her fingertips and toes looked as if they were blushing.

Score   Number correct _____ × 10 = _____ %

Verbs

■ Combined Mastery Test 1

Each sentence contains a mistake involving (1) standard English or irregular verb forms, (2) subject-verb agreement, or (3) consistent verb tense. Cross out the incorrect verb and write the correct form in the space provided.

torn   1. The razor-sharp coral had ~~tore~~ a hole in the hull of the flimsy boat.

warn   2. The signs in the park ~~warns~~ that litterers will be fined.

start   3. I cringe in embarrassment every time I ~~started~~ my car because its broken exhaust makes it sound like a hot rod.

keeps   4. Somebody in the dorm ~~keep~~ the radio on all night long.

hesitates 5. Mike wants to overcome his shyness but ~~hesitated~~ to meet new people because he fears he won't have anything interesting to say.

expects 6. Each of my professors ~~expect~~ a term paper to be turned in before the holidays.

sworn   7. The judge reminded the witness that she had ~~swore~~ to tell the truth.

was   8. There ~~were~~ a heavy load of soggy clothes to be washed when Janet got home from camp.

typed   9. Thelma ~~type~~ the final word and fell back in her chair; her report was finished at last.

bitten 10. Someone called Elaine at the office to tell her that her son had been ~~bit~~ by a stray dog.

Score	Number correct _____ × 10 = _____ %

Verbs

■ **Combined Mastery Test 2**

Each sentence contains a mistake involving (1) standard English or irregular verb forms, (2) subject-verb agreement, or (3) consistent verb tense. Cross out the incorrect verb and write the correct form in the space provided.

hidden   1. Karen searched for the fifty-dollar bill she had ~~hid~~ in the thick book.

feel   2. After I leave the dentist's office, my jaw and mouth ~~feels~~ numb.

reeled   3. After he stirred the thick paint for several minutes, Walt ~~reels~~ backward as the strong fumes made his head spin.

grown   4. My nephew must have ~~grew~~ a foot since I last saw him.

were   5. Hovering overhead at the scene of the accident ~~was~~ several traffic helicopters.

stung   6. When the nurse gave him the injection, Alfonso felt as if a huge bee had just ~~stinged~~ him.

talked   7. When I caught my little boy pulling the dog's ears, I sat him down and ~~talk~~ to him about being kind to animals.

sold   8. McDonald's has ~~selled~~ enough hamburgers to reach to the moon.

motioned   9. When he noticed Helen holding only a quart of milk, the man ahead of her in the checkout line ~~motions~~ for Helen to take his place.

were   10. Leaping out of the patrol car ~~was~~ two police officers with their guns drawn.

> **Score**   Number correct _____ × 10 = _____ %

Pronouns

■ Combined Mastery Test 1

Choose the sentence in each pair that uses pronouns correctly. Then write the letter of that sentence in the space provided.

___b___ 1. a. If someone wants to try out for the women's softball team, they should go to the practice field today after class.
         b. If someone wants to try out for the women's softball team, she should go to the practice field today after class.

___b___ 2. a. At the hardware store, they told me I would need specially treated lumber to build an outdoor deck.
         b. At the hardware store, the clerks told me I would need specially treated lumber to build an outdoor deck.

___a___ 3. a. Those greedy squirrels ate all the sunflower seeds in the bird feeder.
         b. Them greedy squirrels ate all the sunflower seeds in the bird feeder.

___b___ 4. a. Each of the student waiters had to write a report about their employment experience.
         b. Each of the student waiters had to write a report about his employment experience.

___b___ 5. a. We liked the price of the house, but you would have to do too much work to make it livable.
         b. We liked the price of the house, but we would have to do too much work to make it livable.

Score Number correct _____ × 20 = _____ %

Pronouns

■ Combined Mastery Test 2

In the spaces provided, write *PE* for each of the nine sentences that contain pronoun errors. Write *C* for the sentence that uses pronouns correctly. Then cross out each pronoun error and write the correction above it.

____PE____   1. Bobby, Earl, and ~~me~~ are studying for the math test together. [I]

____PE____   2. Someone in the women's aerobics class complained that ~~their~~ back was sore. [her]

____PE____   3. If I fail the final exam, does that mean that ~~you~~ automatically fail the course? [I]

____C____   4. Each of the twins had her name printed on her sweatshirt.

____PE____   5. I enjoy my word processing work, but ~~you~~ tend to have eyestrain by the end [I]

of the day.

____PE____   6. When Juanita got her job as a waitress, ~~they~~ told her she would have to buy [the manager]

her own uniforms.

____PE____   7. Tom read the paper while eating his lunch and then threw the rest of ~~it~~ away. [the paper]

____PE____   8. At the minicar racetrack, I proved that my reaction time was quicker than ~~her's~~. [hers]

____PE____   9. If anyone walks to the cafeteria, will ~~they~~ bring me a cup of coffee? [he or she]

____PE____   10. Since I've been up until two o'clock the last few nights and feel fine, I'm

convinced that ~~you~~ need only six hours of sleep. [I]

Score   Number correct _____ × 10 = _____ %

Faulty Modifiers and Parallelism

■ **Combined Mastery Test 1**

In the spaces provided, indicate whether each sentence contains a misplaced modifier (*MM*), a dangling modifier (*DM*), or faulty parallelism (*FP*). Then correct the error in the space under the sentence.

Rewritten sentences may vary.

FP   1. Before she went to bed, Sue brushed her teeth, took out her contact lenses, and was setting the alarm for six o'clock.
set the alarm for six o'clock.

DM   2. After enjoying the fabulous meal, the bill dampened our spirits.
After we had enjoyed the fabulous meal,

MM   3. Carmen read an article about exploring outer space in the dentist's office.
In the dentist's office, Carmen read an article about exploring outer space.

DM   4. While watching my favorite show, the smoke detector emitted a whistle.
While I was watching my favorite show,

FP   5. The wind blew over the card table, and the cups and plates were scattered.
and scattered the cups and plates.

DM   6. Backfiring and stalling, we realized that the car needed a tune-up.
We realized that the car, which was backfiring and stalling, needed a tune-up.

DM   7. Being left-handed, scissors seem upside down to me.
Since I am left-handed,

MM   8. A month ago, the Wallaces moved into the house next door from Ohio.
A month ago, the Wallaces moved from Ohio into the house next door.

MM   9. I found an antique necklace in the old carton worn by my grandmother.
In the carton, I found an antique necklace worn by my grandmother.

FP   10. The salesperson said we could pay for the furniture with cash, a credit card, or writing a check.
or a check.

Score   Number correct _____ × 10 = _____ %

Faulty Modifiers and Parallelism

■ **Combined Mastery Test 2**

In the spaces provided, indicate whether each sentence contains a misplaced modifier (*MM*), a dangling modifier (*DM*), or faulty parallelism (*FP*). Then correct the error in the space under the sentence.

Rewritten sentences may vary.

DM
1. Working in her vegetable garden, a bee stung Debbie on the shoulder.
   Working in her vegetable garden, Debbie was stung on the shoulder by a bee.

FP
2. Our boss is smart and with plenty of dedication but coldhearted.
   dedicated

MM
3. Mr. Harris said he would be leaving the company during the meeting.
   During the meeting, Mr. Harris said he would be leaving the company.

MM
4. The delivery boy placed the pizza on the couch with anchovies.
   The delivery boy placed the pizza with anchovies on the couch.

DM
5. Covered with wavy lines, the technician suggested that our computer monitor needed adjusting.
   The technician suggested that our computer monitor, which was covered
   with wavy lines, needed adjusting.

DM
6. Twisted in several places, Karl straightened out the garden hose.
   Karl straightened out the garden hose, which was twisted in several places.

FP
7. As I waited, the secretary typed, filed, and was talking on the telephone.
   talked on the telephone

MM
8. Jasmin saw a dress she was dying to wear in the department store window.
   In the department store window, Jasmin saw a dress she was dying to wear.

DM
9. Weighing three tons, my neighbor pays an added registration fee for his truck.
   My neighbor pays an added registration fee for his truck, which weighs
   three tons.

MM
10. While sitting in the traffic jam, I almost read the entire newspaper.
    While sitting in the traffic jam, I read almost the entire newspaper.

Score   Number correct _____ × 10 = _____ %

Capital Letters and Punctuation

■ **Combined Mastery Test 1**

Each of the following sentences contains an error in capitalization or punctuation. Refer to the box below and write, in the space provided, the letter identifying the error. Then correct the error.

a. missing capital letter	c. missing quotation marks
b. missing apostrophe	d. missing comma

_____d_____ 1. The elevator was stuck for more than an hour, but all the passengers stayed calm.

_____c_____ 2. "When I step onto dry land after weeks at sea,"said the sailor, "I feel as if I'm standing on a sponge."

_____a_____ 3. He doesn't talk about it much, but my uncle has been a member of $\overset{A}{\chi}$lcoholics Anonymous for ten years.

_____b_____ 4. My parents always ask me where I'm going and when I'll be home.

_____d_____ 5. Whenever Paul eats peanuts,he leaves a pile of shells in the ashtray.

_____b_____ 6. In the schools "food band," the children used pumpkins for drums and bags of pretzels for shakers.

_____c_____ 7. "Stop making a fool of yourself," said Emily,"and put that sword back on the wall."

_____d_____ 8. The sweating,straining horses neared the finish line.

_____d_____ 9. The children,a costumed horde of Halloween pirates and hoboes, fanned out through the neighborhood.

_____a_____ 10. I decided to drink a glass of milk rather than order a $\overset{P}{\chi}$epsi.

Score Number correct _____ × 10 = _____ %	

Capital Letters and Punctuation

■ **Combined Mastery Test 2**

Each of the following sentences contains an error in capitalization or punctuation. Refer to the box below and write, in the space provided, the letter identifying the error. Then correct the error.

a. missing capital letter	c. missing quotation marks
b. missing apostrophe	d. missing comma

_____d_____ 1. She had never seen anyone put mustard,ketchup, and mayonnaise on French fries.

_____b_____ 2. The school's janitor received nothing but a plaque for his loyal service.

_____c_____ 3. "Using these chopsticks," said Wayne, "is like trying to eat soup with a fork."

_____a_____ 4. Some people don't know that M̸anhattan is an island.

_____d_____ 5. Wanting to make a good impression, Bill shaved twice before his date.

_____a_____ 6. Crumpled sheets of paper and a spilled bottle of B̸ayer aspirin littered Laurie's desk.

_____c_____ 7. "German," said the history instructor,"came within one vote of being named the official language of the United States."

_____b_____ 8. My mother's checks are printed with pictures of endangered wild animals.

_____d_____ 9. Feeling brave and silly at the same time, Art volunteered to go onstage and help the magician.

_____a_____ 10. My Uncle Tyrone fought in the Battle of the Bulge during World W̸ar II.

Score Number correct _____ × 10 = _____ %

Word Use

■ **Combined Mastery Test 1**

Each of the following sentences contains a mistake identified in the left-hand margin. Underline the mistake and then correct it in the space provided.

Rewritten versions may vary.

Slang
1. At 50 percent off, this suit is a real <u>steal</u>.
   bargain

Wordiness
2. Although Yvette was on a <u>reducing diet to lose weight</u>, she splurged on some ice cream.
   diet

Cliché
3. Ken knew his friends would be <u>green with envy</u> when they saw his new car.
   envious

Pretentious language
4. We must complete the <u>decision-making process</u>.
   make a decision (or reach a decision, or decide)

Adverb error
5. I tied the knot <u>slow</u>, making sure it wouldn't come loose again.
   slowly

Error in comparison
6. I felt <u>more thirstier</u> than I ever had in my life.
   thirstier

Confused word
7. "<u>Its</u> the tallest building in the world," the guide said.
   It's

Confused word
8. <u>There</u> parking the car in one of those enclosed garages.
   They're

Confused word
9. He's the center <u>who's</u> teammates throw him the ball every time.
   whose

Confused word
10. If you keep your wallet sticking out of a rear pocket, <u>your</u> bound to lose it to a pickpocket.
    you're

Score Number correct _____ × 10 = _____ %

Word Use

■ Combined Mastery Test 2

Each of the following sentences contains a mistake identified in the left-hand margin. Underline the mistake and then correct it in the space provided.

Rewritten versions may vary.

Slang
1. After his workout at the gym, Paul was too <u>wiped out</u> to cook dinner.
   tired

Wordiness
2. I asked the attendant at the gas station to fill up <u>my tank with gas as far as possible.</u>
   my gas tank

Cliché
3. I try to <u>turn the other cheek</u> instead of getting angry.
   stay calm

Pretentious language
4. Next fall, I plan to <u>matriculate</u> at a nearby college.
   enroll

Adverb error
5. Elizabeth hadn't been feeling <u>good</u> ever since the buffet lunch.
   well

Error in comparison
6. Sharon was <u>more happier</u> after she quit her job.
   happier

Confused word
7. Charles knew he was <u>all ready</u> late for the interview, so he ran up the steps.
   already

Confused word
8. Michael's <u>principle</u> fault is his tendency to lose his temper.
   principal

Confused word
9. The rabbi tried to <u>advice</u> the confused teenager.
   advise

Confused word
10. Before the operation, the surgeon will carefully study <u>you're</u> x-rays.
    your

Score   Number correct _____ × 10 = _____ %

Editing and Proofreading Tests

The passages in this section can be used in either of two ways:

1 As Editing Tests   Each passage contains a number of mistakes involving a single sentence skill. For example, the first passage (on page 479) contains five fragments. Your instructor may ask you to proofread the passage to locate the five fragments. Spaces are provided at the bottom of the page for you to indicate which word groups are fragments. Your instructor may also have you correct the errors, either in the text itself or on separate paper. Depending on how well you do, you may also be asked to edit the second and third passages for fragments.

There are two passages for each skill area, and there are twelve skills covered in all. Here is a list of the skill areas:

2 As Guided Composition Activities

To give practice in proofreading as well, your instructor may ask you to do more than correct the skill mistakes in each passage. You may be asked to rewrite the passage, correcting it for skill mistakes *and also* copying the rest of the passage perfectly. Should you miss one skill mistake or make even one copying mistake (for example, omitting a word, dropping a verb ending, misspelling a word, or misplacing an apostrophe), you may be asked to rewrite a different passage that deals with the same skill.

Here is how you would proceed. You would start with fragments, rewriting the first passage, proofreading your paper carefully, and then showing it to your instructor. He or she will check it quickly to see that all the fragments have been corrected and that no copying mistakes have been made. If the passage is error-free, the instructor will mark and initial the appropriate box in the progress chart on pages 587–588 and you can proceed to run-ons.

If even a single mistake is made, the instructor may question you briefly to see if you recognize and understand it. (Perhaps he or she will put a check beside the line in which the mistake appears, and then ask if you can correct it.) You may then be asked to write the second passage under a particular skill.

You will complete the program in guided composition when you successfully work through all twelve skills. Completing the twelve skills will strengthen your understanding of the skills, increase your ability to transfer the skills to actual writing situations, and markedly improve your proofreading.

In working on the passages, note the following points:

a   For each skill, you will be told how many mistakes appear in the passages. If you have trouble finding the mistakes, turn back and review the pages in this book that explain the skill in question.

b   Here is an effective way to go about correcting a passage. First, read it over quickly. Look for and mark off mistakes in the skill area involved. For example, in your first reading of a passage that has five fragments, you may locate and mark only three fragments. Next, reread the passage carefully so you can find the remaining errors in the skill in question. Finally, make notes in the margin about how to correct each mistake. Only at this point should you begin to rewrite the passage.

c   Be sure to proofread with care after you finish a passage. Go over your writing word for word, looking for careless errors. Remember that you may be asked to do another passage involving the same skill if you make even one mistake.

■ Test 1: Fragments

Mistakes in each passage: 5

Passage A

[1]My best friend Linda recently bought a dog. [2]A German shepherd named Hindenburg which likes getting into fights. [3]In fact, Hindenburg wins every fight that he gets into. [4]One day, Linda was walking her new dog. [5]When she saw a man coming toward her with a big dog of his own. [6]The dog had a long tail and very short legs. [7]As soon as Hindenburg noticed the other dog, he went after it. [8]And began to snarl and to nip at its tail. [9]Being positive her dog would win, Linda did not interfere and let the fight continue. [10]Soon Hindenburg was bleeding from ear to ear. [11]The other dog was at his throat and was getting ready. [12]To finish him off with one savage bite of his sharp teeth. [13]Linda panicked and yelled at the man to pull his dog away. [14]Then she asked him what kind of dog it was. [15]"That's not an ordinary dog," Linda insisted. [16]"You're absolutely right," the man replied. [17]"Before he got his nose job. [18]He was an alligator."

Word groups with fragments: __2__   __5__   __8__   __12__   __17__

Corrections (wording may vary):

Passage A

My best friend Linda recently bought a dog, a German shepherd…
One day, Linda was walking her new dog when she saw…
As soon as Hindenburg noticed the other dog, he went after it and began to…
The other dog was at his throat and was getting ready to finish him off…
Before he got his nose job, he was an alligator.

Passage B

¹Walter won't admit that he is out of a job. ²Last month, Walter was laid off by the insurance company. ³Where he had been working as a salesperson. ⁴But Walter hasn't told anyone. ⁵And continues to go downtown every morning. ⁶Waiting at the bus stop with his newspaper folded under his arm and his briefcase on the sidewalk beside him. ⁷He looks at his watch as if he were worried about being late. ⁸When he gets downtown. ⁹Walter goes to an arcade. ¹⁰He plays video games for an hour or two. ¹¹Then he visits the public library. ¹²To lose himself in the latest spy novel. ¹³At five o'clock, Walter catches the bus for home. ¹⁴His newspaper is still folded under his arm. ¹⁵He has not opened the paper to look at the want ads. ¹⁶I feel sorry for Walter, but I understand his desire to live in a fantasy world.

Word groups with fragments: ___3___ ___5___ ___6___ ___8___ ___12___

Corrections (wording may vary):

Passage B

Last month, Walter was laid off by the insurance company where he had been...
But Walter hasn't told anyone and continues to go downtown every morning.
Waiting at the bus stop with his newspaper folded under his arm and his briefcase on the sidewalk beside him, he looks at his watch...
When he gets downtown, Walter goes to an arcade.
Then he visits the public library to lose himself in the latest spy novel.

■ Test 2: Fragments

Mistakes in each passage: 5

Passage A

¹Are you experiencing car trouble? ²Is your transmission acting up or your muffler rattling? ³By tuning in to your radio. ⁴You can find help. ⁵A Sunday-evening program mixing serious car advice and humor. ⁶Has become popular all over the country. ⁷The show began in Boston when a radio station invited a number of mechanics to take live calls on car problems. ⁸Although a large group of mechanics was expected. ⁹Only Tom and Ray showed up. ¹⁰Tom and Ray are two brothers who liked fixing cars in their spare time. ¹¹And had opened a garage. ¹²The response to the show was so great that it became a weekly event. ¹³With no advance preparation, Tom and Ray take all car questions that the audience asks. ¹⁴They delight listeners with their wit, their down-to-earth philosophy, and their good car sense.

Word groups with fragments: __3__   __5__   __6__   __8__   __11__

Corrections:

Passage A

By tuning into your radio, you can find . . .
A Sunday-evening program mixing serious car advice and humor has become. . .
Although a large group of mechanics was expected, only Tom and Ray . . .
Tom and Ray are two brothers who liked fixing cars in their spare time and had opened . . .

Passage B

[1]For thousands of years. [2]Humans have used certain animals to carry heavy loads. [3]The ox, the elephant, the donkey, and the mule are examples of these "beasts of burden." [4]Although they have a reputation for being stubborn at times. [5]These animals normally work very hard for long hours. [6]One beast of burden, however, refuses to be overworked. [7]The llama, a South American animal much like the camel, has very definite ideas of what it's willing to do. [8]Knowing just how much it can carry comfortably, the llama will sit down and refuse to budge. [9]If even an extra half pound is placed on its back. [10]In addition, the llama will carry a burden only a certain distance. [11]For example, nothing will persuade it to continue. [12]After it travels twenty miles. [13]Sometimes its owner tries to prod the llama with a stick once the animal has decided to quit. [14]When it is disturbed in this fashion. [15]The llama has an unusual way of striking back. [16]It puckers its lips and spits in its owner's face.

Word groups with fragments: __1__   __4__   __9__   __12__   __14__

Corrections:

Passage B

For thousands of years, humans have . . .
Although they have a reputation for being stubborn at times, these animals . . .
Knowing just how much it can carry comfortably, the llama will sit down and refuse to budge if even an extra half pound . . .
For example, nothing will persuade it to continue after it travels . . .
When it is disturbed in this fashion, the llama has . . .

■ Test 3: Run-Ons (Fused Sentences)

Mistakes in each passage: 5

Passage A

[1]How would you like to live in the most expensive part of New York City without paying any rent? [2]Recently, a fifty-five-year-old man did just that he set up residence on a thirty-five-foot-long traffic island in the middle of East River Drive. [3]His furniture was made from storage crates his stove was an oil drum. [4]His only protection from the weather was the elevated highway overhead. [5]People waved to him as they drove by some even donated food and beer. [6]Local television stations soon began to feature this unusual resident. [7]He was pictured relaxed and reading a book the traffic streamed by on both sides of him. [8]Social workers wanted to put him in a city shelter he refused, saying it was a pigpen. [9]Finally, the police took him away, but not before he had become a hero. [10]He had achieved the ultimate American dream; for a little while, he had beaten the system.

Sentences with run-ons: ___2___ ___3___ ___5___ ___7___ ___8___

Corrections (wording may vary):

Passage A

Recently, a fifty-five-year-old man did just that. He...
His furniture was made from storage crates; his...
People waved to him as they drove by, and some...
He was pictured relaxed and reading a book. The...
Social workers wanted to put him in a city shelter, but he...

Passage B

¹Many common expressions have interesting origins one of these is the phrase "the real McCoy." ²In fact, the real McCoy was not really named McCoy he was a farmer's son from Indiana named Norman Selby who got tired of farming and left home around 1890. ³One year later, he began a boxing career, using the name Kid McCoy soon he was fighting every month. ⁴He was willing to meet any opponent anywhere in the country. ⁵He soon had a long string of victories most of them were knockouts. ⁶A number of other fighters began calling themselves "Kid McCoy," thinking the name would get them more boxing matches and more money. ⁷However, on March 24, 1899, the Kid defeated another great champion the fight lasted twenty rounds and cost the Kid three broken ribs. ⁸In his report of the fight, the *San Francisco Examiner's* sportswriter wrote, "Now you've seen the real McCoy!" ⁹From them on, people have said "the real McCoy" whenever they have meant that something is not a fake.

Sentences with run-ons: __1__   __2__   __3__   __5__   __7__

Corrections (wording may vary):

Passage B

Many common expressions have interesting origins. One...
In fact, the real McCoy was not really named McCoy. He...
One year later, he began a boxing career, using the name Kid McCoy, and soon...
He soon had a long string of victories; most...
However, on March 24, 1899, the Kid defeated another great champion. The...

■ Test 4: Run-Ons (Comma Splices)

Mistakes in each passage: 5

Passage A

[1]One evening, a group of friends got together for a dinner party, after dinner they began telling stories. [2]As the evening wore on, the stories got wilder and wilder. [3]Some of the stories involved unusual scientific experiments, others were about strange creatures, such as werewolves and vampires. [4]The friends competed to see who could tell the most exciting story. [5]In the group was a young woman named Mary, who had recently been married. [6]When Mary went to bed that night, she had a frightening dream. [7]In her dream, a hideous monster came to life, she saw it bending over her. [8]The next morning, Mary told her dream to her new husband, Percy, he persuaded her to write it down. [9]After he read her account, Percy was so impressed that he urged her to expand it into a book. [10]The novel that Mary Shelley finally wrote, *Frankenstein,* is probably the most famous horror story of all time, hundreds of monster movies have been inspired by it.

Sentences with run-ons: __1__   __3__   __7__   __8__   __10__

Corrections (wording may vary):

Passage A

One evening, a group of friends got together for a dinner party, and after…
Some of the stories involved unusual scientific experiments; others…
In her dream, a hideous monster came to life, and…
The next morning, Mary told her dream to her new husband, Percy. He…
The novel that Mary Shelley finally wrote, <u>Frankenstein</u>, is probably the most famous horror story of all time. Hundreds…

Passage B

[1]One of the coldest, snowiest, windiest places on earth is not in the Himalayas or the Arctic, it is on Mount Washington in the pleasant state of New Hampshire. [2]The top of this rather small mountain experiences hurricane-force winds, they slice through human beings like razors. [3]The world's highest wind speed was recorded on the mountain one April day in 1934, that speed was 231 miles per hour! [4]Snow is always possible, even in summer. [5]Supercooled fog, called *rime,* hugs the mountain, there is almost no visibility 55 percent of the time. [6]At least sixty people have lost their lives on Mount Washington in the last hundred years. [7]However, people continue to climb to the top, some take the auto route, open only in the summer. [8]The more foolish attempt to climb the mountain at other times of the year. [9]A warning sign on the mountain reads, "People don't die on this mountain. They perish."

Sentences with run-ons: __1__ __2__ __3__ __5__ __7__

Corrections (wording may vary):

Passage B

One of the coldest, snowiest, windiest places on earth is not in the Himalayas or the Arctic; it...
The top of this rather small mountain experiences hurricane-force winds, which slice...
The world's highest wind speed was recorded on the mountain one April day in 1934. That...
Supercooled fog, called rime, hugs the mountain, and there...
However, people continue to climb to the top. Some...

■ Test 5: Standard English Verbs

Mistakes in each passage: 5

Passage A

¹The scenes of flood damage on the network news tonight were horrible. ²Two weeks of steady, heavy rains had ~~raise~~ *raised* the waters of several Midwestern rivers past the levels of their banks, and they had ~~overflow~~ *overflowed* onto the surrounding houses and fields. ³Extensive damage had resulted, with some buildings actually torn from their foundations and ~~suck~~ *sucked* helplessly into the swirling flood waters. ⁴Here and there a rooftop could be seen as it ~~float~~ *floated* by with one or two frightened survivors clinging to it. ⁵Many people's lives had been disrupted, and many millions of dollars' worth of damage had been ~~cause~~ *caused*. ⁶It would be several days yet until the waters receded. ⁷They say that "into every life some rain must fall," but no one could have predicted all this.

Sentences with nonstandard verbs (write the number of a sentence twice if it contains two nonstandard verbs):

  2   2   3   4   5

Passage B

¹I read an odd item in the newspaper about a pet snail that nearly ~~frighten~~ *frightened* its owner to death. ²Actually, the owner did not even know that he had been keeping a pet. ³The snail, which was very fancy, had been ~~varnish~~ *varnished* and made into an ornament. ⁴Its owner had bought the snail at a gift shop and ~~place~~ *placed* it on his desk. ⁵Apparently the snail was not really dead but had been ~~seal~~ *sealed* into hibernation by the varnish and was just asleep. ⁶Three years later, when its owner accidentally ~~knock~~ *knocked* the ornament off his desk, chipping the varnish, the snail woke up. ⁷It began moving across the desk as the owner was writing a letter and startled him so much that he jumped out of his chair. ⁸The owner is feeding his former ornament on cabbage before taking it back to the seashore where it belongs.

Sentences with nonstandard verbs: __1__   __3__   __4__   __5__   __6__

■ Test 6: Irregular Verbs

Mistakes in each passage: 10

Passage A

¹Vince ~~choosed~~ *chose* a job as a supermarket cashier because he liked people. ²After what happened yesterday, though, he isn't so sure. ³First, after he had ~~rang~~ *rung* up her entire order, a woman ~~throwed~~ *threw* a handful of coupons at him. ⁴Then she ~~give~~ *gave* him a hard time when he ~~shown~~ *showed* her that a few had expired. ⁵She ~~begun~~ *began* making nasty comments about stupid supermarket help. ⁶The next person in line thought Vince had put the eggs on the bottom and would not leave until Vince had ~~took~~ *taken* everything out of the bag and repacked it. ⁷Later, two teenagers ~~fighted~~ *fought* with Vince over the price of a bag of M&Ms, saying that it could never have ~~rose~~ *risen* so high in one week. ⁸Vince ~~gone~~ *went* home in a terrible mood, wondering how he would ever force himself to come in the next day.

Sentences with irregular verbs (write the number of a sentence twice if it contains two irregular verbs):

1	3	3	4	4
5	6	7	7	8

Passage B

1A college professor has ~~wrote~~ *written* a book about what he calls "urban legends." 2These are folktales that have ~~spreaded~~ *spread* all over the country. 3They usually have a moral to teach or touch on a basic fear ~~holded~~ *held* by many Americans. 4In one of the more gruesome legends, a young couple parked on a lovers' lane ~~heared~~ *heard* a report on their car radio about a one-armed killer stalking the area. 5The couple ~~leaved~~ *left*; after they ~~gotten~~ *got* home, they ~~seen~~ *saw* a bloody hook hanging on the car's door handle. 6The moral of this urban legend? 7Don't park on lovers' lanes! 8In another story, a man ~~finded~~ *found* pieces of fried rat mixed in with his take-out fried chicken. 9The professor has ~~sayed~~ *said* that this story is related to the American consumer's fear of being contaminated with some dreadful substance. 10No one can find a factual basis for any of these stories, although many tellers have ~~swore~~ *sworn* they are true.

Sentences with irregular verbs (write the number of a sentence twice or more if it contains two or more irregular verbs):

1	2	3	4	5
5	5	8	9	10

■ Test 7: Faulty Parallelism

Mistakes in cach passage: 5

Passage A

¹Some people today are "survivalists." ²These people, because they fear some great disaster in the near future (like economic collapse or nuclear war), are preparing for a catastrophe. ³Hoarding food, stockpiling weapons, and the achievement of self-sufficiency are some of the activities of survivalists. ⁴In Arkansas, for example, one group has built a mountain fortress to defend its supplies and staying safe. ⁵Arkansas, the group feels, is the best place to be for several reasons: it is an unlikely target for nuclear attack; it offers plentiful supplies of food and water; a good climate. ⁶Some Americans feel that the attitude of survivalists is selfish and greed. ⁷These people say that such a philosophy turns society into a "dog-eat-dog" race for life. ⁸Other people believe that after a nuclear war, the world, with radiation and where there would be disease, wouldn't be worth living in.

Sentences with faulty parallelism: __3__ __4__ __5__ __6__ __8__

Corrections:

Passage A

    achieving self-sufficiency
    to stay
    it has a good climate
    greedy
    with radiation and disease

Passage B

[1]Doing your own painting is easy, inexpensive, and you will enjoy it, if you know what you're doing. [2]First, you must properly prepare the surface you are going to paint. [3]This means removing dirt, rust, or mildew. [4]Also, you should get rid of loose paint and to fill any cracks with spackling compound. [5]Primers or sealers should be used on bare wood or over stains. [6]Another important rule to follow is to buy the right amount of paint. [7]Some painters guess how much paint they need and are failing to measure accurately. [8]Then they might buy too little or an excessive amount of paint for the job. [9]The result is making an extra trip to the hardware store or to have a lot of paint left over. [10]Finally, before you begin to paint, read the directions on the container. [11]These hints will save you time and money.

Sentences with faulty parallelism: __1__ __4__ __7__ __8__ __9__

Corrections:

Passage B

enjoyable
and fill
and fail
too much paint
or having

■ Test 8: Capital Letters

Mistakes in each passage: 10

Passage A

¹Last ⁿovember, ʲjoanne ᶠfisher put her turkey in the oven and drove into town to see the ᵀthanksgiving ᴰday parade. ²Parking downtown was almost impossible. ³Joanne saw the sign warning visitors not to park on the private lot at Tenth ˢstreet, but she thought that since it was a holiday, nobody would mind. ⁴When she returned after the parade, her ᴰdatsun was missing. ⁵It had been towed to a lot in a faraway section of the city. ⁶When Joanne finally got to the lot, the owner insisted on a cash payment and refused to accept a check for fifty dollars. ⁷Joanne lost her temper and screamed, "ᴬall right, go ahead and call the police, but I'm going to drive out of here!" ⁸A police car arrived immediately, and Joanne had visions of spending the next month in jail. ⁹But the officer, ˢsgt. Roberts of the Sixteenth ᴾprecinct, agreed to cash her check so she could pay the fine. ¹⁰Joanne was delighted until she got home and found that her turkey had burned to a crisp.

Sentences with missing capitals (write the number of a sentence as many times as it contains capitalization mistakes):

1	1	1	1	1
3	4	7	9	9

Passage B

¹Liza never realized how expensive it was going to be to have a baby. ²Before the birth, Liza visited dr. willis, her obstetrician, eleven times. ³After her baby was born, a multiple-page bill from valley hospital arrived. ⁴There were charges not only from Liza's own doctor, but also from a Dr. David, the anesthesiologist, and a Dr. Ripley, the hospital pediatrician. ⁵After she had brought the baby home, Liza found herself visiting the supermarket more often. ⁶She loaded her cart with boxes of expensive pampers, dozens of cans of enfamil formula, and lots of smaller items like johnson's baby powder and oil. ⁷Liza realized that she would have to return to her job at richmond insurance company if she was going to make ends meet.

Sentences with missing capitals (write the number of a sentence as many times as it contains capitalization mistakes):

2	2	3	3	6
6	6	7	7	7

■ Test 9: Apostrophes

Mistakes in each passage: 10

Passage A

¹Two Minnesota brothers, Ed and Norman, are engaged in a war. ²It all started when Ed's wife gave him a pair of pants that didn't fit. ³Ed wrapped up the pants and put them under Norman's Christmas tree. ⁴When Norman opened the box, he recognized the unwanted pants. ⁵The next year, he gave them back to Ed, sealed in a heavy carton tied with knotted ropes. ⁶The War of the Pants was on. ⁷Each year, on one of the brothers' birthdays, or on Christmas, the dreaded pants reappear. ⁸The war has escalated, however, with each brother trying to top the other's pants delivery of the previous year. ⁹Two years ago, Norman bought an old safe, put the pants in it, welded it shut, and delivered it to Ed's house. ¹⁰Somehow, Ed retrieved the pants (one of the war's rules is that the pants must not be damaged). ¹¹Last year, Ed went to an auto junkyard. ¹²The pants were placed in an ancient Ford's backseat, and the car went through the huge auto crusher. ¹³On his birthday, Norman found a four-foot square of smashed metal on his doorstep; he knew it could only be Ed's doing and the pants must be inside. ¹⁴Norman is still trying to get at the pants and prepare next year's "topper."

Sentences with missing apostrophes (write the number of a sentence twice if it contains two missing apostrophes):

2	2	3	7	8
9	10	12	13	14

Passage B

¹Sometimes I wish the telephone hadn't been invented. ²When I come home after class or work, all I'm interested in is lying down for an hour's nap. ³Typically, five minutes after I've closed my eyes, the phone rings. ⁴Someone I've never met is trying to sell me a subscription to *Newsweek*. ⁵Or I may have just begun to mix up some hamburger when I hear the phone's insistent ringing. ⁶It won't stop, so I wipe the ground meat off my hands and run to answer it. ⁷Yesterday, when this happened, it was my mother's best friend. ⁸She'd found some clothes in her attic. ⁹And she wanted to know if I could use an old evening gown. ¹⁰Even if it's someone I want to talk to, the phone call always seems to come at a bad time.

Sentences with missing apostrophes (write the number of a sentence twice if it contains two missing apostrophes):

1	2	2	3	4
5	6	7	8	10

■ Test 10: Quotation Marks

Quotation marks needed in each passage: 10 pairs

Passage A

1 Tony and Lola were driving home from the movies when they saw a man staggering along the street. 2 "I wonder if he's all right," Tony said.

3 "Let's stop and find out," Lola suggested. 4 They caught up to the man, who was leaning against a tree.

5 "Are you OK?" Lola asked. 6 "Is there anything we can do?"

7 "There's nothing the matter," the man answered. 8 "I guess I had a few too many after work. 9 Now I can't seem to find my front door."

10 Tony steadied the man and asked, "Do you live anywhere near here?"

11 He responded, "Yes, if this is Forrest Avenue, I live at 3619."

12 Tony and Lola walked the man to his door, where he fumbled in his pockets, took out a key, and began to stab wildly with it at the lock.

13 "Let me hold your key, and I'll let you in," Tony offered.

14 The man refused, saying, "Oh, no, I'll hold the key—you hold the house."

Sentences or sentence groups with missing quotation marks:

2	3	5	6	7
8–9	10	11	13	14

Passage B

1 When Martin found a large dent in his new Datsun, he took it back to the agency. 2 "We can fix that," the smiling mechanic said. 3 "Just leave it for a few days."

4 Martin waited three days and then called. 5 "Is my car ready yet?" he asked.

6 "Not yet," the mechanic said. 7 "Try the end of the week."

8 The following Monday, Martin called again. 9 "Is my car ready?"

10 The mechanic sounded apologetic. 11 "Not yet. 12 We'll have it Friday for sure."

13 On Friday, when Martin picked up his car, he noticed a new cigarette burn in the upholstery. 14 "We'll fix that, but it takes a week to match the material," the manager said.

15 Martin took the bus home, fuming. 16 A few minutes later, the phone rang.

17 It was the mechanic. 18 "You left your owner's card here. 19 Want us to mail it?"

20 Martin said, "You may as well keep it. 21 You're using the car more than I am."

Sentences or sentence groups with missing quotation marks:

2	3	5	6	7
9	11–12	14	18–19	20–21

■ Test 11: Commas

Mistakes in each passage: 10

Passage A

¹Frank has a hard time studying,so he plays little games to get himself to finish his assignments. ²He will begin by saying to himself,"Whenever I finish an assignment,I'll give myself a prize." ³Frank has all kinds of prizes; his favorites are watching a detective show on television,drinking a cold beer, and spending an hour with his girlfriend. ⁴Of course,too many of these rewards will mean that Frank won't get much else done. ⁵So Frank uses other strategies. ⁶He will,for example,set the stove timer for one hour. ⁷Then he will work at the kitchen table until the timer buzzes. ⁸Also,he puts a paper clip on every tenth page of the book he is studying. ⁹As soon as he reaches the clip,he can take a five-minute break.

Sentences with missing commas (write the number of a sentence as many times as it contains comma mistakes):

1	2	2	3	3
4	6	6	8	9

Passage B

[1]When Cara gets bored with her secretarial job,she has a whole assortment of things to do to pass the time until five o'clock. [2]First of all,she cleans out her desk. [3]Desk drawers, she has found,contain all sorts of hidden treasure. [4]Cara found her old diary,the gold chain bracelet she had gotten for Christmas,and two unread murder mysteries the last time she "cleaned house." [5]Another thing Cara likes to do is read the company directory. [6]She looks through all the names of the junior executives,and she picks out three she'd like to meet at the next company picnic. [7]In the secretaries' lounge,Cara can make a cup of coffee,read the job opportunities on the bulletin board,or talk to a coworker about what she is going to do after work. [8]These little pleasures help Cara keep her sanity.

Sentences with missing commas (write the number of a sentence as many times as it contains comma mistakes):

1	2	3	3	4
4	6	7	7	7

■ Test 12: Commonly Confused Words

Mistakes in each passage: 10

Passage A

¹Did you know that until May 5 of every year, ~~your~~ [you're] not really working for yourself? ²A group in Washington, D.C., has learned that it takes workers an average of four months and four days to earn enough to pay ~~there~~ [their] taxes. ³The group found in ~~it's~~ [its] study that taxes eat up 34 per~~cent of~~ [their] all the income in the United States. ⁴So, if workers used they're entire income for taxes, they would not be ~~threw~~ [through] paying them until May. ⁵~~Being that~~ [Because] May 5 is the first day people really work for themselves, the study group has some ~~advise~~ [advice]. ⁶It would like a bill ~~past~~ [passed] naming May 5 "Tax Freedom Day." ⁷On that day, you would give yourself a ~~brake, irregardless~~ [break] [regardless] of how hard you worked. ⁸For, from May 5 on, you would finally be your own boss.

Sentences with commonly confused words (write the number of a sentence twice if it contains two commonly confused words):

1	2	3	4	4
5	5	6	7	7

Passage B

¹Did you ever daydream about writing ~~you're~~ *your* life story? ²Do you think that your life is ~~to~~ *too* dull, or you can't ~~right~~ *write*? ³Anyone's life story is filled with fascinating events, and writing them down in the best way you know can give you a sense of accomplishment and, perhaps, leave a valuable inheritance to your family. ⁴The first thing to do is to buy a ~~lose~~ *loose*-leaf notebook. ⁵Each page of the book should be titled with a significant milestone in your life—from your first dog to your proudest moment. ⁶You should ~~than~~ *then* jot down a few key words in the book whenever a memory comes back to you. ⁷The idea is *not* to begin with "I was born…" and try to write a chronological history of your ~~hole~~ *whole* life. ⁸Just delve into your ~~passed~~ *past* at random; one memory will trigger another. ⁹Writing will become ~~quiet~~ *quite* easy after a while. ¹⁰~~Its~~ *It's* also important to write in your own language. ¹¹~~Plane~~ *Plain*, honest writing is the goal.

Sentences with commonly confused words (write the number of a sentence twice if it contains two commonly confused words):

1	2	2	4	6
7	8	9	10	11

Combined Editing Tests

Editing for Sentence-Skills Mistakes

The twelve editing tests in this section will give you practice in finding a variety of sentence-skills mistakes. People often find it hard to edit a paper carefully. They have put so much work, or so little work, into their writing that it's almost painful for them to look at the paper one more time. You may simply have to *force* yourself to edit. Remember that eliminating sentence-skills mistakes will improve an average paper and help ensure a high grade on a good paper. Further, as you get into the habit of editing your papers, you will get into the habit of using the sentence skills consistently. They are a basic part of clear, effective writing.

In tests 3 through 8, the spots where errors occur have been underlined; your job is to identify each error. In tests 1 and 2 and 9 through 12, you must locate as well as identify the errors. Use the progress chart on page 589 to keep track of your performance on these tests.

■ Combined Editing Test 1

Identify the five mistakes in paper format in the student paper on the next page. From the box below, choose the letters that describe the five mistakes and write those letters in the spaces provided.

---

a. The title should not be underlined.

b. The title should not be set off in quotation marks.

c. There should not be a period at the end of a title.

d. All the major words in a title should be capitalized.

e. The title should just be several words and not a complete sentence.

f. The first line of a paper should stand independent of the title.

g. A line should be skipped between the title and the first line of the paper.

h. The first line of a paper should be indented.

i. The right-hand margin should not be crowded.

j. Hyphenation should occur only between syllables.

	"Noise in quiet places"
	The quietest places make the most noise. A library is one exam-
	ple. If you crinkle a bag of potato chips in a quiet library, people
	will stare at you as if you had lit a firecracker under their feet.
	But you could drop a food tray in a noisy cafeteria and nobody
	would pay much attention to you. Then, there's the cough in church.
	A muffled cough bounces off the stained glass windows like a sonic
	boom. But you could cough up a storm at a rock concert and not
	one head would turn. Finally, elevators are hushed places. If you
	ask someone for the time in an elevator, everyone will look at his
	or her watch. Ask the same question on a busy city street, and
	chances are that no one will hear you. It takes a quiet place for
	sound to be really heard.

1. __b__   2. __d__   3. __g__   4. __h__   5. __i__

■ Combined Editing Test 2

Identify the five mistakes in paper format in the student paper on the next page. From the box below, choose the letters that describe the five mistakes and write those letters in the spaces provided.

a. The title should not be underlined.

b. The title should not be set off in quotation marks.

c. There should not be a period at the end of a title.

d. All the major words in a title should be capitalized.

e. The title should just be several words and not a complete sentence.

f. The first line of a paper should stand independent of the title.

g. A line should be skipped between the title and the first line of the paper.

h. The first line of a paper should be indented.

i. The right-hand margin should not be crowded.

j. Hyphenation should occur only between syllables.

	"Bus Travel"
	It is the worst way to get to work or school in the mo-
	rning. First, the weather is unpredictable. Many bus stops are
	not sheltered, and the rider must wait in rain, cold, and heat.
	Another unpleasant thing about bus riding is the wait. It
	seems that buses are on time only when you're running late.
	Next, there is the matter of having exact change. If you try to
	enter without the right change, the driver looks at you as if
	your hair is on fire. Last, there's the problem of finding a seat.
	The elderly folks are saving seats for their friends, and most
	people look as if they will bite your nose if you sit next to them.
	Chances are that the only seat open will be next to a strange-
	smelling person with a wild look in his eye.

1. __a__   2. __b__   3. __f__   4. __g__   5. __j__

■ Combined Editing Test 3

Identify the sentence-skills mistakes at the underlined spots in the selection that follows. From the box below, choose the letter that describes each mistake and write it in the space provided. (The same mistake may appear more than once.) Then, in the spaces provided between the lines, correct each mistake.

a. fragment	e. incorrect end mark
b. run-on	f. missing apostrophe
c. dropped verb ending	g. missing comma
d. misplaced modifier	

Methods of correction may vary. Possibilities appear below.

When I was little, I really *hated* hate visiting Aunt Martha. She was my *father's* fathers sister and
₁   ₂

had never married. Since she had no children of her own, she *didn't* didnt know what to do with
₃

me. I remember the *sofa, which was dark brown and filled with horsehair, in her living room.* sofa in her living room, which was dark brown. And filled with
₄   ₅

horsehair. Every time I sat on it, I got stabbed by the stuffing. I had to plump up the cushion

when I got *up. Otherwise* up otherwise, she would frown at me. She would sit opposite me with a stiff
₆

smile on her face and ask me what I was *learning* learn in school or if I had been *good. They were things* good? Things
₇   ₈

that I didn't want to talk about. I couldn't wait to say *good-bye, plump* good-bye plump up the cushion, and
₉   ₁₀

escape.

1. _c_	3. _f_	5. _a_	7. _c_	9. _a_
2. _f_	4. _d_	6. _b_	8. _e_	10. _g_

■ Combined Editing Test 4

See if you can identify the sentence-skills mistakes at the underlined spots in the selection that follows. From the box below, choose the letter that describes each mistake and write it in the space provided. The same mistake may appear more than once. Then, in the space provided between the lines, correct each mistake. In one case, there is no mistake.

a. fragment	f. missing capital letter
b. run-on	g. missing quotation marks
c. dropped verb ending	h. missing comma
d. irregular verb mistake	i. no mistake
e. dangling modifier	

Methods of correction may vary. Possibilities appear below.

In the unending war of people versus machines, a blow was ~~striked~~ *struck* by a man in

Pennsylvania

~~pennsylvania~~ who had a run-in with an automatic banking machine. At about ten o'clock
                                                                                  2

one night, he approached the machine to make a withdrawal. After he inserted his ~~card the~~ *card, the*
                                                                                                      3

                                                                    happened
machine spat it back at him. The same thing then ~~happen~~ a second time. He put his card in
                                                                                                  4

again. This
~~again, this~~ time the machine kept the ~~card. And~~ *card and* did not give him the money he had
      5   6

                                                              Even after he hit
requested. By now the customer was totally disgusted. ~~Hitting~~ the machine with all his
                                                                                              7

                                                          straw. He
strength, the card still did not come back. This was the last ~~straw he~~ grabbed a metal trash
                                                                              8

can and proceeded to beat up the machine. Unfortunately, the machine still had his card,
      9

and the man was later arrested and charged with causing $2,500 worth of damage. He didn't

                        often," he
mind. "I've been ripped off so ~~often, he~~ said, "that it was time for me to get even."
                                        10

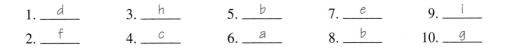

1. ___d___   3. ___h___   5. ___b___   7. ___e___   9. ___i___

2. ___f___   4. ___c___   6. ___a___   8. ___b___   10. ___g___

■ Combined Editing Test 5

See if you can identify the sentence-skills mistakes at the underlined spots in the selection that follows. From the box below, choose the letter that describes each mistake and write it in the space provided. The same mistake may appear more than once. Then, in the space provided between the lines, correct each mistake. In one case, there is no mistake.

a. fragment	f. mistake in subject-verb agreement
b. run-on	
c. omitted word	g. irregular verb mistake
d. misplaced modifier	h. no mistake
e. missing capital letter	

Methods of correction may vary. Possibilities appear below.

        asked to name
If you were ~~asked name~~ our most dangerous insects or animals, which ones would you
      1

                                     scorpions, just
list? You might jot down black widow spiders, rattlesnakes, and ~~scorpions. Just~~ to list a few.
                                                    2

                                   bee. More
However, our Public Enemy Number One is the ~~bee, more~~ people die from bee and wasp
                                     3

                                                   New
stings every year than are killed by animals. Not too long ago in Camden, ~~new~~ Jersey, over
                                                            4

                   taken   *after being*
twenty-seven people were ~~took~~ to hospitals ~~who had been~~ stung by a runaway swarm of
                      5   6

                                                                     were
bees. The bees, which had escaped from a hive that had fallen off a truck, ~~was~~ maddened
                                                                           7

by what they thought was an attack on their hive and would have destroyed anyone who

                                           hive, bees
came near them. If there is no threat to their ~~hive. Bees~~ will usually not sting, for once they
    8   9

                                                                are
lose their stingers, they die. Wasps and yellow jackets, however, ~~is~~ able to sting repeatedly
                                                                               10

with no danger to themselves. For that 1 percent of the population allergic to insect stings,

such attacks can be fatal.

1. _c_	3. _b_	5. _g_	7. _f_	9. _a_
2. _a_	4. _e_	6. _d_	8. _h_	10. _f_

■ Combined Editing Test 6

See if you can identify the sentence-skills mistakes at the underlined spots in the selection that follows. From the box below, choose the letter that describes each mistake and write it in the space provided. The same mistake may appear more than once. Then, in the space provided between the lines, correct each mistake. In one case, there is no mistake.

a. fragment	e. mistake in parallelism
b. run-on	f. apostrophe mistake
c. irregular verb mistake	g. missing comma
d. inconsistent verb tense	h. no mistake

Methods of correction may vary. Possibilities appear below.

As she walked into the dimly lit ~~room~~. *room,* Julie was more nervous than usual. This was
⎯⎯⎯⎯⎯⎯⎯⎯⎯⎯⎯⎯⎯⎯⎯⎯⎯
         1

the first time she had ever ~~went~~ *gone* to a singles bar, and she wasn't sure how she should behave.
                    ⎯⎯⎯
                     2

She stood near the back wall and waited for her ~~eyes'~~ *eyes* to adjust to the darkness. In a minute
                     ⎯⎯⎯⎯   ⎯⎯⎯⎯
                       3   4

or so, she could see what was going on. Several women were sipping drinks at the ~~bar,~~ *bar.*
                                                      ⎯⎯⎯
                                                       5

~~nearby~~, *Nearby* unattached men were whispering and glancing at the women. Seated at small ~~tables~~ *tables,*
⎯⎯⎯⎯⎯⎯   ⎯⎯⎯⎯⎯
                                                                      6

pairs of men and women were talking animatedly and ~~smiled~~ *smiling* at each other. They looked as
⎯⎯⎯⎯⎯   ⎯⎯⎯⎯⎯
                                  7

if they were having a good time. Julie ~~watches~~ *watched* for a few minutes and then went to find the
                    ⎯⎯⎯⎯⎯⎯
                       8

~~ladies~~ *ladies'* room. Joining the singles scene, she ~~thought could~~ *thought, could* wait just a little longer.
⎯⎯⎯⎯   ⎯⎯⎯⎯⎯⎯⎯⎯⎯⎯⎯
  9   10

1. _a_   3. _h_   5. _b_   7. _e_   9. _f_

2. _c_   4. _f_   6. _g_   8. _d_   10. _g_

■ Combined Editing Test 7

See if you can identify the sentence-skills mistakes at the underlined spots in the selection that follows. From the box below, choose the letter that describes each mistake and write it in the space provided. The same mistake may appear more than once. Then, in the space provided between the lines, correct each mistake. In one case, there is no mistake.

---

a. fragment

b. run-on

c. mistake in pronoun reference

d. mistake in subject-verb agreement

e. dangling modifier

f. mistake in parallelism

g. missing comma

h. missing quotation marks

i. no mistake

Methods of correction may vary. Possibilities appear below.

A clerk who works in a computerized office was complaining to me the other day

about how impersonal his workplace has become. "It's just not the same," he ~~insisted "as~~ *insisted, "as*
                                                                                                    1

it was before ~~they~~ put in all the new ~~systems~~. One of the things that really bother him ~~are~~ *is*
       the technicians 2   *systems."* 3   4

the computer terminal on which he has to type his figures. ~~Cold and impersonal~~, he finds *Because it is cold and impersonal,*
                                                            5

it much more threatening than the typewriter he used before the managers decided to

modernize. He also misses the walls and shelf he had in his old ~~office. Before~~ the *office, before*

department was reorganized as an open office without partitions. Now he ~~don't~~ have any *doesn't*
                                                6   7

place to put his trophies and the pictures of his ~~family, he~~ feels vulnerable out there in the *family. He*
                                                  8   9

open where everyone can see him. The new office may be more streamlined and ~~with~~ *more*

~~efficiency~~, but something is definitely missing—perhaps the feeling that it is a place where *efficient,*
  10

people can be people.

1. __g__   3. __h__   5. __e__   7. __d__   9. __i__

2. __c__   4. __d__   6. __a__   8. __b__   10. __f__

■ Combined Editing Test 8

See if you can identify the sentence-skills mistakes at the underlined spots in the selection that follows. From the box below, choose the letter that describes each mistake and write it in the space provided. The same mistake may appear more than once. Then, in the space provided between the lines, correct each mistake. In one case, there is no mistake.

a. fragment	e. apostrophe mistake
b. run-on	f. missing comma
c. mistake in parallelism	g. dropped -*ly* ending (adverb mistake)
d. missing capital letter	h. no mistake

Methods of correction may vary. Possibilities appear below.

What would you do if you were driving to work during the morning rush hour and you

saw a family of geese blocking the road? The adult ~~canada~~ *Canada* goose and her goslings had been
                                                        1

standing on the west side of River Drive, looking at the water on the other side. When a

slight break in traffic ~~occurred the~~ *occurred, the* mother started across. Traffic ~~slowed brakes~~ *slowed, brakes* squealed,
                         2   3

and all the babies except one made it to the other side. That one stood right in the middle

of the ~~highway. Blocking~~ *highway, blocking* one of the lanes. Meanwhile, the mother goose honked ~~helpless~~ *helplessly*
        4   5

from the safety of the riverbank. Not a single car moved as all the ~~driver's~~ *drivers* waited for the
                                                                    6

gosling to cross. Then, just as one driver opened his door to get out and rescue the little
                    7

~~one the~~ *one, the* mother gave a deafening ~~honk, the~~ *honk. The* gosling quickly hurried over to join her. The
8   9

drivers restarted their motors and ~~were continuing~~ *continued* on their way, proud that they had helped
                                   10

save a life.

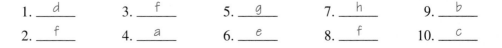

1. __d__   3. __f__   5. __g__   7. __h__   9. __b__

2. __f__   4. __a__   6. __e__   8. __f__   10. __c__

■ Combined Editing Test 9

See if you can locate and correct the ten sentence-skills mistakes in the following passage. The mistakes are listed in the box below. As you locate each mistake, write the number of the word group containing it in the space provided. Then, in the spaces between the lines, correct each mistake.

2 fragments __7__ __15__	1 missing comma after a
2 run-ons __4__ __6__	quotation __25__
1 irregular verb mistake __2__	2 missing apostrophes __10__
1 dangling modifier __4__	__17__
	1 missing quotation mark __12__

¹Our daughter was a happy, pleasant child until she reached the age of two. ²Then,

began

she ~~begun~~ having tantrums—and not just any tantrums. ³No, Tasha would thrash on the

floor, knock her head against the wall, and let out a bloodcurdling scream that pierced our

we decided

eardrums like an ice pick. ⁴Consulting our child-care books, ~~the decision was made~~ to

screams. Tasha's

ignore the ~~screams, Tasha'a~~ attempts to capture our attention might then stop. ⁵Have you

ever tried to ignore a toddler whose howls and moans make the walls shake? ⁶We had to

cells. It

think of something before Tasha drove us to a pair of padded ~~cells, it~~ was then that I came

up with a notion of a "screaming place." ⁷The next time that Tasha started the low, siren-

scream, I

like wail that preceded a full-fledged ~~scream. ⁸I~~ carried her to the bathroom. ⁹I said,

you'll

"Tasha, this is your screaming place. ¹⁰It's small, so ~~youll~~ hear your screams nice and loud.

¹¹You can roll around on the soft carpet. ¹²You can even get a drink if your throat feels

dry."

~~dry.~~ ¹³ Tasha came barreling out of the bathroom in about ten seconds—screaming—and

I gently pushed her back in. ¹⁴When she came out the next time, she had stopped screaming. [15]After a few more episodes like ~~this.~~ ^(this, Tasha's) [16] ~~Tasha's tantrums~~ started to subside. [17]Apparently, the private screaming place wasnt as ~~much~~ ^(wasn't) fun as the more public parts of the house. [18]I knew my system had triumphed when, one day, I passed Tasha's room and heard some muffled moans. [19]I poked my head in the door and asked her why she was crying. [20]"I'm not crying, Daddy," she said. [21]"Brownie's crying." [22]Brownie is the name of Tasha's teddy bear. [23]"But where is Brownie?" I asked. [24] Tasha walked over to the closet and opened it, revealing a rather lonely stuffed bear. [25]"He's in his screaming ~~place."~~ ^(place,") she replied.

■ Combined Editing Test 10

See if you can locate and correct the ten sentence-skills mistakes in the following passage. The mistakes are listed in the box below. As you locate each mistake, write the number of the word group containing it in the space provided. Then, in the spaces between the lines, correct each mistake.

2 fragments __4__ __9__	1 dangling modifier __6__
2 run-ons __8__ __15__	1 apostrophe mistake __18__
1 dropped verb ending __12__	1 mistake in parallelism __15__
1 irregular verb mistake __17__	1 missing capital letter __5__

¹In 1940, an unusual young man was buried in a custom-built ten-foot-long casket.

²The young man needed such a gigantic casket because he himself was a giant. ³He was

just a shade under nine feet ~~tall. ⁴And~~ *tall and* weighed almost five hundred pounds. ⁵Robert Wadlow,

an ~~american~~ *American* born in 1918, lived a tragic, pain-filled life. ⁶Weighing eight pounds at birth,

~~Robert's mother had given birth to a~~ *Robert was a* normal infant. ⁷But by the age of five, Robert stood

over five feet tall. ⁸His exceptional growth never ~~stopped he~~ *stopped; he* grew three inches every year

until he died. ⁹Because a human's internal organs can't support an excessively large ~~body~~ *body,*

¹⁰~~Robert~~ *Robert* was doomed to an early death. ¹¹Just before he died, he was fitted with ankle

braces to help support his enormous weight. ¹²One of the braces cut into an ankle,

triggering an infection that ~~overload~~ *overloaded* his already strained nervous system.

¹³The Wadlow family's reaction to Robert's plight was an intelligent and loving one.

¹⁴They refused to let him be exploited, turning down offers from freak shows and greedy

promoters. ¹⁵Robert's parents attempted to give him a normal ~~life they~~ *life. They* encouraged him

to read, to join the Boy Scouts, and ~~playing sports~~ *to play sports.* ¹⁶When the company that made Robert's shoes offered to employ him as a traveling representative, Mr. Wadlow drove his son more than 300,000 miles—all over the United States—on behalf of the shoe company. [17]The Wadlows helped Robert to stay cheerful and avoid the depression and gloom he could so easily have ~~sinked~~ sunk into. [18]Robert's life is an example of tremendous courage and persistence in the face of incredible ~~handicap's~~ handicaps.

■ Combined Editing Test 11

See if you can locate and correct the ten sentence-skills mistakes in the following passage. The mistakes are listed in the box below. As you locate each mistake, write the number of the word group containing it in the space provided. Then, in the spaces between the lines, correct each mistake.

---

1 fragment __18__

1 run-on __2__

1 mistake in subject-verb
   agreement __1__

2 missing commas around an
   interrupter __8__   __8__

1 missing commas after
   introductory words __16__

2 clichés __1__   __12__

1 mistake in parallelism __11__

1 irregular verb mistake __5__

---

suffers   _depressed_
[1]Everyone ~~suffer~~ from an occasional bad mood, but I get ~~down in the dumps~~ more

often than other people. [2]As a result, I've developed a list of helpful hints for dealing with

depression. One
~~depression, one~~ thing I've learned to do is to keep a mood diary. [3]About four times a day,

I jot down a one-word description of my mood at that moment—sad, tired, frustrated,

happy, and so on. [4]Then I ask myself questions like, "What event preceded this mood?

drunk
[5]Have I just eaten a lot of junk food or ~~drank~~ a lot of coffee? [6]Have I felt this way before?"

found,
[7]After keeping this diary for a while, I've begun to see patterns in my moods. [8]I've ~~found~~

for example, that
~~for example that~~ consuming a lot of salty foods like chips or pretzels makes me feel tense.

[9]Another way I've found to control my moods is to exercise every day. [10]Exercise seems

to prevent depression; it also helps me to sleep better. [11]Any type of exercise works,

just walking
including jogging, dancing, and even ~~just to walk~~ around the block. [12]I can also overcome

are low
depression by giving myself a small treat at those times when my spirits ~~are under the~~

~~weather.~~ [13]For instance, I might go to a movie, listen to a CD, or buy a new shirt. [14]Finally,

I try not to go to sleep in a bad mood. [15]I find that I will probably wake up in the same mood that I fell asleep in. ¹⁶Before getting into ~~bed I'll~~ ^{bed, I'll} do some relaxation techniques like

deep breathing or stretching exercises. ¹⁷Sometimes, I'll try soaking in a hot ~~tub. ¹⁸Which~~ ^{tub, which}

seems to ease the tension in my muscles. ¹⁹If I still feel miserable, I try to remain hopeful,

for no bad mood lasts forever.

■ Combined Editing Test 12

See if you can locate and correct the ten sentence-skills mistakes in the following passage. The mistakes are listed in the box below. As you locate each mistake, write the number of the word group containing it in the space provided. Then, in the spaces between the lines, correct each mistake.

2 fragments __4__ __8__	1 mistake in pronoun agreement __6__
1 run-on __15__	
1 dropped verb ending __1__	1 missing capital letter __10__
1 mistake in subject-verb agreement __13__	2 missing commas around an interrupter __12__ __12__
	1 apostrophe mistake __17__

                                                                      explains
¹A former advertising copywriter named Paul Stevens ~~explain~~ in a book called *I Can Sell You Anything* how advertisers use "weasel words" to persuade people to buy. ²Weasel words are slippery, sneaky words that may not really mean what they imply. ³Some of them make you believe things that have never been stated.

                                        Take, for example,
⁴~~For example,~~ the weasel words *help* and *like.* ⁵How many ads can you think of that include the phrases *helps stop, helps prevent,* or *helps fight?*

                                                                      its
⁶A toothpaste company couldn't possibly say that ~~their~~ product will "stop cavities forever," so that weasel word *helps* is put in front of the claim. ⁷Now

                        impressive but
the ad sounds ~~impressive. ⁸But~~ doesn't actually guarantee anything. ⁹The same is true of

        If
like. ¹⁰~~if~~ a household cleanser claims that it cleans "like a white tornado," are you impressed? ¹¹The image of a powerful, dirt-sucking whirlwind may have gripped your

        However, if   it, a
mind. ¹²~~However~~ if you think about ~~it a~~ tornado springing out of a bottle is clearly

                are
impossible. ¹³Then there ~~is~~ the weasel words that don't have any particular meaning.

¹⁴Words like *taste, flavor,* and *good looks* are all based on subjective standards that vary

                                                                      best." Every
with each individual. ¹⁵The truth is that every cigarette in the world can "taste ~~best" every~~

car manufacturer can claim the "most advanced design." [16]There's just no scientific way to measure qualities like these. [17]Advertisers, using weasel words, manipulate language to win the trust (and the cash) of ~~consumer's.~~ consumers.

APPENDIXES

Introduction

Six appendixes follow. Appendix A consists of Parts of Speech, and Appendix B is a series of ESL Pointers. Appendixes C and D consist of a diagnostic test and an achievement test that measure many of the skills in this book. The diagnostic test can be taken at the outset of your work; the achievement test can be used to measure your progress at the end of your work. Appendix E supplies answers to the introductory projects and the practice exercises in Part Two. The answers, which you should refer to only after you have worked carefully through each exercise, give you responsibility for testing yourself. (To ensure that the answer key is used as a learning tool only, answers are *not* given for the review tests in Part Two or for the reinforcement tests in Part Three. These answers appear only in the Instructor's Manual; they can be copied and handed out at the discretion of your instructor.) Finally, Appendix F provides handy progress charts that you can use to track your performance on all the tests in the book and the writing assignments as well.

Parts of Speech

14.1

Words—the building blocks of sentences—can be divided into eight parts of speech. *Parts of speech* are classifications of words according to their meaning and use in a sentence.

This chapter will explain the eight parts of speech:

1. Nouns
2. Pronouns
3. Verbs
4. Prepositions
5. Adjectives
6. Adverbs
7. Conjunctions
8. Interjections

Nouns

A *noun* is a word that is used to name something: a person, a place, an object, or an idea. Here are some examples of nouns:

Nouns			
woman	city	pancake	freedom
Alice Walker	street	diamond	possibility
Steve Martin	Chicago	Corvette	mystery

Most nouns begin with a lowercase letter and are known as *common nouns.* These nouns name general things. Some nouns, however, begin with a capital letter. They are called *proper nouns.* While a common noun refers to a person or thing in general, a proper noun names someone or something specific. For example, *woman* is a common noun—it doesn't name a particular woman. On the other hand, *Alice Walker* is a proper noun because it names a specific woman.

Practice 1

Insert any appropriate noun into each of the following blanks.
Answers will vary.

1. The shoplifter stole a(n) _____ from the department store.

2. _____ threw the football to me.

3. Tiny messages were scrawled on the _____.

4. A _____ crashed through the window.

5. Give the _____ to Keiko.

Singular and Plural Nouns

A *singular noun* names one person, place, object, or idea. A *plural noun* refers to two or more persons, places, objects, or ideas. Most singular nouns can be made plural with the addition of *s*.

Some nouns, like *box*, have irregular plurals. You can check the plural of nouns you think may be irregular by looking up the singular form in a dictionary.

Singular and Plural Nouns	
Singular	*Plural*
goat	goats
alley	alleys
friend	friends
truth	truths
box	boxes

- For more information on nouns, see "Subjects and Verbs," pages 89–98.

Practice 2

Underline the three nouns in each sentence. Some are singular, and some are plural.

1. Two <u>bats</u> swooped over the <u>heads</u> of the frightened <u>children</u>.

2. The <u>artist</u> has purple <u>paint</u> on her <u>sleeve</u>.

3. The lost <u>dog</u> has <u>fleas</u> and a broken <u>leg</u>.

4. Tiffany does her <u>homework</u> in green <u>ink</u>.

5. Some <u>farmers</u> plant <u>seeds</u> by <u>moonlight</u>.

Pronouns

A *pronoun* is a word that stands for a noun. Pronouns eliminate the need for constant repetition. Look at the following sentences:

> The phone rang, and Malik answered the phone.
>
> Lisa met Lisa's friends in the music store at the mall. Lisa meets Lisa's friends there every Saturday.
>
> The waiter rushed over to the new customers. The new customers asked the waiter for menus and coffee.

Now look at how much clearer and smoother these sentences sound with pronouns.

> The phone rang, and Malik answered *it*.
>
> (The pronoun *it* is used to replace the word *phone*.)
>
> Lisa met *her* friends in the music store at the mall. *She* meets *them* there every Saturday.
>
> (The pronoun *her* is used to replace the word *Lisa's*. The pronoun *she* replaces *Lisa*. The pronoun *them* replaces the words *Lisa's friends*.)
>
> The waiter rushed over to the new customers. *They* asked *him* for menus and coffee.
>
> (The pronoun *they* is used to replace the words *the new customers*. The pronoun *him* replaces the words *the waiter*.)

Following is a list of commonly used pronouns known as personal pronouns:

Personal Pronouns						
I	you	he	she	it	we	they
me	your	him	her	its	us	them
my	yours	his	hers		our	their

Practice 3

Fill in each blank with the appropriate personal pronoun.

1. André feeds his pet lizard every day before school. _____He_____ also gives _____it_____ flies in the afternoon.

2. The reporter interviewed the striking workers. _____They_____ told _____him (or her)_____ about their demand for higher wages and longer breaks.

3. Students should save all returned tests. _____They_____ should also keep _____their_____ review sheets.

4. The pilot announced that we would fly through some air pockets. _____He (or She)_____ said that we should be past _____them_____ soon.

5. Adolfo returned the calculator to Sheila last Friday. But Sheila insists that _____she_____ never got _____it_____ back.

There are several types of pronouns. For convenient reference, they are described briefly in the box below.

Types of Pronouns

Personal pronouns can act in a sentence as subjects, objects, or possessives.

> *Singular*: I, me, my, mine, you, your, yours, he, him, his, she, her, hers, it, its
>
> *Plural*: we, us, our, ours, you, your, yours, they, them, their, theirs

Relative pronouns refer to someone or something already mentioned in the sentence.

> who, whose, whom, which, that

Interrogative pronouns are used to ask questions.

> who, whose, whom, which, what

Demonstrative pronouns are used to point out particular persons or things.

> this, that, these, those

Note: Do not use *them* (as in *them* shoes), *this here, that there, these here,* or *those there* to point out.

Continued

Reflexive pronouns are those that end in *-self* or *-selves*. A reflexive pronoun is used as the object of a verb (as in *Cary cut **herself***) or the object of a preposition (as in *Jack sent a birthday card to **himself***) when the subject of the verb is the same as the object.

> *Singular:* myself, yourself, himself, herself, itself
>
> *Plural:*   ourselves, yourselves, themselves

Intensive pronouns have exactly the same forms as reflexive pronouns. The difference is in how they are used. Intensive pronouns are used to add emphasis. (***I myself** will need to read the contract before I sign it.*)

Indefinite pronouns do not refer to a particular person or thing.

> each, either, everyone, nothing, both, several, all, any, most, none

Reciprocal pronouns express shared actions or feelings.

> each other, one another

- For more information on pronouns, see "Pronoun Types," pages 205–217.

Verbs

Every complete sentence must contain at least one verb. There are two types of verbs: action verbs and linking verbs.

Action Verbs

An *action verb* tells what is being done in a sentence. For example, look at the following sentences:

> Mr. Jensen *swatted* at the bee with his hand.
> Rainwater *poured* into the storm sewer.
> The children *chanted* the words to the song.

In these sentences, the verbs are *swatted, poured*, and *chanted*. These words are all action verbs; they tell what is happening in each sentence.

- For more about action verbs, see "Subjects and Verbs," pages 89–98.

Practice 4

Insert an appropriate word in each blank. That word will be an action verb; it will tell what is happening in the sentence.

Answers will vary.

1. The surgeon _____ through the first layer of skin.

2. The animals in the cage _____ all day.

3. An elderly woman on the street _____ me for directions.

4. The boy next door _____ our lawn every other week.

5. Our instructor _____ our papers over the weekend.

Linking Verbs

Some verbs are *linking verbs*. These verbs link (or join) a noun to something that is said about it. For example, look at the following sentence:

The clouds *are* steel-gray.

In this sentence, *are* is a linking verb. It joins the noun *clouds* to words that describe it: *steel-gray*.

Other common linking verbs include *am, is, was, were, look, feel, sound, appear, seem,* and *become.*

- For more about linking verbs, see "Subjects and Verbs," pages 89–98.

Practice 5

In each blank, insert one of the following linking verbs: *am, feel, is, look, were.* Use each linking verb once.

1. The important papers _____ *were* _____ in a desk drawer.

2. I _____ *am* _____ anxious to get my test back.

3. The bananas _____ *look* _____ ripe.

4. The grocery store _____ *is* _____ open until 11 P.M.

5. Whenever I _____ *feel* _____ angry, I go off by myself to calm down.

Helping Verbs

Sometimes the verb of a sentence consists of more than one word. In these cases, the main verb will be joined by one or more *helping verbs*. Look at the following sentence:

The basketball team *will be leaving* for the game at six o'clock.

In this sentence, the main verb is *leaving*. The helping verbs are *will* and *be*.
Other helping verbs include *do, has, have, may, would, can, must, could,* and *should*.

- For more information about helping verbs, see "Subjects and Verbs," pages 89–98, and "Irregular Verbs," pages 161–171.

Practice 6

In each blank, insert one of the following helping verbs: *does, must, should, could, has been*. Use each helping verb once.

1. You ___should (or must)___ start writing your paper this weekend.
2. The victim ___could___ describe her attacker in great detail.
3. You ___must (or should)___ rinse the dishes before putting them into the dishwasher.
4. My neighbor ___has been___ arrested for drunk driving.
5. The bus driver ___does___ not make any extra stops.

Prepositions

A *preposition* is a word that connects a noun or a pronoun to another word in the sentence. For example, look at the following sentence:

A man *in* the bus was snoring loudly.

In is a preposition. It connects the noun *bus* to *man*. Here is a list of common prepositions:

Prepositions

about	before	down	like	to
above	behind	during	of	toward
across	below	except	off	under
after	beneath	for	on	up
among	beside	from	over	with
around	between	in	since	without
at	by	into	through	

The noun or pronoun that a preposition connects to another word in the sentence is called the *object* of the preposition. A group of words beginning with a preposition and ending with its object is called a *prepositional phrase.* The words *in the bus*, for example, are a prepositional phrase.

Now read the following sentences and explanations.

An ant was crawling *up the teacher's leg.*

The noun *leg* is the object of the preposition *up. Up* connects *leg* with the word *crawling.* The prepositional phrase *up the teacher's leg* describes *crawling.* It tells just where the ant was crawling.

The man *with the black moustache* left the restaurant quickly.

The noun *moustache* is the object of the preposition *with.* The prepositional phrase *with the black moustache* describes the word *man.* It tells us exactly which man left the restaurant quickly.

The plant *on the windowsill* was a present *from my mother.*

The noun *windowsill* is the object of the preposition *on.* The prepositional phrase *on the windowsill* describes the word *plant.* It describes exactly which plant was a present.

There is a second prepositional phrase in this sentence. The preposition is *from*, and its object is *mother.* The prepositional phrase *from my mother* explains *present.* It tells who gave the present.

- For more about prepositions, see "Subjects and Verbs," pages 89–98, and "Sentence Variety II," pages 245–258.

Practice 7

In each blank, insert one of the following prepositions: *of, by, with, in, without.*
Use each preposition once.

1. The letter from his girlfriend had been sprayed _____with_____ perfume.

2. The weed killer quickly killed the dandelions _____in_____ our lawn.

3. _____Without_____ giving any notice, the tenant moved out of the expensive apartment.

4. Donald hungrily ate three scoops _____of_____ ice cream and an order of French fries.

5. The crates _____by_____ the back door contain glass bottles and old newspapers.

Adjectives

An *adjective* is a word that describes a noun (the name of a person, place, or thing). Look at the following sentence.

> The dog lay down on a mat in front of the fireplace.

Now look at this sentence when adjectives have been inserted.

> The *shaggy* dog lay down on a *worn* mat in front of the fireplace.

The adjective *shaggy* describes the noun *dog*; the adjective *worn* describes the noun *mat*. Adjectives add spice to our writing. They also help us to identify particular people, places, or things.

Adjectives can be found in two places:

1 An adjective may come before the word it describes (a *damp* night, the *moldy* bread, a *striped* umbrella).

2 An adjective that describes the subject of a sentence may come after a linking verb. The linking verb may be a form of the verb *be* (he *is* **furious**, I *am* **exhausted**, they *are* **hungry**). Other linking verbs include *feel, look, sound, smell, taste, appear, seem,* and *become* (the soup *tastes* **salty**, your hands *feel* **dry**, the dog *seems* **lost**).

Note   The words *a, an,* and *the* (called *articles*) are generally classified as adjectives.

- For more information on adjectives, see "Adjectives and Adverbs," pages 218–224.

Practice 8

Write any appropriate adjective in each blank.

Answers will vary.

1. The _____ pizza was eaten greedily by the _____ teenagers.

2. Melissa gave away the sofa because it was _____ and _____.

3. Although the alley is _____ and _____, Jian often takes it as a shortcut home.

4. The restaurant throws away lettuce that is _____ and tomatoes that are _____.

5. When I woke up in the morning, I had a(n) _____ fever and a(n) _____ throat.

Adverbs

An *adverb* is a word that describes a verb, an adjective, or another adverb. Many adverbs end in the letters *-ly*. Look at the following sentence:

The canary sang in the pet store window as the shoppers greeted each other.

Now look at this sentence after adverbs have been inserted.

The canary sang *softly* in the pet store window as the shoppers *loudly* greeted each other.

The adverbs add details to the sentence. They also allow the reader to contrast the singing of the canary and the noise the shoppers are making.

Look at the following sentences and the explanations of how adverbs are used in each case.

The chef yelled *angrily* at the young waiter.

(The adverb *angrily* describes the verb *yelled*.)

My mother has an *extremely* busy schedule on Tuesdays.

(The adverb *extremely* describes the adjective *busy*.)

The sick man spoke *very* faintly to his loyal nurse.

(The adverb *very* describes the adverb *faintly*.)

Some adverbs do not end in *-ly*. Examples include *very, often, never, always,* and *well*.

- For more information on adverbs, see "Adjectives and Adverbs," pages 218–224.

Practice 9

Fill in each blank with any appropriate adverb.

Answers will vary.

1. The water in the pot boiled _____.

2. Carla _____ drove the car through _____ moving traffic.

3. The telephone operator spoke _____ to the young child.

4. The game show contestant waved _____ to his family in the audience.

5. Wes _____ studies, so it's no surprise that he did _____ poorly on his finals.

Conjunctions

A *conjunction* is a word that connects. There are two types of conjunctions: coordinating and subordinating.

Coordinating Conjunctions

Coordinating conjunctions join two equal ideas. Look at the following sentence:

Kevin *and* Steve interviewed for the job, *but* their friend Anne got it.

In this sentence, the coordinating conjunction *and* connects the proper nouns *Kevin* and *Steve*. The coordinating conjunction *but* connects the first part of the sentence, *Kevin and Steve interviewed for the job,* to the second part, *their friend Anne got it.*

Following is a list of all the coordinating conjunctions. In this book, they are simply called *joining words*.

Coordinating Conjunctions (Joining Words)

and	so	nor	yet
but	or	for	

- For more on coordinating conjunctions, see information on joining words in "Run-Ons," pages 119–136, and "Sentence Variety I," pages 137–151.

Practice 10

Write a coordinating conjunction in each blank. Choose from the following: *and, but, so, or, nor.* Use each conjunction once.

1. Either Jerome _____*or*_____ Alex scored the winning touchdown.

2. I expected roses for my birthday, _____*but*_____ I received a vase of plastic tulips from the discount store.

3. The cafeteria was serving liver and onions for lunch, _____*so*_____ I bought a sandwich at the corner deli.

4. Kristina brought a pack of playing cards _____*and*_____ a pan of brownies to the company picnic.

5. Neither my sofa _____*nor*_____ my armchair matches the rug in my living room.

Subordinating Conjunctions

When a *subordinating conjunction* is added to a word group, the words can no longer stand alone as an independent sentence. They are no longer a complete thought. For example, look at the following sentence:

Karen fainted in class.

The word group *Karen fainted in class* is a complete thought. It can stand alone as a sentence. See what happens when a subordinating conjunction is added to a complete thought:

When Karen fainted in class

Now the words cannot stand alone as a sentence. They are dependent on other words to complete the thought:

When Karen fainted in class, we put her feet up on some books.

In this book, a word that begins a dependent word group is called a *dependent word.* Subordinating conjunctions are common dependent words. Below are some subordinating conjunctions.

Subordinating Conjunctions

after	even if	unless	where
although	even though	until	wherever
as	if	when	whether
because	since	whenever	while
before	though		

Following are some more sentences with subordinating conjunctions:

After she finished her last exam, Irina said, "Now I can relax."
(*After she finished her last exam* is not a complete thought. It is dependent on the rest of the words to make up a complete sentence.)

Lamont listens to books on tape *while* he drives to work.
(*While he drives to work* cannot stand by itself as a sentence. It depends on the rest of the sentence to make up a complete thought.)

Since apples were on sale, we decided to make an apple pie for dessert.
(*Since apples were on sale* is not a complete sentence. It depends on *we decided to make an apple pie for dessert* to complete the thought.)

- For more information on subordinating conjunctions, see information on dependent words in "Fragments," pages 99–118; "Run-Ons," pages 119–136; "Sentence Variety I," pages 137–151; and "Sentence Variety II," pages 245–258.

Practice 11

Write a logical subordinating conjunction in each blank. Choose from the following: *even though, because, until, when, before.* Use each conjunction once.

1. The bank was closed down by federal regulators ____because____ it lost more money than it earned.

2. ____When____ Paula wants to look mysterious, she wears dark sunglasses and a scarf.

3. ____Even though____ the restaurant was closing in fifteen minutes, customers sipped their coffee slowly and continued to talk.

4. ____Before____ anyone else could answer it, Leon rushed to the phone and whispered, "Is that you?"

5. The waiter was instructed not to serve any food ____until____ the guest of honor arrived.

Interjections

An *interjection* is a word that can stand independently and is used to express emotion. Examples are *oh, wow, ouch,* and *oops.* These words are usually not found in formal writing.

"*Hey!*" yelled Maggie. "That's my bike."
Oh, we're late for class.

A Final Note

A word may function as more than one part of speech. For example, the word *dust* can be a verb or a noun, depending on its role in the sentence.

I *dust* my bedroom once a month, whether it needs dusting or not. (verb)
The top of my refrigerator is covered with an inch of *dust*. (noun)

ESL Pointers

This section covers rules that most native speakers of English take for granted but that are useful for speakers of English as a second language (ESL).

Articles

Types of Articles

An *article* is a noun marker—it signals that a noun will follow. There are two kinds of articles: indefinite and definite. The indefinite articles are *a* and *an*. Use *a* before a word that begins with a consonant sound:

> **a d**esk, **a p**hotograph, **a u**nicycle
>
> *(A* is used before *unicycle* because the *u* in that word sounds like the consonant *y* plus *u,* not a vowel sound.)

Use *an* before a word beginning with a vowel sound:

> **an e**rror, **an o**bject, **an h**onest woman
>
> *(Honest* begins with a vowel sound because the *h* is silent.)

The definite article is *the:*

> **the** sofa, **the** cup

An article may come right before a noun:

> **a** magazine, **the** candle

Or an article may be separated from the noun by words that describe the noun:

> **a** popular magazine, **the** fat red candle

Note There are various other noun markers, including quantity words (*a few, many, a lot of*), numerals (*one, thirteen, 710*), demonstrative adjectives (*this, these*), adjectives (*my, your, our*), and possessive nouns (*Raoul's, the school's*).

Articles with Count and Noncount Nouns

To know whether to use an article with a noun and which article to use, you must recognize count and noncount nouns. (A *noun* is a word used to name something— a person, place, thing, or idea.)

Count nouns name people, places, things, or ideas that can be counted and made into plurals, such as *pillow, heater*, and *mail carrier* (*one pillow, two heaters, three mail carriers*).

Noncount nouns refer to things or ideas that cannot be counted and therefore cannot be made into plurals, such as *sunshine, gold,* and *toast*. The box below lists and illustrates common types of noncount nouns.

Common Types of Noncount Nouns

Abstractions and emotions: justice, tenderness, courage, knowledge, embarrassment

Activities: jogging, thinking, wondering, golf, hoping, sleep

Foods: oil, rice, pie, butter, spaghetti, broccoli

Gases and vapors: carbon dioxide, oxygen, smoke, steam, air

Languages and areas of study: Korean, Italian, geology, arithmetic, history

Liquids: coffee, kerosene, lemonade, tea, water, bleach

Materials that come in bulk or mass form: straw, firewood, sawdust, cat litter, cement

Natural occurrences: gravity, sleet, rain, lightning, rust

Other things that cannot be counted: clothing, experience, trash, luggage, room, furniture, homework, machinery, cash, news, transportation, work

---

The quantity of a noncount noun can be expressed with a word or words called *qualifiers*, such as *some, more,* or *a unit of*. In the following two examples, the qualifiers are shown in *italic* type, and the noncount nouns are shown in **bold-face** type.

How *much* **experience** have you had as a salesclerk?

Our tiny kitchen doesn't have *enough* **room** for a table and chairs.

Some words can be either count or noncount nouns depending on whether they refer to one or more individual items or to something in general:

Three **chickens** are running around our neighbor's yard.

(This sentence refers to particular chickens; *chicken* in this case is a count noun.)

Would you like some more **chicken**?

(This sentence refers to chicken in general; in this case, *chicken* is a noncount noun.)

Using *A* or *An* with Nonspecific Singular Count Nouns

Use *a* or *an* with singular nouns that are nonspecific. A noun is nonspecific when the reader doesn't know its specific identity.

A photograph can be almost magical. It saves a moment's image for many years.

(The sentence refers to any photograph, not a specific one.)

An article in the newspaper today made me laugh.

(The reader isn't familiar with the article. This is the first time it is mentioned.)

Using *The* with Specific Nouns

In general, use *the* with all specific nouns—specific singular, plural, and noncount nouns. A noun is specific—and therefore requires the article *the*—in the following cases:

- When it has already been mentioned once:

  An article in the newspaper today made me laugh. **The** article was about a talking parrot who frightened away a thief.
  (*The* is used with the second mention of *article*.)

- When it is identified by a word or phrase in the sentence:

  The CD that is playing now is a favorite of mine.
  (*CD* is identified by the words *that is playing now*.)

- When its identity is suggested by the general context:

  The service at Joe's Bar and Grill is never fast.
  (*Service* is identified by the words *at Joe's Bar and Grill*.)

- When it is unique:

  Some people see a man's face in **the** moon, while others see a rabbit. (Earth has only one moon.)

- When it comes after a superlative adjective (for example, *best, biggest,* or *wisest)*:

  The funniest movie I've seen is *Young Frankenstein.*

Omitting Articles   Omit articles with nonspecific plurals and nonspecific noncount nouns. Plurals and noncount nouns are nonspecific when they refer to something in general.

  Stories are popular with most children.

  Service is almost as important as food to a restaurant's success.

  Movies can be rented from many supermarkets as well as video stores.

Using *The* with Proper Nouns   Proper nouns name particular people, places, things, or ideas and are always capitalized. Most proper nouns do not require articles; those that do, however, require *the.* Following are general guidelines about when not to use *the* and when to use *the.*

  Do not use *the* for most singular proper nouns, including names of the following:

- *People and animals* (Ronald Reagan, Fluffy)
- *Continents, states, cities, streets, and parks* (South America, Utah, Boston, Baker Street, People's Park)
- *Most countries* (Cuba, Indonesia, Ireland)
- *Individual bodies of water, islands, and mountains* (Lake Michigan, Captiva Island, Mount McKinley)

Use *the* for the following types of proper nouns:

- *Plural proper nouns* (the Harlem Globetrotters, the Marshall Islands, the Netherlands, the Atlas Mountains)
- *Names of large geographic areas, deserts, oceans, seas, and rivers* (the Midwest, the Kalahari Desert, the Pacific Ocean, the Sargasso Sea, the Nile River)
- *Names with the format* "the _____ of _____" (the King of Morocco, the Strait of Gibraltar, the University of Illinois)

Practice

Underline the correct word or words in parentheses.

1. (Indiana, The Indiana) is a state where basketball is extremely popular.
2. (Dictionaries, The dictionaries) provide both the spelling and the definition of words.
3. On Friday, I'll be going to (a birthday party, the birthday party).
4. (A birthday party, The birthday party) will be held at an Italian restaurant.
5. Theo spends all his spare time playing (soccer, the soccer).
6. Rice, coconuts, and pineapples are some important products of (Philippines, the Philippines).
7. (Amazon River, The Amazon River) carries more water than any other river in the world.
8. (Lucky man, The lucky man) won a two-week trip to Paris.
9. The name of (the National Organization of Women, National Organization of Women) is often abbreviated as NOW.
10. (Cereal, The cereal) my sister likes has tiny blue and pink marshmallows in it.

Subjects and Verbs

Avoiding Repeated Subjects

In English, a particular subject can be used only once in a word group with a subject and a verb (that is, a clause). Don't repeat a subject in the same word group by following a noun with a pronoun.

Incorrect: My *parents they* live in Miami.
Correct: My **parents** live in Miami.
Correct: **They** live in Miami.

Even when the subject and verb are separated by several words, the subject cannot be repeated in the same word group.

Incorrect: The *windstorm* that happened last night *it* damaged our roof.
Correct: The **windstorm** that happened last night **damaged** our roof.

Including Pronoun Subjects and Linking Verbs

Some languages omit a subject that is a pronoun, but in English, every sentence other than a command must have a subject. In a command, the subject *you* is understood: (You) Hand in your papers now.

> Incorrect: The soup tastes terrible. *Is* much too salty.
> Correct: The soup tastes terrible. **It is** much too salty.

Every English sentence must also have a verb, even when the meaning of the sentence is clear without the verb.

> Incorrect: The table covered with old newspapers.
> Correct: The table **is** covered with old newspapers.

Including *There* and *Here* at the Beginning of Sentences

Some English sentences begin with *there* or *here* plus a linking verb (usually a form of *to be: is, are,* and so on). In such sentences, the verb comes before the subject.

> **There are** ants all over the kitchen counter.
> (The subject is the plural noun *ants*, so the plural verb *are* is used.)
>
> **Here is** the bug spray.
> (The subject is the singular noun *spray*, so the singular verb *is* is used.)

In sentences like those above, remember not to omit *there* or *here*.

> Incorrect: *Are* several tests scheduled for Friday.
> Correct: **There are** several tests scheduled for Friday.

Not Using the Progressive Tense of Certain Verbs

The progressive tenses are made up of forms of *be* plus the *-ing* form of the main verb. They express actions or conditions still in progress at a particular time.

> The garden **will be blooming** when you visit me in June.

However, verbs for mental states, the senses, possession, and inclusion are normally not used in the progressive tense.

> Incorrect: I **am knowing** a lot about auto mechanics.
>
> Correct: I **know** a lot about auto mechanics.
>
> Incorrect: Gerald **is having** a job as a supermarket cashier.
>
> Correct: Gerald **has** a job as a supermarket cashier.

Common verbs not generally used in the progressive tense are listed in the following box.

Common Verbs Not Generally Used in the Progressive

Verbs relating to thoughts, attitudes, and desires: agree, believe, imagine, know, like, love, prefer, think, understand, want, wish

Verbs showing sense perceptions: hear, see, smell, taste

Verbs relating to appearances: appear, seem, look

Verbs showing possession: belong, have, own, possess

Verbs showing inclusion: contain, include

Using Gerunds and Infinitives after Verbs

Before learning the rules about gerunds and infinitives, you must understand what they are. A *gerund* is the *-ing* form of a verb that is used as a noun:

> **Reading** is a good way to improve one's vocabulary.
>
> (*Reading* is the subject of the sentence.)

An *infinitive* is *to* plus the basic form of the verb (the form in which the verb is listed in the dictionary), as in **to eat**. The infinitive can function as an adverb, an adjective, or a noun.

> On weekends, Betsy works at a convenience store **to make** some extra money.
>
> (*To make some extra money* functions as an adverb that describes the verb *works*.)

I need a pencil **to write down** your telephone number.

(*To write down your telephone number* functions as an adjective describing the noun *pencil*.)

To forgive can be a relief.

(*To forgive* functions as a noun—it is the subject of the verb *can be*.)

Some verbs can be followed by only a gerund or only an infinitive; other verbs can be followed by either. Examples are given in the following lists. There are many others; watch for them in your reading.

Verb + gerund (*enjoy + skiing*)
Verb + preposition + gerund (*think + about + coming*)

Some verbs can be followed by a gerund but not by an infinitive. In many cases, there is a preposition (such as *for, in,* or *of*) between the verb and the gerund. Following are some verbs and verb-preposition combinations that can be followed by gerunds but not by infinitives:

admit	deny	look forward to
apologize for	discuss	postpone
appreciate	dislike	practice
approve of	enjoy	suspect of
avoid	feel like	talk about
be used to	finish	thank for
believe in	insist on	think about

Incorrect: The governor *avoids to make* enemies.
Correct: The governor **avoids making** enemies.

Incorrect: I *enjoy to go* to movies alone.
Correct: I **enjoy going** to movies alone.

Verb + infinitive (*agree* + *to leave*)

Following are common verbs that can be followed by an infinitive but not by a gerund:

agree	decide	manage
arrange	expect	refuse
claim	have	wait

Incorrect: I *arranged paying* my uncle's bills while he was ill.

Correct: I **arranged to pay** my uncle's bills while he was ill.

Verb + noun or pronoun + infinitive (*cause* + *them* + *to flee*)

Below are common verbs that are followed first by a noun or pronoun and then by an infinitive, not a gerund.

cause	force	remind
command	persuade	warn

Incorrect: The flood *forced them leaving their home.*

Correct: The flood **forced them to leave their home.**

Following are common verbs that can be followed either by an infinitive alone or by a noun or pronoun and an infinitive:

ask	need	want
expect	promise	would like

Rita **expects to go** to college.

Rita's parents **expect her to go** to college.

Verb + gerund or infinitive (*begin* + *packing* or *begin* + *to pack*)

Following are verbs that can be followed by either a gerund or an infinitive:

begin	hate	prefer
continue	love	start

The meaning of each of the above verbs remains the same or almost the same whether a gerund or an infinitive is used.

I love **to sleep** late.
I love **sleeping** late.

With the verbs below, the gerunds and the infinitives have very different meanings.

forget	remember	stop

Yuri **forgot putting money** in the parking meter.
(He put money in the parking meter, but then he forgot that he had done so.)

Yuri **forgot to put money** in the parking meter.
(He neglected to put money in the parking meter.)

Practice

Underline the correct word or words in parentheses.

1. The waitress (she looks, <u>looks</u>) grumpy, but she is really quite pleasant.
2. Our picnic will have to be put off until another day. (Is raining, <u>It is raining</u>) too hard to go.
3. (Are, <u>There are</u>) some good articles in this magazine.
4. A very famous writer (coming, <u>is coming</u>) to talk to our class on Friday.
5. I (<u>have</u>, am having) a few questions to ask you.
6. Lila's mother (<u>prefers</u>, is preferring) that we call her by her first name.

7. If your boss is so unpleasant, you should think about (<u>getting</u>, to get) another job.

8. Standing in front of the mirror, Omar practiced (to give, <u>giving</u>) his speech for hours.

9. Because she was angry at her boyfriend, Delores refused (going, <u>to go</u>) to the movies with him.

10. Now that he's done it for several weeks, Sergei is used to (ride, <u>riding</u>) the city buses.

Adjectives

Following the Order of Adjectives in English

Adjectives describe nouns and pronouns. In English, an adjective usually comes directly before the word it describes or after a linking verb (a form of *be* or a "sense" verb such as *look, seem,* or *taste*), in which case it modifies the subject of the sentence. In each of the following two sentences, the adjective is **boldfaced** and the noun it describes is *italicized*.

Marta has **beautiful** *eyes*.

Marta's *eyes* are **beautiful**.

When more than one adjective modifies the same noun, the adjectives are usually stated in a certain order, though there are often exceptions. Following is the typical order of English adjectives:

Typical Order of Adjectives in a Series

1 Article or other noun marker: a, an, the, Helen's, this, seven, your

2 Opinion adjective: rude, enjoyable, surprising, easy

3 Size: tall, huge, small, compact

4 Shape: triangular, oval, round, square

5 Age: ancient, new, old, young

6 Color: gray, blue, pink, green

7 Nationality: Greek, Thai, Korean, Ethiopian

8 Religion: Hindu, Methodist, Jewish, Islamic

9 Material: fur, copper, stone, velvet

10 Noun used as an adjective: book (as in *book report*), picture (as in *picture frame*), tea (as in *tea bag*)

Here are some examples of the order of adjectives:

an exciting new movie

the petite young Kenyan woman

my favorite Chinese restaurant

Greta's long brown leather coat

In general, use no more than two or three adjectives after the article or other noun marker. Numerous adjectives in a series can be awkward: **that comfortable big old green velvet** couch.

Using the Present and Past Participles as Adjectives

The present participle ends in *-ing*. Past participles of regular verbs end in *-ed* or *-d;* a list of the past participles of many common irregular verbs appears on pages 163–164. Both types of participles may be used as adjectives. A participle used as an adjective may come before the word it describes:

There was a **frowning** *security guard.*

A participle used as an adjective may also follow a linking verb and describe the subject of the sentence:

The *security guard* was **frowning**.

While both present and past participles of a particular verb may be used as adjectives, their meanings differ. Use the present participle to describe whoever or whatever causes a feeling:

a **disappointing** *date*
(The date *caused* the disappointment.)

Use the past participle to describe whoever or whatever experiences the feeling:

the **disappointed** *neighbor*
(The neighbor *is* disappointed.)

Here are two more sentences that illustrate the differing meanings of present and past participles.

The waiter was **irritating**.

The diners were **irritated**.

(The waiter caused the irritation; the diners experienced the irritation.)

Following are pairs of present and past participles with similar distinctions.

annoying, annoyed	exhausting, exhausted
boring, bored	fascinating, fascinated
confusing, confused	surprising, surprised
depressing, depressed	tiring, tired
exciting, excited	

Practice

Underline the correct word or wording in parentheses.

1. We were glad to find such a (young helpful, <u>helpful young</u>) guide to show us the new city.

2. The children spent hours stacking the (<u>little square yellow</u>, yellow little square) blocks into different arrangements.

3. Our family attends the (old Orthodox Greek, <u>old Greek Orthodox</u>) church on Maple Avenue.

4. After his long workday, Ezra is often very (<u>tired</u>, tiring).

5. The (tired, <u>tiring</u>) journey lasted for almost five days.

Prepositions Used for Time and Place

The use of a preposition in English is often not based on the prepositions' common meaning, and there are many exceptions to general rules. As a result, the correct prepositions use must be learned gradually through experience. Following is a chart showing how three of the most common prepositions are used in some customary references to time and place:

Using *On*, *In*, and *At* to Refer to Time and Place

Time

On *a specific day:* on Wednesday, on January 11, on Halloween

In *a part of a day:* in the morning, in the daytime (but *at* night)

In *a month or a year:* in October, in 1776

In *a period of time:* in a second, in a few days, in a little while

At *a specific time:* at 11 P.M., at midnight, at sunset, at lunchtime

Place

On *a surface:* on the shelf, on the sidewalk, on the roof

In *a place that is enclosed:* in the bathroom, in the closet, in the drawer

At *a specific location:* at the restaurant, at the zoo, at the school

Practice

Underline the correct preposition in parentheses.

1. Kids like to play tricks (<u>on</u>, at) April Fool's Day.
2. The baby usually takes a nap (on, <u>in</u>) the afternoon.
3. (<u>In</u>, At) a few minutes, the show will begin.
4. You'll find paper clips (on, <u>in</u>) the cup on my desk.
5. I didn't see anyone I knew (on, <u>at</u>) the party.

■ Review Test

Underline the correct word or words in parentheses.

1. At the beach, the children enjoyed playing in the (<u>sand</u>, sands).
2. (Are, <u>There are</u>) more stars in the sky tonight than I have ever seen.
3. Doesn't watching such a sad movie make you feel (<u>depressed</u>, depressing)?
4. On my way to the restaurant I had a (depressed, <u>depressing</u>) thought: I had no money.

5. I'll never throw away my (<u>favorite old denim</u>, old favorite denim) jacket.

6. The girl's parents suspect her of (to use, <u>using</u>) drugs.

7. The old woman carefully hung the picture of her grandchildren (in, <u>on</u>) the wall.

8. That umbrella by the door (<u>belongs</u>, is belonging) to my uncle.

9. (<u>Happiness</u>, The happiness) is something everyone hopes to find in life.

10. Many people dislike (to wait, <u>waiting</u>) in a long line.

Sentence-Skills Diagnostic Test

Part 1

This diagnostic test will help check your knowledge of a number of sentence skills. In each item below, certain words are underlined. Write *X* in the answer space if you think a mistake appears at the underlined part. Write *C* in the answer space if you think the underlined part is correct.

The headings within the test ("Fragments," "Run-Ons," and so on) will give you clues to the mistakes to look for. However, you do not have to understand the heading to find a mistake. What you are checking is your own sense of effective written English.

Fragments

___X___   1. Because I didn't want to get wet. I waited for a break in the downpour. Then I ran for the car like an Olympic sprinter.

___C___   2. The baby birds chirped loudly, especially when their mother brought food to them. Their mouths gaped open hungrily.

___X___   3. Trying to avoid running into anyone. Cal wheeled his baby son around the crowded market. He wished that strollers came equipped with flashing hazard lights.

___X___   4. The old woman combed out her long, gray hair. She twisted it into two thick braids. And wrapped them around her head like a crown.

Run-Ons

___X___   5. Irene fixed fruits and healthy sandwiches for her son's lunch, he traded them for cupcakes, cookies, and chips.

___X___   6. Angie's dark eyes were the color of mink they matched her glowing complexion.

___C___   7. My mother keeps sending me bottles of vitamins, but I keep forgetting to take them.

_X_ 8. The little boy watched the line of ants march across the <u>ground, he</u> made a wall of Popsicle sticks to halt the ants' advance.

Standard English Verbs

_C_ 9. When she's upset, Mary <u>tells</u> her troubles to her houseplants.

_X_ 10. The street musician counted the coins in his donations basket and <u>pack</u> his trumpet in its case.

_X_ 11. I tried to pull off my rings, but they <u>was</u> stuck on my swollen fingers.

_X_ 12. Bella's car <u>have</u> a horn that plays six different tunes.

Irregular Verbs

_X_ 13. I've <u>swam</u> in this lake for years, and I've never seen it so shallow.

_X_ 14. The phone <u>rung</u> once and then stopped.

_C_ 15. Five different people had <u>brought</u> huge bowls of potato salad to the barbecue.

_C_ 16. The metal ice cube trays <u>froze</u> to the bottom of the freezer.

Subject-Verb Agreement

_X_ 17. The records in my collection <u>is</u> arranged in alphabetical order.

_C_ 18. There <u>was</u> only one burner working on the old gas stove.

_X_ 19. My aunt and uncle <u>gives</u> a party every Groundhog Day.

_X_ 20. One of my sweaters <u>have</u> moth holes in the sleeves.

Consistent Verb Tense

_C_ 21. After I turned off the ignition, the engine <u>continued</u> to sputter for several minutes.

_X_ 22. Before cleaning the oven, I lined the kitchen floor with newspapers, <u>open</u> the windows, and shook the can of aerosol foam.

Pronoun Reference, Agreement, and Point of View

_C_ 23. All visitors should stay in <u>their</u> cars while driving through the wild animal park.

_X_ 24. At the library, <u>they</u> showed me how to use the microfilm machines.

_X_ 25. As I slowed down at the scene of the accident, <u>you</u> could see long black skid marks on the highway.

Pronoun Types

_X_____ 26. My husband is more sentimental than <u>me</u>.

_C_____ 27. Andy and <u>I</u> made ice cream in an old-fashioned wooden machine.

Adjectives and Adverbs

_X_____ 28. Brian drives so <u>reckless</u> that no one will join his car pool.

_C_____ 29. Miriam pulled <u>impatiently</u> at the rusty zipper.

_X_____ 30. I am <u>more happier</u> with myself now that I earn my own money.

_C_____ 31. The last screw on the license plate was the <u>most worn</u> one of all.

Misplaced Modifiers

_X_____ 32. I stretched out on the lounge chair <u>wearing my bikini bathing suit</u>.

_X_____ 33. I replaced the shingle on the roof <u>that was loose</u>.

Dangling Modifiers

_X_____ 34. <u>While doing the dishes</u>, a glass shattered in the soapy water.

_C_____ 35. <u>Pedaling as fast as possible</u>, Todd tried to outrace the snapping dog.

Faulty Parallelism

_X_____ 36. Before I could take a bath, I had to pick up the damp towels on the floor, gather up the loose toys in the room, and <u>the tub had to be scrubbed out</u>.

_X_____ 37. I've tried several cures for my headaches, including drugs, meditation, exercise, and <u>massaging my head</u>.

Capital Letters

_C_____ 38. This <u>fall</u> we plan to visit Cape Cod.

_X_____ 39. Vern ordered a set of tools from the <u>spiegel</u> catalog.

_C_____ 40. When my <u>aunt</u> visits us, she insists on doing all the cooking.

_X_____ 41. Maureen asked, "<u>will</u> you split a piece of cheesecake with me?"

Numbers and Abbreviations

_X_____ 42. Before I could stop myself, I had eaten <u>6</u> glazed doughnuts.

_C_____ 43. At <u>10:45</u> A.M., a partial eclipse of the sun will begin.

_____X_____ 44. Derrick, who is now over six <u>ft.</u> tall, can no longer sleep comfortably in a twin bed.

End Marks

_____C_____ 45. Jane wondered if her husband was telling the <u>truth.</u>

_____C_____ 46. Does that stew need some <u>salt?</u>

Apostrophe

_____X_____ 47. <u>Elizabeths</u> thick, curly hair is her best feature.

_____X_____ 48. I tried to see through the interesting envelope sent to my sister but <u>couldnt.</u>

_____C_____ 49. <u>Pam's</u> heart almost stopped beating when Roger jumped out of the closet.

_____X_____ 50. The <u>logs'</u> in the fireplace crumbled in a shower of sparks.

Quotation Marks

_____C_____ 51. Someone once <u>said, "A lie has no legs and cannot stand."</u>

_____X_____ 52. <u>"This repair job could be expensive, the mechanic warned."</u>

_____C_____ 53. <u>"My greatest childhood fear," said Sheila, "was being sucked down the bathtub drain."</u>

_____X_____ 54. <u>"I was always afraid of everybody's father, said Midori, except my own."</u>

Comma

_____X_____ 55. The restaurant's "sundae bar" featured bowls of <u>whipped cream chopped nuts and chocolate sprinkles.</u>

_____C_____ 56. My <u>sister, who studies karate,</u> installed large practice mirrors in our basement.

_____X_____ 57. When I remove my thick <u>eyeglasses</u> the world turns into an out-of-focus movie.

_____C_____ 58. Gloria wrapped her son's presents in pages from the comics <u>section, and</u> she glued a small toy car atop each gift.

Spelling

_____X_____ 59. When Terry <u>practises</u> scales on the piano, her whole family wears earplugs.

_____X_____ 60. I wondered if it was <u>alright</u> to wear sneakers with my three-piece suit.

_____X_____ 61. The essay test question asked us to describe two different <u>theorys</u> of evolution.

_____X_____ 62. A <u>theif</u> stole several large hanging plants from Marlo's porch.

Omitted Words and Letters

C   63. After dark, I'm afraid to look in the closets or under the bed.

X   64. I turned on the television, but baseball game had been rained out.

X   65. Polar bear cubs stay with their mother for two year.

Commonly Confused Words

X   66. Before your about to start the car, press the gas pedal to the floor once.

X   67. The frog flicked it's tongue out and caught the fly.

X   68. I was to lonely to enjoy the party.

C   69. The bats folded their wings around them like leather overcoats.

Effective Word Choice

X   70. If the professor gives me a break, I might pass the final exam.

X   71. Harry worked like a dog all summer to save money for his tuition.

X   72. Because Monday is a holiday, sanitation engineers will pick up your trash on Tuesday.

C   73. Our family's softball game ended in an argument, as usual.

X   74. As for my own opinion, I feel that nuclear weapons should be banned.

X   75. This law is, for all intents and purposes, a failure.

Part 2 (Optional)

Do the following at your instructor's request. This second part of the test will provide more detailed information about skills you need to know. On separate paper, number and correct all the items you have marked with an *X*. For example, suppose you had marked the word groups below with an *X*. (Note that these examples are not taken from the actual test.)

4. <u>When I picked up the tire.</u> Something in my back snapped. I could not stand up straight as a result.

7. The phone started <u>ringing, then</u> the doorbell sounded as well.

15. <u>Marks</u> goal is to save enough money to get married next year.

29. Without checking the rearview <u>mirror the</u> driver pulled out into the passing lane.

Here is how you should write your corrections on a separate sheet of paper:
Many answers will vary; see Instructor's Manual for corrected sentences.

4. When I picked up the tire, something in my back snapped.

7. The phone started ringing, and then the doorbell sounded as well.

15. Mark's

29. mirror, the

There are over forty corrections to make in all.

Sentence-Skills Achievement Test

Part I

This achievement test will help you check your mastery of a number of sentence skills. In each item below, certain words are underlined. Write *X* in the answer space if you think a mistake appears at the underlined part. Write *C* in the answer space if you think the underlined part is correct.

The headings within the test ("Fragments," "Run-Ons," and so on) will give you clues to the mistakes to look for.

Fragments

_____X_____ 1. <u>When the town bully died.</u> Hundreds of people came to his funeral. They wanted to make sure he was dead.

_____C_____ 2. <u>Suzanne adores junk foods, especially onion-flavored potato chips.</u> She can eat an entire bag at one sitting.

_____X_____ 3. My brother stayed up all night. <u>Studying the rules in his driver's manual.</u> He wanted to get his license on the first try.

_____X_____ 4. Hector decided to take a study break. He picked up *TV Guide*. <u>And flipped through the pages to find that night's listings.</u>

Run-Ons

_____X_____ 5. Ronnie leaned forward in his <u>seat,</u> he could not hear what the instructor was saying.

_____X_____ 6. Our television set obviously needs <u>repairs the</u> color keeps fading from the picture.

_____C_____ 7. Nick and Fran enjoyed their trip to <u>Chicago, but</u> they couldn't wait to get home.

_____X_____ 8. I tuned in the weather forecast on the <u>radio, I</u> had to decide what to wear.

Standard English Verbs

___C___   9. My sister Louise <u>walks</u> a mile to the bus stop every day.

___X___   10. The play was ruined when the quarterback <u>fumble</u> the handoff.

___X___   11. When the last guests left our party, we <u>was</u> exhausted but happy.

___X___   12. I don't think my mother <u>have</u> gone out to a movie in years.

Irregular Verbs

___X___   13. My roommate and I <u>seen</u> a double feature this weekend.

___X___   14. My nephew must have <u>growed</u> six inches since last summer.

___C___   15. I should have <u>brought</u> a gift to the office Christmas party.

___C___   16. After playing touch football all afternoon, Al <u>drank</u> a quart of Gatorade.

Subject-Verb Agreement

___X___   17. The cost of those new tires <u>are</u> more than I can afford.

___C___   18. Nick and Fran <u>give</u> a New Year's Eve party every year.

___X___   19. There <u>was</u> only two slices of cake left on the plate.

___X___   20. Each of the fast-food restaurants <u>have</u> a breakfast special.

Consistent Verb Tense

___C___   21. After I folded the towels in the basket, I <u>remembered</u> that I hadn't washed them yet.

___X___   22. Before she decided to buy the wall calendar, Joanne <u>turns</u> its pages and looked at all the pictures.

Pronoun Reference, Agreement, and Point of View

___C___   23. All drivers should try <u>their</u> best to be courteous during rush hour.

___X___   24. When Bob went to the bank for a home improvement loan, <u>they</u> asked him for three credit references.

___X___   25. I like to shop at factory outlets because <u>you</u> can always get brand names at a discount.

Pronoun Types

_____X_____ 26. My brother writes much more neatly than <u>me</u>.

_____C_____ 27. Vonnie and <u>I</u> are both taking Introduction to Business this semester.

Adjectives and Adverbs

_____X_____ 28. When the elevator doors closed <u>sudden</u>, three people were trapped inside.

_____C_____ 29. The bag lady glared <u>angrily</u> at me when I offered her a dollar bill.

_____X_____ 30. Frank couldn't decide which vacation he liked <u>best</u>, a bicycle trip or a week at the beach.

_____C_____ 31. I find proofreading a paper much <u>more difficult</u> than writing one.

Misplaced Modifiers

_____X_____ 32. The car was parked along the side of the road <u>with a flat tire</u>.

_____X_____ 33. We bought a television set at our neighborhood video store <u>that has stereo sound</u>.

Dangling Modifiers

_____X_____ 34. <u>While looking for bargains at Sears</u>, an exercise bike caught my eye.

_____C_____ 35. <u>Hurrying to catch the bus</u>, Donna fell and twisted her ankle.

Faulty Parallelism

_____X_____ 36. Before she leaves for work, Ana makes her lunch, does fifteen minutes of calisthenics, and <u>her two cats have to be fed</u>.

_____X_____ 37. Three remedies for insomnia are warm milk, <u>taking a hot bath</u>, and sleeping pills.

Capital Letters

_____C_____ 38. Every <u>Saturday</u> I get up early, even though I have the choice of sleeping late.

_____X_____ 39. We stopped at the drugstore for some <u>crest</u> toothpaste.

_____C_____ 40. Rows of crocuses appear in my front yard every <u>spring</u>.

_____X_____ 41. The cashier said, "<u>sorry</u>, but children under three are not allowed in this theater."

Numbers and Abbreviations

___X___ 42. Our train finally arrived—2 hours late.

___C___ 43. Answers to the chapter questions start on page 293.

___X___ 44. Three yrs. from now, my new car will finally be paid off.

End Marks

___C___ 45. I had no idea who was inside the gorilla suit at the Halloween party.

___X___ 46. Are you taking the make-up exam.

Apostrophe

___X___ 47. My fathers favorite old television program is *Star Trek*.

___X___ 48. I couldnt understand a word of that lecture.

___C___ 49. My dentist's recommendation was that I floss after brushing my teeth.

___X___ 50. Three house's on our street are up for sale.

Quotation Marks

___C___ 51. Garfield the cat is fond of saying, "I never met a carbohydrate I didn't like."

___X___ 52. "This restaurant does not accept credit cards, the waiter said."

___X___ 53. Two foods that may prevent cancer," said the scientist, "are those old standbys spinach and carrots."

___X___ 54. "I can't get anything done," Dad complained, if you two insist on making all that noise."

Comma

___X___ 55. The snack bar offered overdone hamburgers rubbery hot dogs and soggy pizza.

___C___ 56. My sister, who regards every living creature as a holy thing, cannot even swat a housefly.

___X___ 57. When I smelled something burning I realized I hadn't turned off the oven.

___C___ 58. Marge plays the xylophone at parties, and her husband does Dracula imitations.

Spelling

_____X_____ 59. No one will be <u>admited</u> without a valid student identification card.

_____X_____ 60. Trisha <u>carrys</u> a full course load in addition to working as the night manager at a supermarket.

_____X_____ 61. Did you feel <u>alright</u> after eating Rodolfo's special chili?

_____X_____ 62. My parents were disappointed when I didn't enter the family <u>busines</u>.

Omitted Words and Letters

_____C_____ 63. <u>Both high schools in my hometown offer evening classes for adults.</u>

_____X_____ 64. <u>I opened new bottle of ketchup and then couldn't find the cap.</u>

_____X_____ 65. <u>Visiting hour for patients at this hospital are from noon to eight.</u>

Commonly Confused Words

_____X_____ 66. Shelley has always been <u>to</u> self-conscious to speak up in class.

_____X_____ 67. <u>Its</u> not easy to return to college after raising a family.

_____X_____ 68. "Thank you for <u>you're</u> generous contribution," the letter began.

_____C_____ 69. Nobody knew <u>whose</u> body had been found floating in the swimming pool.

Effective Word Choice

_____X_____ 70. My roommate keeps <u>getting on my case</u> about leaving clothing on the floor.

_____X_____ 71. Karla decided to <u>take the bull by the horns</u> and ask her boss for a raise.

_____X_____ 72. Although Lamont <u>accelerated his vehicle</u>, he was unable to pass the truck.

_____C_____ 73. When the movie <u>ended suddenly</u>, I felt I had been cheated.

_____X_____ 74. <u>In light of the fact that</u> I am on a diet, I have stopped eating between meals.

_____X_____ 75. <u>Personally, I do not think</u> that everyone should be allowed to vote.

Part 2 (Optional)

Do the following at your instructor's request. This second part of the test will provide more detailed information about which skills you have mastered and which skills you still need to work on. On separate paper, number and correct all the items you have marked with an *X*. For example, suppose you had marked the word groups below with an *X*. (Note that these examples were not taken from the actual test.)

4. <u>When I picked up the tire.</u> Something in my back snapped. I could not stand up straight as a result.

7. The phone started <u>ringing, then</u> the doorbell sounded as well.

15. <u>Marks</u> goal is to save enough money to get married next year.

29. Without checking the rearview <u>mirror the</u> driver pulled out into the passing lane.

Here is how you should write your corrections on a separate sheet of paper:
Many answers will vary; see Instructor's Manual for corrected sentences.

4. When I picked up the tire, something in my back snapped.

7. The phone started ringing, and then the doorbell sounded as well.

15. Mark's

29. mirror, the driver

There are more than forty corrections to make in all.

Answers to Introductory Activities and Practice Exercises in Part Two

This answer key can help you teach yourself. Use it to find out why you got some answers wrong—to uncover any weak spot in your understanding of a skill. By using the answer key in an honest and thoughtful way, you will master each skill and prepare yourself for many tests in this book that have no answer key.

SUBJECTS AND VERBS

Introductory Activity (page 89)

Answers will vary.

Practice 1 (91)

1. Fran froze
2. company offered
3. announcer talked
4. Brenda peeled
5. sunshine felt
6. backyard is
7. Alicia snagged
8. comb scratched
9. pen leaked
10. store carries

Practice 2 (92)

1. shows . . . were
2. burp is
3. sunglasses . . . look
4. voice sounds
5. Tamika became
6. lotion smells
7. Visitors . . . appear
8. vibrations are
9. cold feels
10. change . . . seems

Practice 3 (92)

1. light glowed
2. kite soared
3. Manuel caught
4. skaters shadowed
5. lights emphasized
6. Tracy reads
7. glasses slipped
8. Jane allowed
9. squirrel jumped
10. Carpenters constructed

Practice (94)

1. Stripes of sunlight glowed on the kitchen floor.
2. The black panther draped its powerful body along the thick tree branch.
3. A line of impatient people snaked from the box office to the street.
4. At noon, every siren in town wails for fifteen minutes.
5. The tops of my Bic pens always disappear after a day or two.
6. Joanne removed the lint from her black socks with Scotch tape.
7. The mirrored walls of the skyscraper reflected the passing clouds.
8. Debris from the accident littered the intersection.
9. Above the heads of the crowd, a woman swayed on a narrow ledge.
10. The squashed grapes in the bottom of the vegetable bin oozed sticky purple juice.

Practice (95)

1. Einstein could have passed
2. She could have been killed
3. children did not recognize
4. strikers have been fasting
5. I could not see
6. People may be wearing
7. He should have studied

8. Rosa has been soaking
9. lines . . . were flying
10. brother can ask

Practice (96)

1. trees creaked and shuddered
2. girl fell . . . and landed
3. I will vacuum . . . and change
4. sun shone . . . and turned
5. Sam and Billy greased
6. man and . . . friend rode
7. sister and I . . . race
8. Nia breathed and . . . began
9. Phil draped . . . and pretended
10. wrestler and opponent strutted . . . and pounded

FRAGMENTS

Introductory Activity (99)

1. verb
2. subject
3. subject . . . verb
4. express a complete thought

Practice 1 (103)

Answers will vary.

Practice 2 (104)

Note   The underlined part shows the fragment (or that part of the original fragment not changed during correction).

1. Since she was afraid of muggers, Barbara carried a small can of Mace on her key ring.
2. When I began watching the TV mystery movie, I remembered that I had seen it before.
3. Tulips had begun to bloom until a freakish spring snowstorm blanketed the garden.
4. Whenever I'm in the basement and the phone rings, I don't run up to answer it. If the message is important, the person will call back.
5. Since she is a new student, Carla feels shy and insecure. She thinks she is the only person who doesn't know anyone else.

Practice 1 (106)

1. Julie spent an hour at her desk, staring at a blank piece of paper.
2. Rummaging around in the kitchen drawer, Tyrone found the key he had misplaced a year ago.
3. As a result, I lost my place in the checkout line.

Practice 2 (107)

Rewritten versions may vary.

1. I tossed and turned for hours.
    Or: Tossing and turning for hours, I felt like a blanket being tumbled dry.
2. It fluffed its feathers to keep itself warm.
    Or: A sparrow landed on the icy windowsill, fluffing its feathers to keep itself warm.
3. The reason was that she had to work the next day.
    Or: Alma left the party early, the reason being that she had to work the next day.
4. Grasping the balance beam with her powdered hands, the gymnast executed a handstand.
5. To cover his bald spot, Walt combed long strands of hair over the top of his head.

Practice 1 (109)

1. For instance, he folds a strip of paper into the shape of an accordion.
2. Marco stuffed the large green peppers with hamburger meat, cooked rice, and chopped parsley.
3. For example, he craves Bugles and Doritos.

Practice 2 (109)

Rewritten versions may vary.

1. For instance, he has his faded sweatshirt from high school.
2. For example, she borrows my sweaters.
3. To improve her singing, Amber practiced some odd exercises, such as flapping her tongue and fluttering her lips.
    Or: She flapped her tongue and fluttered her lips.
4. For example, she had put on forty pounds.
5. Stanley wanted a big birthday cake with candles spelling out STAN.

Practice (111)

Rewritten answers may vary.

1. Then she quickly folded her raggedy towels and faded sheets.
2. Wally took his wool sweaters out of storage and found them full of moth holes.
   Or: He found them full of moth holes.
3. Also, she is learning two computer languages.
4. Then he hides under the bed.
5. A tiny bug crawled across my paper and sat down in the middle of a sentence.
   Or: And it sat down in the middle of a sentence.

RUN-ONS

Introductory Activity (119)

1. period
2. but
3. semicolon
4. although

Practice 1 (122)

1. coffee. His
2. way. She
3. coughing. A
4. me. It
5. time. The
6. machine. We
7. closely. They
8. Lauren. She
9. victims. They
10. late. The

Practice 2 (123)

1. cockroaches. Both
2. blood. The
3. counselor. She's
4. death. He
5. seen. One
6. beautiful. Now
7. penalty. The
8. down. It
9. Germany. In
10. request. He

Practice 3 (123)

Answers will vary.

Practice 1 (125)

1. drawer, but
2. paper, for
3. therapy, so
4. drive, for
5. on, and
6. summer, so
7. truck, so
8. break, but
9. map, for
10. fit, so

Practice 2 (125)

Answers will vary.

Practice (127)

1. backward; his
2. indestructible; it
3. cards; she
4. moth; it
5. book; it

Practice 1 (128)

Answers may vary.

1. month; on the other hand, they
2. sick; therefore, she (*or* consequently *or* as a result *or* thus)
3. hydrant; however, she
4. guests; furthermore, he (*or* also *or* moreover *or* in addition)
5. money; consequently, she (*or* therefore *or* as a result *or* thus)

Practice 2 (128)

1. wait; however, she
2. computers; as a result, she
3. abused; moreover, many
4. smoking; otherwise, I
5. carefully; nevertheless, the

Practice 1 (130)

Answers may vary.

1. After
2. before
3. When
4. If
5. until

Practice 2 (130)

1. Even though I had a campus map, I still could not find my classroom building.
2. When a cat food commercial came on, Marie started to sing along with the jingle.
3. Since the phone in the next apartment rings all the time, I'm beginning to get used to the sound.
4. After Michael gulped two cups of coffee, his heart began to flutter.
5. As a car sped around the corner, it sprayed slush all over the pedestrians.

SENTENCE VARIETY I

The Simple Sentence

Practice (138)

Answers will vary.

The Compound Sentence

Practice 1 (138)

Answers may vary; possible answers are given.

1. I am studying computer science, and my sister is majoring in communications.
2. The children started hitting each other, so I made them turn off the TV.
3. Betsy put masking tape on her forehead at night, for she wanted to stop wrinkles from forming.
4. The pizza was covered with salty anchovies and pepperoni, but he picked up the salt shaker as usual.
5. She felt faint, so she grabbed the metal lamppost.

Practice 2 (139)

Answers will vary.

The Complex Sentence

Practice 1 (141)

Answers may vary; possible answers are given.

1. Because the movie disgusted Dena, she walked out after twenty minutes.
2. After the house had been burglarized, Dave couldn't sleep soundly for several months.
3. When my vision begins to fade, I know I'd better get some sleep.
4. Since the family would need a place to sleep, Fred told the movers to unload the mattresses first.
5. When the hurricane hit the coast, we crisscrossed our windows with strong tape.

Practice 2 (142)

Answers may vary; possible answers are given.

1. Although the muffler shop advertised same-day service, my car wasn't ready for three days.
2. Because the high-blood-pressure pills produced dangerous side effects, the government banned them.
3. While Phil lopped dead branches off the tree, Michelle stacked them into piles on the ground below.
4. Anne wedged her handbag tightly under her arm because she was afraid of muggers.
5. Although Ellen counted the cash three times, the total still didn't tally with the amount on the register tape.

Practice 3 (142)

Answers may vary; possible answers are given.

1. The boy who limps was in a motorcycle accident.
2. Raquel, who is my neighbor, is a champion weight lifter.
3. The two screws that held the bicycle frame together were missing from the assembly kit.
4. The letter that arrived today is from my ex-wife.
5. The tall hedge which surrounded the house muffled the highway noise.

Practice 4 (144)

Answers will vary.

The Compound-Complex Sentence

Practice 1 (144)

Answers will vary.

1. Since . . . for
2. When . . . and
3. until . . . so
4. When . . . or
5. but . . . because

Practice 2 (144)

Answers will vary.

Review of Coordination and Subordination

Practice (145)

Answers will vary. Many other combinations are possible.

1. I needed butter to make the cookie batter, but I couldn't find any, so I used vegetable oil instead.
2. Although Tess had worn glasses for fifteen years, she decided to get contact lenses. She would be able to see better, and she would look more glamorous.
3. When the children at the day-care center took their naps, they unrolled their sleeping mats, and they piled their shoes and sneakers in a corner.
4. When Jerry dialed the police emergency number, he received a busy signal. He dropped the phone and ran, for he didn't have time to call back.

5. Louise disliked walking home from the bus stop, for the street had no overhead lights, and it was lined with abandoned buildings.

6. When the rain hit the hot pavement, plumes of steam rose from the blacktop. Cars slowed to a crawl, for the fog obscured the drivers' vision.

7. While his car went through the automated car wash, Harry watched from the sidelines. Floppy brushes slapped the car's doors, and sprays of water squirted onto the roof.

8. Since the pipes had frozen and the heat had gone off, we phoned the plumber. He couldn't come for days because he had been swamped with emergency calls.

9. When my car developed an annoying rattle, I took it to the service station. The mechanic looked under the hood, but he couldn't find what was wrong.

10. The childproof cap on the aspirin bottle would not budge even though the arrows on the bottleneck and cap were lined up. When I pried the cap with my fingernails, one nail snapped off, and the cap still adhered tightly to the bottle.

STANDARD ENGLISH VERBS

Introductory Activity (152)

played . . . plays

hoped . . . hopes

juggled . . . juggles

1. past time . . . -ed or –d
2. present time . . . . -s

Practice 1 (154)

1.	wears	6.	distributes
2.	says	7.	C
3.	subscribes	8.	feeds
4.	believes	9.	overcooks
5.	sees	10.	polishes

Practice 2 (155)

Lou works for a company that delivers singing telegrams. Sometimes he puts on a sequined tuxedo or wears a Cupid costume. He composes his own songs for birthdays, anniversaries, bachelor parties, and other occasions. Then he shows up at a certain place and surprises the victim. He sings a song that includes personal details, which he gets in advance, about the recipient of the telegram. Lou loves the astonished looks on other people's faces; he also enjoys earning money by making people happy on special days.

Practice 1 (156)

1.	turned	6.	washed
2.	bounced	7.	cracked
3.	paged	8.	collected
4.	crushed	9.	pulled
5.	C	10.	lacked

Practice 2 (156)

Mrs. Bayne strolled across the street to her neighbor's yard sale. She examined the rack of used clothes, checked the prices, and accidentally knocked a blouse off its hanger. She poked through a box of children's toys, spilling a carton full of wooden blocks. She leafed through some old magazines, ripping a few of the brittle pages. At a table of kitchen equipment, she pushed down the buttons on a toaster and forced them up again. Mrs. Bayne then wandered off without buying anything.

Practice 1 (158)

1.	is	6.	was
2.	has	7.	had
3.	is	8.	was
4.	does	9.	did
5.	did	10.	was

Practice 2 (159)

1.	is	6.	do
2.	has	7.	do
3.	has	8.	has
4.	are	9.	does
5.	are	10.	are

Practice 3 (159)

My friend Tyrell is a real bargain-hunter. If any store has a sale, he runs right over and buys two or three things, whether or not they are things he needs. Tyrell does his best, also, to get something for nothing. Last week, he was reading the paper and saw that the First National Bank's new downtown offices were offering gifts for new accounts. "Those freebies sure do look good," Tyrell said. So he went downtown, opened an account, and had the manager give him a Big Ben alarm clock. When he got back with the clock, he was smiling. "I am a very busy man," he told me, "and I really need the free time."

IRREGULAR VERBS

Introductory Activity (161)

1. R . . . screamed . . . screamed
2. I . . . wrote . . . written
3. I . . . stole . . . stolen
4. R . . . asked . . . asked
5. R . . . kissed . . . kissed
6. I . . . chose . . . chosen
7. I . . . rode . . . ridden
8. R . . . chewed . . . chewed
9. I . . . thought . . . thought
10. R . . . danced . . . danced

Practice 1 (165)

1. took
2. chosen
3. caught
4. stolen
5. saw
6. gone
7. fallen
8. sworn
9. shrunk
10. spoken

Practice 2 (165)

1. (a) loses
   (b) lost
   (c) lost
2. (a) brings
   (b) brought
   (c) brought
3. (a) swim
   (b) swam
   (c) swum
4. (a) goes
   (b) went
   (c) gone
5. (a) begins
   (b) began
   (c) begun
6. (a) hides
   (b) hid
   (c) hidden
7. (a) choose
   (b) chose
   (c) chosen
8. (a) speak
   (b) spoke
   (c) spoken
9. (a) takes
   (b) took
   (c) taken
10. (a) wake
    (b) woke
    (c) woken

Practice (168)

1. laid
2. lay
3. laid
4. lying
5. lay

Practice (169)

1. set
2. set
3. sit
4. set
5. setting

Practice (170)

1. rise
2. raised
3. raised
4. rose
5. raised

SUBJECT-VERB AGREEMENT

Introductory Activity (172)

Correct: There were many applicants for the position.

Correct: The pictures in that magazine are very controversial.

Correct: Everybody usually watches the lighted numbers in an elevator.

1. applicants . . . pictures
2. singular . . . singular

Practice (174)

1. leaders of the union have
2. One of Omar's pencil sketches hangs
3. days of anxious waiting finally end
4. members of the car pool chip
5. woman with the teased, sprayed hairdo looks
6. addition of heavy shades to my sunny windows allows
7. houses in the old whaling village have
8. stack of baseball cards in my little brother's bedroom is
9. puddles of egg white spread
10. box of Raisinets sells

Practice (175)

1. were . . . trucks
2. are . . . coyotes
3. are rows
4. are . . . boots
5. was . . . boy
6. was . . . animal
7. is . . . shampooer
8. was . . . stream
9. is . . . box
10. is . . . sign

Practice (176)

1. is
2. remembers
3. fit
4. has
5. wanders
6. needs
7. keeps
8. sneaks
9. is
10. eats

Practice (177)

1. look
2. are
3. confuse
4. are
5. star

Practice (177)

1. roam
2. begins
3. thunder
4. fear
5. tastes

CONSISTENT VERB TENSE

Introductory Activity (182)

Mistakes in verb tense: Alex discovers . . . calls a . . . present . . . past

Practice (183)

1. smeared
2. started
3. breathed
4. saw
5. rolled
6. points
7. swallows
8. pushed
9. coat
10. notices

ADDITIONAL INFORMATION ABOUT VERBS

Practice (Tense; 189)

1. had watched
2. has written
3. am taking
4. had lifted
5. has improved
6. are protesting
7. have dreaded
8. has vowed *or* is vowing
9. were peeking
10. are getting *or* have gotten

Practice (Verbals; 190)

1. P
2. G
3. I
4. G
5. I
6. P
7. P
8. P
9. G
10. I

Practice (Active and Passive Verbs; 191)

Answers may vary.

1. The beautician snipped off Carla's long hair.
2. The parents protested the teachers' strike.
3. The alert bank teller tripped the silent alarm.
4. Relentless bloodhounds tracked the escaped convicts.
5. A famous entertainer donated the new CAT scanner to the hospital.
6. A stock clerk dropped a gallon glass jar of pickles in the supermarket aisle.
7. A car struck the deer as it crossed the highway.
8. My doctor referred me to a specialist in hearing problems.
9. Family photographs cover one wall of my living room.
10. Fear gripped the town during the accident at the nuclear power plant.

PRONOUN REFERENCE, AGREEMENT AND POINT OF VIEW

Introductory Activity (194)

1. b
2. b
3. b

Practice (196)

Note The practice sentences could be rewritten in various ways; the following are examples.

1. When we pulled into the gas station, the attendant told us one of our tires looked soft.
2. Nora broke the heavy ashtray when she dropped it on her foot.
3. Vicky asked for a grade transcript at the registrar's office, and the clerk told her it would cost three dollars.
4. Don't touch the freshly painted walls with your hands unless the walls are dry.
5. Maurice's habit of staying up half the night watching <u>Chiller Theater</u> really annoys his wife.

6. Robin went to the store's personnel office to be interviewed for a sales position.

7. Leon told his brother, "You need to lose some weight."

8. I wrote to the insurance company but haven't received an answer.

9. I went to the doctor to see what he could do about my itchy, bloodshot eyes.

10. I took the loose pillows off the chairs and sat on the pillows.
    Or: I sat on the loose pillows, which I had taken off the chairs.

Practice (198)

1. it
2. them
3. they
4. their
5. it

Practice (200)

1. her
2. he
3. his
4. his
5. she
6. its
7. her
8. his
9. their
10. his

Practice (202)

1. we saw
2. I can buy
3. we were given
4. we relax
5. they serve
6. I get depressed
7. I save
8. he or she could make
9. she can buy
10. I can stop

PRONOUN TYPES

Introductory Activity (205)

Correct sentences:
Andy and I enrolled in a computer course.
The police officer pointed to my sister and me.
Lola prefers men who take pride in their bodies.
The players are confident that the league championship is theirs.
Those concert tickets are too expensive.
Our parents should spend some money on themselves for a change.

Practice 1 (208)

2. I (*S*)
3. her (*O*)
4. me (*O*)
5. her and him (*O*)
6. I (*can* is understood) (*S*)
7. We (*S*)
8. she (*S*)
9. me (*O*)
10. he (*S*)

Practice 2 (209)

Answers will vary. Below are some possibilities.

2. me *or* her *or* him *or* them
3. I *or* she *or* he
4. I *or* she *or* he *or* they
5. me *or* him *or* her *or* them
6. I *or* he *or* she *or* they
7. them
8. him *or* her *or* them
9. I *or* he *or* she
10. I *or* she *or* he

Practice 1 (211)

1. who
2. which
3. whom
4. who
5. who

Practice 2 (211)

Answers will vary.

Practice (213)

1. hers
2. mine
3. ours
4. its
5. their

Practice 1 (214)

1. This
2. Those
3. These
4. Those
5. that

Practice 2 (214)

Answers will vary.

Practice (215)

1. ourselves
2. himself
3. themselves
4. yourself
5. ourselves

ADJECTIVE AND ADVERBS

Introductory Activity (218)

Answers will vary for 1–4.

adjective . . . adverb . . . *ly* . . . *er* . . . *est*

Practice 1 (220)

1. kinder . . . kindest
2. more ambitious . . . most ambitious
3. more generous . . . most generous
4. finer . . . finest
5. more likable . . . most likeable

Practice 2 (221)

1. thickest
2. lazier
3. harshest
4. more flexible
5. worse
6. best
7. less
8. less vulnerable
9. most wasteful
10. shinier

Practice (222)

1. hesitantly
2. easily
3. sharply
4. abruptly
5. aggressive
6. regretfully
7. quickly
8. messily
9. envious
10. terribly

Practice (223)

1. well
2. good
3. well
4. good
5. well

MISPLACED MODIFIERS

Introductory Activity (225)

1. Intended: The farmers were wearing masks.
   Unintended: The apple trees were wearing masks.
2. Intended: The woman had a terminal disease.
   Unintended: The faith healer had a terminal disease.

Practice 1 (226)

Note In the corrections below, the underlined part shows what had been a misplaced modifier. In some cases, other corrections are possible.

1. Driving along the wooded road, we noticed several dead animals.
2. In her mind, Maya envisioned the flowers that would bloom.
3. In my tuxedo, I watched my closest friends being married.
4. Zoe carried her new coat, which was trimmed with fur, on her arm.
5. We just heard on the radio that all major highways were flooded.
6. Fresh-picked blueberries covered almost the entire kitchen counter.
7. Making sounds of contentment, Betty licked the homemade peach ice cream.
   Or: Betty, making sounds of contentment, licked the homemade peach ice cream.
8. With a grin, the salesman confidently demonstrated the vacuum cleaner.
9. Dressed in a top hat and tails, Natasha is delivering singing telegrams.
10. The local drama group badly needs people to build scenery.

Practice 2 (228)

1. With a pounding heart, I opened my mouth for the dentist.
2. Newspapers all over the world announced that the fighter jets had landed.
3. Newborn kangaroos, which resemble blind, naked worms, crawl into their mothers' pouches.
4. Bruce Springsteen's latest album has sold almost five million copies.
5. Tanya proudly deposited in her savings account the fifty dollars she had earned typing term papers.

DANGLING MODIFIERS

Introductory Activity (231)

1. Intended: The giraffe was munching leaves.
   Unintended: The children were munching leaves.
2. Intended: Michael was arriving home.
   Unintended: The neighbors were arriving home.

Practice 1 (233)

1. The dog warden had the stray, which was foaming at the mouth, put to sleep.
2. Marian finally found her slippers, which had been kicked carelessly under the bed.
3. I tried out the old swing set, which was rusty with disuse.
4. The manager decided to replace his starting pitcher, who had given up four straight hits.
5. The farmers lost their entire tomato crop, which had frozen on the vines.
6. *C*
7. The audience cheered wildly as the elephants, which were dancing on their hind legs, paraded by.
8. Marta took the overdone meat loaf, which was burned beyond all recognition, from the oven.
9. We decided to replace the dining room wallpaper, which was tattered, faded, and hanging in shreds.
10. A person can keep membership cards clean by sealing them in plastic.
    Or: When sealed in plastic, membership cards can be kept clean.

Practice 2 (234)

Answers will vary.

FAULTY PARALLELISM

Introductory Activity (237)

Correct sentences:

   I use my computer to write papers, to search the Internet, and to play video games.

   One option the employees had was to take a cut in pay; the other was to work longer hours.

   Dad's favorite chair has a torn cushion, a stained armrest, and a musty odor.

Practice 1 (239)

1. waved pennants
2. to stay indoors

3. make a cream sauce
4. turn down the heat
5. overdone hamburgers
6. coughed
7. demanding
8. drinking two milk shakes
9. puts a frozen waffle into the toaster
10. to leave the company

Practice 2 (240)

Answers will vary.

SENTENCE VARIETY II

-ing Word Groups

Practice 1 (246)

Answers may vary; possible answers are given.

1. Fluffing out its feathers, the sparrow tried to keep warm.
2. Squeezing the tube as hard as I could, I managed to get enough toothpaste on my brush.
3. Checking the glass-faced gauges, the janitor started up the enormous boiler.
4. Staring straight ahead, the runner set his feet into the starting blocks.
5. The produce clerk, chatting with each customer, cheerfully weighed bags of fruit and vegetables.

PRACTICE 2 (246)

Answers will vary.

-ed Word Groups

Practice 1 (247)

Answers may vary; possible answers are given.

1. Bored with the talk show, I dozed off.
2. Crinkled with age, the old dollar bill felt like tissue paper.
3. Crowded into a tiny, windowless room, the students acted nervous and edgy.
4. Loaded down with heavy bags of groceries, I waited for someone to open the door.
5. Tired of his conservative wardrobe, Ron bought a green-striped suit.

Practice 2 (248)

Answers may vary.

-ly Openers

Practice 1 (248)

1. Abruptly, Clarissa hung up on the telemarketer.
2. Casually, the thief slipped one of the watches into her coat sleeve.
3. Swiftly, I tugged on my shoes and pants as the doorbell rang.
4. Gruffly, the defense lawyer cross-examined the witnesses.
5. Carefully, Estelle poked the corner of a handkerchief into her eye.

Practice 2 (249)

Answers will vary.

To Openers

Practice 1 (250)

1. To anchor the flapping tablecloth, we set bricks on the ends of the picnic table.
2. To break up the coating of ice, Darryl scraped the windshield with a plastic credit card.
3. To make the basketball game more even, we gave our opponents a ten-point advantage.
4. To give my wife a rest, I offered to drive the next five hundred miles.
5. To feed the unexpected guests, Fran added Hamburger Helper to the ground beef.

Practice 2 (250)

Answers will vary.

Prepositional Phrase Openers

Practice 1 (251)

Suggested combinations are shown below. Other combinations are possible.

1. On the bus, the old man wrote down my address with a stubby pencil.

2. During the day, special bulletins about the election returns interrupted regular programs.
3. At 6:00 A.M., my clock radio turned itself on with a loud blast of rock music.
4. At the concert, the security guard looked in Sue's pocketbook for concealed bottles.
5. On the highway, a plodding turtle crawled toward the grassy shoulder of the road.

Practice 2 (252)

Answers will vary.

Series of Items: Adjectives

Practice 1 (252)

1. Impatient and excited, the child gazed at the large, mysterious gift box.
2. Sticky juice squirted out of the fuzzy crushed caterpillar.
3. The battered car dangled from the gigantic yellow crane.
4. Patty squeezed her swollen, tender, sunburned feet into the tight shoes.
5. The tall white-aproned cook flipped the thick, juicy hamburgers on the grooved metal grill.

Practice 2 (254)

Answers will vary.

Series of Items: Verbs

Practice 1 (254)

1. The bank robber donned his gloves, twirled the lock, and opened the door of the vault.
2. Fans at the rock concert popped balloons, set off firecrackers, and dropped bottles from the balcony.
3. The doctor slid the needle into Gordon's arm, missed the vein, and tried again.
4. The magician walked over hot coals, lay on a bed of nails, and stuck pins into his hands.
5. The journalists surrounded the president, shouted questions, and snapped pictures.

Practice 2 (255)

Answers will vary.

PAPER FORMAT

Introductory Activity (259)

In "A," the title is capitalized and centered and has no quotation marks around it; there is a blank line between the title and the body of the paper; the first line is indented; there are left and right margins around the body of the paper; no words are incorrectly hyphenated.

Practice 1 (261)

2. Do not use quotation marks around the title.
3. Capitalize the major words in the title (Too Small to Fight Back).
4. Skip a line between the title and the first line of the paper.
5. Indent the first line of the paper.
6. Keep margins on both sides of the paper.

Practice 2 (261)

Here are some possible titles:

1. My First-Grade Teacher
2. My Hardest Year
3. My Father's Sense of Humor
4. Ways to Conserve Energy
5. Violence in the Movies

Practice 3 (262)

1. Lack of communication is often the reason why a relationship comes to an end.
2. Educational TV programs are in trouble today for several reasons.
3. Correct
4. The worst vacation I ever had began when my brother suggested that we rent a large van and drive to Colorado.
5. Most professional athletes have been pampered since grade school days.

CAPITAL LETTERS

Introductory Activity (264)

1–13: Answers will vary, but all should be capitalized.
14–16: On . . . "Let's . . . I

Practice (266)

1. Fourth . . . July . . . Veterans' Day

2. When . . . I
3. Toyota . . . Long Island Expressway
4. *Guide . . . Sixty Minutes*
5. National Bank . . . General Electric
6. Melrose Diner . . . Business Institute
7. A Sound . . . Thunder
8. Pacific School . . . Cosmetology
9. Sears . . . Ninth Street
10. Tang . . . Swift's

Practice (270)

1. Uncle Harry
2. Bic . . . Snoopy
3. Congressman Hughes
4. Native . . . West Coast
5. Introduction . . . Astronomy . . . General Biology

Practice (271)

1. high school . . . principal . . . discipline
2. father . . . creature . . . wing
3. skull . . . hair . . . bones
4. monument . . . settlers' . . . plague . . . locusts
5. motorcycle . . . tractor-trailer . . . motel

NUMBERS AND ABBREVIATIONS

Introductory Activity (276)

Correct choices:

First sentence: 8:55 . . . 65 percent
Second sentence: Nine . . . forty-five
Second sentence: brothers . . . mountain
Second sentence: hours . . . English

Practice (278)

1. five
2. eight . . . fifty-six
3. 10:30
4. five o'clock
5. 65
6. seventy-two
7. 12
8. 600 . . . 80
9. November 3, 1992,
10. *The Three Musketeers* . . . two

Practice (279)

1. department . . . purchase
2. Route . . . Florida
3. America . . . pounds
4. pair . . . inch
5. appointment . . . doctor . . . month
6. library . . . minutes . . . magazine
7. teaspoon . . . French
8. license . . . driving . . . road
9. finish . . . assignment . . . point
10. limit . . . senator . . . representative

END MARKS

Introductory Activity (281)

1. depressed.   3. parked.
2. paper?   4. control!

Practice (283)

1. house?   6. working?"
2. it.   7. Shark!"
3. tiger!   8. bottle.
4. mower?   9. drain.
5. chip.   10. leaflets.

APOSTROPHE

Introductory Activity (285)

1. To show ownership or possession
2. To indicate missing letters and shortened spellings
3. Because *families* signals a plural noun, while *family's* indicates ownership or possession

Apostrophe in Contractions

Practice 1 (286)

shouldn't	won't	who's
doesn't	they're	wouldn't
isn't	can't	aren't

Practice 2 (287)

1. you'll . . . it's   4. I'm . . . I'm
2. hadn't . . . couldn't   5. Where's . . . who's
3. isn't . . . doesn't

Practice 3 (287)

Answers will vary.

Practice (288)

1. It's . . . it's   4. whose . . . who's
2. they're . . . their   5. it's . . . your . . . who's
3. You're . . . your

Apostrophe to Show Ownership or Possession

Practice 1 (289)

1. The assassin's rifle   6. the president's wife
2. his mother's inheritance 7. The mugger's hand
3. Ali's throat   8. Harry's briefcase
4. Sam's parking space   9. Sandy's shoulder bag
5. The chef's hat   10. The dog's leash

Practice 2 (290)

2. instructor's   7. Brian's
3. astrologer's   8. Nita's
4. Ellen's   9. Ted's
5. lemonade's   10. hypnotist's
6. sister's

Practice 3 (291)

Sentences will vary.

2. friend's   4. teammate's
3. cashier's   5. brother's

Apostrophe versus Simple Plurals

Practice (292)

1. diners: diner's, meaning "the hamburgers of the diner"
   hamburgers: simple plural meaning more than one hamburger
   steaks: simple plural meaning more than one steak
2. San Franciscos: San Francisco's, meaning "the cable cars of San Francisco"
   cars: simple plural meaning more than one car
   hills: simple plural meaning more than one hill
3. brothers: brother's, meaning "the collection of my brother"
   cards: simple plural meaning more than one card
   boxes: simple plural meaning more than one box

4. toothpicks: simple plural meaning more than one toothpick
   years: year's, meaning "the fashions of this year"
   fashions: simple plural meaning more than one fashion
5. Pedros: Pedro's, meaning "the blood pressure of Pedro"
   minutes: simple plural meaning more than one minute
   spaces: simple plural meaning more than one space
6. write-ups: simple plural meaning more than one write-up
   Rubys: Ruby's, meaning "the promotion of Ruby"
   coworkers: simple plural meaning more than one co-worker
7. sons: son's, meaning "the fort of my son"
   pieces: simple plural meaning more than one piece
   nails: simple plural meaning more than one nail
   shingles: simple plural meaning more than one shingle
8. mayors: mayor's, meaning "the double-talk of the mayor"
   reporters: simple plural meaning more than one reporter
   heads: simple plural meaning more than one head
   notebooks: simple plural meaning more than one notebook
9. cuts: simple plural meaning more than one cut
   boxers: boxer's, meaning "the left eye of the boxer"
   rounds: simple plural meaning more than one round
10. cafeterias: cafeteria's, meaning "the loudspeakers of the cafeteria"
    loudspeakers: simple plural meaning more than one loudspeaker
    exams: simple plural meaning more than one exam

Apostrophe with Plural Words Ending in -s

Practice (294)

1. stores' windows
2. friends' problems
3. Cowboys' new quarterback
4. students' insect collections
5. voters' wish

QUOTATION MARKS

Introductory Activity (299)

1. Quotation marks set off the exact words of a speaker.
2. Commas and periods following quotations go inside quotation marks.

Practice 1 (301)

1. "This is the tenth commercial in a row," complained Niko.

2. The police officer said sleepily, "I could really use a cup of coffee."
3. My boss asked me to step into his office and said, "Joanne, how would you like a raise?"
4. "I'm out of work again," Miriam sighed.
5. "I didn't know this movie was R-rated!" Lorraine gasped.
6. "Why does my dog always wait until it rains before he wants to go out?" Donovon asked.
7. A sign over the box office read, "Please form a single line and be patient."
8. "Unless I run three miles a day," Marty said, "my legs feel like lumpy oatmeal."
9. "I had an uncle who knew when he was going to die," claimed Dan. "He saw the date in a dream."
10. The unusual notice in the newspaper read, "Young farmer would be pleased to hear from young lady with tractor. Send photograph of tractor."

Practice 2 (301)

1. The officer said, "I'm giving you a ticket."
2. "Please wait your turn," the frantic clerk begged.
3. Phil yelled, "Where's the Drano?"
4. "These directions don't make any sense," Lin muttered.
5. "Inside every fat person," someone once said, "is a thin person struggling to get out."

Practice 3 (302)

Answers will vary.

Practice 1 (303)

2. Marian exclaimed, "It was the worst day of my life."
3. Lew said, "Tell me all about it."
4. Marian insisted, "You wouldn't understand my job problems."
5. Lew said, "I will certainly try."

Practice 2 (303)

1. He said that he needed a vacation.
2. Gretchen said that purple was her favorite color.
3. She asked the handsome stranger if she could buy him a drink.
4. My brother asked if anyone had seen his frog.
5. Fran complained that she married a man who falls asleep during horror movies.

Practice (305)

1. My recently divorced sister refused to be in the talent show when she was told she'd have to sing "Love Is a Many-Splendored Thing."

2. Disgusted by the constant dripping noise, Brian opened his copy of Handy Home Repairs to the chapter entitled "Everything about the Kitchen Sink."

3. My little brother has seen the movie Star Wars at least eight times.

4. Before they bought new car tires, Nick and Fran studied the article "Testing Tires" in the February, 1993, issue of Consumer Reports.

5. Many people mistakenly think that Huckleberry Finn and The Adventures of Tom Sawyer are children's books only.

6. I just found out that the musical My Fair Lady is taken from a play by George Bernard Shaw called Pygmalion.

7. The ending of Shirley Jackson's story "The Lottery" really surprised me.

8. I sang the song "Mack the Knife" in our high school production of The Threepenny Opera.

9. Unless he's studied the TV Guide listings thoroughly, my father won't turn on his television.

10. Stanley dreamed that both Time and Newsweek had decided to use him in their feature article "Man of the Year."

COMMA

Introductory Activity (309)

1. a.   news, a movie, a *Honeymooners* rerun,
        check, write your account number on the back,

2. b.   indoors,
        car,

3. c.   opossum, an animal much like the kangaroo,
        Derek, who was recently arrested,

4. d.   pre-registration, but
        intersection, and

5. e.   said, "Why
        interview," said David, "I

6. f.   1,500,000
        Highway, Jersey City, New Jersey, . . . January 26, 1998,

Practice 1 (311)

1. rackets, a volleyball, and a first-aid kit
2. comics, the sports page, and the personals
3. birdbath, two stone deer, a flagpole, and a plastic daisy

Practice 2 (311)

1. A metal tape measure, a pencil, a ruler, and a hammer dangled from the carpenter's pockets.

2. The fortune-teller uncovered the crystal ball, peered into it, and began to predict my future.

3. That hairdresser is well-known for her frizzy perms, butchered haircuts, and brassy hair colorings.

Practice 1 (312)

1. hands,
2. storm,
3. help,

Practice 2 (312)

1. In order to work at that fast-food restaurant, you have to wear a cowboy hat and six-guns. In addition, you have to shout "Yippee!" every time someone orders the special Western-style double burger.

2. Barely awake, the woman slowly rocked her crying infant. While the baby softly cooed, the woman fell asleep.

3. When I painted the kitchen, I remembered to cover the floor with newspapers. Therefore, I was able to save the floor from looking as if someone had thrown confetti on it.

Practice 1 (314)

1. gadget, ladies and gentlemen,
2. Tigers, because they eat people,
3. dummy, its straw-filled "hands" tied with rope,314

Practice 2 (314)

1. My brother, who likes only natural foods, would rather eat a soybean patty than a cheeseburger.

2. That room, with its filthy rug and broken dishwasher, is the nicest one in the building.

3. My aunt, who claims she is an artist, painted her living room ceiling to look like the sky at midnight.

Practice (315)

1. hour, or
2. fine, but
3. releases, and
4. one, but
5. C
6. C
7. housecleaning, and
8. melted, and
9. telephone, but
10. C

Practice 1 (316)

1. asked, "Do
2. wrote, "2
3. of," said Richie, "is

Practice 2 (316)

1. "Could you spare a quarter," the boy asked passersby in the mall, "for a video game?"
2. "Man does not live by words alone," wrote Adlai Stevenson, "despite the fact that sometimes he has to eat them."
3. "That actress," said Velma, "has promoted everything from denture cleaner to shoelaces."

Practice (318)

1. sorry, sir, but
2. May 6, 1954, Roger
3. June 30, 2004, will
4. Seven Seas, P.O. Box 760, El Paso, Texas
5. Leo, turn

Practice (319)

1. A new bulletproof material has been developed that is very lightweight.
2. The vet's bill included charges for a distemper shot.
3. Since the firehouse is directly behind Ken's home, the sound of its siren pierces his walls.
4. Hard sausages and net-covered hams hung above the delicatessen counter.
5. The students in the dance class were dressed in a variety of bright tights, baggy sweatshirts, and woolly leg warmers.
6. A woman in the ladies' room asked me if she could borrow a safety pin.

7. Telephone books, broken pencils, and scraps of paper littered the reporter's desk.
8. The frenzied crowd at the game cheered and whistled.
9. Splitting along the seams, the old mattress spilled its stuffing on the ground.
10. To satisfy his hunger, Enrique chewed on a piece of dry rye bread.

OTHER PUNCTUATION MARKS

Introductory Activity (324)

1. list:
2. life-size
3. (1856–1939)
4. track;
5. breathing—but alive.

Practice (325)

1. follows:
2. things:
3. life:

Practice (326)

1. outlets; otherwise,
2. spider; he
3. 9 A.M.; . . . 10:00;

Practice (327)

1. well—
2. see—
3. hoped—no, I prayed—

Practice (328)

1. first-rate . . . brand-new
2. worn-out . . . wall-to-wall
3. great-looking . . . two-bit

Practice (328)

1. prices (fifty to ninety dollars) made
2. election (the April primary), only
3. you (1) two sharpened pencils and (2) an eraser.

DICTIONARY USE

Introductory Activity (330)

1. fortutious (fortuitous)
2. hi/er/o/glyph/ics
3. be
4. oc/to/ge/nar'/i/an
5. (1) an identifying mark on the ear of a domestic animal
   (2) an identifying feature or characteristic

Answers to the activities are in your dictionary. Check with your instructor if you have any problems.

SPELLING IMPROVEMENT

Introductory Activity (339)

Misspellings:

akward . . . exercize . . . buisness . . . worryed . . . shamful . . . begining . . . partys . . . sandwichs . . . heros

Practice (342)

1. carried
2. revising
3. studies
4. wrapping
5. horrified
6. permitted
7. gliding
8. angrily
9. rebelling
10. grudges

Practice (343)

1. crashes
2. matches
3. doilies
4. crosses
5. dozens
6. potatoes
7. twenties
8. wives
9. passersby
10. media

OMITTED WORDS AND LETTERS

Introductory Activity (348)

bottles . . . in the supermarket . . . like a windup toy . . . his arms . . . an alert shopper . . . with the crying

Practice (349)

1. In the rest room, Jeff impatiently rubbed his hands under the mechanical dryer, which blew out feeble puffs of cool air.

2. On February 10, 1935, *The New York Times* reported that an eight-foot alligator had been dragged out of a city sewer by three teenage boys.

3. Dave dressed up as a stuffed olive for Halloween by wearing a green plastic garbage bag and a red knitted cap.

4. Mrs. Chan nearly fainted when she opened the health insurance bill and saw an enormous rate increase.

5. At 4 A.M., the all-night supermarket where I work hosts an assortment of strange shoppers.

6. With a loud hiss, the inflated beach ball suddenly shrank to the size of an orange.

7. The boiling milk bubbled over the sides of the pot, leaving a gluey white film on the stove top.

8. Susan turned to the answer page of the crossword book, pretended to herself that she hadn't, and turned back to her puzzle.

9. In order to avoid stepping on the hot blacktop of the parking lot, the barefoot boy tiptoed along the cooler white lines.

10. The messy roommates used hubcaps for ashtrays and scribbled graffiti on their own bathroom walls.

Practice 1 (350)

1. shaves . . . blades
2. legs . . . hurdles
3. fads . . . ants
4. owners . . . monkeys
5. photographers . . . sharks
6. spores . . . leaves
7. cages . . . plants
8. pounds . . . grapes . . . cents
9. soles . . . shoes
10. cheeseburgers . . . shakes

Practice 2 (351)

Answers will vary.

COMMONLY CONFUSED WORDS

Introductory Activity (353)

1. Incorrect: your   Correct: you're
2. Incorrect: who's   Correct: whose
3. Incorrect: there   Correct: their
4. Incorrect: to   Correct: too
5. Incorrect: Its   Correct: It's

Homonyms (354)

Answers will vary for sentences only.

already . . . all ready
brake . . . break
course . . . coarse
hear . . . here
whole . . . hole
It's . . . its
knew . . . new
know . . . no
pair . . . pear
passed . . . past
peace . . . piece
plane . . . plain
principal . . . principle
right . . . write
then . . . than
There . . . their . . . they're
through . . . threw
two . . . to . . . too
where . . . wear
weather . . . whether
whose . . . Who's
your . . . you're

Other Words Frequently Confused (362)

Answers will vary for sentences only.

an . . . a
accept . . . except
advise . . . advice
effect . . . affect
Among . . . between
Besides . . . beside
can . . . may
cloths . . . clothes
desert . . . dessert
dose . . . does
fewer . . . less
former . . . latter
learn . . . teach
loose . . . lose
quiet . . . quite
Though . . . thought

Incorrect Word Forms (368)

being that (368)

1. Because the boss heard my remark,
2. because my diet
3. since his dad

can't hardly, couldn't hardly (369)

1. They could hardly
2. I can hardly
3. We could hardly

could of, must of, should of, would of (369)

1. Thelma must have
2. You should have
3. I would have
4. No one could have

irregardless (369)

1. Regardless of what anybody else does,
2. Regardless of the weather,
3. Regardless of what my parents say,

EFFECTIVE WORD CHOICE

Introductory Activity (372)

Correct sentences:
1. After a disappointing movie, we devoured a pizza.
2. Mourning the death of his best friend, Tennyson wrote the moving poem "In Memoriam."
3. Psychological tests will be given on Wednesday.
4. I think the referee made the right decision.

    1 . . . 2 . . . 3 . . . 4

Note   The answers may vary for all of the following word-choice practices.

Practice (374)

1. The scene in the movie where Rocky ate six raw eggs made me sick.
2. Ex-offenders have a hard time adjusting after leaving prison.
3. Manny went through the multiple-choice questions quickly but had trouble with the essay section.

4. The professional assassin killed over twenty victims before someone informed on him.

5. That book on suicide is depressing; it really bothered me.

Practice 1 (375)

1. Substitute <u>make me very angry</u> for <u>make my blood boil</u>.
2. Substitute <u>depressed</u> for <u>down in the dumps</u>.
3. Substitute <u>wonderful</u> for <u>one in a million</u>.
4. Substitute <u>have a celebration</u> for <u>roll out the red carpet</u>.
5. Substitute <u>free</u> for <u>free as a bird</u>.

Note   The above answers are examples of how the clichés could be corrected. Other answers are possible.

Practice 2 (376)

Answers will vary.

Practice (377)

1. I do not understand that person's behavior.
2. He erased all the mistakes in his notes.
3. She thought about what he said.
4. The police officer stopped the car.
5. Inez told the counselor about her career hopes.

Practice (379)

1. I am a vegetarian.
2. Last Tuesday, I started going to college full time.
3. Since I'm broke, I can't go to the movies.
4. I repeated that I wouldn't go.
5. Everything I say and do annoys my father.

Progress Charts

Progress Charts for Mastery Tests

Enter Your Score for Each Test in the Space Provided

Individual Tests	1 Mastery	2 Mastery	3 Mastery	4 Mastery	5 IM	6 IM
Subjects and Verbs						
Fragments						
Run-Ons						
Sentence Variety I						
Standard English Verbs						
Irregular Verbs						
Subject-Verb Agreement						
Consistent Verb Tense						
Additional Information About Verbs						
Pronoun Reference, Agreement, and Point of View						
Pronoun Types						
Adjectives and Adverbs						
Misplaced Modifiers						
Dangling Modifiers						

Individual Tests Continued	1 Mastery	2 Mastery	3 Mastery	4 Mastery	5 IM	6 IM
Faulty Parallelism						
Sentence Variety II						
Capital Letters						
Numbers and Abbreviations						
End Marks						
Apostrophe						
Quotation Marks						
Comma						
Other Punctuation Marks						
Dictionary Use						
Spelling Improvement						
Omitted Words and Letters						
Commonly Confused Words						
Effective Word Choice						

Combined Tests	1 Mastery	2 Mastery	3 Mastery	4 Mastery	5 IM	6 IM
Fragments and Run-Ons						
Verbs						
Pronouns						
Faulty Modifiers and Parallelism						
Capital Letters and Punctuation						
Word Use						

Progress Chart for
Editing and Proofreading Tests

Date	Test	Step	Comments	To Do Next	Instructor's Initials
9/27	1	1a	Missed -ing frag; 3 copying mistakes	1b	JL
9/27	1	1b	No mistakes—Good job!	2a	JL

Progress Chart for Editing and Proofreading Tests (Continued)

Date	Test	Step	Comments	To Do Next	Instructor's Initials

Progress Chart for Combined Editing Tests

Enter Your Score for Each Test in the Space Provided

Combined Test 1		Combined Test 7	
Combined Test 2		Combined Test 8	
Combined Test 3		Combined Test 9	
Combined Test 4		Combined Test 10	
Combined Test 5		Combined Test 11	
Combined Test 6		Combined Test 12	

Progress Chart for Writing Assignments

Date	Paper	Comments	To Do Next
10/15	Worst job	Promising but needs more support. Also, 2 frags and 2 run-ons.	Rewrite

Date	Paper	Comments	To Do Next

Index